INFIDELS AND EMPIRES IN A NEW WORLD ORDER

Before international relations in the West, there were Christian–infidel relations. *Infidels and Empires in a New World Order* decenters the dominant story of international relations beginning with Westphalia in 1648 by looking a century earlier to the Spanish imperial debate at Valladolid addressing the conversion of native peoples of the Americas. In addition to telling this crucial yet overlooked story from the colonial margins of Western Europe, this book examines the Anglo-Iberian Atlantic to consider how the ambivalent status of the infidel other under natural law and the law of nations culminating at Valladolid shaped subsequent international relations in explicit but mostly obscure ways. From Hernán Cortés to Samuel Purchas, and Bartolomé de las Casas to New England Puritans, a host of unconventional colonial figures enter into conversation with Francisco de Vitoria, Hugo Grotius, and John Locke to reveal astonishing religious continuities and dissonances in early modern international legal thought with important implications for contemporary global society.

David M. Lantigua is Assistant Professor of Moral Theology and Christian Ethics at the University of Notre Dame. He was previously a faculty member at The Catholic University of America and was a former graduate fellow at the Notre Dame Institute for Advanced Study. He co-authored, with Darrell Fasching and Dell deChant, *Comparative Religious Ethics: A Narrative Approach to Global Ethics*, Second Edition (2011). He is also co-editor of *Bartolomé de las Casas and the Defense of Amerindian Rights: A Brief History with Documents* (2020), part of the Atlantic Crossings series.

LAW AND CHRISTIANITY

The Law and Christianity series publishes cutting-edge work on Catholic, Protestant, and Orthodox Christian contributions to public, private, penal, and procedural law and legal theory. The series aims to promote deep Christian reflection by leading scholars on the fundamentals of law and politics, to build further ecumenical legal understanding across Christian denominations, and to link and amplify the diverse and sometimes isolated Christian legal voices and visions at work in the academy. Works collected by the series include groundbreaking monographs, historical and thematic anthologies, and translations by leading scholars around the globe.

Books in the series

The Possibility of Religious Freedom: Early Natural Law and the Abrahamic Faiths
Karen Taliaferro

Catholic Social Teaching: A Volume of Scholarly Essays
edited by Gerard Bradley and E. Christian Brugger

The Immortal Commonwealth: Covenant, Community, and Political Resistance in Early Reformed Thought
David P. Henreckson

Great Christian Jurists in American History
edited by Daniel L. Dreisbach and Mark David Hall

Great Christian Jurists and Legal Collections in the First Millennium
Philip L. Reynolds

English Ecclesiastical Lawyers: A History of Their Life and Work
R. H. Helmholz

Law, Love and Freedom: From the Sacred to the Secular
Joshua Neoh

Great Christian Jurists in French History
Olivier Descamps and Rafael Domingo

Church Law in Modernity: Toward a Theory of Canon Law Between Nature and Culture
Judith Hahn

Common Law and Natural Law in America: From the Puritans to the Legal Realists
Andrew Forsyth

Care for the World: Laudato Si' and Catholic Social Thought in an Era of Climate Crisis
edited by Frank Pasquale

Church, State, and Family: Reconciling Traditional Teachings and Modern Liberties
John Witte, Jr.

Great Christian Jurists in Spanish History
Rafael Domingo and Javier Martínez-Torrón

Under Caesar's Sword: How Christians Respond to Persecution
edited by Daniel Philpott and Timothy Samuel Shah

God and the Illegal Alien
Robert W. Heimburger

Christianity and Family Law
John Witte, Jr., and Gary S. Hauk

Christianity and Natural Law
Norman Doe

Great Christian Jurists in English History
edited by Mark Hill, QC, and R. H. Helmholz

Agape, Justice, and Law
edited by Robert F. Cochran, Jr, and Zachary R. Calo

Calvin's Political Theology and the Public Engagement of the Church
Matthew J. Tuininga

God and the Secular Legal System
Rafael Domingo

How Marriage Became One of the Sacraments
Philip L. Reynolds

Christianity and Freedom (Volume I: Historical Perspectives, Volume II: Contemporary Perspectives)
edited by Timothy Samuel Shah and Allen D. Hertzke

The Western Case for Monogamy Over Polygamy
John Witte, Jr.

The Distinctiveness of Religion in American Law
Kathleen A. Brady

Pope Benedict XVI's Legal Thought
Marta Cartabia and Andrea Simoncini

Infidels and Empires in a New World Order

EARLY MODERN SPANISH CONTRIBUTIONS TO INTERNATIONAL LEGAL THOUGHT

DAVID M. LANTIGUA
University of Notre Dame

CAMBRIDGE
UNIVERSITY PRESS

CAMBRIDGE
UNIVERSITY PRESS

University Printing House, Cambridge CB2 8BS, United Kingdom

One Liberty Plaza, 20th Floor, New York, NY 10006, USA

477 Williamstown Road, Port Melbourne, VIC 3207, Australia

314–321, 3rd Floor, Plot 3, Splendor Forum, Jasola District Centre, New Delhi – 110025, India

79 Anson Road, #06–04/06, Singapore 079906

Cambridge University Press is part of the University of Cambridge.

It furthers the University's mission by disseminating knowledge in the pursuit of education, learning, and research at the highest international levels of excellence.

www.cambridge.org
Information on this title: www.cambridge.org/9781108498265
DOI: 10.1017/9781108633499

First published 2020

Printed in the United Kingdom by TJ International Ltd. Padstow Cornwall

A catalogue record for this publication is available from the British Library.

Library of Congress Cataloging-in-Publication Data
NAMES: Lantigua, David M., author.
TITLE: Infidels and empires in a new world order : early modern Spanish contributions to international legal thought / David Lantigua, University of Notre Dame, Indiana.
DESCRIPTION: Cambridge, United Kingdom ; New York, NY, USA Cambridge University Press, 2020. | Series: Law and Christianity | Includes bibliographical references and index.
IDENTIFIERS: LCCN 2019049169 (print) | LCCN 2019049170 (ebook) | ISBN 9781108498265 (hardback) | ISBN 9781108633499 (epub)
SUBJECTS: LCSH: International law – Spain – History – 16th century. | Indigenous peoples (International law) – History – 16th century. | Indians – Legal status, laws, etc. – History – 16th century. | Casas, Bartolomé de las, 1484–1566 – Influence.
CLASSIFICATION: LCC KZ1242 .L36 2020 (print) | LCC KZ1242 (ebook) | DDC 341.4/85209031–dc23
LC record available at https://lccn.loc.gov/2019049169
LC ebook record available at https://lccn.loc.gov/2019049170

ISBN 978-1-108-49826-5 Hardback

For Marisa Ann

Contents

Figures

Acknowledgments

The ancient world acknowledged dependence on parents, the *patria*, and God. My parents, immigrants to a new world, have been an unfailing source of inspiration, teaching me the rewards of sacrifice and discipline. I am most grateful for their gifts of love and encouragement in my vocation as scholar and teacher. I also thank my amazingly talented sister Jacqueline and my dear brothers Carlos and Mitch for their love over the years. Without my parents, I would not have the level of gratitude for my *patria* and, especially, my Lord and my God. I would like to acknowledge another source of dependence to express my sincere gratitude – the academy. The professional colleagues and friends who have taken the time to converse, inquire, challenge, and, above all, share with me their brilliance and talents humbles and inspires me. There are too many to do justice to, but I shall try to thank a few.

First, my mentor and now colleague and neighbor, Jean Porter. Her careful guidance, judiciousness, and loyalty, combined with profound kindness, have exemplified the true way of being an academic scholar. Without her brilliant wisdom of Aquinas and ethics, I would never have entered the fascinating world of Spanish scholasticism. Her continual support and encouragement have given me confidence and trust to follow through this project. Other mentors and colleagues include Jerry McKenny and David Clairmont, both of whom have not only been sagacious guides professionally, but have also always shown me the dignity of being appreciated and welcomed. I look forward to many more cigars (or pipes) and glasses of rum with them over the years. I also wish to especially thank Tim Matovina and Matt Ashley for their support as chairs of the Department of Theology at Notre Dame, facilitating my time for researching and writing this book. Other colleagues I thank for various reasons include Peter Casarella, William Mattison, Mary Keys, Neil Arner, Steven Battin, Fr. Kevin Grove, Todd Whitmore, Cyril O'Regan, Joseph Wawrykow, Fr. Paul Kollman, Ken Oakes, and John Cavadini.

There are others on my journey to whom I owe gratitude who have now passed into eternity. Darrell Fasching (2017), my mentor at the University of South Florida, taught me to think of Christianity always in terms of its other. And Sabine MacCormack (2012), a dear conversation partner who bridged for me the classical and early modern worlds thereby expanding my imagination about colonial Latin America. Another person who still graces us on earth is Gustavo Gutiérrez, OP. Padre Gustavo has taught me precious truths about the Christian faith. He is my teacher of Bartolomé de las Casas and I cherish the personal conversations with him about all things theological. There is also Ramón Hernández Martín, OP, whom I had the great pleasure of meeting and conversing with at San Esteban in Salamanca during my research. He pointed me to "*las fuentes*" that united the sixteenth-century Spanish Dominicans.

Indeed, there are so many others who have given me inspiration in various ways over the years. I am grateful to my friend Victor Carmona during my time as a graduate student, who helped inspire my interest in the topic, and also to Jennifer Herdt for her ecumenical wisdom of the Christian moral tradition. To Luis Vera, Deonna Neal, Andrew Prevot, Mike Griffin, and Jordan Wales, thank you all for your friendships and conversations. To my friend David Elliot, whose fearless theological inquiry I wish only to emulate. Others from whom I have benefitted with conversations and exchanges include Tim Shah, Paolo Carozza, Russell Hittinger, Matt Tapie, José Cárdenas, David Decosimo, Scott Davis, Ileana Porras, Daniel Brunstetter, Ángel Gallardo, and Garry Sparks. Fellow travelers to the Spanish scholastic world with whom I have greatly enjoyed talking include Elisabeth Kincaid, Catherine Kuiper, and Barrett Turner, who provided helpful feedback on a portion of the manuscript. I would also like to thank the assistance of Nick Ogle and the enriching conversations with Liam de los Reyes and Fr. Dominic Verner. I am especially grateful for the undeserving support and encouragement from a scholar's scholar, Robert Wilken.

Two fellow followers of Las Casas to whom I owe a great deal of gratitude are David Orique, OP, and Larry Clayton. They have inspired me through their work on Latin American colonial history. Fr. David is the embodiment of the Dominican spirit and he has become more than just a scholarly companion, but an incredibly thoughtful friend. Similarly, Larry has become a guide and friend over the last near decade. Gratitude belongs to other scholars who have provided me invaluable feedback on portions of the manuscript and the research: James Muldoon, Daniel Philpott, Luke Glanville, Luis Valenzuela-Vermehren, and

Brian Tierney. I am especially grateful to conversation partner William Bain for his incisive and helpful comments on part of the manuscript. Others who have supported this project from The Catholic University of America include Fr. Mark Morozowich, Joe Capizzi, Josh Benson, Chad Pecknold, Bill Barbieri, Tom Cohen, Julia Young, and John Grabowski. The Strake Fund provided generous support in acquiring research materials.

I am incredibly grateful for Luis Fraga and the Institute for Latino Studies at Notre Dame, without which I would not have completed this manuscript. Tremendous thanks also go to Denise Wright and the Kellogg Institute for International Studies for providing me with resources to conduct research in Spain as a graduate student. And to the librarians at the priory of San Esteban in Salamanca, Miguel and Lita, for their patient assistance. For the Notre Dame Institute for Advanced Study, my academic home for a year, and its fantastic leadership and guidance then under Donald Stelluto, Vittorio Hösle, and Carolyn Sherman, I am so grateful. Thanks also to Julie Tanaka at the University of Notre Dame's Hesburgh Library.

Finally, I give my utmost thanks to John Witte as Series Editor for Law and Christianity at Cambridge University Press. Witte is a consummate scholar, teacher, administrator, and mentor. His immensely patient support and guidance has taken this project from its beginning stages and seeing it through to the end. It is my privilege and honor to share it with his series at Cambridge University Press. The editors at Cambridge have also been tremendously patient and helpful as the baton has passed from John Berger to Jackie Grant. I also wish to thank Sunantha Ramamoorthy, Helen Baxter, and the anonymous reviewer whose comments were instrumental to reconceiving this manuscript at an early stage.

Beyond the academy, there is gratitude for dependence on one's home and family. My dearest wife and best friend, Marisa, to you I dedicate this book. I am grateful to your parents, Jack and Maria, for their continual support and encouragement. You are my compass and guide for navigating an uncharted future together with our children. Your love, perseverance, and faith have simply made possible what was impossible. Through you, and through our children – Sofia, Natalia, Elena, and Lilia – I realize every day that the Kingdom of Heaven is near. We did it, as a team.

1

Introduction: International Relations Beyond Westphalia

The modern age ... begins in the Renaissance and Reformation when the nations defied the universal authority of the church.[1]

The universal "rights of man" and the international "system of states" often appear as the crowning achievements of the Western political imagination for modern international relations. The quelling of religious wars across Europe under a stronger policy of toleration and the rise of territorial sovereignty set the tone for a form of international relations breaking free from Latin Christendom and the grip of the papacy. Yet long-standing scholarly attention on political citizenship and national sovereignty within Reformation Europe after the iconic 1648 Peace of Westphalia often disregards the ideological underside of universal natural rights claims in extra-European contexts of imperial conquest and colonial settlement. European assertions of a natural right to punish and subjugate populations deemed unfit to govern themselves and an exclusive right to private property in foreign lands, bolstered by biblical and theological justifications, provided legal armor to early modern and modern expansion in the Americas, Africa, and Asia.[2]

The development of universal rights, along with international law, has a checkered colonial past admitting both Western imperial aggression against non-Europeans but also its critique by Europeans extending the same concepts of universal rights and international law to all.[3] That ambivalence marking modern international relations has sometimes inhabited single

[1] Reinhold Niebuhr, *The Structure of Nations and Empires* (Charles Scribner's Sons, 1959), p. 148.

[2] Camilla Boisen and David Boucher, "The Medieval and Early Modern Legacy of Rights: The Rights to Punish and to Property," in *Medieval Foundations of International Relations*, ed. William Bain (Routledge, 2017), pp. 149–50.

[3] For attention to the ambivalent European legal concepts of *res nullius* and *ius gentium*, respectively, see Andrew Fitzmaurice, *Sovereignty, Property and Empire, 1500–2000*

individuals, such as eighteenth-century Swiss jurist Emer de Vattel, whose treatise *The Law of Nations* (*Droit des gens*) received popular transatlantic acclaim. Vattel adamantly endorsed an international society comprised of free and equal states in possession of autonomous independence. On this principled basis, he saw the Spanish conquest of the Inca and Aztec empires as a "notorious usurpation."[4] However, when it came to "savage nations," prone to war and theft, the rules of conduct in the law of nations did not apply to them as they deserved punishment and even extermination by a confederacy of more civilized nations.[5] The ambivalence of defending equal liberty and supporting colonial subjugation in the history of international relations typically rested, as in Vattel's case, on a distinct category of otherness for uncivilized non-Europeans. Recognition of political equality and universal rights only held among civilized nations, not savage ones outside the law of nations.

Before savages occupied Western thinking about international relations beyond Europe in ambivalent terms, there were the infidels of Latin Christendom. *Infidels and Empires in a New World Order* argues that the ambivalence of modern international relations identified here had its ideological roots in the Western European past of Christian–infidel relations. Through the prism of the infidel other in frontier colonial settings, the ambivalent nature of universal rights inscribed in a world order comes into sharper focus during the early modern period of European expansion, especially in Spain. The infidel other, a legal category and not merely a moral or rhetorical designation, was distinct from the "barbarian foreigner" or "natural slave" of ancient Greco-Roman cultures. It was also distinct from the "uncivilized savage" of modern Western European societies even as both shared some overlapping features.

Because infidels were a robust legal category in the Latin Christian tradition, they were the political subjects of rights in a manner unlike classical barbarians or natural slaves. The notion of infidel rights offers a unique vantage point for investigating how early modern European Christians, indebted to Roman classical and medieval scholastic-juristic notions of natural law and the law of nations, conceptualized humanity and its proper due beyond religious, cultural, and political borders. This book examines the extension and application of infidel rights to the native peoples of the New World justifying both their political freedom and their political dispossession.

(Cambridge University Press, 2014), and Jennifer Pitts, *Boundaries of the International: Law and Empire* (Harvard University Press, 2018).

4 Emer de Vattel, *The Law of Nations*, eds. Béla Kapossy and Richard Whatmore (Liberty Fund, 2008), Book 1, chap. 7, p. 130.

5 Vattel, *The Law of Nations*, Book 3, chap. 3, p. 487.

By focusing on Christian–infidel relations outside Europe as constitutive of international relations, this study decenters the dominant Westphalian narrative of international society that moves from Europe outward.[6] It thereby introduces a different story from the colonial margins about the emergence of international relations and its ambivalent legacy for Western legal thought.

Most Anglophone treatments of early modern/modern rights for infidels in the Christian tradition explore north transatlantic debates about the toleration of Christian heretics, wherein the right of individual conscience against papal power or established state religion became a crucial catalyst for modern democratic liberties and sovereign independence. John Locke's protracted epistolary debate with Jonas Proast and Roger Williams's rhetorical battle with John Cotton are key historical examples from England and colonial America about liberty's struggle against religious coercion. Alternatively, *Infidels and Empires in a New World Order* widens the analytical lens by turning to an unprecedented sixteenth-century Spanish debate about the rights of those outside Latin Europe: unbaptized indigenous peoples across the Atlantic who had never before encountered Europeans, much less heard of Christianity.

The anchor point of this overlooked Iberian past of international legal thought was the sixteenth-century junta in Valladolid, Spain between Bishop Bartolomé de las Casas and the imperial humanist Juan Ginés de Sepúlveda. The main contention of the debate under imperial auspices, which was moderated by theologian of the Second Scholastic Domingo de Soto, concerned the alleged lawfulness of making religious war against idolatrous infidels to bring about their widespread conversion to the Christian faith. Although both sides of the debate acknowledged infidels as human beings, the account of natural law and universal world order informing each diverged greatly. Natural law and the law of nations could serve as a basis for both affirming and denying the rationality of Amerindians and, correlatively, their rights of jurisdiction and sovereignty. The Valladolid junta brought into relief the historically contested politics and strategic uses of natural law and the law of nations in the European Christian encounter with infidels. As this book demonstrates, the Spanish debate about infidel rights exposed the inherent yet seldom recognized ambivalence marking the emergence of international relations with non-Europeans in the West.

6 *The Expansion of International Society*, eds. Hedley Bull and Adam Watson (Oxford University Press, 1984), p. 1. Consider the opening words of this influential study: "The purpose of this book is to explore the expansion of the international society of European states across the rest of the globe, and its transformation from a society fashioned in Europe and dominated by Europeans into the global international society of today."

When European Protestant natural lawyers and philosophers in the latter half of the sixteenth and seventeenth century reconfigured international relations along a legal humanist axis instead of scholasticism and canon law, the doctrine of infidel rights receded into the background along with the exposed ambivalence won at Valladolid. These international thinkers retained conflicting aspects of Spanish views on infidels represented at the Valladolid junta, recognizing the natural rights of non-Europeans but also the superiority of European civilization. International thinkers such as Locke, but also Hugo Grotius and Alberico Gentili, characteristically discarded the ongoing foundational role of the universal Church and papacy in safeguarding world order. Juridical independence from papal power generated new claims to freedom of trade, commerce, and settlement against European competitors by inaugurating a political discourse about universal natural rights in frontier colonial spaces lacking a sovereign judge. These thinkers also increasingly denied idolatry a critical role in the moral grammar of their international thought. On the one hand, this had the advantage of eliminating idolatry as a cause of interconfessional strife within Europe, and wars against infidels outside Europe, like in North America. On the other, the dwindling discourse of idolatry in English colonization would have the adverse effect of weakening the overall self-critique of westward expansion and wealth accumulation. As the idolatrous infidel diminished from later seventeenth-century international thinking, the savage and nonindustrious Indian would proliferate in its absence.

The Dominican theologians considered in this book, by contrast, continued to apprise themselves of the moral category of idolatry as a reflexive device to rebuke the voracious thirst for wealth and profit plaguing Spanish colonization of the Indies. They also restricted idolatry as a lawful cause for waging war against non-Christians. From a different geopolitical and confessional standpoint than Protestant humanists and natural lawyers, the Spanish theologians engaged in this book similarly rejected the logic of coercion undergirding religious war endorsed by papal theocracy and imperial tyranny. Moreover, they did so on the basis of *human* natural rights supporting the rationality and political authority of non-Christian peoples more than a century prior to Westphalia. Remarkably, their reformatory resistance to overreaching claims of Pope and emperor in temporal matters recognized the autonomous polity as a boundary to empire without abandoning the definitive role of Christian belief in the promotion of justice and solidarity among peoples of the world. The normative claim of this book is that the Spanish theologians developed reliable ethical principles for international thought to chasten empire, repudiate colonial abuses, promote solidarity with non-Europeans, and empower indigenous political agency. They did so not by eliding their religious convictions, but by creatively affirming them in a New World context responsive to bringing the Gospel peacefully to all nations.

THEOLOGY AND THE UNIVERSAL CHURCH

Infidels and Empires in a New World Order features the historic legacy of the sixteenth-century theological conception of world order articulated by Spanish Dominicans (members of the Order of Preachers) responding to "the affair of the Indies." During the reign of Emperor Charles V, Las Casas, Soto, and Francisco de Vitoria, among others, appropriated and expanded a scholastic-juristic account of natural law and the law of nations chiefly indebted to St. Thomas Aquinas and the medieval *ius commune* tradition to promote the basic rights and freedoms of individuals and peoples under God. In an unprecedented way, they appealed to a universal juridical order and ecclesiastical forum transcending Spanish imperial power to protect non-Europeans from unjust political aggression and colonial oppression.

Their scholastic-theological conception of world order hinged on the belief that the divine image belonged to all human beings, even infidels, as spiritual and rational creatures. The image of God naturally impressed upon every individual, and restored to perfection through Jesus Christ, punctuated an objective safeguard and horizon for expressing the subjective rights of non-Christian peoples. It affirmed a universal natural law protected and vindicated by the rule of Christ over the Church and creation. As theologian Oliver O'Donovan has suggested, this belief signaled "the last and greatest of the legal accomplishments of Christendom," which was "the conception that there exists, not merely as an ideal but in fact, an international law, dependent on no regime and no statute."[7]

Extending Richard Tuck's treatment of "scholasticism" in his foundational study of international thought and Annabel Brett's comprehensive work on the "Dominican moment" of the Catholic Second Scholastic, this book considers the ideas and practices informing the political judgments about the Indies by Spanish theologians.[8] The book mines the political context and canon legal

7 Oliver O'Donovan, *The Desire of the Nations: Rediscovering the Roots of Political Theology* (Cambridge University Press, 1996), p. 236.

8 Richard Tuck, *The Rights of War and Peace: Political Thought and the International Order from Grotius to Kant* (Oxford University Press, 1999); Annabel S. Brett, *Liberty, Right and Nature: Individual Rights in Later Scholastic Thought* (Cambridge University Press, 1997) and *Changes of State: Nature and the Limits of the City in Early Modern Natural Law* (Princeton University Press, 2011).

background of the Indies affair to elucidate Christian theological contributions of the Dominicans. In particular, the Valladolid debate, which receives insufficient treatment in histories of international thought, contextualizes the book's organizing theme on the rights of infidels as constitutive of a new world order in contrast to the theory and practice of empire. The enigmatic slaveholder-turned-lawyer advocate of the Amerindians, Fray Bartolomé de las Casas (1484–1566), provides the microhistorical reference point for this wider narrative of infidel rights focused on Valladolid and the early modern development of international relations.

Despite Las Casas's signal theological and legal contributions to international thought, he has been woefully underappreciated if not disregarded by historians of international political thought, even those attentive to Spanish scholastics.[9] Perhaps this has been due to a reduction of him to that of propagandist because of his usable history for the Black Legend by European colonial competitors with Spain. Or perhaps it is because scholars who have seen his importance remain unconvinced that he was a foremost legal thinker and political theorist in his own right. *Infidels and Empires in a New World Order* rectifies this inadequacy and places Las Casas in conversation with his Dominican confreres Vitoria, Soto, and Melchor Cano, and his main interlocutors and opponents, in order to appreciate both his singularity and the broader Spanish contributions to international legal thought.

The Valladolid junta represented the culmination of a decades-long conflict about the proper method of spreading the Gospel to the native peoples of the Indies. It also symbolized a centuries-long Christian debate about missionary war against infidels within Latin Christendom. This was indeed a great moment of evangelical and political crisis for the Dominicans resulting in the development of a Spanish theological conception of world order reliant on the scholastic tradition of Thomas Aquinas. Without attention to the intricacies of this moment of crisis, the Dominican theological response to the whole affair risks envelopment under grand narratives and genealogies that purportedly trace the origin of modern liberal internationalism, modern capitalism, or modern racialized

[9] Consider the dismissal by Andrew Fitzmaurice when he writes, "Las Casas was not a Salamanca theologian and his arguments did not employ the same natural law reasoning." *Sovereignty, Property and Empire*, p. 61. Even though Georg Cavallar treats Las Casas in colonial context, he, too, concludes that Las Casas offers, at best "the rudimentary elements of a theory of aggression, of collective self-determination or political independence, and of self-defense" more fully developed in Vitoria. See his *The Rights of Strangers* (Ashgate Publishing, 2002), p. 80.

colonialism.[10] Instead, our focus on the conflicting Christian accounts of world order yields a richer analysis of the normative contribution of Spanish Dominicans, and their critical interlocutors, for international relations in Western Europe.

Four scholastic theses help theorize the Spanish theological conception of world order considered throughout this book: (1) The spiritual transcendence of temporal political powers by ecclesiastical authority. (2) The recognition of the political integrity and right of peoples as a boundary to empire. (3) The natural and mystical unity of all persons made in the divine image. (4) The moral defense and juridical protection of innocent and dispossessed non-Christian peoples. All the aforementioned theses operated within a theological political framework according to the Thomistic dictum: *grace does not abolish nature, but perfects it.*[11] This Thomistic axiom distinctly outlined a scholastic theological approach to world order emerging from the crisis of the Indies by affirming the reality of divine grace from Christ through the universal Church, but also the universal integrity of natural reason. Las Casas had this axiom precisely in mind when he argued for infidel rights at Valladolid: "[T]he law of grace perfects the acts of nature; it does not overturn or abolish them. This is the teaching of all the schools, all theologians, and all doctors. And thus it is lawful for pagan rulers to protect their borders as well as to exercise jurisdiction, since, in this respect, their jurisdiction is no less natural than the jurisdiction of Christian rulers."[12]

Although the Thomistic axiom and scholastic theses provided a common repository for international thought among the Spanish Dominicans, it did not mean that each theologian's moral ideas were identical or that they arrived at the same political judgments concerning the Indies affair. Neither did it preclude the evolution of their ideas and opinions during their lives due to changing circumstances and maturation of thought. Jointly, however, the sixteenth-century Spanish theologians opted for an ethical commitment to world order over the imperial jurisdiction of the Crown. It rested on the spiritual authority of Christ and the Church, and natural law and the law of nations derived from human reason. They did not conceive of a political unit

[10] Respectively, see James Brown Scott, *The Spanish Origin of International Law: Francisco de Vitoria and His Law of Nations* (Clarendon Press, 1934); Alejandro A. Chafuen, *Faith and Liberty: The Economic Thought of Late Scholastics* (Lexington Books, 2003); Walter D. Mignolo, *The Darker Side of Western Modernity: Global Futures, Decolonial Options* (Duke University Press, 2011), chap. 2.

[11] Thomas Aquinas, *Summa theologiae* (*ST* hereafter) I, q. 1, a. 8 *ad* 2.

[12] Bartolomé de las Casas, *In Defense of the Indians*, trans. Stafford Poole (Northern Illinois University Press, 1992), chap. 9, p. 83.

of empire that could legitimately hold universal political power in its classical or medieval sense.[13] Neither did they adhere to a curialist conception of universal dominium that granted excessive or unbecoming latitude to the papacy in temporal political matters.

Although the Church and the papacy had to retain a certain extraordinary measure of power from Christ to intervene on behalf of pressing spiritual matters as defined in canon law, this presupposed a recognition of the integrity of temporal political powers and the limits of Christian jurisdiction over infidels. The prospect of unjust intervention on the world stage of non-European peoples prompted the Spanish theologians to place still greater emphasis on the moral constraint of states, rather than greater freedom of states to act against one another.[14] They generated Christian political arguments derived from theology, canon law, and Roman law, for restraining empire and condemning European colonial domination. Most prominent among their colonial repertoire for protecting native sovereignty and property were redeployments of the canon legal principle of infidel (or outsider) immunity from political judgment and the Roman law of occupation.

The Spanish Dominicans articulated a scholastic theological conception of world order that could properly chasten the conceits of both European imperialism and theocratic papalism. They did so by locating the temporal authority over the newly traversed Atlantic world in its indigenous occupants, not in the papacy or empire of Latin Christendom.[15] Their reliance on the medieval legal tradition in both its scholastic and canonistic expressions enabled them to take measure of an alternative "world order defined not as a universal government but as a unified law," anchored in theological convictions rather than imperial might.[16] O'Donovan has further identified the normative importance of this scholastic-juristic tradition inherited and appropriated by the Spanish theologians, which elevated Christ as sole ruler of the nations without erecting a world government in his place yet giving his rule a clear institutional witness through the Church.[17]

The moral stance of Spanish Dominicans in the New World during the early colonial period suggests another theological basis for world order resting

[13] Brett, "Scholastic Political Thought and the Modern Concept of the State," in *Rethinking the Foundations of Modern Political Thought*, eds. Annabel Brett and James Tully with Holly Hamilton Bleakley (Cambridge University Press, 2006), p. 144.

[14] Tuck, "Grotius, Hobbes, and Pufendorf on Humanitarian Intervention," in *Just and Unjust Military Intervention: European Thinkers from Vitoria to Mill*, eds. Stefano Recchia and Jennifer Welsh (Cambridge University Press, 2013), p. 102.

[15] O'Donovan, *The Ways of Judgment* (Eerdmans Publishing, 2005), pp. 216–217.

[16] O'Donovan, *The Desire of the Nations*, p. 267.

[17] O'Donovan, *The Desire of the Nations*, pp. 267–268.

on infidel rights as a counter to the ancient practice of unjustly making empire through dispossession. In a momentous shift in Roman ecclesiastical policy, Pope Paul III (1534–1549) communicated such an inclusive vision of world order in his letters addressing the affair of the Indies.[18] These papal letters of 1537, directed to the universal Church and specific bishops, outlined the proper method of evangelizing extra-European nonbelievers based on respect of their fundamental rights as rational creatures capable of receiving the Christian faith. The Pope undermined preceding medieval papal doctrine and the practice of spreading Christianity through an aggressive civilizing mission. He also gave clear ecclesial witness by requiring bishops in the New World to withhold sacraments from any Christian who refused to set free oppressed infidel peoples.

The most well-known of Paul III's letters, the encyclical *Sublimis Deus*, targeted Satan's corruption of those within the Church – namely, European Catholics who employed fear, greed, war, and enslavement to convert those outside the Church by subjugation and dispossession. As the Vicar of Christ on earth, Paul III believed his papal duty was to protect all of Christ's sheep, especially "the Indians of the West and South" beyond the visible fold of the Church.[19]

> Those Indians (and all other peoples who will be discovered by Christians in the future), although they are outside the faith, should not be deprived of their freedom and their ownership of things. Indeed, they can use, control, and enjoy their liberty and ownership freely and lawfully. Nor should they be reduced to slavery. If the contrary were to happen, it would be void and useless, having neither force nor influence. We declare that those same Indians and other peoples should be attracted to the proper faith of Christ by the preaching of God's word and by good example.[20]

For historian Helen Parish, Pope Paul III's letter *Sublimis Deus* marked "the true beginning of international law in the modern world: the first intercontinental proclamation of the inherent rights of all humans and the liberty of peoples."[21] Even if this overestimated the papacy's historical role for

[18] The following letters of Paul III addressing the Amerindian question coincidedin 1537 over the course of three consecutive months: *Pastorale officium* (May 29), *Sublimis Deus* (June 2), *Altitudo divini consilii* (July 1).

[19] Jn 10:16, where Jesus as the Good Shepherd teaches his followers: "I have other sheep that do not belong to this fold. I must bring them also, and they will listen to my voice. So there will be one flock, one shepherd."

[20] *Sublimis Deus*, in *Las Casas en México*, Helen Rand Parish and Harold Weidman (Fondo de Cultura Económica, 1992), Appendix 14 in Latin and Spanish translation, p. 310.

[21] Parish, *Las Casas en México*, p. 18. Historian Lawrence Clayton has also referred to the letter as "the magna carta of Indian rights." See his *Bartolomé de las Casas: A Biography* (New York: Cambridge University Press, 2012), p. 239.

international law, Paul III's threefold commitment to the right of freedom, self-rule, and property stemming from a recognition of the dignity of the rational creature was a watershed moment in Christian–infidel relations outside Europe. So was his threat to excommunicate Christian oppressors in defense of a peaceful method of evangelization. This point was not lost on the founder of modern Catholic social teaching, Pope Leo XIII, who commemorated Paul III in 1888 to celebrate Brazil's abolition of slavery.[22] Remarkably, Spanish Dominican missionaries and theologians were the direct inspiration of Pope Paul III's views on the Indies affair.

The juridical locus of international society for Pope Paul III and the Spanish Dominicans was not the issue of heresy and interconfessional strife within Reformation Europe, but instead the European encounter with infidels in a New World. From this theological standpoint, the moral basis for the juridical unity of humankind was the mystical Body of Christ, comprised of individuals scattered among the nations. And yet, the dominant origin story of international relations and the modern states system has made Christian theological contributions to world order and universal rights exceedingly inconsequential, outmoded, or a mere antecedent to thinkers of the modern political canon. Its narrative premise about formal anarchy among nations jettisons the complex theological heritage of Christian thinking about world order.

INTERNATIONAL RELATIONS, WESTPHALIA, AND ANARCHY

The Roman Church's support of international right may seem an irony of history when considering that the papacy extricated itself from the most symbolic founding event of international law – the 1648 Peace of Westphalia ending the Thirty Years' War. The treaties between equal French, German, Dutch, and Swedish states seeking greater independence from the authority of the Holy Roman Empire and the Roman papacy revolutionized the politics of sovereignty and national legitimacy in the West.[23] Pope Innocent X declared the treaties underlying the iconic origin of the modern states system legally null, void, and invalid for all times due to the Protestant incursion on traditional ecclesiastical authority and property.[24] The papacy zealously sought to

22 Pope Leo XIII, *In plurimis* (1888), §16.

23 Daniel Philpott, *Revolutions in Sovereignty: How Ideas Shaped Modern International Relations* (Princeton University Press, 2001), chap. 5; Ian Clark, *Legitimacy in International Society* (Oxford University Press, 2005), p. 49, and chap. 3.

24 Pope Innocent X, *Zelo domus Dei* (1648), in *Church and State through the Centuries*, eds. Sidney Ehler and John Morrall (Newman Press, 1954), pp. 194–198.

reassert its dwindling temporal influence in European politics but to no avail – a new form of international legitimacy among independent states won out.

Westphalia signals a transformation of medieval Western Europe becoming "modern" by leaving behind the *respublica Christiana* under papal unity for independent sovereign states, and the pacification of wars of religion through civic unity and toleration. Its mythical status has even been directly associated with the sovereign equality of states necessary for establishing the UN Charter of Nations. As one observer noted in 1948, the tercentenary year marked by the UN Universal Declaration of Human Rights, Westphalia marked "the end of an epoch and the opening of another," representing "a majestic portal which leads from the old into the new world."[25] Although subject to overstatement, the myth's hold on discussions over the origins of international law and the modern states system has been significant, especially after the Second World War.[26] European abandonment of a higher authority, whether earthly in the Habsburg monarchy or spiritual in the universal papacy, supposedly enabled the emergence of international law and the balance of power between equally sovereign states.[27]

The Westphalian theoretical paradigm has often set the terms for analyzing various political "traditions" in the study of international relations (IR), a discipline emerging in the twentieth century that rapidly evolved in postwar Europe to address the new global context of international law and decolonization. The concept of tradition used here gives the impression of stable theoretical frameworks for understanding normative principles and laws underlying alternative conceptions of relations between governments and peoples on the historical stage of world politics to illuminate the present. These traditions, sometimes called types, usually come in duos and trinities. Realism versus idealism, and sovereigntism versus cosmopolitanism, portray divergent political ideologies concerning the nature of obligation to public authority at the national and international levels, the grounds for armed conflict and its authorization, and the juridical basis and extent of individual rights. The nub of the duel between *raison d'état* and utopian cosmopolis is whether world politics revolves around the brute fact of international anarchy or the potential for world community.

25 Leo Gross, "The Peace of Westphalia: 1648–1948," *The American Journal of International Law* 42, no. 1 (1948), 28.

26 Sebastian Schmidt, "To Order the Minds of Scholars: The Discourse of the Peace of Westphalia in International Relations Literature," *International Studies Quarterly* 55, no. 3 (2011), 601–623.

27 Gross, "The Peace of Westphalia," 29.

In the English School of IR theory identified with pioneering figures like Martin Wight and Hedley Bull, the "broad middle road" of rationalism runs in between realist and utopian approaches to world politics.[28] Wight's tripartite distinction between realist, rationalist, and revolutionist "patterns of thought" generally corresponds to Bull's Hobbesian, Grotian, and Kantian traditions.[29] A certain normative preference here belongs to the Grotian rationalist tradition of international relations. This bears the important influence of Hersch Lauterpacht on the English School, a Cambridge Professor of International Law and Judge of the International Court of Justice who identified Hugo Grotius's *On the Rights of War and Peace* (*De jure belli ac pacis*) as "the first comprehensive and systematic treatment on international law."[30] Lauterpacht saw in Grotius a viable postwar alternative to political realism's excessive focus on the moral bankruptcy of states reflected, for example, in the Christian theologian Reinhold Niebuhr and historian E. H. Carr.[31]

According to the types devised by the English School IR theory, the sociability of nature thesis of Grotius avoids Hobbes's materialist view of nature as "a war of all against all," the latter of which implies that each artificially constructed state is like an island unto itself. The Grotian tradition recognizes a society of states sharing norms of morality and law, yet without succumbing to Kantian universalistic aspirations of establishing a cosmopolitan world community that overestimates individuals to states. In between Hobbesian international anarchy and Kantian cosmopolitan society stands Grotian anarchical society – a society of states and individuals without central institutions and a central government.[32] Grotius's idea of international society overlaps ideologically with Westphalia, according to Bull, therefore earning the Dutch lawyer the intellectual patrimony of the founding event that occurred only a few years after his death.[33]

Christian theological views on world order gain prominence in the story of international relations when we do not confine the early modern Spanish

28 Martin Wight, *International Theory: The Three Traditions* (Continuum, 2002), pp. 14–15.

29 Wight, "An Anatomy of International Thought," *The Review of International Studies* 13 (1987), 221–227; Hedley Bull, *The Anarchical Society: A Study of Order in World Politics*, 4th edn (Columbia University Press, 2002), pp. 23–24.

30 Hersch Lauterpacht, "The Grotian Tradition of International Law," *British Yearbook of International Law* (1946), 17.

31 Barry Buzan, *An Introduction to the English School of International Relations* (Polity, 2004), pp. 28–29.

32 Bull, "The Importance of Grotius in the Study of International Relations," in *Hugo Grotius and International Relations*, eds. Hedley Bull, Benedict Kingsbury, and Adam Roberts (Oxford University Press, 2002), p. 72.

33 Bull, "The Importance of Grotius," 75.

theologians within a standard Westphalian paradigm or portray them simply as scholastic predecessors to Grotian rationalism. Bull's brief remarks about the Spanish theologians, particularly Vitoria, stifles recognition of their unique contribution to international political thought by assuming that all interactions between Europeans and Indians were simply anarchical, or "absent any common framework of rules and institutions."[34] Recovering the moral significance of supranational society that can account for both its natural and mystical dimensions therefore demands a different template of world order than the anarchical international politics presumed in the Westphalian paradigm.

Christian theology provides resources for reimagining and reconfiguring space and time to enable a new mode of engaging international relations.[35] From a theological perspective, God's sovereign rule in Christ, the desire of all the nations, renders anarchical society ontologically inert and cosmopolitan society spiritually tenuous. The world order affirmed by Pope Paul III in 1537 recognized the freedom and independence of peoples everywhere, even infidels, all of whom were capable of receiving the faith as rational creatures. The idea of *world order* provides the organizing normative principle for appreciating the importance of a universal or supranational society such as the Church or humankind as such. World order, articulated yet undeveloped by Bull, grants moral priority to the individual human being as a member of the whole of human society. Therefore, it is more comprehensive and primordial than the specific form of *international order* associated with the modern European system of states.[36] The fundamental unit for analyzing world order in a Christian theological sense similarly is not the sovereign state, but the individual human being made in the divine image who possesses a rational social nature.[37] The idea of world order can elucidate the normative contributions of theology for international relations beyond the sovereign state at the center of the Westphalian myth. Even so, the Westphalian myth of

34 Bull, *Anarchical Society*, p. 42.

35 William T. Cavanaugh, *Theopolitical Imagination* (T&T Clark, 2002), p. 4.

36 Bull, *Anarchical Society*, p. 21.

37 For articles that begin to theorize the Spanish scholastic conception of world order associated with Vitoria and its importance in the history of international relations concerning the issues of sovereign authority, war and intervention, see G. Scott Davis, "Conquest and Conscience: Francisco de Vitoria on Justice in the New World," *Modern Theology* 13, no. 4 (1997): 475–500; Luis Valenzuela-Vermehren, "The Politics of Legitimacy and Force in International Relations: Vitoria and Rawls on the 'Law of Peoples' and Recourse to War," *Revista de ciencia política*, 32.2 (2012): 449–478, and William Bain, "Saving the Innocent, Then and Now: Vitoria, Dominion and World Order," *History of Political Thought*, 34.4 (2013): 588–613.

international relations rests on a crucial idea that demands further consideration for this inquiry.

More than Grotius, Hobbes provided the political terms for Westphalia with his idea of the international state of nature.[38] Before Hobbes, the natural law and the law of nations of the Christian European *ius commune*, with roots in Roman jurisprudence and canon law, were conceptual conduits for delineating the moral and juridical unity of humanity.[39] According to the canonistic tradition of Latin Christianity shaped by the Roman legal heritage, the law of nations (*ius gentium*) identified customs and practices concerning war, occupation of territory, treaties, enslavement, and truces found among "almost all nations."[40] Natural law (*ius naturale*), in distinction, was "common to all nations" because it denoted a universal "instinct of nature" bearing on matters that included union of men and women, childrearing, the common possession of all things, the identical liberty of all, and repaying violence with force.[41]

In contrast, Hobbes did not seek to abolish *ius naturale* as wrest it from ideas of ontological perfection and any universal moorings in scholastic metaphysics, canon law, or the papacy. "Natural law" for Hobbes was a dictate of reason that served the remedial role of constantly reminding individuals to seek peace by escaping the bellicose state of nature, and to defend themselves by establishing alliances.[42] Hobbes inscribed war within the natural state of affairs, thus representing a marked departure from Latin Christianity's treatment of war as part of the law of nations. He thereby devalued the anthropological axiom of sociable nature indicative of Aristotle, the Stoics, and the scholastics.

38 Wight, *International Theory*, p. 30. Wight recognized that Hobbes was the first to provide the terms in which the question "*What is international society?*" would be answered: "It seems to have been Hobbes who first laid down the equation: *international relations/society equals the state of nature*, and from the mid-seventeenth century this became the basic assumption of international theory."

39 The Christian European *ius commune* represented a common body of European law known by trained jurists that was chiefly comprised of Roman law and canon law. It developed during the Latin Middle Ages and dominated European legal education until the early modern period. The *ius commune* was a transnational source of law in Europe, standing above "the rules of the different courts, the particular lands, and even the individual legislative bodies among which European jurisdictions were divided." R. H. Helmholz, *The Spirit of Classical Canon Law* (University of Georgia Press, 1996), p. 20.

40 Gratian, *The Treatise on Laws*, trans. Augustine Thompson (Catholic University of America Press, 1993), Dist. 1, c. 9. Gratian cited Isidore of Seville's *Etymologies*, V.vi.

41 Gratian, *Treatise on Laws*, Dist. 1, c. 7, citing Isidore's *Etymologies*, V.iv.

42 Hobbes, *On the Citizen*, eds. Richard Tuck and Michael Silverthorne (Cambridge University Press, 1998), chap. 2, §2, p. 34; *Leviathan*, ed. J. C. A. Gaskin (Oxford University Press, 1996), Part I, chap. 14, p. 87.

Mutual fear and not mutual dependence, he surmised, was the most basic passion driving humans to form society.[43]

Hobbes's evisceration of humanity's social nature simultaneously contributed to a fundamental revision of "natural right." Christian juristic teaching on "the common possession of all things" as part of the *ius naturale* had always entailed a duty and obligation to share with others in times of necessity. Right in its characteristically Christian mode was indexed to sociable human nature. For Hobbes, the common right of all appeared terrifyingly different under his individualist anthropology that defined *ius* as each man's power to preserve his own nature. With the primordial right of individual self-preservation providing the basic axiom of liberty in the Hobbesian universe, the "common right of all things" was recalibrated into everyone's license "to everything, even to one another's body," for the sake of personal security.[44] This primeval "right to all things" (*ius in omnia*) was virtually synonymous with a "right of war."[45] The ancient cynicism of Plato's Thrasymachus and the Greek historian Thucydides prevailed in the Hobbesian state of nature, meaning that everyone must yield to the rational and physical powers of self-preservation. Hobbes eloquently stated this realist revision of *ius* in his *Elements of Law*: "[I]rresistible might in the state of nature is right."[46]

Hobbes's invention of the state of nature occupied by individuals in equal possession of an untrammeled right of self-preservation radically rewrote the story of Western European political thought. A crucial part of what made Hobbes's claims so radical was his unconventional yet intuitive deduction: "To this war of every man against every man, this is also consequent; that nothing can be unjust. The notions of right and wrong, justice and injustice have there no place. Where there is no common power, there is no law: where no law, no injustice."[47] Common right without an underlying social nature or an overarching authoritative power amounts to the superior right of every individual using might. The Hobbesian state of nature is a pugnacious space where the proverbial saying from Cicero holds, *inter arma silent leges*.[48] Hobbes's conclusion that individuals in such a dreadful, muted state need civil society and its positive laws for protection and adjudication carries the

43 Hobbes, *On the Citizen*, chap. 1, §§1–2, pp. 21–24.

44 *Leviathan*, Part 1, chap. 14, p. 87.

45 Hobbes, *On the Citizen*, chap. 5, §1, p. 69.

46 Hobbes, *Elements of Law*, in *Three-Text Edition of Thomas Hobbes's Political Theory*, ed. Deborah Baumgold (Cambridge University Press, 2017), Part 1, chap. 14, p. 140.

47 Hobbes, *Leviathan*, Part 1, chap. 14, p. 85.

48 Hobbes, *Elements of Law*, Part 1, chap. 19, p. 198. "Among [times of] arms, the laws become silent." This is a reference to Cicero's oration, *Pro Milone*.

greatest rhetorical force. Hobbes relied on a standard of civilization here as the benchmark for real political societies under law (or *imperium*) in contrast to the precarious anarchical state of nature.[49]

The anarchic state of nature as an encounter between inherently conflictual, even deadly, individuals in possession of their own right without a common superior authority was a mainstay of not only Western modernity's domestic politics but also international politics. Consider Hobbes's treatment of the law of nations, which he did not interpret as a conceptual placemark between natural law and civil law. Instead, the brief and sparse references to the law of nations by Hobbes in his mature writings were tersely summarized in *Leviathan*: "[T]he law of nations, and the law of nature, is the same thing."[50] The natural law and the law of nations, both unwritten, were mere "prudential rules for survival," although now at the level of commonwealths instead of individuals in the state of nature.[51] Rather than providing a normative basis for regulating interstate relations for mutual benefit within a universal community, as seen in his scholastic Jesuit contemporary Francisco Suárez (1548–1617), this new law of nations was patently self-referential just like the natural law. Hobbes opened the prospect of imagining the international arena of states as made up of artificial persons inhabiting the unruly realm of natural right where each state sought strictly to preserve itself.

The absence of a common power must necessarily yield an international state of nature wherein the liberty of autonomous commonwealths clash and overrule one another. Hobbes's portrayal of this international politics of anarchy resting on self-interest relied on classical historical examples like the Athenians and Romans, commonwealths possessing the freedom to resist and invade other commonwealths.[52] Hobbes was more than willing to exchange papal dominion and the universal society of the Church for an arena of independent commonwealths under "continual jealousies, and in the state and posture of gladiators" to attain greater stability at the domestic level of civil society.[53] Since natural law dictated to individuals outside civil society the formation of alliances and treaties for self-protection, the same held for

49 Robert Kraynak, "Hobbes on Barbarism and Civilization," in *The Journal of Politics* 45, no. 1 (1983), 86–109; Brett Bowden, *The Empire of Civilization: The Evolution of an Imperialist Idea* (University of Chicago Press, 2009), pp. 40–41.

50 Hobbes, *Leviathan*, Part 2, chap. 30, p. 325. Cf. *On the Citizen*, chap. 14, p. 156, where the law of nations is considered the "natural law of commonwealths."

51 Bull, "Hobbes and the International Anarchy," *Social Research* 48, no. 4 (1981), 723.

52 Hobbes, *Leviathan*, Part 2, chap. 21, pp. 142–3.

53 Hobbes, *Leviathan*, Part 1, chap. 13, p. 85.

commonwealths in the international state of nature.[54] But this was no summons to fulfill Christian duties of justice and love rooted in humanity's sociable nature made in the divine image. Leagues between commonwealths without a higher arbiter represented pragmatic arrangements beneficial to each participant for their respective survival.[55] Even if total and constant warfare did not strictly characterize the international state of nature, it still contained "an omnipresent *potential* for conflict."[56]

The state of nature was much more than a hypothetical or abstract notion in Hobbes's political thought and the Westphalian traditions more broadly. The Englishman presented a rhetorically powerful descriptive account of it with clear normative implications. As a translator of Thucydides's *Peloponnesian War*, Hobbes drew from specific literary records of ancient Greece despite his observation that there was never a time in which the whole world generally was a war of all against all.[57] The violent interactions and wars between sovereign states throughout the course of history also represented the state of nature. But these historical and literary examples were mere glimpses of it. According to Hobbes and the Westphalian political traditions generally, the most palpable empirical proof for the existence of the state of nature was not in some relic of the past. It was observable among "the savage people in many places of America."[58]

In the broadly generalized terms of *De cive* (*On the Citizen*), Hobbes's identification of "the Americans" as concrete examples of the poor and brutish state of nature served the rhetorical function of sharply distinguishing them from civil society.[59] Several years before the peace treaties, Hobbes clearly expounded a standard of civilization that would cast a shadow on Westphalia's historic legacy. The distinction was visibly manifest in the bottom half of the frontispiece to the 1642 Paris edition of *De cive*.[60] It depicted the magnificent Lady Justice holding her sword and scales while standing on the pedestal of *IMPERIUM* on one side, and a native Algonquian woman, featured as a an unseemly crone, holding a bow and spear standing on *LIBERTAS* on the

[54] Noel Malcolm, *Aspects of Hobbes* (Oxford University Press, 2002), pp. 449–452; William Bain, "Thomas Hobbes as a Theorist of Anarchy: A Theological Interpretation," *History of European Ideas* 41.1 (2015), 24.

[55] Hobbes, *Leviathan*, Part 2, chap. 22, p. 157.

[56] Stephen C. Neff, *Justice among Nations: A History of International Law* (Harvard University Press, 2014), p. 169.

[57] David Boucher, *Political Theories of International Relations: From Thucydides to the Present* (Oxford University Press, 1998), pp. 155–157.

[58] Hobbes, *Leviathan*, Part 1, chap. 13, p. 85.

[59] Hobbes, *On the Citizen*, chap. 1, p. 30.

[60] See Figure 1.1.

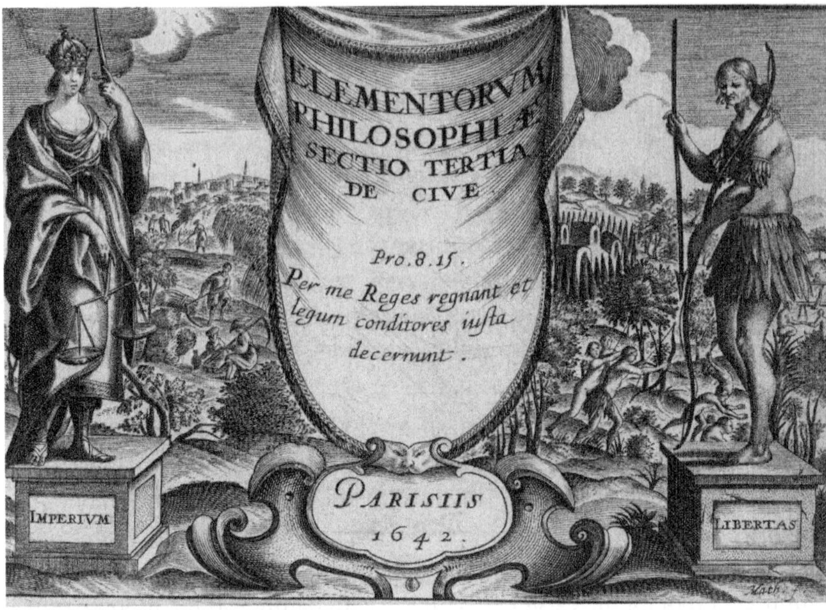

FIGURE 1.1 "Frontispiece of Hobbes's *De Cive*." (Source: Wikimedia Commons, Frontispiece: Elementorum philosophiae sectio tertia de cive, Paris: 1642, by Thomas Hobbes. *EC65 H6525 642e, Houghton Library, Harvard University)

other.[61] Behind the figures were illustrations of their respective modes of life: *IMPERIUM* represented peaceful society, aimed at the cultivation of land with cities in the background; whereas *LIBERTAS* expressed the untamed nature of savages at war with each other in a vast wilderness filled with trees and small dwellings. The frontispiece image reinforced Hobbes' partitioning of the world in two, contrasting the rule of European civil society in the old world with the wild liberty of Native Americans occupying the state of nature in the New World.[62]

The Eurocentric rational standard of Hobbes also undermined native pleas for maintaining traditional ways of life due to the savage portrayal of them. In shocking contrast to the civilized mode of acquiring food through agriculture, native people appear to squat before a roasting human limb. Native savage cannibals were in a perpetual conflict. Hence, "Anyone who believes that one

61 Quentin Skinner, *Hobbes and Republican Liberty* (Cambridge University Press, 2008), pp. 99–102; Theodor Christov, *Before Anarchy: Hobbes and his Critics in Modern International Thought* (Cambridge University Press, 2016), pp. 36–43.

62 Pat Moloney, "Hobbes, Savagery, and International Anarchy," *American Political Science Review* 105, no. 1 (2011), 192–193.

should remain in that state, in which all is allowed to all, is contradicting himself."[63] By deduction, unyielding Amerindians were irrational for refusing to abide by the natural law precepts of peace and security that lead individuals out of the natural state. The prospects for colonial justifications flung open wide once basic natural law precepts were no longer "rationally" evident among wildly free foreign peoples.

Hobbes, who served as a member of the Virginia Company in his early career and received land in the new colony, confronted the parochial limits of Leviathan from his background in colonial politics. Aside from self-implosion, nothing in principle detracted a monarch from acquiring diverse nations by war and conquest, especially when there was a demographic and socioeconomic need to settle "countries not sufficiently inhabited."[64] Expansion into less inhabited spaces was not a license to exterminate those already present there. Hobbes recommended instead that foreigners "constrain" any original inhabitants "to inhabit closer together, and not range a great deal of ground . . . but to court each little plot with art and labor" for sustenance and development.[65] Yet read in a colonial context, this was but a dire warning to native inhabitants about encroaching foreigners.[66] More striking still, if the land became overpopulated and resources scarce, war was the only logical conclusion. Through Hobbes, the anarchical politics of Westphalia was beginning to show its colonial underbelly.

The Westphalian myth of sovereignty, which operates on the assumption that no supremely spiritual or temporal authority exists to adjudicate international relations, offers a lively commentary on the Hobbesian state of nature. At the national level, Hobbes provided an explanatory paradigm for the transition from a prepolitical condition to organized civil society. He clearly partitioned uncivilized and civilized worlds corresponding to life before and after the sovereign. At the international level, the anarchical state of nature, or coexistence without a superior authority, has remained the *sine qua non* of relations between governments in the modern states system. Of course, Hobbes's domestic analogy only went so far. He never concluded free sovereign commonwealths should escape the international state of nature by

63 Hobbes, *On the Citizen*, chap. 1, p. 30.

64 Hobbes, *Leviathan*, Part 2, chap. 3, p. 230. Richard Tuck has argued that Hobbes's colonial view here reflected "the culmination of a humanist tradition" developing from Thomas More, Alberico Gentili, and Hugo Grotius. See Tuck's *The Rights of War and Peace*, p. 138.

65 Hobbes, *Leviathan*, Part 2, chap. 3, p. 230.

66 Malcolm's treatment of Hobbes on international relations offers a far too generous reading removed from historical context when he writes, "[C]olonists were under a moral duty to treat the native people humanely, and to encourage them to use greater productivity to compensate for the loss of territory." See *Aspects of Hobbes*, p. 442.

creating a world Leviathan because that would undermine their exclusive domestic power.

Hobbes's international state of nature and its pervasive potential for conflict yielded a spectrum of possibilities for later Westphalian political thinkers. John Locke, despite showing more affinity for sociability like Grotius and unlike Hobbes, still considered the meeting of independent rulers to be plain examples of the international state of nature.[67] Regardless of entering treaties and trade, separate governments belong to the state of nature, according to Locke, as individuals lacking a single political society. Vattel similarly conceived of nations as free and equal individuals living in the state of nature yet under the impulse to cultivate the bond of human society.[68] Even Kant's international political theory began from the Hobbesian construal of the natural state in hostile terms, only to foreground the urgent ethical demand of establishing a cosmopolitan federation of peoples short of a world government.[69]

What has dominated modern international relations based on the states system mythologized in Westphalia has been a parochialism indebted to focusing on ideal relations between legitimate peoples inside Europe. This implicit "orthodox theory" of international order operated on the principle of toleration between free and equal sovereign states.[70] Outside Europe, these same sovereign states in practice abided by an ordering principle of civilization to establish imperial and colonial relations with non-European peoples. Hobbes's scant but rhetorically salient references to savage Americans in need of civil society attested this historical fact. Subsequent Westphalian thinkers such as Locke, Vattel, and Kant confirm it. It also demonstrates how the state of nature – a central idea of modern Western political sovereignty – was conceived through European interactions with non-European others, beginning with the gaze of Spaniards. To go beyond Westphalia and the politics of anarchy in international thought, the question of the non-European other in the face of European colonial powers must receive analytical priority by moving from the periphery to the center of investigation.[71] Only then can

67 John Locke, *Two Treatises of Government*, ed. Ian Shapiro (Yale University Press, 2003), chap. 2, §14. Locke's view on independent sovereigns entering into leagues with one another for safety and trade in the international state of nature was a clear endorsement of Hobbes.

68 Vattel, *The Law of Nations*, Preliminaries, p. 68.

69 Immanuel Kant, *Toward Perpetual Peace*, ed. Pauline Kleingeld (Yale University Press, 2006), p. 78.

70 Edward Keene, *Beyond the Anarchical Society: Grotius, Colonialism, and Order in World Politics* (Cambridge University Press, 2002), chap. 1.

71 For an important work that exemplifies this approach in contemporary IR scholarship attentive to the historical practice of dispossessing non-European others and its continuing

we embark on a new search for an alternative Christian politics of world order in which the authentic proclamation of the Gospel to all nations framed the discussion.

VALLADOLID AND INFIDELS IN A NEW WORLD ORDER

Despite the Westphalian paradigm for international relations in the English School, Martin Wight made a remarkably underappreciated claim about the theological roots of modern international relations in his analysis of the three traditions. When Wight broached the topic of colonialism in his international political theory, he arrived at a surprising conclusion:

> Rationalism in Europe begins with the great debate in Spain in the second quarter of the sixteenth century about the Indians, which was the origin of modern international law. Sepúlveda, the chaplain of Charles V and tutor of Phillip II, wrote the first reasoned treatise of Realism about barbarians, justifying the subjugation of primitive peoples by those more civilized. Las Casas, a Dominican and great humanitarian, made fourteen journeys to America collecting information, and he pleaded with Charles V and the Pope for just and humane treatment of the Indians. In 1550 there was a public dispute between Sepúlveda and Las Casas at Valladolid before a committee of theologians and jurists, on the question of whether it was permitted to make war on American Indians to subject them to Spanish rule and Christianity ... This "great debate", in the long run, transformed the Spanish Empire ... [.]
>
> This "great debate" also laid the foundations for modern international law. It was not the development of the diplomatic system in Europe, nor war in Europe, nor the disintegration of Christendom and the need for its reunion that provided the occasion for international law; it was this problem of the barbarians. The first great treatises on international law were by Vitoria, O.P., professor of theology at Salamanca. His "Relectiones de Indis" were lectures of 1539, investigating the legality and morality of Spanish rule in the Indies, and explicitly condemning much of the Conquest.[72]

Wight, unfortunately, expanded little beyond this contrarian point about an earlier Hispanic origin to international law the very assertion of which dethroned Grotius and displaced Westphalian Europe. Wight's anachronistic imposition of the rationalist and realist types to the "great debate" at Valladolid between 1550 and 1551 notwithstanding, it was astonishing that the event

influence, see Paul Keal, *European Conquest and the Rights of Indigenous Peoples* (Cambridge University Press, 2003).

72 Wight, *International Theory*, pp. 69–70.

occupied a place at all in his etiological narrative of international law, and a central one at that.[73] Although Francisco de Vitoria (1483–1546) did not live long enough to join the dispute at Valladolid, Wight directly associated him with the Spanish contribution to international law. This egregious, epoch-defining crucible of conflict was known as *la duda indiana* ("the Amerindian question"). Wight's provocative invitation orients our study of the infidel other as the touchstone for understanding world order and international society in Western Europe's colonial past.

Throughout the twentieth century, Iberoamerican scholars reclaimed the Spanish scholastic origins of international law and its distinction from the political realism of Machiavelli and Hobbes. In Spain, Camilo Barcia Trelles identified "the Spanish international school" of the sixteenth-century theologians, contrasting it with the Westphalian "error" that posited the strict contingent states system at the expense of universal community.[74] On this view, Vitoria was a progenitor of modern international law who anticipated a global future that avoided the extremes of cosmic imperial universalism and national monarchical atomism.[75] Across the Atlantic, the Mexican diplomat and scholar Antonio Gómez Robledo not only celebrated the modernity of Vitoria's "right of peoples" (*derecho de gentes*), but also his ongoing relevance for thinking about *ius cogens* norms having peremptory force.[76] Vitoria was the first scholastic thinker to ground the *ius gentium* on the authority "of the whole world" (*totius orbis*).[77] These Hispanist retrievals, seeking to displace the dominant Westphalian narrative, agreed that the principal inspiration for international relations among the Spanish theologians was none other than the European encounter with peoples of the New World.[78]

73 Some IR scholars have signaled Valladolid's historical importance for distinct purposes in international law. See Keal, *European Conquest*, p. 91; G. C. Marks, "Indigenous Peoples in International Law: The Significance of Francisco de Vitoria and Bartolomé de Las Casas," *Australian Yearbook of International Law* 13 (1990–1991), 22–34; Timothy Dunne, "Colonial Encounters in International Relations: Reading Wight, Writing Australia," *Australian Journal of International Affairs* 51, no. 3 (1997), 315; Neta Crawford, *Argument and Change in World Politics: Ethics, Decolonization, and Humanitarian Intervention* (Cambridge University Press, 2002), pp. 152–158; Clark, *Legitimacy in International Society*, p. 42.

74 Camilo Barcia Trelles, *Interpretación del Hecho Americano por la España Universitaria del Siglo XVI* (Institución cultural Española de Uruguay, 1949), p. 22.

75 Barcia Trelles, *Interpretación del Hecho Americano*, p. 56.

76 Antonio Gómez Robledo, *Fundadores del Derecho Internacional: Vitoria, Gentili, Suárez, Grocio* (Universidad Nacional Autónoma de México, 1989), pp. 35–36.

77 Francisco de Vitoria, *On Civil Power*, in *Political Writings*, eds. Anthony Pagden and Jeremy Lawrance (Cambridge University Press, 1991), q. 3, a. 4, p. 40.

78 Barcia Trelles, *Interpretación del Hecho Americano*, p. 81; Gómez Robledo, *Fundadores del Derecho Internacional*, pp. 34–35. For a comparable argument from the twentieth-century

The foundational role of the Spanish theologians in the history of international legal thought has not gone unnoticed in the Anglophone world either. James Brown Scott, a longtime secretary of the Carnegie Endowment for International Peace who helped establish the World Court at The Hague in 1920, raised scholarly awareness of the Spanish school of international thought by making available key English translations and commentaries of Vitoria and Suárez. Remarkably, the North American was a Protestant expositor of the Catholic conception of international law, praising Vitoria as the one who first sketched the "Temple of International Justice to which Grotius was to add with his own hand the details of the completed drawing."[79] According to Scott, Vitoria's modern law of nations anticipated the Permanent Court of International Justice four centuries by declaring the native principalities of America equal members of the international community with the same rights and duties of European Christian states. At the height of Woodrow Wilson's foreign policy of internationalism, Scott turned Vitoria's so-called "liberal law of nations" into a politics of the present moment. The Spanish school was a blueprint for the activities of the League of Nations and its support of the Mandates System to improve backward societies, or "children of nature," in order to place them on equal footing with "enlightened states."[80]

From a very different normative perspective after the middle of the twentieth century, other lawyers and scholars have identified Vitoria with the insidious colonial origins of international law. Carl Schmitt's 1950 *Der Nomos der Erde* (*The Nomos of the Earth*) offset earlier appraisals of Vitoria with a trenchant thesis that modern European international law was established by a singular course of events: the conquest and dispossession of the New World.[81] Critical histories and postcolonial studies of international law in Schmitt's wake argue that Vitoria's law of nations provided a secular justification of the civilizing mission of imperial Spain independent of papal approval that has continued up to the present day.[82] Instead of elevating native peoples

German political philosopher, Heinrich Rommen, see *The State in Catholic Thought: A Treatise in Political Philosophy* (Lexington, KY: Cluny Media, 2006), pp. 585–586.

79 Scott, *The Spanish Origin of International Law*, p. 288. Also see Oxford Professor James Brierly, who considered international law a "subordinate offshoot of theology." *The Basis of Obligation in International Law and Other Papers* (Oxford: Clarendon Press, 1958), pp. 366–369.

80 Scott, *The Spanish Origin of International Law*, pp. 282–287.

81 Carl Schmitt, *The Nomos of the Earth*, trans. G. L. Ulmen (Telos Publishing, 2006), p. 101.

82 Robert Williams, *The American Indian in Western Legal Thought* (Oxford University Press, 1990), pp. 93–108; Antony Anghie, *Imperialism, Sovereignty, and the Making of International Law* (Cambridge University Press, 2007), chap. 1. It is worth noting these legal scholars contrast with Schmitt, who did not identify Vitoria as a "secular" forerunner to modern

to an equal status, Vitoria's colonial international thought, along with other Spanish theologians, laid out the modern imperial and commercial architecture for foreign domination and assimilation. Critics assail Vitoria's affirmation of human reason and natural rights among Amerindians for only appearing benign. Vitoria's ideas instead rationalized European expansion through the enforcement of supposedly "universal" norms and duties on the international community's newest colonized members.

These Anglophone American scholars have tended to turn Vitoria's scholastic thought into a usable past, the alleged predecessor to liberal internationalism or neocolonialism. Neither contrasting interpretation places Vitoria and the Spanish theologians in their proper historical context or the broader history of international relations attentive to important ideological and political transformations occurring in Western Europe. By putting Valladolid in conversation with Westphalia, the task of Chapters 5 and 6, *Infidels and Empires in a New World Order* unearths a more complex yet revealing history of transnational continuities and discontinuities in early modern international thought. Unlike the Westphalian paradigm of legitimate sovereign states in Christian Europe, the Amerindian question demanded the moral and political recognition of infidels within a world order extending beyond Europe. According to Spanish Dominicans, especially Vitoria and Las Casas, the Church's task of witnessing to a new world order transcending the rule and practice of imperial rule rested on two claims of universality: the universal proclamation of the Gospel to all nations and the universal inclusivity of the Body of Christ.

The principal religious justification for Spanish Christian presence across the Atlantic was the conversion of native peoples. One year after the Admiral Christopher Columbus first made Caribbean landfall in 1492, Pope Alexander VI wrote the bull *Inter caetera* entrusting the Catholic Monarchs of Spain, Ferdinand and Isabel, with the duty of bringing the ecclesial faith to the natives of newly discovered islands and the Central and South American mainland, or the "Indies."[83] Among other things, the 1493 papal bull of Alexander VI inaugurated early modern disputes about European expansion into new worlds by Portuguese, Dutch, and English traders and settlers. For the Spaniards, it set the terms or the state of the question for their colonial debates. The spiritual rationale of Spanish expansion contained in the bull

international law, but instead located the Dominican theologian within a spiritual worldview belonging to the Christian Middle Ages. See *The Nomos of the Earth*, chap. 2.

83 *Inter caetera* (May 4, 1493), in Eugene Shiels, SJ, *King and Church: The Rise and Fall of the Patronato Real* (Loyola University Press, 1961), pp. 78–81.

would certainly augment theocratic universalist arguments in favor of the colonial dispossession and enslavement of Amerindians, as we will consider in the next chapter. Yet the same spiritual objective would also sustain mendicant critiques of colonial abuses evident in war and the forced labor institution known as the *encomienda*, the focus of Chapter 3.

Already in 1516, the former *encomendero*-priest of Cuba, Bartolomé de las Casas, pleaded the native cause before the Council of the Indies:

> The principal end by which everything has been ordered . . . is the salvation of the Indians . . . There is and has been a great defect however in the administration of this task among those Spaniards entrusted with Indians, who do not know what to teach. Even those who do know, with the little love that they have, fail to show it because they prefer money over the salvation of souls.[84]

For Las Casas, and the New World Dominicans who had initially reformed his thoughts and feelings, the principal end of salvation trumps profit and brings all other temporal considerations in the Indies under spiritual judgment. In opposition to the crusader-like method of missionary war, the Spanish Dominicans advanced a peaceful method of evangelization conforming to the biblical norm and example given by Jesus Christ to the apostles.

In January of 1539, Vitoria began his famous *Relectio de Indis* delivered at the University of Salamanca by "rereading" the Great Commission of Christ to preach the Gospel to all nations in the context of the New World (*novi orbis*).[85] Vitoria's lecture rejected all the commonly rehearsed Spanish titles justifying war against Amerindians. The Great Commission could not be a pretext for both Christian imperial and papal theocratic expansion and subjugation of foreign peoples. The Salmantine theologian, along with many of his Dominican confreres, ruled out religious wars in principle for international relations because it violated the true spirit of the Gospel. "[W]ar is no argument for the truth of the Christian faith," he wrote. "Hence, the barbarians cannot be moved by war to believe, but only to pretend that they believe and accept the Christian faith; and this is monstrous and sacrilegious."[86]

84 Las Casas, *Memorial de remedios para las indias* (1516), in *Obras completas* (hereafter OC), vol. 13, eds. Paulino Castañeda Delgado et al. (Alianza Editorial, 1995), p. 40.

85 Mt 28:19.

86 Francisco de Vitoria, *On the American Indians*, in *Political Writings*, q. 2, a. 4, p. 272. I have crosschecked the Pagden and Lawrance edition with the Latin transcription of the *relectiones* from Teofilo Urdanoz in *Obras de Franscisco de Vitoria* (Biblioteca de Autores Cristianos, 1960) making slight and occasional modifications as needed to reflect the meaning and translation of specific terms more clearly. All other Latin and Spanish translations are my own unless indicated otherwise.

Contrary to Hobbes, the Spanish theologians did not view the Church as a temporal political unit coextensive with the commonwealth.[87] Rather, as the mystical Body of Christ, the Church inhabited an eschatological space transcending time that included people from every nation in every age, both believers and nonbelievers who were always members of it in a potential sense.[88] The dogma was not abstract but had moral and juridical importance for affirming individual dignity and freedom in distinctive ways. Vitoria's two university lectures (or *relectiones*) on ecclesiastical power given in 1532 and 1533 defended the dualism of the spiritual and temporal powers against any inkling of political or ecclesiastical monism. Since the nature of ecclesiastical power directs the faithful toward eternal happiness, the mystical Body of Christ requires a jurisdictional *potestas* to govern and discipline Christians among the various nations over the course of history.[89]

In scholastic analogical fashion, Vitoria took inspiration from Aquinas to show the comparative limits between the mystical Body (*corpus mysticum*) of Christ and the natural body of a single organism.[90] The social implications of this dissimilitude were crucial for Vitoria's affirmation of the worth of the individual within a single commonwealth and, by extension, the community of the whole world. Whereas "the parts of a natural body are disposed entirely for the good of the whole," the individual member of the Church exists "for God" and "for themselves" (*propter se*). Similar to Aquinas, Vitoria's ecclesiology enabled him to identify an end transcending political society whereby "the good of a private man is not even principally, let alone entirely, ordained for the good of the whole community."[91] Vitoria's conception of world order, in which the good of the individual avoids complete subordination to any political community, could offer "a powerful antidote" to absolutist forms of sovereignty.[92]

At the Valladolid junta, further discussed in Chapter 4, Las Casas extracted another important teaching from Aquinas on the mystical Body of Christ to include all of humanity, particularly Amerindians, within an ecclesial vision of world order. Las Casas applied the scholastic act–potency distinction to substantiate the freedom of Amerindian peoples apart from Christian claims of political sovereignty. Christ is not only the head of the visible Church, but

87 Hobbes, *On the Citizen*, chap. 17, pp. 221, 228.

88 Cavanaugh, *Theopolitical Imagination*, p. 5.

89 Vitoria, *On the Power of the Church* (Part I), in *Political Writings*, q. 2, a. 1, p. 58.

90 Aquinas, *ST* III, q. 8, a. 1 *ad* 2; q. 8, a. 3.

91 Vitoria, *On the Power of the Church* (Part II), in *Political Writings*, q. 1, a. 1, p. 119. Cf. *ST* I-II, q. 21, a. 4 *ad* 3.

92 Bain, "Saving the Innocent," 610.

also the universal head of humanity through the Incarnation. Therefore, those who are only potential members of the Church still belong to him, but not in the same manner as actual members of the Church.[93] Actual members of the Church are those baptized members subject to ecclesiastical power and discipline.

In contrast, indigenous nonbelievers "who have never accepted the faith of Christ are not *in actuality* subject to Christ and therefore not to the Church or its authority."[94] That is because nonbelievers belong individually as members of Christ *in potentia*. Las Casas distinguished between the sovereign power of Christ over the world and the proper juridical authority of the Church defined by its evangelical mission. He concluded that Christians must absolutely respect the freedom of infidels since "this potency is based on the power of Christ, who does not force anyone, as well as upon the freedom of the will, which cannot be forced either."[95] Christ, who is Lord of all creation and humanity, thereby anchors world order, safeguarding the possibility of salvation for every individual free to accept or deny the gift of faith entrusted to the Church. Vitoria and Las Casas similarly appropriated Aquinas's mystical Body teaching to affirm the primacy of the individual person within a single political community and the world community.

The Church's authentic proclamation of the Good News of salvation outside the old world set the moral parameters for a Christian theological conception of a new world order. No matter the necessity of conversion for receiving eternal life, the means of bringing the message of salvation to infidels must never violate the universal order of reason inhering in the natural right and the right of peoples vindicated by Jesus Christ. According to the Spanish Dominicans, the freedom of every single rational creature to receive the faith without coercion stood as a theological prerequisite for the Church's presence and its activity in the Indies. The rest of this book considers why their contributions and that of their Spanish interlocutors revolving around Valladolid mattered for international legal thought, a history conventionally told through the strict conceptual parameters of Westphalia.

93 Aquinas, *ST* III, q. 8, a. 3 *ad* 1.

94 Las Casas, *In Defense of the Indians*, trans. Stafford Poole (Northern Illinois University Press, 1992), chap. 6, p. 55.

95 Las Casas, *In Defense of the Indians*, chap. 6, pp. 60–61.

PART I

THE NEW WORLD CRUCIBLE OF INFIDEL RIGHTS

2

Theocratic World Order and Religious Wars

The conquests of the Indians began once the conquests of the Moors ended because Spaniards always wage war against infidels.[1]

Before international relations in the West, there were Christian–infidel relations. Latin Christendom was an incorporating society that rationalized and regulated the difference of religious identity within Europe and beyond.[2] The incorporation of others into a Christian political order presumed legal boundaries between insiders and outsiders of the institutional Church, the definitive identity marker of which was baptism. Church law, or canon law, generated a normative vocabulary of difference contrasting the orthodox faithful from heretics and schismatics among the baptized. For those outside the Church, religious difference was subsumed under the general category of the infidel (*infidele*), which included Jews, Muslims, and pagans.[3] Both defense and denigration of unbaptized infidels typified the ambivalent ecclesiastical policy of incorporation. Overall, this medieval and early modern canonistic regulation was more influential in its power to restrain than to protect infidels.

This book focuses on the legal and political status of infidels outside the Church to analyze divergent European Christian conceptions of world order

[1] Francisco López de Gómara, *Historia General de las Indias* (Comisión Nacional del V Centenario del Descubrimiento de América Encuentro de Dos Mundos, 1993): "*Comenzaron las conquistas de indios acabada la de moros, porque siempre guerreasen españoles contra infieles.*"

[2] Jonathan Boyarin, *The Unconverted Self: Jews, Indians, and the Identity of Christian Europe* (University of Chicago Press, 2009), p. 12.

[3] Although heretics generally belonged to the category of unbelievers, their baptismal status made them a different juridical case than non-Christians. Muslims and pagans were often used interchangeably in medieval canon legal literature to denote Saracen Muslims as idol-worshipping pagans. See Benjamin Z. Kedar, "*De Iudeis et Sarracenis*: On the Categorization of Muslims in Medieval Canon Law," in *Studia in Honorem Eminentissimi Cardinalis Alphonsi M. Stickler*, eds. José Rosalio and Castillo Lara (LAS, 1992), pp. 207–213.

in the early modern Anglo-Iberian Atlantic. It was not the case that Christian Europe in the West, or Latin Christendom, construed relations with infidels strictly in terms of hostility according to an insurmountable legal gulf.[4] The medieval Christian roots of world order emerged in the thirteenth-century canonistic account of infidel dominium amidst a wider development in the language of subjective rights.[5] Infidels had rights, which attested to a belief in the oneness of rational humanity and the universal potentiality for salvation, as well as the legitimate political orders and properties of non-Christian peoples and their right to defend themselves from injustice. It also meant that unbelievers as rational creatures were accountable to a universal standard of law providing grounds for intervention and just war.

Appropriation of these ideas by lawyers and theologians addressing the early modern encounter with extra-European peoples cut in two directions for and against colonial practices of dispossession. The theological category of the infidel demarcated those who either rejected the Christian faith or had never received it in the first place and were therefore outside proper ecclesiastical jurisdiction. Consequently, Christian posture toward infidels was always evangelically oriented toward conversion, which could additionally serve as both a justification and a rebuke of colonial subjugation. The discussion of infidel rights was as much about the extent and limits of ecclesiastical power as it was about the proper way to evangelize non-Christians without denigrating the possibility of salvation for all and the authentic witness of the faith.

The infidel of Latin Christendom inhabited a highly ambivalent political space punctuated by periods of both accommodation and intolerance. On the one hand, the politics of difference could foment the social repression of infidels and war making against declared enemies during an era of Crusades and Reconquista. By extension, Jews symbolized the internal enemies of Christendom and Muslim "Saracens" its external enemies. Canon law cast relations with these infidels in generally conflictual terms because of the belief that each group's rejection of the faith posed distinct threats to the stability and unity of Latin Europe. On the other hand, the baptismal identity marker also provided a buffer from Christian political judgments and legal recognition of traditional non-Christian religious customs. Remarkably, canon law also contained important principles for guarding the internal spiritual matters of non-Christians from coercion by setting limits on ecclesiastical jurisdiction.[6]

4 Cf. Pitts, *Boundaries of the International*, pp. 19–20.

5 Brian Tierney, *The Idea of Natural Rights* (Eerdmans, 1997), chap. 2.

6 Mario Condorelli, *I Fondamenti Giuridici della Tolleranza Religiosa Nell'elaborazione Canonistica dei Secoli XII–XIV* (Milan, 1960), pp. 24–25. Solomon Grayzel, "Introduction" in *The Church and the Jews in the XIIIth Century* (Wayne State University, 1989), p. 12;

Although the ancient Roman Empire had a policy of tolerating the rites and customs of subject peoples to pacify civil discord, the Christian Latin West developed legal norms for it based on the Bible and theological claims. Chief among those teachings was St. Paul's setting boundaries on ecclesiastical power by instructing Christians not to judge those outside the Church (1 Cor 5:12–13): "For why should I judge those who are outside [*qui foris sunt*]? Is it not your business to judge those within? God will judge those outside." Centuries later, St. Augustine echoed this teaching about the spiritual immunity of those outside the community of the baptized in a sermon advising Christians to attract unbelievers to the truth of the faith through gentleness.[7] Gratian, the pioneering monk of medieval canon law, turned this early Church teaching on the difference between insiders and outsiders into a juridical norm for tolerating non-Christians, or those who belong to a different law than the Church.[8] Even scholastic theologians adopted this norm, as seen in Thomas Aquinas's restriction on the spiritual judgment of non-Christians who posed no threat to the common good.[9] Remarkably, the Spanish Dominican theologians considered in Chapter 3 translated this canon legal norm into a political principle for defending free Amerindian peoples from the judgment and punishment of European powers.

CRUSADES AND THE RIGHTS OF INFIDELS

At the center of the ambivalent premodern construal of Christian–infidel relations was the institution of the papacy, Latin Christendom's spiritual and political figurehead. Pope Gregory the Great (590–604), whose leadership anticipated the prominent social role of the medieval papacy, illustrated an uneasy tension in his respective treatment of Jews and pagans. With respect to Jews, Pope Gregory's teachings often set the legal standard for positive Christian relations with them during the Middle Ages.[10] Similar to Augustine's homily, Gregory, in a famous letter protecting the Jews of

István Bejczy, "Tolerantia: A Medieval Concept," *Journal of the History of Ideas* 58, no. 3 (1997): 365–384.

7 *Patrologia Latina*, 38, 420, Sermon 62, cap. 7. Homilies on the Gospel of Matthew. Referring to pagan outsiders, Augustine cites 1 Cor 5:12 and then remarks: "Those [pagans] are to be attracted gently, so that they may hear the truth" (*Blandiendum est illis, ut audiant veritatem*).

8 Gratian, *Decretum*, Causa 23, q. 4, cc. 16–17.

9 Aquinas, *ST*, II-II, q. 12, a. 2: "Now it is not within the competency of the Church to punish unbelief in those who have never received the faith, according to the saying of the Apostle (1 Cor 5:12): *What have I to do to judge them that are without?*"

10 For a full Latin register with accompanying English translations, see Amnon Linder, *The Jews in the Legal Sources of the Early Middle Ages* (Wayne State University Press, 1997), pp. 417–443.

Naples, mandated that "outsiders" must be drawn to the faith by "enticements, not harshness." Pope Gregory's firm support of fourth-century Roman imperial legislation respecting Jewish worship would set a benchmark for medieval canon law, codified in Gratian's *Decretum*.[11]

Opposing those Christians who hindered Jews from practicing their ancient customs, Gregory once asked the bishop of Naples, "What is the advantage" (*quid utilitas est*) of religious coercion if it frustrates the possibility of genuine conversion? The protection of infidels from overreaching Christian authorities was not merely for the sake of avoiding conflict but was also for preserving the Gospel message from any association with scandalous violence. The long-standing custom and dogma of respecting free will in the reception of faith in the heart, encapsulated by the Augustinian formula that "man cannot believe unless he is willing," required vigilant observance.[12] Transgression of this teaching in medieval Christendom did not lessen its orthodoxy or the Christian desire of conforming to it.

Gregory the Great's evangelical concerns had a salutary effect on Christian relations with Jews, but it also widened the parameters for conflict with pagans. In a striking example, Pope Gregory advised his bishops on the island of Sardinia to impose heavy taxes on obstinate pagan peasants for the sake of hastening their conversion.[13] In another, Gregory wrote a letter to the African exarch Gennadius on the margins of the Roman Empire, praising his military campaigns and war effort to bring the faith to subjugated peoples.[14] Carl Erdmann, the twentieth-century historian of Crusades, argued that Pope Gregory introduced the idea here of an *indirect* missionary war, which overcame the apparent contradiction between conquest and evangelization. Missionary war would not be achieved "by direct imposition of faith," a flagrant violation of mainstream Church tradition, "but by the detour of political subjugation" to secure a safe path for preaching.[15] Overall, Gregory's letters on Jews and pagans represented the ambivalent political status of infidels that later marked the teachings of medieval popes and canonists.[16]

[11] Gratian, *Decretum*, Dist. 45, c. 3. For an English translation, see Robert Chazan, *Church, State and Jew in the Middle Ages* (Behrman House, 1980), p. 20.

[12] Augustine, *Homilies on the Gospel of John*, Tractate 26, §2: "[C]*redere non potest homo nisi volens*."

[13] Pope Gregory I, Book IV, Letter 26, trans. James Barmby, in *Nicene and Post-Nicene Fathers of the Christian Church, Second Series*, vol. 12, eds. Philip Schaff and Henry Wace (Christian Literature, 1895).

[14] Pope Gregory I, Book I, Letter 75.

[15] Carl Erdmann, *The Origin of the Idea of Crusade*, trans. Marshall Baldwin and Walter Goffart (Princeton University Press, 1977), pp. 10–11.

[16] Gratian, *Decretum*, Causa 23, q. 6.

Nothing in the Middle Ages shaped Christian–infidel relations more than the papal Crusades and holy war. Pope Gregory VII (1073–1085) was a medieval catalyst for the ecclesiastical politics favoring religious war against enemies of the faith.[17] Well-known for his struggle to preserve Church immunity from secular control during the investiture crisis, Gregory VII conferred an unprecedented sacred value on war from his supreme spiritual authority. The reformist Pope hoped to liberate Byzantium from the Turks by leading the charge of soldiers for Christ (*milites Christi*). In part, this vision came to fruition a few years later at Clermont in 1095 when Pope Urban II delivered a fiery sermon against the Muslim enemies of the Church in the East. Pope Urban institutionalized holy war through the crusader vow, a binding religious commitment on the part of knights seeking spiritual merit and remission of sins for defeating the Saracen enemy. By the Fourth Lateran Council (1215), the canons of the Church stipulated that wars against heretics in Christendom would receive the same spiritual reward as wars against infidels in the Holy Land. Additionally, the Council decreed that priests and crusaders were the respective spiritual and material arms of the Church's fight against enemies of the faith.[18]

Holy war's growing popularity vitiated Christian–infidel relations by corrupting the peaceful ethic of evangelization taught by Jesus, the apostles, and the early Church. The violent excesses of the First Crusade were a major turning point. Marauding bands of armed pilgrims who decimated certain Jewish and Muslim communities from Germany to Egypt represented egregious examples of forcible baptism under a policy of conversion or death.[19] Latin chroniclers of the First Crusade, cognizant of these brutal events, commonly identified the principal aim of holy war with the eradication of pagan idolatry and unbelief.[20] The popular crusading poem *The Song of Roland*, which recounted the legendary eighth-century Frankish conquest of Muslim Iberia for a medieval audience, similarly portrayed holy war as a sacred act to convert infidels and defend the faith against the evil of idolatry.[21]

17 Erdmann, *The Origin of the Idea of Crusade*, chap. 5; James Brundage, "Holy War and Medieval Lawyers," in *The Holy War*, ed. Thomas Patrick Murphy (Ohio State University Press, 1976), pp. 104–5.

18 Respectively, Canons 3 and 71.

19 Jonathan Riley-Smith, *The First Crusade and the Idea of Crusading* (University of Pennsylvania Press, 1986).

20 John Tolan, *Saracens: Islam in the Medieval European Imagination* (Columbia University Press, 2002), chap. 5.

21 Gerard J. Brault, *Song of Roland: An Analytical Edition* (Pennsylvania State University Press, 1978), laisse 266, lines 3660–3670, pp. 223–225.

Despite the popularization of forced conversion on shocking display in the First Crusade, clerics attempted to curb such exploits by strengthening ecclesiastical oversight of holy war through canon law. The Christian teaching on just war offered an effective means of doing so but this doctrine would undergo significant reformulation in order to accommodate the reality of crusading mission. Gratian's *Decretum*, for example, began to include God's direct authorization for war (as seen in numerous Old Testament examples) in addition to mere public authority and just cause.[22] The assimilation of divine authority to ecclesiastical authority, in turn, sacralized the cause of defending the faith against enemies. Arguably, this opened the possibility of legitimate wars to extend the reach of Christendom.[23]

Both the First and the Second Crusades summoned by Pope Eugenius III may have constituted traditional causes of war for recovering lands from Muslims in Palestine and Edessa. However, the doctrine of missionary war was coalescing into an independent criterion for crusading popes, and secular and clerical proponents. The Second Crusade sent knights not only to the East, but also into Iberia against the Moors and the Baltic region against unbelievers. Notably, the extension of Christendom over the Wendish people through a religious war gained theological and pastoral support from St. Bernard of Clairvaux, a teacher and advisor to Pope Eugenius.[24] Although Bernard's popular preaching resolutely opposed the mistreatment of Jews, he proposed an indirect strategy of converting pagan Slavs by subjugating them through conquest and destroying their religious rites. The elimination of their idolatry – an obstacle invented by the devil – would open an effective path to preaching and salvation.[25]

The evolution of just war into a legitimate instrument of Christian mission under papal leadership would attain its most articulate exposition in the canon lawyer Sinibaldo Fieschi, later Pope Innocent IV (1243–1254). The future Pope Innocent treated the subject of Christian–infidel relations in his commentary on a papal letter (or decretal) *Quod super his, de voto*, the main subject of which was the crusader vow. His opening question set the terms for a new discussion about war: "There is no doubt that it is licit for the pope, by

22 Gratian, *Decretum*, Causa 23, q. 2.

23 Frederick H. Russell, *The Just War in the Middle Ages* (Cambridge University Press, 1975), pp. 72–73.

24 Jonathan Phillips, *The Second Crusade: Extending the Frontiers of Christendom* (Yale University Press, 2007), chap. 12.

25 Jospeh Lecler, *Toleration and the Reformation*, trans. T. L. Westow, vol. 1 (Association Press, 1960), pp. 76–77; Friedrich Lotter, "The Crusading Idea and the Conquest of the Region East of the Elbe," in *Medieval Frontier Societies*, eds. Robert Bartlett and Angus MacKay (Clarendon Press, 1989), pp. 290–292.

persuading the faithful and granting indulgences, to defend the Holy Land and all the faithful inhabiting it. But is it ever licit to invade lands which are held or owned by infidels?"[26] In the commentary, Innocent moved the discussion of just war beyond its classic rationales of reclaiming stolen goods or repaying violence with violence. The canonist Pope raised the prospect of expansionary wars of intervention that presumed the lawful dominium of infidels. His rather brief but systematic answer laying out the Christian criteria of war with infidels became the *communis opinio* for subsequent canon legal thinking.[27] It outlined the basic principles for a theocratic conception of world order resting on a doctrine of infidel rights yet strongly curtailed by the universal temporal claims of papal authority.

Innocent IV began his commentary *Quod super his* with a reflection on the theological origins of property and political rule to establish the universal rights of all peoples, even infidels. The first chapter of Genesis revealed the special place within God's creation of human beings as "rational creatures for whom He made all things."[28] Innocent made the canonist's point that the world, belonging entirely to God from the beginning, was once a common possession of everyone. Even so, the division and appropriation of things was a good that contributed to a greater concern for possessions and the avoidance of conflict. Property came about through the usage (*usibus*) of things among the earliest humans. In accordance with natural law and the Golden Rule, it is therefore unlawful to occupy land that already belongs to another following the division of the earth that goes back biblically to Abraham and Lot in Genesis 13. Innocent also made the standard Christian theological claim that human beings were not property in themselves since "by nature all men are free." Slavery was not present in the beginning but emerged later, presumably because of war, under the force of human custom expressed through civil law and the law of nations.

Political rule and civil jurisdiction also originated with the sovereignty of God over all creation although Innocent remained unclear about the first expression of divine–human communication of jurisdictional authority – the legitimate power to punish others. Perhaps it began from the sword given to an

26 Pope Innocent IV, *Quod super his, de voto*, X 3.34.8, §1. For an English translation of most of *Quod super his*, see *The Ethics of War: Classic and Contemporary Readings*, eds. Gregory Reichberg, Henrik Syse, and Endre Begby (Blackwell, 2006), pp. 152–155. Latin terms are from the Frankfurt edition unless noted otherwise. *Commentaria Innocentii super libros quinque Decretalium* (Frankfurt, 1570).

27 James Muldoon provides singular treatment of Pope Innocent IV's theory of Christian-infidel relations and its subsequent importance in the Latin West in *Popes, Lawyers, and Infidels: The Church and the Non-Christian World, 1250–1550* (University of Pennsylvania Press, 1979).

28 Pope Innocent IV, *Quod super his*, X 3.34.8, §1, p. 152.

individual or group for meting out justice on offenders, or perhaps from a father's ruling authority over the family. Regardless, the issue of jurisdiction among the earliest humans mattered little to the canonist Pope. For him, if the prepolitical mode of jurisdiction currently existed at all in the world, it would only be in the rarest of instances. Significantly, the dominant mode of transferring political power in most societies, he claimed, was a people's election or choice of ruler. Innocent drew biblical inspiration from King Saul's election by the people of Israel. At this point, Innocent provided his classic statement on infidel rights to property and self-rule:

> The aforesaid dominions, possessions, and jurisdictions may licitly and without sin be held by the infidels, for these were ordained not only for the faithful, but for every rational creature, as "He maketh his sun to rise on the good and evil," and "he feeds the fowls of the air," Matthew, chapter 5 near the end [verse 45], and chapter 6 [verse 26]. And therefore we say that it is not legitimate for the pope or the faithful to dispossess the infidels of either dominion or jurisdiction, because they possess them without sin.[29]

By invoking God as sovereign ruler and owner of the created world, no Christian emperor, not even the Pope, had the unqualified right to seize the lands and possessions of unbelievers.

The theological foundation of infidel dominium was its greatest strength but also its greatest temptation. Pope Innocent IV was among the strongest medieval proponents of the Church's hierocratic power over temporal matters. In the effort to depose and launch a crusade against Emperor Frederick II, an ally to Saracens and heretics, he appealed to canon law's "by reason of sin" (*ratione peccati*) justification for intervention, which granted the Church power in temporal matters. Yet Innocent identified the Church's temporal power directly with the unparalleled sovereignty of Christ. As the natural Lord from all eternity, Christ by natural right could pass judgment to depose rulers or anyone else.[30] Christ granted this divine power and jurisdictional authority to his vicar on earth, the Pope. Consequently, if the seat of the emperor were ever vacant, the Pope could inhabit the earthly role and attain full jurisdiction over secular matters.[31] The temporal power of the Pope over secular matters

29 Pope Innocent IV, *Quod super his*, X 3.34.8, §3, p. 153.

30 R. W. and A. J. Carlyle, A *History of Medieval Political Theory in the West*, vol. 5 (William Blackwood & Sons, 1928), p. 319.

31 Tierney, *The Crisis of Church and State 1050–1300* (University of Toronto Press, 1988), pp. 153–155.

therefore stemmed from a natural right founded on the natural kingship of Christ.

The world reach of Innocent's theocratic papalism was most applicable to Christian–infidel relations. As he writes in *Quod super his*, "Everyone, both faithful and infidel, are Christ's sheep through creation, although they are not in the sheepfold of the church."[32] The papacy wields the natural universal jurisdiction of Christ and therefore has "full power over all" (*plenam potestatem super omnes*) in principle, although not de facto. After designating humans as rational creatures under the order of creation, and equipping the papacy with jurisdictional authority over everyone, Innocent deployed a concept that had universal scope – the natural law. The universal jurisdiction of natural law inscribed in the sovereignty of Christ extended papal power to the ends of creation, which principally served a spiritual task of caring for all souls.[33] Innocent's radical invention of a papal politics of natural law, for better and for worse, made possible his legal theory of Christian–infidel relations. In principle, infidels belong to the human family because they are rational creatures subject to the rule and requirements of natural law. The Pope as caretaker could therefore judge and intervene in their affairs through the conferred power of Christ, the natural Lord of creation, when their authorities failed to do so.

Innocent IV's papal politics of intervening in the affairs of Jews within Christendom generalized the case of all infidels. Although somewhat reticent of his predecessor Gregory IX's policy of burning the books of the Talmud, Pope Innocent eventually decided in its favor. He referred to the destruction of the Talmud in *Quod super his* as an example of papal intervention and punishment of moral violations of the Mosaic Law by Jews.[34] Scripture authoritatively validated permissible cases of intervention. God's punishment of Sodom for sins against the natural law in Genesis 19 provided a more than sufficient model. The vicar of Christ therefore may rightly punish pagans who have "no law except the law of nature." In addition to the sins of Sodom, the sin of idolatry can also authorize intervention when it goes unpunished.

32 Pope Innocent IV, *Quod super his*, X 3.34.8, §4, p. 153.

33 Muldoon, *Popes, Lawyers, and Infidels*, pp. 10–11.

34 Pope Innocent IV, *Quod super his*, X 3.34.8, §5. Although the Frankfurt edition of the *Apparatus* included reference to violating the law of the Gospel (*contra legem evangelii*), Benjamin Kedar has definitively shown that such a policy would have amounted to an extreme proscription of Judaism within Christendom. By adhering to an older, more reliable manuscript, Kedar concludes: "Innocent IV claims papal jurisdiction over Jews not in cases where they contravene Gospel morality, but where they transgress Old Testament legislation on moral matters and their leaders fail to punish them." See "Canon Law and the Burning of the Talmud," *Bulletin of Medieval Canon Law* 9 (1979): 81.

Worship of idols constitutes a violation of the natural law because "it is natural to worship the one and only God, the Creator, and not creatures."[35] The singular importance of punishing idolatry as a cause for religious war in Christian imperial expansion is difficult to overstate, as will be evident later in the chapter.

Innocent craftily extended the *ratione peccati* principle of ecclesiastical intervention in temporal matters to those outside the Church. This "new and truly revolutionary opinion" of punishing violations of the natural law among infidels, even in religious matters, had dire consequences for the papalist conception of world order in the Latin West.[36] Applied to non-Christian societies where religion and political life were inseparable, Innocent's rationale for intervention outlined a doctrine of missionary warfare under an indirect strategy of punishing sins that could evade the crusader dilemma of forcible baptism. The "Innocentian linkage" between warfare and conversion, or arms and preaching, became the normative view for Christian–infidel relations beyond Europe among popes and canonists.[37]

The canonistic subtleties of Pope Innocent enabled him to draw a logical distinction between direct and indirect forms of coercion in order to justify missionary warfare. Similar to his policy of bringing Jews under Christian judgment by interpreting their violation of the Mosaic Law, he also ratified a policy of James I of Aragon forcing Jews to listen to Christian sermons.[38] According to standard canonistic opinion, neither one of these policies of punishment and forced listening directly violated the freedom of the will in the act of faith. Rather, both employed the force of law and fear of punishment to remove obstacles that stood in the way of receiving the Gospel. Innocent once again generalized from the particular case of Jews to defend his missionary warfare doctrine among infidels in non-Christian lands. The forced listening of Jews translated into a rationale of forced preaching outside Christendom. If the sin of pagan idolatry could be punished, so, too, could the sin of obstructing preachers, since both abided by a valid, indirect form of coercion.

> [A]lthough infidels ought not be forced to accept the faith, since everyone's free will ought to be respected, and this conversion should [come about] only

35 Pope Innocent IV, *Quod super his*, X 3.34.8, §4, p. 153.

36 Condorelli, *I Fondamenti Giuridici*, 126. Walter Ullmann referred to Innocent's theocratic conception of world order as a method and policy of "infiltration." See *Medieval Papalism: The Political Theories of the Medieval Canonists* (Methuen, 1949), p. 121.

37 Kedar, *Crusade and Mission: European Approaches toward the Muslims* (Princeton University Press, 1988), chap. 5.

38 Jeremy Cohen, *Living Letters of the Law* (University of California Press, 1999), p. 163.

> by the grace of God (*Decretum* Dist. 45 *De Iudaeis*) ... yet the pope may command the infidels to admit preachers of the Gospel to the lands under their jurisdiction; for, since every rational creature is created to praise God, they sin if they stop the preachers from preaching, and therefore they ought to be punished.[39]

With these two goals supplied by the canon lawyer-pope – removal of idolatry and admission of preachers – the legal doctrine of missionary war became firmly entrenched in the crusader ideology of the Latin West. In each case, punishment of unbelievers for violating the law of nature contributed to abolishing their sinful customs and forcing them to consider the truth of the Christian faith. According to the parameters of canon law, both of these actions were coercive but did not constitute forcible conversion. The resulting political conclusion was that if unbelievers did not yield to the supreme authority of the Pope on these matters, then they should fear the threat of war and slavery. Oppositely, Muslims and other infidels were certainly not on equal footing with Christians to preach their religion in public. Innocent more or less held that "error" had no right.[40] In the acute words of Jewish scholar Jonathan Boyarin, "Innocent IV's articulation of the extension of the papal vicariate to every human being was a key moment in the ideological prehistory of early modern European imperialism."[41] The papal directives, royal decrees, legal arguments, and popular chronicles of Iberian conquest beyond the European continent in the Atlantic bore out the encumbered legacy of Innocent IV's theocratic papalist conception of world order.

PAPALIST WORLD ORDER UNDER IBERIAN RULE

The political transmutation of a papal crusading mission into an imperial civilizing mission came about through Iberian Catholic expansion into Africa and the Atlantic during the fifteenth and sixteenth centuries. The spread of new trade and commerce, colonial revenues and tributes from acquired lands, and prisoners of war, refashioned the Iberian kingdoms of Portugal and Spain into transatlantic imperial powers. In these two centuries of alliance between throne and altar, ecclesiastical oversight of the practice of Iberian missionary war weakened considerably, largely due to the papacy itself. Facing the internal challenge of heresy on matters of ecclesiastical power, and the external fear of the Ottoman Turks after the Fall of Constantinople,

39 Pope Innocent IV, *Quod super his*, X 3.34.8, §8, p. 154.

40 Pope Innocent IV, *Quod super his*, X 3.34.8, §10, pp. 154–155.

41 Boyarin, *The Unconverted Self*, p. 46.

fifteenth-century popes were desperate for protection and reform. They favored a royal patronage system that conceded the Catholic crown a right to administer the Church in their kingdoms by appointing bishops, spearheading reform, and extending missionary activity to new territories. The practice of royal patronage had a medieval precedent in the papal concession of privileges and rights to secular powers sponsoring the Reconquista and Crusades.[42]

Despite the growing attenuation of papal power over missionary warfare, Pope Innocent IV's theocratic papalist conception of world order still provided the imperial legal rubric for intervention and incorporation of non-European peoples through the universal jurisdiction of natural law. Innocent IV offered a *dilatatio* thesis for widening or enlarging the borders of Christendom that justified use of force as a prerequisite to facilitate conversion.[43] The canonist Pope, as we observed, presented Christian–infidel relations in unavoidably conflictual terms, if not "a permanent state of war" with respect to Muslims and pagan idolaters.[44] However, unlike the Hobbesian state of international anarchical politics, theocratic papalism embraced supranational society and the idea of singular humanity to the fullest extent possible. Humans held a privileged place in creation and were destined to worship the one God. Moreover, the papacy was committed with the task of feeding Christ's sheep everywhere (John 21:17), even those sheep belonging to another fold (John 10:16).

Applied outside of its original historical context, Innocent's papalist conception of world order provided ideological armature for colonial subjugation and imperial expansion. Strictly speaking, however, Innocent's theory was mostly cautious and reserved about armed conflict with infidels outside the paradigmatic case of recovering the Holy Land. First, Innocent IV reiterated throughout the *Quod super his* commentary that the papacy was the only authority to declare war against infidels, similar to the Crusades. He acknowledged that the Pope could make decrees against infidels who persecute the Church in lands formerly belonging to Christians, and even strip infidels of their political jurisdiction over Christians. Yet the Pope must carry this out with supreme discretion under extreme conditions. Tolerance, or "to put up with them" as much as possible without risking great danger to Christians,

42 W. Eugene Shiels, *King and Church: The Rise and Fall of the Patronato Real* (Loyola University Press, 1961), pp. 4–5.

43 Neff, *Justice among Nations*, pp. 102–103. Although Neff does not acknowledge the *dilatatio* theory of Pope Innocent IV, he rightly locates the development of it in the fourteenth-century Portuguese conquest of the Canary Islands.

44 Joseph Höffner, *La etica colonial española del siglo de oro* (Ediciones Cultura Hispanica, 1957), p. 80.

remained the political norm.[45] Additionally, Innocent suggested that in the case of a community converting, an infidel ruler did not automatically lose political authority over the new Christians, assuming he did not persecute converts. At the end of the commentary, Innocent claimed that the Church's reception of universal dominium from Christ de iure was ultimately for the purpose of securing and protecting humanity: "[T]he pope and the churches possess all things in the name of all men so that they may come to the aid of anyone in need."[46]

Although Innocent's papalist conception of world order framed the early modern expansion of imperial Christendom ideologically, his notion of infidel dominium could also support a protectionist aim for non-Christians thereby demonstrating its inherent ambivalence. During the Council of Constance (1414–1418), a debate ensued about the legitimacy of dispossessing pagan Lithuanians under Polish Catholic jurisdiction. The crusading order of Teutonic Knights claimed a papal right from Alexander IV to extend the faith by war against enemy infidels. The basic argument of the Knights was akin to the teachings of Jan Hus and John Wyclif declared heretical and subversive at the council. They taught that mortal sin deprives true dominium among prelates and bishops.[47] For different political purposes, this quasi-Donatist view resembled the "dominium founded in grace" doctrine shared by certain medieval hierocratic papalists like the theologian Giles of Rome and the canon lawyers Alanus Anglicus and Cardinal Hostiensis. Each of them, ironically labeled political Augustinians, had argued that outside the Church, there could be no true dominium and political authority.

The Polish representative of the king who opposed the Teutonic Order of Knights at the council was Paulus Vladimiri, a canon lawyer from the University of Cracow. Vladimiri portrayed the Polish conflict with the Knights in stark canonistic terms as a choice between Pope Innocent IV and his student, Cardinal Hostiensis (Henry of Susa). In contrast to Innocent IV, Hostiensis denied the foundation of infidel dominium in the rational creature and instead claimed that the arrival of Christ automatically dispossessed infidel property and political rule and transferred it over to the Church.[48] Vladimiri associated this "opinion of Hostiensis" with the Teutonic Knights. He proceeded to defend infidel rights according to Innocent's teaching while deploying other sources too, especially Aquinas, in that effort. His *Opinio*

45 Pope Innocent IV, *Quod super his*, X 3.34.8, §7, p. 154.
46 Pope Innocent IV, *Quod super his*, X 3.34.8, §10, p. 155.
47 Muldoon, *Popes, Lawyers, and Infidels*, chap. 6.
48 Muldoon, *Popes, Lawyers, and Infidels*, pp. 16–17.

Hostiensis, which offered a repudiation of Teutonic missionary warfare, plainly stated: "It is unlawful to use arms or oppress infidels to compel them [the Lithuanians] to the Christian faith. The reason is because this method expresses injury to the neighbor, and evil cannot be done so that good may come."[49] Echoing Gratian and Gregory the Great's teaching on the Jews, Vladimiri also argued that the proper way to evangelize and convert infidels was through gentleness, not punishments.

But it was Vladimiri's claim about infidel rights that proved most striking and innovative. Although he relied on Innocent's claim that infidel dominium was founded on the rational creature, against Hostiensis he appended this argument with Aquinas's political axiom from Question 10, Article 10, from the *Secunda secundae*: "[D]*ominium et prelatio introducta sunt ex iure humano* (*scilicet ex iure gentium*). *Distinctio autem fidelium et infidelium est ex iure divino. Ius autem divinum, quod est ex gratia, non tollit ius humanum, quod est ex naturali ratione.*"[50] Vladimiri further established the property and jurisdiction of infidels on "a right of human society" (*humanae societatis ius*), which fundamentally protected them from infractions of justice such as theft and murder.[51] No distinction existed between Christians and infidels with respect to the duties of justice and love toward neighbor.[52] Remarkably, believers could rightly unite with peaceful infidels without incurring sin to defend themselves against aggressors, Christian or otherwise, just as the Jewish Maccabees allied with the Romans against the Seleucid ruler Antiochus IV.[53] The Polish were therefore in the right to make an alliance with the Lithuanians in opposition to the Teutonic Order.

Vladimiri's defense of Christian–infidel alliances in war was a notable precedent to Vitoria and Grotius in the history of international relations.[54] In addition, the Polish canonist expanded the horizon for infidel dominium

49 *Opinio Hostiensis*, in *Paulus Vladimiri and His Doctrine Concerning International Law and Politics*, ed. Stanislaus F. Belch (Mouton & Co., 1965), p. 877: "*Non est licitum infideles armis, vel oppressionibus, ad fidem compellere christianam. Ratio: quia hic modus est cum iniuria proximi, et non sunt facienda mala, ut eveniant bona.*"

50 *Opinio Hostiensis*, p. 884.

51 *Opinio Hostiensis*, p. 883.

52 *Opinio Hostiensis*, p. 877: "[P]*roximi enim nostri sunt tam infideles quam fideles indistincte.*"

53 *Opinio Hostiensis*, p. 882. "*Princeps christianus, necessitate imminente, sine peccato ad sui defensionem et suae terrae uti potest auxilio infidelium, non solum sibi subiectorum, sed etiam aliorum, intelligendo de infidelibus pacificis, non habentibus nobiscum guerram active vel passive.*"

54 Vitoria, *On the American Indians*, q. 3, aa. 5 and 7, pp. 287–289, where he referred to the problematic case of Hernán Cortés making an alliance with native Tlaxcalans against the Aztecs using the threat of war as a possible cause for Spanish intervention. The other example of infidel alliance from Vitoria entailed the case of assisting those held under tyranny by their

by demonstrating the more positive aspirations of an incorporating society inclusive of all humanity. His legacy, unfortunately, would remain minimal if not absent from subsequent Iberian debates concerning Christian–infidel relations. Even at the Council of Constance, Vladimiri's argument did not entirely win over Pope Martin V (1417–1431). The Pope may have conceded the common opinion of Innocent IV on infidel dominium, but he also affirmed its strong theocratic orientation and curtailment of infidel rights. Contrary to Vladimiri's stance, Martin V confirmed the previous papal privileges for the crusading Teutonic Knights signaling the fifteenth- and sixteenth-century practice of European colonial expansion according to the papal distribution of infidel lands.[55]

Martin's theocratic papalist stance was further evident in his interests beyond Christendom's frontiers. While the Council of Constance convened in continental Europe, the Portuguese were conquering the Muslim-controlled city of Ceuta in the northern region of another continent, Africa. The Portuguese crusading *Orden de Cristo*, whose leader was Prince Enrique the Infante, sought papal backing for enlarging Christendom as the Teutonic Knights had done. They received it in Martin V's *Rex regum* (1418), a bull since lost that granted indulgences to Portuguese crusaders in Africa. Pope Martin in this instance widened papal missionary warfare against infidels overseas. Under papal directives, the Portuguese pursuit of new Christian subjects and markets of exchange was the primary catalyst for the early modern age of overseas European expansion.[56]

The papacy also figured importantly in the Iberian colonization of the Canary Islands off the coast of Africa, a strategic battleground between the Spanish and Portuguese beginning in the fourteenth century. It was specifically in the Canaries context of the European encounter with native islanders that missionary war against infidels clearly shifted from a crusading mission to a civilizing one. King Duarte, the brother of Prince Enrique, petitioned Pope Eugenius IV (1431–1447) to endorse the Portuguese occupation of infidel lands in the Canaries. In that effort, King Duarte invoked another justification of

own rulers. For a case more comparable to Vladimiri's support of infidel alliances against even Christians yet shaped by strong commercial interests, see Hugo Grotius, who cited Vitoria on this point, in the *Commentary on the Law of Prize and Booty (De jure praedae)*, ed. Martine Julia van Ittersum (Liberty Fund, 2006), chap. 13, p. 434. For more on Vladimiri's importance in legal history, see C. H. Alexandrowicz, "Paulus Vladimiri and the Development of the Doctrine of Coexistence of Christian and Non-Christian Countries," in *The Law of Nations in Global History*, eds. David Armitage and Jennifer Pitts (Oxford University Press, 2017).

55 Belch, *Paulus Vladimiri*, vol. 1, p. 89.

56 John H. Elliott, *Empires of the Atlantic World* (Yale University Press, 2006), p. 18.

conquest with fateful consequences. The crusader doctrine of missionary warfare linking evangelization and conquest seemed viable against Muslims – cast as perpetual enemies of Christendom – even in North Africa. However, addressing unbelievers posing no political threat to the unity of Christendom whatsoever required another justification for expansion. Duarte proposed a new cause for a civilizing mission that involved baptism of infidel natives, and imparting good customs and just laws.[57]

King Duarte's letter in 1436 to Eugenius IV laid out the parameters for a civilizing mission of incorporating infidels into a transatlantic Christendom. But the king needed the spiritual leader of Christendom on his side, whose fullness of power extended "over the entire world."[58] Duarte risked excommunication and sedition without the approval of Pope Eugenius IV. That was because the Pope had previously banned, at the suggestion of a local bishop, Christian colonization of the Canaries in reaction to the violence perpetrated against natives by a group of famished Portuguese settlers awaiting food supply. The Pope threatened any Christian invader of the islands with ecclesiastical censure. Eugenius expressed his judgment of the matter in his 1434 bull *Creator omnium rerum*. Eugenius' bull affirmed the common humanity of infidels and believers, and annulled Martin V's permission of expansionary crusading following Christian pillaging and enslavement of the natives on the islands. Eugenius believed the papacy was responsible for spreading the faith without causing scandal.[59]

Duarte attempted to counteract the Pope with a renewed policy of missionary warfare beneficial, most of all, to the natives. According to Duarte, the Portuguese had little material interests in these lands inhabited by simpletons having "no kind of metal or money." The primary intention of Portuguese interventions was to rescue the natives spiritually and culturally. This provided a rationale for conquest priding itself on both evangelical and humanitarian concerns. Conversion to the Christian religion would contribute greatly to civilizing and educating primitive peoples described as "nearly wild men" living "like animals" and lacking common religion, law codes, and normal social intercourse. Although backward infidels could not be forced to become Christians, they could at the very least be taught and disciplined by a superior Christian civilization. It was therefore a duty of Portuguese society to

57 Muldoon, *Popes, Lawyers, Infidels*, pp. 121–124.

58 "Letter of King Duarte to Eugenius IV," in *The Expansion of Europe: The First Phase*, ed. James Muldoon (University of Pennsylvania Press, 1977), p. 56.

59 Norman Housley, *Religious Warfare in Europe, 1400–1536* (Oxford University Press, 2002), pp. 183–184.

subjugate primitive peoples of the islands, not for "personal gain," but "for the salvation of the souls of the pagans."[60]

To make the case for the Pope, Duarte offered the example of his younger brother, Prince Enrique, also known as "Henry the Navigator," who arrived with a fleet to the Canary Islands. Soon after Enrique's soldiers stepped upon the shore carrying weapons in hand, nearly 400 infidels received baptism whereas many others fled in terror at the mere sight of the armed men. This example made armed aggression appear necessary and incredibly useful for precipitating infidel conversion. As previously noted, subjugation by fear and threat of punishment already belonged to an indirect mode of coercion outlined by Innocent IV. When Enrique arrived on the islands, Duarte attested, he not only brought Christianity to the native Guanches, but also gave them "civil laws and an organized form of society" so that they could become loyal servants of the Portuguese crown. Duarte pleaded with the Pope to lift the ban prohibiting colonization, which he called "the last obstacle" to civilizing and converting infidels.[61] The Canary Islands offered Duarte an exemplary case combining the religious right of preaching outside Christendom and the superior right of conquering those without civilization and unfit to rule themselves.

Duarte's letter was a momentous political device. What made it unprecedented in the history of Christian–infidel relations was its impact on reversing papal policy, thus signaling a new imperial age of European expansion. After receiving Duarte's letter, Eugenius IV responded with his bull *Romanus Pontifex* (1436). Pope Eugenius's new letter revoked his earlier ban and granted Portugal the sole right of conquering the Canary Islands for the propagation of the faith.[62] The theocratic papalist conception of world order that informed Eugenius, although attentive to the humanity and protection of infidels, ultimately succumbed to a policy of missionary warfare under Iberian rule. A striking feature about the policy shift of Eugenius IV from protection of non-European Canary islanders to the permission of Duarte's Christianization by force of arms was the legal discussion that preceded it. Before penning *Romanus Pontifex*, Pope Eugenius sought canon legal advice from two Bolognese jurists, both of whom applied Innocent's papalist conception of world order to justify armed expansion into extra-European lands.[63]

60 "Letter of King Duarte to Eugenius IV," pp. 54–55.

61 "Letter of King Duarte to Eugenius IV," pp. 55–56.

62 Housley, *Religious Warfare in Europe*, p. 184.

63 The formulation of the problem was "whether or not it was lawful to wage war against infidels who occupied lands that had never belonged to Christians." See Muldoon, *Popes, Lawyers, and Infidels*, pp. 124–128, and Paulino Castañeda Delgado, *La teocracía pontifical en las*

According to the missionary warfare doctrine evolving out of the Crusades and applied to Iberian overseas expansion, conquest and evangelization were compatible, mutually supportive practices. And they remained so for the next one hundred years of papal confirmation of Iberian transatlantic politics until Pope Paul III's *Sublimis Deus* in 1537. The most notable example during that century was Pope Nicholas V, who returned to the crusader idea of waging wars in North Africa against enemies of Christ in his version of *Romanus Pontifex* (1455). Not only Saracens but also other pagan infidels in "further and more remote areas" were subject to perpetual slavery and dispossession of goods and lands for being enemies of Christ.[64] Nicholas approved Portuguese expansion and right of conquest to incorporate sheep into the papacy's universal fold without restriction for the defense and enlargement of the faith.[65] Under royal patronage, the Portuguese Crown could spread the faith indefinitely by subjugating new peoples, constructing new churches, and making ecclesiastical appointments. Relatedly, the papacy approved the crown's civilizing mission to dispose and govern the natives by imposing laws, statutes, and tributes. All of this served the specific aim of converting infidels. Even infidel slaves, among them black bodies from Africa captured by force or traded through exchange, could be "acquired for Christ."[66]

The European civilizing mission took on a particularly Spanish character with the formation of the Crown of Ferdinand of Aragon and Isabel of Castile – *los Reyes Católicos* – in 1474. Their devout commitment to renew the religious and cultural identity of a unified Spain was incredibly successful and most impressive in scope. The Catholic Monarchs received full papal endorsement of their religious project of reform and expansion through Pope Innocent VIII's Reconquista bull of Granada *Orthodoxe fidei propagationem* (1486), which transferred the ecclesiastical wherewithal to make rapid religious changes effectively and authoritatively under the *Patronato Real*.[67] The retaking of old political dominions on the Peninsula and new ones undreamt of across the Atlantic made 1492 a world-changing year for Christian Europe.

On January 6, Ferdinand and Isabel concluded an 800-year Reconquista campaign by taking the last Muslim stronghold in Granada. Out of their

controversias sobre el Nuevo Mundo (Universidad Nacional Autónoma de Mexico, 1996), pp. 292–295.

64 Pope Nicholas V, *Romanus Pontifex* (1455), in *Church and State through the Centuries*, p. 150.

65 Pope Nicholas V, *Romanus Pontifex*, p. 146.

66 Pope Nicholas V, *Romanus Pontifex*, p. 148. For a bracing account of the early modern Catholic soteriological roots of racial ideology, see Willie James Jennings, *The Christian Imagination* (Yale University Press, 2010), chap. 1.

67 A complete English translation of the bull is in Shiels, *King and Church*, pp. 66–70.

religious fervor to purify Christendom, they would institute a policy of baptism or exile upon Jews and Muslims and a *General Inquisición* to oversee orthodoxy. But their pursuits were not strictly spiritual since Granada was, at the time, a wealthy kingdom specializing in silk production, jewels, ceramics, and arms.[68] Acquisition of these industries could help offset the impending economic loss from the expulsion of Jews, who were important contributors to Castilian economy. Furthermore, the soldiers contracted for these wars were in need of repayment for their services. Half of the kingdom of Granada was divided up among them and nobility.

At least since the eleventh century, the Iberian Reconquista generated a political system out of the royal duty of rewarding and granting privileges to soldiers distinguishing themselves in combat.[69] This system of granting royal rewards such as land and spoils to military leaders and their orders responsible for reconquering Moorish territories came under the legal title of a contract with the Crown. It offered recompense for their personal services and financial expenditures. These contracts or agreements appeared to be the customary basis for *capitulaciones* in extra-European lands.[70] The *capitulación* was the fundamental legal charter for new settlements established by explorers and conquistadors under the Spanish Crown. It supplied the backbone for a sea-based royal commercial enterprise beginning with the Canary Islands.

Geopolitically, the Canaries were "a natural link between the Reconquista in Spain and the conquest of America" that represented the latest chapter of "Castile's holy war against the infidel."[71] Already in 1478, following the Portuguese cession of rights over the islands to the Spanish Crown, Ferdinand and Isabel had sent an expedition from Seville to the islands off the African coast. After unsuccessful incursions, the Spaniard Alonso Fernández de Lugo finally took control of La Palma in 1492. Lugo could not have accomplished such a feat without the assistance of merchants from Seville who financed the expedition in coordination with the Spanish Crown. Lugo received his rewards (*mercedes*) from the Crown, which included both bounty and administrative responsibilities. Appointed governor of the island (or *adelantado*), Lugo could distribute the land according to the Spanish patronage tradition from the Reconquista. This practice of distribution or dividing land, known as *repartimiento*, established an island fiefdom of

68 Fernández-Armesto, *1492: The Year the World Began* (HarperCollins, 2009), p. 29.

69 Mario Góngora, *Studies in the Colonial History of Spanish America*, trans. Richard Southern (Cambridge University Press, 1975), chap. 1.

70 Elliott, *Imperial Spain, 1469–1716* (Penguin Books, 1963), p. 59.

71 Elliott, *Imperial Spain*, p. 58.

sorts, granting European control over production and export of goods and slaves in exchange for loyalty to the Crown.[72]

Two royally approved letters presented before the Spanish council already indicated the Crown's promotion of conversion by means of conquest "against the Canary infidel enemies of the faith."[73] Spain's medieval legal code, the *Siete Partidas* of Alfonso X, had identified the just cause of waging expansionary religious wars against infidels amidst the Reconquista struggle against Moorish presence.[74] The eventual conquest of Tenerife in the Canaries between 1495 and 1496 followed this traditional policy when Lugo's forces came into conflict with a resistant native chief. Transplanting the practice of missionary warfare onto the islands, Lugo presented a violent ultimatum to the Guanche peoples: conversion or dispossession.[75] This baptism-or-enslavement policy assumed the indigenous would become Christian and submit to the authority of the Spanish Crown. If they chose neither, war ensued with the outcome of enslavement anyway or worse, extermination. Unable to accept the terms of conquest, the native chief elected his own death by ritual suicide.[76] Evidently, Lugo's missionary war in Tenerife followed a coercive model of infidel relations already evident in the expulsions at Granada. To formalize rule over their new subjects, the Spaniards stomped upon the ground and cut off tree branches to symbolize the new possession of the Crown.[77]

The end of the Reconquista, the initial conquest of the Canaries, and the "discovery" of the Indies uncannily overlapped in 1492. Practices of dividing land and political subjugation in the Canaries had an intractable force connecting the Spanish Reconquista of the past with Spain's uncharted future in the Indies. Both the forced labor system of the *encomienda* and the legal protocol termed the Requirement (*Requerimiento*) would enshrine a policy of missionary war that made

72 Kathleen Deagan and José María Cruxent, *Columbus's Outpost among the Taínos* (Yale University Press, 2002), p. 9.

73 Silvio Zavala, *Las conquistas de Canarias y América* (Cabildo Insular de Gran Canaria, 1991), p. 20.

74 *Las Siete Partidas* ed. Robert I. Burns, S. J., vol. 2 (University of Pennsylvania Press, 2001), II, Title 23, Law II, p. 440: "The right to maintain a just war, is as the ancient sages explained, based upon three considerations; first, to expand the religion of the people, and to destroy those who wish to oppose it; second, for the sake of their lord, by desiring to loyally serve, honor, and defend him; third, in order to protect themselves and aggrandize and honor the country in which they dwell."

75 Zavala, *Las conquistas*, pp. 31–33.

76 Fernández-Armesto, 1492, p. 286.

77 Elliott, *Empires of the Atlantic World*, p. 31.

the Spanish civilizing mission to take possession of the New World highly effective and unyieldingly exploitative.

TAKING POSSESSION OF THE INDIES

Possession was an expansive legal notion in the West based on the physical control of appellations. During the early modern age of European expansion, the Roman legal notion of possession (*possessio*) framed European claims over land, things, and even people.[78] The unclaimed thing (*res nullius*) and unoccupied land (*terra nullius*) were subject to the original occupant who first discovered it. But it was not enough simply to see something with one's eye, as the young lawyer Hugo Grotius astutely noted.[79] One had to acquire it. For Grotius and his philological sources, "to discover" (*invenire*) and "to take possession of" (*occupare*) were, therefore, synonymous terms. The rational consensus among jurists was that a title for claiming something from discovery must entail factual possession, meaning that movable things had to be seized and what was immovable, namely, land, had to be marked off by boundaries and guarded.

European claims of possession and control over the New World generally tracked onto two distinguishable modes of colonial domination in the Spanish and English cases. Whereas the Spanish claims in the Indies often gravitated toward the seizure of precious metals, gold and silver most prominently, English claims in North America capitalized on setting boundaries to cultivable land otherwise considered vacant or wasted space.[80] When Europeans made these claims at all, they did not do so within a vacuum. Aside from staving off other European imperial competitors, they had to reckon with the native peoples already present on the American continents and islands of the Caribbean. Colonial possession of the Indies navigated between these intra-European and extra-European political spheres. The establishment of settlements, the construction of forts, and the planting of flags and erecting monuments all provided the initial symbolic acts of colonial possession productive of legal effects and titles. These acts were exclusive signs of possession to other Europeans and Amerindians.

78 Lauren Benton and Benjamin Straumann, "Acquiring Empire by Law: From Roman Doctrine to Early Modern Practice," *Law and History Review* 28, no. 1 (2010): 1–38.

79 Grotius, *Commentary on the Law of Prize*, chap. 12, pp. 306–307.

80 For a generalized although insightful comparative reading of European colonization in the Americas attentive to Spanish and English, but also Portuguese and French examples, see Patricia Seed, *American Pentimento: The Invention of Indians and the Pursuit of Riches* (University of Minnesota Press, 2001).

Spain's early colonial debates focused on the issue of whether Amerindian peoples could legitimately govern themselves independently of the Crown or if they had forfeited their right to do so because of their incivility. The English settlers, by contrast, started with the question of what constituted private property before asking if such a view of ownership was actually present among Native Americans to claim land against European colonies. The distinct emphasis on taking possession through *political rule* and taking possession through *private property* had far-reaching implications for respective Spanish and English relations with Amerindians. In broadly unique colonial patterns, whereas the Spanish sought to incorporate "*indios*" within the political rule of transatlantic Christendom, the English mostly displaced nonpropertied "savages" to make room for Western civilization.[81]

The early Spanish colonial discourse and literature of taking territorial possession primarily turned on the right to conquer the newly discovered peoples of the Indies.[82] Spain was thoroughly a legal culture, meticulous in the recording of details about everything from business contracts to court proceedings. It was also in every sense religious, led by a Catholic Crown that was irrepressibly expansive in its mission to proclaim the Gospel abroad and utterly possessive over those entrusted to its care. During the reigns of Ferdinand and Isabel and Emperor Charles V, the "struggle for justice" in the New World preoccupied the intellects of theologians and jurists who regularly scrutinized Spanish activities in an official capacity.[83] No Spaniard questioned the Crown's divine right, assigned by Pope Alexander VI, to bring the Christian faith to the infidels across the Atlantic. From this agreed upon religious title unfolded the subsequent legal dispute regarding the claim of taking political possession in the Indies.[84] At the core of these debates about the justice of conquest was the canon legal tradition of infidel dominium stemming from Pope Innocent IV.[85] Although it would take several decades following the initial discoveries and conquests to bring the legal dimension of

81 Anthony Pagden, *The Burdens of Empire: 1539 to the Present* (Cambridge University Press, 2015), pp. 122–123.

82 Rolena Adorno, *The Polemics of Possession in Spanish American Narrative* (Yale University Press, 2007), p. 4.

83 See the classic treatment in Lewis Hanke, *The Spanish Struggle for Justice in the Conquest of America* (Southern Methodist University Press, 2002).

84 *Recopilación de leyes de los reynos de las Indias* (Centro de Estudios Políticos y Constitutionales, 1998), III, t. 1, l. 1. The law read: "By the donation of the Holy Apostolic See, and other just and legitimate titles, we are the Sovereign ruler of the West Indies … which are incorporated into the Royal Crown of Castile."

85 James Muldoon, *The Americas in the Spanish World Order* (University of Pennsylvania Press, 1994), p. 22.

the Spanish debate into perspicuous view, the colonial practices of possession from the beginning reached down into the subterranean roots of Christian–infidel relations shaped by the Crusades and Reconquista.

The Genoese "Admiral" of the Ocean Sea, Christopher Columbus, was the first explorer contracted by the Crown to advance the Spanish civilizing mission in the islands and lands to be discovered and acquired across the Atlantic.[86] The *Capitulaciones de Santa Fe* appointed Columbus as the official viceroy of the Crown, which entitled him, by virtue of royal concession, to all the honors and jurisdictions accorded the conquerors of the Canaries. Usage of the terms "to discover" (*descubrir*) and "to acquire" (*ganar*) were legal cues indicating the goals of Spanish possession through occupancy and conquest. Additionally, the *Santa Fe* contract permitted the Crown to collect one-tenth (*décima*) of the "pearls, gems, gold, silver, spices, or goods of any kind" the Admiral discovered, traded, and obtained during his voyage. The opening of lucrative trade routes and the exchange of merchandise were especially worthy pursuits for a Crown interested in strengthening a fragile Castilian economy.

Columbus, along with the Crown, believed that his mission was part of a wider providential plan for the expansion of Christendom.[87] The same day of the *Santa Fe* contract, the Admiral received a formal passport from the royal court to show rulers he met on his journey of his spiritual commitment "to the service of God and also to extend the orthodox faith."[88] Starting with the first log of his diary, the aim of Columbus's Westward voyage to China through India was incandescent: to ascertain the manner of bringing about infidel conversion to the Christian faith.[89] In Columbus' opinion, the realization of this spiritual aim could only succeed through political control of the Indies. His desire, as indicated in an October 15 entry written less than a week after his first landfall, was "not to pass any island without taking possession of it"[90] (see Figure 2.1).

The expression "taking possession" was an eminently legal claim suffused with an infatuating motivation for economic wealth. In that same diary entry of October 15, the Admiral indicated: "These islands are very green and fertile

86 "The Capitulations of Santa Fe" (April 17, 1492), in *New Iberian World: A Documentary History of the Discovery and Settlement of Latin America to the Early 17th Century*, vol. 2, eds. John H. Parry and Robert G. Keith (Times Books, 1984), pp. 18–19.

87 David Brading, *The First America* (Cambridge University Press, 1993), pp. 13–14.

88 Vicente D. Sierra, "En torno a las Bulas Alejandrinas de 1493," *Missionalia Hispanica* X, no. 28 (1953): 89.

89 Christopher Columbus, *The Journal of Christopher Columbus*, trans. Cecil Jane (Clarkson N. Potter, 1960), p. 4.

90 Columbus, "October 15 (1492)," in *The Journal*, p. 28.

FIGURE 2.1 "Christopher Columbus Landing by Luigi Gregori." (Source: photograph of Columbus Murals, University of Notre Dame by David Lantigua)

and the breezes are very soft, and it is possible that there are in them many things, of which I do not know, because I do not wish to delay in finding gold, by discovering and going about many islands."[91] The quest for gold was a constant theme in Columbus's writings about the voyages. Especially noteworthy was the spiritual representation of his quest as a prayer to a God whose very goodness would lead him to find gold mines.[92] But the search would not stop at the plush island of Española filled with its many "rivers of gold." Columbus had reason to believe there were other islands containing infinite amounts. His overriding desire, so spiritually tinged, was to see and discover more and more islands. Tzvetan Todorov's pensive study of Columbus' psychology of the voyages has made the arresting point that for the Admiral the verbs "to discover" and "to take possession" become *intransitive*.[93]

Toward the end of his fourth and final voyage, the spiritualization of gold as the source of freedom's power was unimpeachable: "Gold is most excellent. Gold constitutes treasure and he who possesses it may do what he will in the world, and may so attain as to bring souls to Paradise."[94] Columbus and the many who followed him were quite adamant about bringing salvation to the peoples of the Indies by means of taking physical possession of the islands and everything in them. The Admiral first acknowledged that the natives, especially the Taínos of Española, were prime candidates for Christian instruction and conversion. They did not appear to have a creed or observable idolatry.[95] Conveniently, they also exhibited a gentle disposition, which made them defenseless in the face of European military might. For Columbus, this meant they were not only capable of receiving the faith but would also be subordinate to the superior culture of Catholic Spain as their caretakers. Their almost natural subordination was most fitting for Spanish trusteeship and exploitation. Consider Columbus's clear outline to the Crown of the Spanish civilizing mission taken from his journal entry on December 16, 1492:

> Your Highnesses ... you may believe that this island [Española] and all the others are as much your own as Castile, so that there is lacking here nothing except a settlement and then to command them [the Indians] to do what you wish. For I, with these people whom I carry with me, who are not many, could go about all these islands without meeting opposition, for now I have seen

91 Columbus, "October 15 (1492)," p. 30.

92 Columbus, "December 23 (1492)," p. 117.

93 Tzvetan Todorov, *The Conquest of America: The Question of the Other*, trans. Richard Howard (University of Oklahoma Press, 1999), p. 13.

94 Columbus, "Columbus's Letter to the Sovereigns from Jamaica (1503)," in *New Iberian World*, 2:118.

95 Columbus, "October 16 (1492)," p. 33.

> three of these sailors to land alone, where there was a crowd of Indians, and they have all fled, without anyone wishing to harm them. They have no arms and are all naked and without any knowledge of war, and very cowardly, so that a thousand of them would not face three. And they are also fitted to be ruled and to be set to work, to cultivate the land and to do all else that may be necessary, and you may build towns and teach them to go clothed and adopt our customs.[96]

Beginning with the first voyage, Columbus set the parameters for a regime of imposed mutual beneficence by which "the natives would be "civilized" in the Spaniards' image, and the colonists would be teachers as well as masters" ready to reap rewards from the natives and the land's deposits.[97] The establishment of forts and settlements beginning with La Navidad, but also including La Isabela, Santo Tomás, Magdalena, and Santo Domingo, were essential to the civilizing process of living alongside natives. Spanish belief that God had commissioned them to make a new Christian civilization according to their image sanctioned possession of the Indies in the strongest possible terms.

Pope Alexander VI's apostolic intervention in 1493 assigning the Spanish Crown the right to evangelize and impart good customs on those inhabitants of the discovered lands granted an authoritative gravitas to the civilizing mission. In order to clarify the sovereign transatlantic domain of Spain from Portugal, the Pope conceded Spain "the full and complete liberty to take physical possession of the indicated islands and lands ... to retain them in perpetuity, and to impede any adverse force, and to defend them ."[98] Although any political action contrary to apostolic authority on the matter was subject to the threat of excommunication, the papal bulls of donation were a ratification of the Iberian civilizing mission well underway. When Spain and Portugal in 1494 established the Treaty of Tordesillas identifying exclusive zones of sovereignty and trading across the Atlantic independent of the papacy, the political signal was loud and clear. The Tordesillas Treaty further illustrated that in the New World the Pope was a *post facto* formal notary to a civilizing project led by secular power. Pope Julius II confirmed the Catholic treaty between Spain and Portugal in his 1506 bull *Ea quae*. Two years later, Julius's *Universalis ecclesiae* gave Ferdinand and his successors a perpetual right to establish religious institutions and make ecclesiastical appointments in the Spanish New World.

96 Columbus, "December 16 (1492)," pp. 101–102.
97 Fernández-Armesto, *1492*, p. 197.
98 Pope Alexander VI, *Dudum siquidem* (September 26, 1493), in Shiels, *King and Church*, p. 86.

Political possession of the Indies presumed the presence of native peoples, and Columbus never ceased to mention their abundance. "I found very many islands, filled with innumerable people," he wrote in a letter after his first voyage, "and I have taken possession of them all for their Highnesses, done by proclamation and with the royal standard unfurled, and no opposition was offered me."[99] If the traditional Roman legal language of what remained "vacant" applied at all in Iberian expansion, it was not in reference to lack of inhabitants or unimproved land, but rather, the absence of political jurisdiction over an unconquered territory containing mineral wealth.[100] The value of land was not measurable so much by its vacancy and cultivability – a prominent feature of English colonization to be considered in Chapter 5 – as by its natural bounty. Accordingly, the Bahamas, or *Lucayas*, were known as "the useless islands" (*las islas inútiles*) for their lack of precious metals.[101]

Taking political possession required a demonstration of the subordinate political status of natives so that the Crown could lawfully assert its authority over them. In this regard, the popular renderings of Amerindian inferiority provided by Columbus and early chroniclers stipulated the indigenous need of European tutelage gained traction. Spaniards characterized Amerindians chiefly in terms of laziness and their sinful abominations. These deficiencies detected among the natives justified the civilizing mission of Spain during the late fifteenth and early sixteenth centuries, which principally relied on two colonial practices having royal oversight: the *encomienda* system of forced labor and the waging of religious wars. With intractable roots in Latin Christendom, both of these violent and coercive practices consolidated the spiritual, humanitarian, and economic interests of the Crown. However, it was not until the harsh mendicant rebuke of native mistreatment considered in the next chapter that the royal regulation of these practices in 1512 and 1513 began to occur under the Law of Burgos and the Requirement.

The *encomienda*, or the practice of "commending" and "entrusting" laborers to individual Spaniards, emerged during the early years of colonization as an economic institution aggressively suited for taking possession of the Indies. Its origins went back to medieval Spain when crusading military orders defending land granted by the Crown had jurisdiction over it and title to receive taxes from the subject population.[102] In the transatlantic context, the

99 "Letter to Santangel (1493)," in *The Journal*, p. 191.

100 Nicolás Wey Gómez, *The Tropics of Empire: Why Columbus Sailed South to the Indies* (MIT Press, 2008), p. 319.

101 Andrés Reséndez, *The Other Slavery: The Uncovered Story of Indian Enslavement in America* (Houghton Mifflin Harcourt, 2016), p. 41.

102 Góngora, *Studies in the Colonial History*, p. 132.

encomienda imposed on native subjects tributary labor in the form of tending land and the more dangerous activities of fishing for pearls and digging in mines. The institution forced the incorporation of natives into a European civil order whereby Indians received protection and instruction in faith from their Spanish overseers or *encomenderos*. By legal standards, the *encomenderos* possessed jurisdiction over the natives. They were neither strictly landowners nor slave-owners in the formal sense.

Initially, Governor Columbus had received permission directly from the Crown in his subsequent transatlantic voyages to distribute land (*repartimientos*) to the settlers for tilling and ranching, yet this did not include Indian laborers.[103] When the early Spanish settlement under Columbus' poor governance faced the brute reality of food shortage, and an unquenched desire for material gain, chaos unfolded.[104] Columbus's company threatened mutiny through the popular leadership of his appointed *adelantado*, Francisco Roldán. On the brink of rebellion, Governor Columbus acceded to Roldán's pressure, which demanded that the Admiral grant Spanish colonists both land allotment and rights of labor over the Indians to work on farms, and in mines and households. Columbus's approval permitted the Spaniards to impose a policy of forced labor upon the native chiefs (*caciques*) and their peoples.[105] The growing power of private *encomenderos* would pose a continual problem for Spanish royal sovereignty by threatening to make the Indies into a transatlantic fiefdom comprised of European hereditary castes. Because the *encomienda* had the function of getting indolent natives to generate royal revenue, its utility seemed all the more obvious.

The European perception of natives as lazy directly entailed the issue of private property. Columbus detected no private ownership among the Indians following his first voyage. Rather, they seemed to hold things in common, so that "all took a share in whatever any one had, especially of eatable things."[106] Columbus was not dreaming about the possibilities of a communist utopia or a Platonic paradise among the natives but was looking instead for clear confirmation of a basic Aristotelian presupposition about organized political life. According to Aristotle, a people without individual property tend to become careless and idle toward what they share in common.[107] When

103 Deagen and Cruxent, *Columbus's Outpost*, p. 202.

104 Lesley Bird Simpson, *The Encomienda in New Spain* (University of California Press, 1966), pp. 6–8.

105 Simpson, *The Encomienda in New Spain*, p. 9.

106 "Letter to Santangel (1493)," p. 200.

107 Aristotle, *The Politics*, trans. Carnes Lord (University of Chicago Press, 1984), Book 2, chap. 3, p. 57; Cf. Aquinas, *ST* II-II, q. 66, a. 2.

Columbus during his second voyage heard from local *caciques* that the natives owned no private property among themselves, he could now say: "[T]hey are lazy to the greatest degree."[108] Consequently, Columbus sent back several hundred native slaves as rewards for those settlers accompanying him on the second voyage. One of those settlers possessing a slave was the father of Bartolomé de las Casas.

Queen Isabel frequently claimed her new transatlantic subjects were "free" and not "slaves," and therefore seemingly protected from harm and oppression. In June of 1500, just before Columbus and his brothers were sent to prison for their failed island administration, Isabel freed the slaves he had sent to Spain, pondering: "By what right does the Admiral give my vassals away?" Efforts to restrain the transatlantic slavery of Indian subjects by a private class of merchants notwithstanding, the Crown made compromises with *encomenderos* to implement its civilizing mission of incorporating the Indies. In order to address the alleged laziness of the natives and collect the royal tax, the Crown sought to regulate, rather than abolish, compulsory labor. After unsuccessful attempts to motivate Indians to work and assimilate with Spaniards on Española by giving them a wage, Queen Isabel issued a *Real cédula* for Governor Nicolás de Ovando in 1503. She gave the instruction for Ovando "to compel and force the Indians" who "wander about idle" so that they would gather and mine gold and other metals, till the fields, and learn the Christian faith from their overseers.[109] Despite the policy, the final codicil she dictated on her deathbed in 1504 reiterated her royal commitment, beginning with Columbus, to convert the peoples of the Indies and to treat them well and with justice.[110]

The native potential to work in the gold mines of Española was precisely why Columbus saw them as "the greatest wealth of the island."[111] As the local Taíno population rapidly deteriorated following decades of Spanish incursion, which tragically drove some natives to suicide, King Ferdinand recommended an ad hoc policy of transplanting native Lucayans from the "useless" islands, which had no gold, to Española, still rich in gold. Not only would the policy pay off the royal-fifth tribute, it would also allow Christians to make use of and teach those natives "so that they will not be idle and idolatrous as they are in those other islands."[112] Tailor-made to address the colonial situation in the

[108] Cited in Wey Gómez, *The Tropics of Empire*, p. 217.
[109] Simpson, *The Encomienda in New Spain*, p. 13.
[110] Simpson, *The Encomienda in New Spain*, pp. 14–15.
[111] Cited in Reséndez, *The Other Slavery*, p. 28.
[112] *Real cédula* (21 July 1511), in *Colección de Documentos para la Historia de la Formación Social de Hispanoamérica, 1493–1810*, ed. Richard Konetzke, vol. 1 (Consejo Superior de Investigaciones Científicas, 1953), pp. 26–27.

Indies, the *encomienda* system could put idle natives to work and civilize those considered idolatrous, all for the glory of God and Crown. Yet such a system needed a war-making procedure with medieval Christian roots to energize it.

RELIGIOUS WARS AGAINST IDOLATRY

Having royal support, the colonial institution of the *encomienda* quickly evolved into a mechanism for taking possession of the Indies through the forced incorporation of infidels. It facilitated a rapacious strategy of native assimilation that fulfilled the Crown's spiritual and economic ambitions to convert infidel subjects and receive their tributes. In actuality, the *encomienda* was almost indistinguishable from slavery because of its violent imposition of excessively burdensome labor on vulnerable native bodies already plagued by deadly European-borne illnesses. The institution was simply unsustainable without a ready labor force. For this reason, slaves captured in war provided an attractive solution to a European colonial culture on the heels of Reconquista. Here, again, Columbus was instrumental, if only by intimation.

When the Admiral wrote a letter to the royal comptroller Luis de Santángel summarizing the results of his first voyage, he made the ill-fated suggestion to give the Crown not only "as much gold as they may need," but also as many slaves as they requested, "who will be from the idolaters."[113] Columbus had in mind the "Caribs," or the Caniba, a fierce and resilient people notorious for eating the flesh of their opponents. During his first voyage, he made an informal Spanish alliance with Taínos, promising them that the Spanish Monarchs would enslave their enemies and abolish the Carib way of life.[114] Soon after, the Admiral requested that the Crown permit slaving raids against the Caribs, especially since they were numerous. He gave several reasons for doing so in order to promote greater incorporation of the Indies.[115] Among them was a reference to his earlier promise to protect other natives who fear the warlike Caribs. Defending indigenous allies against their enemies would prove a popular justification for warfare by the Crown and conquistadors like Hernán Cortés. The inability to fend off enemy tribes also reaffirmed native

113 "Letter to Santangel (1493)," in *The Journal*, p. 201.

114 December 26 (1492), in *The Journal*, p. 125: "The admiral told him by signs that the Sovereigns of Castile would order the destruction of the Caribs and would have all of them brought with their hands bound."

115 For a discussion of the policy, see Luis Rivera Pagán, *A Violent Evangelism: The Political and Religious Conquest of the Americas* (Westminster/John Knox Press, 1992), pp. 98–99. The 1494 report of Columbus containing the recommendation is in *New Iberian World*, 2:179–185.

dependency and vassalage under Spanish lordship. Additionally, the Crown could trade Carib slaves with other Amerindians in exchange for goods.

The Admiral's religious justifications for enslavement were telling. Cannibalism was an inhuman custom demanding suppression. The forced removal and punishment of flesh-eating peoples from their native habitat, Columbus proffered, would enable the inculcation of civilized behavior and conversion to the faith. If the Caribs were sent to Spain, for example, they could learn Castilian and serve as translators for preachers. With greater language facility, they could also receive proper instruction in the faith and eventually baptism. As a precedent, conversion by means of cultural displacement had already occurred with several Taínos Columbus brought back from his first voyage to captivate his royal audience.

Queen Isabel later endorsed Columbus' proposal to enslave the Caribs, which followed the traditional policy of missionary warfare. In August of 1503, Isabel declared in a royal decree:

> [I]n Our desire for them [the Caribs] to be converted to Our Holy Catholic Faith, they had been required many times to become Christians, to be converted and incorporated securely into the communion of the faithful and come under Our overlordship, and not to do any violence to the Indians living in the other islands. They have not only refused to do these things, as was said, but have tried to avoid being taught the things of Our Holy Catholic Faith, and have constantly made war on Our subjects and killed many Christians who have gone to the said islands. And because they are obdurate in their evil and idolatrous course, and because they eat the said Indians, it was decided that I should dispatch this letter concerning the matter.[116]

Isabel also endorsed capturing, displacing, and selling Carib infidels to make instruction in the faith and incorporation into Christendom easier. Failed evangelization of the Caribs due to their resistance and attacks on Spaniards and Indians provided the Crown persuasive legal grounds for waging war and reducing them to slavery. One could even infer that the idolatrous and anthropophagic practices of natives were primary obstacles frustrating conversion. With the Caribs declared perpetual enemies of the Crown, slavery was both a necessary and useful means of forcibly eradicating their entrenched evil customs and civilizing them according to European moral norms.

The Carib policy of missionary warfare overlapped significantly with its predecessor doctrine of crusading. Spain justified conquest and enslavement

[116] "Decree on the Enslavement of Cannibals" (1503), in *New Iberian World*, 2:386–387.

of infidel Caribs and any other natives having similar abominable customs according to the traditional criteria of Innocent IV: the punishment of unnatural sins and the elimination of resistance to preaching. Columbus and his company members already included sodomy among the unnatural vices of Caribs, and other natives.[117] From the Carib policy of missionary war there emerged the "multiplication of the number of alleged cannibals in the accounts of conquerors and adventurers."[118] Nevertheless, the practice of missionary war made justification increasingly reliant on legal rationalization, which became the distinct task of lawyers and theologians. Chief among them was Juan López de Palacios Rubios (1450–1524), the first Spanish jurist to articulate the theocratic papalist conception of world order underlying the European civilizing mission.

Juan López de Palacios Rubios, called "*El Doctor*" for his proficiency and expertise in canon law, served as a legal advisor to the Crown (1504–1524) during the early phase of Spanish colonization. His influence on royal policy over the Indies was notable in the Law of Burgos (1512), which regulated the *encomienda* institution, but most especially in his drafting of the protocol for conquest known as the Requirement (1513). Palacios Rubios provided the most comprehensive canon legal argument defending Spanish possession of the Indies in the seven chapters of his book *De insulis oceanis* (Sp. *De las Islas del Mar Océano*) published in 1516. According to *De insulis*, the 1493 papal donation of Alexander VI was "necessary" because without it neither Spain nor any other secular power would have been justified "to occupy or to wage war in those islands."[119] An astute canonist, Palacios Rubios asserted that the complete and superior right to claim jurisdiction over the islands and its native inhabitants resided exclusively in the Roman papacy, citing the authority of Innocent IV's *Quod super his*.

The reference to Innocent IV's teaching on Christian–infidels relations permitted Palacios Rubios to present the entire project of Spanish colonization as a papally endorsed extension of the Crusades and Reconquista. For "only the Church is able to concede to Christian princes a new conquest against infidels," wrote the Spaniard.[120] Palacios Rubios adhered

[117] "Letter of Michele de Cuneo" (1494), in *New Iberian World*, 2:92.

[118] Rivera Pagán, *A Violent Evangelism*, p. 99.

[119] Juan López de Palacios Rubios, *Libellus de insulis oceanis (De las Islas del Mar Océano)*, trans. Paulino Castañeda Delgado et al. (EUNSA, 2013), cap. 5, §1, pp. 332–334. Interestingly, Palacios Rubios does not mention the papal donation in name. He may have especially had in mind *Dudum siquidem*, which claimed perpetuity and physical possession whereas *Inter caetera* did not.

[120] Palacios Rubios, *De insulis*, cap. 5, §1, p. 334: "[S]*ola Ecclesia potest christianis principibus novam conquestam contra infideles concedere.*"

to the extreme medieval hierocratic model of universal papal jurisdiction whereby the Pope possessed power in spiritual and even temporal matters over believers and infidels. He also elaborated Innocent's view that the Pope is shepherd over all rational creatures according to two modes in virtue of Christ's empowerment of St. Peter. The Pope possesses by right of redemption (*iure redemptionis*) those sheep within the fold, or baptized Christians. And there are sheep outside the fold, infidels, whom the Pope possesses by right of creation (*iure creationis*). Palacios Rubios made the further point that infidels are all capable of becoming members of the Church in the future through conversion, having received as rational creatures the power of the will and freedom of choice.[121]

Palacios Rubios went beyond the canonistic legal opinions available to him although he did eclectically combine Innocent IV and Hostiensis in the process of generating his own unyielding theocratic universalist approach to world order.[122] On the one hand, he sided with Innocent in Chapter 3 of *De insulis* when he claimed that believers and unbelievers alike lawfully have ownership of things (*rerum dominia*).[123] Property belonged to infidels according to positive law, the law of nations, and natural law. Similar to Columbus, Palacios Rubios detected that the form of property held among the natives of the islands was not private, but shared, demonstrated by "certain boundaries of land" cultivated and used in common.[124] The Spanish jurist also defended the *humanitas* of infidels, who are "participants in our nature" and therefore neighbors worthy of love.[125] According to natural right, then, it would be unjust to despoil peaceable infidels of possessions strictly because of their unbelief.[126]

121 Palacios Rubios, *De insulis*, cap. 4, §7, p. 274.

122 My reading is particularly indebted to Castañeda Delgado who held that Palacios Rubios affirmed infidel freedom and property but rejection of their legitimate political rule. See *La teocracía pontifical*, p. 374. I make this point about the early modern Spanish jurist's eclecticism because there has been a tendency to read him as favoring either Innocent IV or Cardinal Hostiensis. For alternative readings, see, respectively, James Muldoon, *Popes, Lawyers, and Infidels*, pp. 142–143, and Silvio Zavala, *The Political Philosophy of the Conquest of America*, trans. Teener Hall (Editorial Cultura, 1953), chap. 2.

123 Palacios Rubios, *De insulis*, cap. 3, p. 126: "*Infideles ergo sicut fideles licite possident ac tenent rerum dominia, quod aperte firmat Innocentius quem ceteri omnes sequntur in praellegato c.* Quod super his, De voto."

124 Palacios Rubios, *De insulis*, cap. 1, §1, p. 52.

125 Palacios Rubios, *De insulis*, cap. 4, §7, p. 280: "*Infideles, enim, dicuntur proximi nostri quos debemus diligere et lucrifacere quantum possumus, ratione humanitatis, cum sint nostrae naturae participes. Unde per appellatione proximorum veniunt Iudaei, Sarraceni et alii infideles.*"

126 Palacios Rubios, *De insulis*, cap. 3, §1, pp. 132, 136.

When it came to the matter of infidel political jurisdiction and rule (*dominium iurisdictionis*), on the other hand, Palacios Rubios strongly favored the opinion of Hostiensis. Unlike the case of property, unbelief did effect a change regarding the legitimacy of infidel rule. The Spanish jurist believed that infidels might have lawfully held jurisdictional power prior to the coming of Christ and the establishment of the Church. After the birth of the Savior, however, infidel rule in its lawful mode ended since all power on earth and in heaven now belonged to Christ.[127] Referring to Hostiensis' commentary of *Quod super his*, infidels still retain a "capacity" (*capaces*) for self-governance, but only if they acknowledge the supreme rule or dominium of the Church, in which case they should be tolerated not by right, but by a precarious permission of the Church.[128] Palacios Rubios stretched Hostiensis here in order to tighten the imperial grip of his theocratic account of world order. Beyond Hostiensis, the Spanish jurist required infidel recognition of superior authority residing not only in ecclesiastical power, but also royal power conceded by the papacy in perpetuity. On this innovative point rested his unique legal sophistry for Spanish missionary war and the logic of the Requirement.

By emphasizing the secular transference of supreme papal power to the Spanish Monarchy in a context of the *Patronato Real*, theocratic world order moved from mere papalism to royalism cum papalism. A divine trustee of the Church in the Indies, Spain undoubtedly relied on the papal donation for expansion and conquest. Yet Palacios Rubios also understood that the Church's missionary task was only as effective as the secular arm conducting its temporal affairs through Christian rulers. In this sense, the papacy needed the Crown, a reality all too easily confirmed by diminishing papal power in Europe. The Church's supreme fullness of power could indeed confer dominium to Christian political authority through a donation, but not the effectuation (*facti*) of it.[129] Palacios Rubios followed the canonistic precedent of construing papal fullness of power over infidels in a de iure, rather than a de facto, mode. As a spiritual and royal institution founded by Christ, the papacy could transfer dominium by right in full, seen most clearly in Alexander VI's *Dudum siquidum*, but could not transfer *possessio*, which consisted in the fact of taking physical control of things, land, and people.[130]

127 Palacios Rubios, *De insulis*, cap. 4, §8, p. 302.

128 Palacios Rubios, *De insulis*, cap. 4, §8, p. 296: "*Haec videtur mens Hostiense, in praellegato* c. Quod super his, De voto, *cum dicit quod tunc erunt infideles iurisdictionis capaces, quando dominium Ecclesiae recognoscant, nam tales sunt ab Ecclesia tollerandi, quia nec ad fidem sunt cogendi.*"

129 Palacios Rubios, *De insulis*, cap. 5, §3, p. 344.

130 Palacios Rubios, *De insulis*, cap. 5, §8, p. 348.

Palacios Rubios argued that the "lawful" possession of the Indies and its inhabitants under the Catholic Monarchs could proceed along the two strategies of incorporation dictated by the colonial circumstances: either by occupation or by a just cause of war. Both legal rationales gained persuasive force in view of the popular Spanish perception of native infidels as lazy and idolatrous. The Spanish jurist did find some use in applying Aristotle's idea of the natural slave to certain peoples on the islands whom he considered "so inept and feeble" that they were utterly incapable of governing themselves.[131] The law of nations and natural law had both introduced this manner of servitude whereby the unskilled submit to the rule of the wiser and experienced because of its convenience and utility.[132] One of the clearest markers for the absence of sufficient political rule was the inability to maintain property in peace. Although the native islanders had property according to natural law and the law of nations, it was only common property held over fields used for planting herb. Native groups took care of these planted lands by defending them from invasion by others.[133] Many wars among them, Palacios Rubios averred, were the result of defending these bounded spaces.[134] What the various island communities apparently lacked was positive law – the most effective safeguard of property against warring groups – enforced by a superior political authority.

Nevertheless, the principal legal device in *De insulis* for taking possession was the act of war. Innocent's canonistic opinion continued to provide Palacios Rubios with the just parameters for intervention and conquest. The focus on war extended the terms of possession beyond taking political control over the Indies to include taking control of native properties through legal enslavement. The justification for war and conquest only impressed itself as Spanish explorers and slavers made their way beyond Caribbean islands and onto the native continent with Requirement in hand to confront the imperial cultures of Mexico and Peru, abounding with sacred treasures.

The political subjugation of infidels and the dispossession of their goods in war relied on appeals to just causes for legitimate enforcement. This legal requisite may seem redundant in view of the papacy's full and complete donation of the Indies. However, infidel participation in the same natural

131 Palacios Rubios, *De insulis*, cap. 2, §1, p. 118: "*[A]liqui eorum ita sunt inepti et imbecilles, quod se nullo modo gubernare sciunt, quapropter, largo modo, possunt dici servi, quasi nati ad serviendum non autem ad imperandum, ut tradit Philosophus, Politicorum, lib.* 1, *et hoc modo, insipientes, servire debent prudentibus, vel subditi dominis.*"

132 Palacios Rubios, *De insulis*, cap. 2, §1, p. 120.

133 Palacios Rubios, *De insulis*, cap. 3, p. 122.

134 Palacios Rubios, *De insulis*, cap. 1, §1, p. 52.

right as believers adhered to a logic of parity that demanded a modicum of respect toward infidels, at least formally. Palacios Rubios could pursue a protective stance of infidels, claiming that, "neither the pope nor anyone else should fight against infidels or seize their goods, since that would be like going against neighbors and sheep entrusted to Peter and his successors."[135] The all-important qualifier being that infidels lived peaceably and recognized the superior authority of the Church and Crown, in which case the Pope as protector had an obligation to defend them against anyone who unjustly attacked or harmed them.

But the defense of infidels from unjust oppression was not really the matter under consideration in *De insulis* as it had been in Paulus Vladimiri's *Opinio Hostiensis*. The Spanish jurist invoked at least three traditional canonistic causes for justifiable intervention against infidels thereby dangerously expanding the papal vicariate over the natives of the New World through royal power. One cause considered infidel rulers who posed a persecutory threat to their Christian subjects, in which case the Pope could commission a secular ruler to wage a war "liberating believers from grave danger."[136] The primary test case for permitting infidels rulers was whether they acquiesced in recognizing the superior dominium of the Church, which they had to demonstrate by the admission of Christian preachers in their territories. In addition to submitting to ecclesiastical power by allowing preachers, they had to acknowledge that the papacy had donated their province to the Spanish Crown, which they must now obey as overseer.

In artful fashion, Doctor Palacios Rubios combined the canonistic opinions of Innocent and Hostiensis to delineate a second cause of war addressing native admission of preachers and submission to the Spanish Crown. This cause took legal expression through the infamous Requirement. *De insulis* expressed the logic of the Requirement as an apparent "choice" of accepting or denying the superior dominium of the Catholic Crown. Palacios Rubios put the matter of refusal in the following way: "If they do not accept, after given the terms for a prudential deliberation, then they can be invaded and conquered by means of war, force, and arms. Their goods can be seized and they can be reduced to slavery because the war is just on the part of Christians."[137] The biblical proof text for the Requirement was Israel's claim over the Promised

[135] Palacios Rubios, *De insulis*, cap. 3, §1, pp. 132–134.

[136] Palacios Rubios, *De insulis*, cap. 3, §4, p. 162.

[137] Palacios Rubios, *De insulis*, cap. 2, §1, p. 116: "*Quod si facere noluerint, dato sibi termino ad deliberandum competenti, tunc bello, vi et armis, invadi et expugnari possunt, bona capi, et personae servituti donari, quia bellum, ex parte christianorum, est iustificatum.*" Palacios Rubios then cited *Quod super his* as the common opinion.

Land (Deuteronomy 20), in which God had commanded the chosen people to encounter others on peaceful terms. However, in cases where gentiles refused to welcome and accept tributary status under the chosen people of God, war was an acceptable response. The Spanish jurist envisioned a policy designed to employ weapons for invoking fear and forcing evangelization upon natives, rather than defending preachers from potential harm.

The proposed just causes of protecting Christians against persecution and the forced admission of preachers in the Indies were, to a certain extent, ancillary to the most important legal rationale for war – punishing sins against the natural law. Strikingly, Palacios Rubios cited the examples of Gregory IX and Innocent IV in favor of burning the Talmud to support the last cause. Just as the Jews were subject to Christian judgment over the morality of their religious laws, so too were pagans liable to punishment when their customs violated the precepts of natural law. Following Innocent, Palacios Rubios used the example of divine judgment from Scripture, where God punished the people of Sodom for their sins against nature. He also identified the worship of idols as an egregious unnatural sin subject to Christian judgment.[138]

The royalist-papalist teaching of Palacios Rubios was thoroughly theocratic and prone to endorsing perpetual war with infidels more extensively than medieval canonists. This extreme theocratic conception of world order gained practicability in the Requirement attributed to the pen of Palacios Rubios and formulated at a 1512 junta of theologians and jurists. Notably, the junta back in Valladolid, Spain at the priory of San Pablo put on hold the largest fleet to the New World, which was assembled and ready to embark under the command of the newly appointed governor of Tierra Firme, Pedrarias Dávila. It boasted some fifteen ships along with notable chroniclers and conquistadors such as Hernando de Soto, Bernal Díaz de Castillo, and Gonzalo Fernández de Oviedo.

In an effort to end the hiatus of the Pedrarias voyage, the novice conquistador, lawyer, and geographer Martín Fernández de Enciso presented a biblical argument for Spanish conquest on the basis of fulfilling a divine right – to acquire the Promised Land ("*la tierra de Promisión*") from pagan idolaters.[139] Before an audience that included Palacios Rubios, Enciso recalled that Moses had sent Joshua "to require" (*requerir*) the inhabitants of Jericho to abandon their city because God had given to the people of Israel.

[138] Palacios Rubios, *De insulis*, cap. 4, §7, p. 278: "*Idem dicit Innocentius quem alii sequuntur, si infideles colant idola, quia illud videtur contra legem naturalem: naturale, quippe, est colere Unum Deum creatorem, non creaturam.*"

[139] Adorno, *The Polemics of Possession*, pp. 265–266.

When they refused, they were decimated. Joshua then went and "took all of the land of Canaan by force of arms [*por fuerza de armas*], killing a countless number of them, and those who were captured were given as slaves to serve the Israelites. And all this was done by the will of God because they were idolaters."[140]

Enciso interpreted the whole affair of the Indies through this biblical narrative of conquest that justified enslavement through religious war. The Spanish Crown received divine concession over infidel lands through the Pope, who stood in the place of God on earth. King Ferdinand could therefore "justly require these idolatrous Indians to relinquish their land, which has been granted by the Pope. If they refuse, then war is acceptable as a means of seizing the land by force and killing them and enslaving those taken as prisoners just as Joshua had done to those inhabiting the Promised Land."[141] According to Enciso's *Memorial* recounting the relevant arguments, the conclusion of the junta was that the right of conquest conceded by the papacy rested on a single cause owing to the canonistic tradition: "[T]hey [the Indians] were idolaters who sacrificed and honored many gods."[142] This cause of eliminating idolatry provided the incontrovertible basis for the Requirement, which now dictated the terms of Spanish possession over the new Promised Land of the Indies.

The Requirement was intended to be read out loud before launching conquests, regardless of native incomprehensibility. It was consistent with the papal missionary warfare doctrine of the preceding centuries. Stipulating that God had granted worldwide dominium to the chair of Peter in Rome, the Requirement functioned like a ritual of taking possession.[143] The popes donated the designated islands and lands across the Atlantic to the Spanish Crown making them the official sovereigns over it. If the Indians accepted Spanish jurisdiction, and along with it, the universal rule of the Church and the freedom to preach, they would be free vassals of Ferdinand and now Queen Juana. Like the story of Joshua, if they refused, they would undergo subjugation by war, their possessions seized, and all the remaining women and children would be sold into slavery. The responsibility for these actions would fall on the Indians, who deny the Requirement thereby making themselves disobedient vassals subject to punishment. After the junta, Pedrarias' fleet

140 *Colección de documentos inéditos relativos al descubrimiento, conquista y organización de las antiguas posesiones españolas de América y Oceanía*, vol. 1 (Manuel B. de Quirós, 1864), pp. 443–444.

141 *Colección de documentos inéditos*, p. 444.

142 *Colección de documentos inéditos*, p. 447.

143 Hanke has provided a translation in *The Spanish Struggle for Justice*, p. 33.

received permission to depart following the royal approval of the Requirement in 1514.

Spanish chronicler and notary Fernández de Oviedo, who joined Pedrarias's company, was one of the original Spaniards to read out loud what he termed the *teología* ("theology") of the Requirement.[144] Oviedo first read the Requirement in 1514 to an empty or unoccupied town thereby indicating its importance as a ritual for taking possession. Although Oviedo benefited from the colonizing project by receiving an *encomienda* for his services, he was skeptical about the Requirement's effective communication to the natives. Nevertheless, the charge of cannibalism against the native Carib islanders framed the Requirement's initial legal context for rationalizing missionary war. Oviedo became a definitive eyewitness source for Spanish colonial legal arguments justifying the Requirement and wars against the natives. As he claimed in his authoritative *Historia General y Natural de las Indias*, the decimation of the native population was a punishment from God because of their "crimes and abominable customs and rites."[145] The alleged crimes of the *indios* recorded in Oviedo's work included idolatry, cannibalism, bestiality, and sodomy, all of which left an indelible imprint on the popular Spanish colonial imagination.

On June 18, 1519, the justice official (*juez de residencia*) Alonso de Zuazo, along with Jeronymite friars (Order of St. Jerome), issued a questionnaire to inquire about the cannibals who were a potential source of labor supply, along with black slaves from Africa. What was significant about this interrogatory directed toward ship officers was that it "broadened the range of legitimate offenses for which Indians could be enslaved."[146] Of the seventeen questions, the second one asked if the Carib-like natives on Tierra Firme were in fact "unbelievers, idolaters, cannibals, and sodomites not subject to the Crown" and "enemies of indigenous allies of the Spaniards."[147] With this development in legal policy, cannibalism no less than idolatry and sodomy could now be invoked as justifiable reasons for war and enslavement of infidels opposed to Spanish imperial rule and its native allies.

In that same year of 1519, Hernán Cortés began his inroads through Mexico by subjugating the native Nahua peoples and incorporating them into transatlantic Christendom. The onset of infectious disease, use of steel and strategic

[144] Hanke, *The Spanish Struggle for Justice*, pp. 33–34.

[145] Gonzalo Fernández de Oviedo, *Historia General y Natural de las Indias* (Madrid: La Real Academia de la Historia, 1851), primera parte, lib. 5, proemio, p. 124.

[146] Adorno, *The Polemics of Possession*, p. 102.

[147] Castañeda Delgado, "La politíca española con los caribes durante el siglo XVI," *Revista de Indias* 30 (1970), p. 84.

native alliances, provided him with the necessary conditions for Spanish domination of the Aztec Empire in less than three years. The "manufactured legal chain of conquest justification" branched out from the native cannibalism on the islands to the accusations of Amerindian mass idolatry on the mainland.[148] War against idolatry was evolving into an organized imperial procedure under the new king of Spain, Charles, also Holy Roman Emperor. Cortés related in one of his letters to the Crown his faithful observance to missionary warfare: "Above all, they were fighting to increase and spread our Faith and to submit to Your Majesty's service all those lands and provinces which had rebelled; this would fill them with courage and desire to conquer or die."[149]

The Indians of Mexico, especially the Aztecs, were not only cannibals, but they also sacrificed humans to their gods. Since this posed a direct obstacle to the spread of Christianity, Cortés declared to his armed company that their "principal motive and intention must be to dislodge and root out idolatry from all the natives of these regions and to bring them, or at least desire to bring them, to salvation [. . .]. For if the said war were fought with any other intent, it would be unjust."[150] The religious war against idolatry formalized in the Requirement had become an unapologetic ground of the Spanish right of conquest according to Cortés. As someone trained in law at a rudimentary level, Cortés also employed the cause of self-defense to justify his skirmishes. This reason included the defense of indigenous allies comparable to the Carib policy of missionary warfare.[151]

The Aztecs were an imperial power with numerous enemies. Among them were the Totonacs and Tlaxcalans, tributary peoples under imperial rule. These tribes became useful allies and were the first incorporated as possessions of the "Sacred Majesty" of Charles, which now stretched from Germany to Mexico.[152] Cortés immediately turned to the project of teaching them faith in the one God and rejecting idolatry. When Cortés learned of the animosity between the Aztecs and their tributary subjects, he was greatly pleased and capitalized on this conflict by pursuing an ancient tactic of conquering by

148 Matthew Restall, *When Montezuma Met Cortés* (HarperCollins, 2018), p. 80.

149 Hernán Cortés, *The Third Letter*, in *Letters from Mexico*, trans. Anthony Pagden (Yale University Press, 1986), p. 207.

150 Cited in Silvio Zavala, "Hernán Cortés ante la justificación de su conquista," *Revista de Historia de América*, vol. 92 (1981), pp. 60–61.

151 Cortés, *The Third Letter*, p. 166. Cortés specifically identified several just causes to inspire courage in his soldiers beginning with religious war: "First, because we were fighting against a barbarian people to spread our Faith; second, in order to serve Your Majesty; third, we had to protect our lives; and, last, many of the natives were our allies and would assist."

152 Cortés, *The Second Letter*, p. 48.

dividing.[153] Similar to the warnings Columbus received about Carib enemies, these communities informed Cortés about the tyranny of the Aztecs who had taken their children and offered them as sacrifices to idols.[154] Such reinforcement and native support would make European domination a reality for the greatly outnumbered Spaniards. The first experiment in war with his new "friends" was a massacre against the Cholulans, which claimed thousands of lives.

Soon after Cortés had defeated the Cholulan warriors, who were other Aztec subjects, he made his way into the imperial capital and island city, Tenochtitlan. The imperial ruler Montezuma cautiously greeted Cortés and his band of soldiers, Spanish and indigenous. While taking residence there, Cortés reported making his way into the city's main temple, a structure whose size surpassed La Giralda, the great bell tower of Seville's gothic cathedral. The magnificent temple housed not only the tombs of chiefs, but also the most important idols of the Aztecs. When Cortés came upon these religious items, he seized them and smashed them across the temple steps (see Figure 2.2).[155] He then cleaned out the fresh blood of the sacrifices. In place of the idols, he installed images of the Blessed Mother and other saints. In spite of the fact that temple priests asked Cortés not to perform such a subversive act at the risk of inciting rebellion, he did it anyway. He later boasted in his fifth letter addressed to the Catholic Monarch and Emperor, Charles: "I have put an end to many idolatries and offenses against our Creator, bringing many of the natives to the knowledge of God and planting in these lands Our Holy Catholic Faith."[156]

With unflinching zeal, Cortés implemented the twofold colonial practices of forced labor and religious war to advance the Spanish civilizing mission over the peoples and lands of Mexico. He marshalled justifications for ongoing conquest based on the elimination of idolatry and the defense of subjugated allies through the policy of the Requirement. Like the Admiral, the conquistador was transparent about the spiritual and economic benefits – or salvation and gold – that transatlantic incorporation would bring to the Crown. At the conclusion of his fifth letter, Cortés referred to a "very barbarous people and not so intelligent," the Chichimecas in the Michoacán region of Mexico, whose ability to learn the faith and recognize Spanish sovereignty was questionable. He concluded that refusal to submit demonstrated their incivility. Consequently, "the Spaniards are

153 Cortés, *The Second Letter*, pp. 69–70, referring to Mt 12:25.
154 Cortés, *The Second Letter*, pp. 50–51.
155 Cortés, *The Second Letter*, p. 106.
156 Cortés, *The Fifth Letter*, p. 442.

FIGURE 2.2 "Spanish attack on Aztec Temple with Tlaxcalan Allies." (Source: Getty Images/UniversalImagesGroup/Contributor)

to make war on them and reduce them to slavery ... By making slaves of this barbarous people, who are almost savages, Your Majesty will be served and the Spaniards will benefit greatly, as they will work in the gold mines, and perhaps by living among us some of them may even be saved."[157]

Although there were certain prospects of material gain for the Crown, Charles did not concede to every whim of the conquistadors' claims to take possession of the New World. The Monarch was increasingly aware of unlawful abuses perpetrated against natives by Spaniards across the Atlantic, especially through the Requirement. Charles stipulated that war was only acceptable if Spaniards were attacked first by Indians. In response, Cortés generated an argument defending the necessity of the *encomienda* that utilized the preexisting tributary system of the Aztecs to distinguish it further from the practice of forced labor in the Caribbean. Under the "tyranny" of the

[157] Cortés, *The Fifth Letter*, p. 446.

Aztecs, Cortés asserted, natives were more fearful of them as rulers than Spaniards. Not only did the Aztecs rob the goods of their subject populations, they also offered their sons and daughters as sacrifices to idols. What might appear as enslavement in one context, Cortés reasoned, looked more like freedom in another. The conquistador recommended that with royal oversight the *encomienda* should be granted in perpetuity to the *encomendero* and his descendants so that they could care for the Indians as their own. Moreover, the maintenance of the *encomienda* system in Mexico with a large labor class and the right technology meant that, "God willing, more gold will be mined in this land alone – so many mines being discovered – than in all the islands put together and as many more."[158] Cortés, like Columbus, was captive to the endless pursuit of gold in the Indies, albeit now on the mainland rather than islands.

Although Cortés did not fully persuade the king, he did manage to plant an unshakeable seed of doubt in royal policy by articulating a mainland *encomendero* position later used in sixteenth-century labor disputes. According to this view, abolishing the *encomienda* was tantamount to the destruction of the Indies. Royal decrees were markedly inconsistent and ambivalent toward the institution, supporting it and restricting it at other times. This culminated in the New Laws of 1542, which prohibited the practice but ultimately failed in its enforcement. What remained consistent were the justifications for war to capture and enslave cannibals and idolaters until the royal repudiation in 1573, which replaced the term "conquest" for "expedition" under King Philip II.[159] The resounding voice that stood directly opposed to the abusive colonial practices of dispossession in the Indies was that of certain Spanish Dominicans committed to justice for, and peaceful evangelization of, the native peoples. Their missionary imperative would give rise to a new scholastic theological conception of world order recognizing the rationality, rights, and cultural difference of infidel others.

158 "Cortés to the Emperor" (1524), in *New Iberian World*, 3:346–347.

159 "Ordinances of New Discoveries" (1573), in *New Iberian World*, 1:368: "The term 'conquest' is not to be used to describe exploring expeditions. These expeditions are to be made in a spirit of peace and love, and we do not wish them to be described by a word that might be thought to authorize the use of force against Indians."

3

Spanish Dominicans and the "Affair of the Indies"

Spanish political possession of the Indies relied on the effective occupation of insufficiently governed land rich in metals and the waging of war against infidels. Rendering the native peoples as lazy and idolatrous justified political subjugation under a European right of conquest forcing them to dig in mines, labor the fields, and fish for pearls. The spiritual goal of converting infidels remained the fundamental title of Spanish imperial expansion, although its interpretation remained deeply contested.[1] On the one hand, this religious title established under the Alexandrine bulls of donation (1493) mustered the widespread appeal, even intractability, of the *encomienda* system of forced labor and religious war during the early period of Spanish colonization. The colonialist invocation of the religious title stripped the Amerindians of political autonomy. On the other, it also mobilized the potent fissure point cracked wide by Spanish Dominicans who questioned the justice over the whole affair of the Indies. For these Dominicans, the religious title secured native independence from colonial dispossession because the unlawful exercise of political coercion thwarted the task of evangelization.

The Spanish Dominican missionaries and theologians considered in this chapter combined a peace ethic of evangelization opposed to religious war with a scholastic juristic account of natural law especially indebted to the moral theology of Thomas Aquinas. Faith and reason for them operated reflexively along the moral axes of idolatry and injustice thus generating a prophetic self-corrective to the colonialist abuse of indigenous peoples across the Atlantic. That there were both grounds and strategies to challenge Spanish colonialism at all was indeed remarkable. The dynamic interplay of private *encomenderos*, an interventionist Crown, an eager papacy, and vocal mendicant missionaries took place within a broader legal culture recognizing

[1] Elliott, *Empires of the Atlantic World*, p. 19.

Indians as juridical subjects, even independent of their membership and incorporation into the Spanish Crown. For transatlantic Spain, the term "*indios*" was not a racial classification, but a legal one designating "*naciones*" (nations or peoples) of the New World with their attendant rights, protections, and duties as vassals under the Crown.[2] Through the local authority of the bishop or the universal authority of the Pope, the institutional Church provided an additional measure of legal recognition to *indios* under the canonistic category of "*miserabiles personae*" (poor, disadvantaged persons).[3]

Our attention to the Indies affair in this chapter uniquely addresses the theological and canonistic category "*infideles*," demarcating legal otherness of unbaptized peoples outside Christian jurisdiction yet still human participants in a universal world order. The Dominican theologians considered here were innovative expositors of an idea and practice of world order affirming the freedom and rights of infidels outside of European Christian political rule. The New World appeared to these theologians as an "Indian world" (*orbe Indiano*) belonging to its first inhabitants. Their moral and juridical reflection on this new world order generated normative resources for international thought.

Natural law, the law of nations, and canon law opened juridical spaces for the Crown and Church to discuss, deliberate, rationalize and reform policy concerning Indians. In the previous chapter, we considered the political deployment of natural law and canon law to authorize religious war and the dispossession of infidels in the medieval and early modern contexts of crusade and expansion in North Africa and the Atlantic world. According to theocratic world order, the circumscription of infidel rights facilitated a European, largely Iberian, civilizing mission. Contrastingly, for Spanish Dominican critics of colonial violence the natural law, the law of nations, and Church law went beyond mere civil law to safeguard the rational agency of free native peoples. These alternative supranational or supra-imperial sources of law and right – inflected with scholastic theological principles indebted to

2 R. Jovita Baber, "Categories, Self-Representation, and the Construction of the Indios," *Journal of Spanish Cultural Studies* 10, no. 1 (2009): 27; Nancy E. van Deusen, *Global Indios: The Indigenous Struggle for Justice in Sixteenth-Century Spain* (Duke University Press, 2015), chap. 1.

3 Castañeda Delgado, "La condición miserable del indio y sus privilegios," *Anuario de estudios Americanos* 28 (1971): 245–335; Thomas Duve, *Sonderrecht in der Frühen Neuzeit: studien zum* ius singulare *und den* privilegia miserabilium personarum, senum, *und* indorum in Alter und Neuer Welt (Vittorio Klostermann, 2008); Caroline Cunill, "El indio miserable: nacimiento de la teoría legal en la América colonial del siglo XVI," *Cuadernos intercambio* 8, no. 9 (2011): 229–248.

Aquinas – provided Dominicans with independent moral norms of justice for Indian political recognition and their advocacy.

Altogether, the Spanish late scholastic theological approach to world order was neither theocratic royalist nor imperial humanist in orientation. Neither was it proto-secularist in outlook. As noted in Chapter 1, it entailed the crucial role of the Church witnessing to world order by authentically proclaiming the Gospel to all peoples and including them as potential members of the mystical Body of Christ. By acknowledging the basic freedom to accept or refuse the Gospel, the Spanish theologians did not cast the Church's evangelical mission in secularizing terms to justify colonization through the punishment of natural law violations. Neither did they advance a civilizing rationale for European expansion that excluded native forms of governance and property from the law of nations.

The Dominican theologians adhered to a Thomistic framework of law arranged according to the twofold order of nature and grace whereby the latter could not abolish or take away the former. Aquinas's theological axiom of *gratia non tollit* ("grace does not destroy") directly informed Dominican political judgments and legal reflection concerning the Indies, as seen most readily in Vitoria's *Relectio de Indis*, but also the writings of Domingo de Soto and Bartolomé de las Casas.[4] Aquinas extrapolated the legal and political significance of this scholastic theological principle in his teaching from the *Summa*: "[J]urisdiction and authority have been introduced by human law, while the distinction between believer and infidel is from divine law. Divine law, which is from grace, does not abolish human law, which is from natural reason."[5] The Spanish scholastic theological conception of world order rested on the congruous relationship between nature and grace, and reason and faith, human law and divine law, as articulated by Aquinas.

Like the polish lawyer Paulus Vladimiri a century prior, the Spanish Dominicans appealed to the Thomistic political axiom in their effort to uphold infidel dominium of jurisdiction and property as a facet of the law of nations, or positive human law. The law of nations was a rational outgrowth of the universal natural law and therefore a juridical source of native independence and sovereignty. Spanish Dominican discourse about the Indies revolved around political freedom and just war – two key aspects of *ius gentium* that applied universally to European Christian and non-European infidels.

4 Brading, *The First America*, pp. 83–84. See also Venancio D. Carro, "The Spanish Theological-Juridical Renaissance and the Ideology of Bartolomé de Las Casas," in *Bartolomé de Las Casas in History: Toward an Understanding of the Man and His Work*, eds. Juan Friede and Benjamin Keen (Northern Illinois University Press, 1971), pp. 251–252.

5 Aquinas, *ST* II-II, q. 10, a. 10.

Their discussion of *ius gentium* will be the primary focus of Chapter 6. This chapter specifically explores their creative interpretation of natural law by considering the role of the image of God, which anchored the subjective natural rights of all peoples, irrespective of baptismal membership in the Body of Christ. From this natural rational basis, the law of nations carried greater moral and juridical weight. The universal power of Christ, or divine law, safeguarded, rather than superseded, subjective natural rights according to the Spanish Dominicans.

INITIAL THEOLOGICAL DEBATES ABOUT CONQUEST

Although the Roman Church's prerogative remained the authoritative backbone of official Spanish colonial expansion, the erosion of papal power in temporal matters made it, at best, a justificatory rationale for imperial intervention. The papacy sanctioned what it could not effect on its own: taking new possessions and expanding Christendom in the transatlantic world. Beginning with King Duarte's successful entreating of Pope Eugenius IV over the conquest of the Canaries, and later illustrated by Pope Alexander VI's posterior letters of concession and the papal ratification of the Tordesillas Treaty more than a decade after its agreement, the papacy had to capitulate to the civilizing mission of Iberian empires overseas. Theocratic royalism, as presented by Juan López de Palacios Rubios in the previous chapter, provided the legal framework for theorizing a Catholic world order under a secular patronage system.

After the death of Queen Isabel in 1504, yet still during the initial phase of Spanish colonization across the Atlantic, theologians and not merely lawyers began responding to the affair of the Indies thus shaping subsequent debates.[6] Two of the earliest and most influential opinions came from scholastic contemporaries outside Spain residing in Paris and Rome, each of whose ideas clashed over the scope of ecclesiastical power and the grounds for European presence in the New World. The Scotsman Johannes Maior, or John Mair (1469–1550), who taught at the University of Paris, provided a different kind of argument for expanding Christendom overseas. Mair's theological opinion immediately strengthened Spanish justifications of a European right of conquest among royalists and imperialists by marshalling Aristotle's category of the natural slave, a long-standing notion in Western thought that now took on a positivist historical tone.

Alternatively, the Italian Dominican Tommaso de Vío Gaetanus, or "Cajetan" (1469–1534), adopted a speculative Thomistic view on the subject.

6 Zavala, *The Political Philosophy of the Conquest*, pp. 30–32.

Cajetan reflected on Christian–infidel relations from Rome when he was Master General of the Order of Preachers (1508–1518). His opinion mobilized Spanish Dominican efforts to resist violent Christian colonialism in a twofold sense: by strengthening the notion of infidel dominium indebted to Aquinas and by promoting a peaceful ethic of evangelization. Cajetan's stunning scholastic intervention introduced a new category of unbelievers beyond the traditional characterization of Christian–infidel relations in mostly conflictual terms, as determined by ongoing interaction with Muslims.

Mair formulated what could be designated a "modern" Christian argument for conquest in his commentary on the *Sentences* of Peter Lombard (c. 1510). His conciliarist commitments – a point of strong contention with his contemporary interlocutor Cajetan – privileged the authority of the ecumenical council over the Pope for the universal Church.[7] Mair's views on politics struck a modern chord that elided papalist conceptions of ecclesiastical power. As he decisively stated: "The supreme pontiff does not have temporal power over kings."[8] Nevertheless, the rejection of theocratic papalism did not translate into a stronger account of infidel dominium for Mair. In fact, Mair was the first theologian to defend, quite unreservedly, the superior right of European Christians over infidels in a post-contact New World. Yet he did so without arguing in favor of the Pope's universal jurisdiction over natural law. Neither did he assert the worldwide dominium of emperors. Instead, Mair "applied himself to the question of legality of empire in the new orb" by invoking "the *nature* of the Indians as a title for subjecting or enslaving them."[9] His novel argument for European domination presented an eclectic admixture of classical, medieval, and modern ideas about Aristotelian natural slavery, missionary warfare, and positivist nominalism.

Christian–infidel relations were in a perpetual state of conflict for Mair. The newly discovered peoples provided an empirical test case for asserting a superior right of conquest over infidels outside Europe. Similar to Pope Innocent IV's *Quod super his* commentary on the crusades addressed in the previous chapter, the Scottish theologian chose to address the topic of

7 John Mair, "A Disputation Concerning the Authority of the Council Over the Supreme Pontiff," in *Conciliarism and Papalism*, eds. J. H. Burns and Thomas M. Izbicki (Cambridge University Press, 1997), p. 286. An overview of the conciliarist view in the political context of the Protestant Reformation can be found in Quentin Skinner, *The Foundations of Modern Political Thought*, vol. 2, *The Age of Reformation* (Cambridge University Press, 1978), pp. 36–47.

8 Cited in Pedro Leturia, "Maior y Vitoria ante la conquista de América," *Anuario de la Asociación Francisco de Vitoria* 3 (1930–1931): 58.

9 Wey Gómez, The Tropics of Empire, p. 102; See also Pagden, *The Fall of Natural Man: The American Indian and the Origins of Comparative Ethnology* (Cambridge University Press, 1982), p. 39; Adorno, *Polemics of Possession*, pp. 102–103.

Christian–infidel relations in his commentary on Book Two of the *Sentences* where he considered the lawfulness of Christians waging war against Saracens, Tartars, and infidels generally.[10] Mair followed Innocent in recognizing the legitimacy of dominium among those infidels outside Christendom but severely curtailed it. Mair's commentary on Book One had distinguished two kinds of extra-European infidel – aggressive and peaceful types – yet both of whom could be rightfully dispossessed of their political authority for rejecting Christianity.[11] In each instance of either obstructing Christian preachers by force or permitting preachers yet refusing to convert, nonbelievers still have cause to lose political legitimacy. Unconvertible infidels were, quite simply, enemies of the Church unfit for life in a commonwealth. According to Mair's positivist reading, there were no historical examples of peaceful infidels who had permitted Christian preaching without converting, as the Mohammedans and Tartars had proved.[12]

When turning to the new peoples encountered across the Atlantic, Mair duplicated the missionary warfare doctrine of theocratic universalism without conceding to its papal conception of power. He had no need of alluding to the Alexandrine bulls allegedly donating the lands across the Atlantic.[13] Due to the language barrier between Europeans and Amerindians, the spread of the faith could not have been possible "without great military presence" to secure protection and permit the inculcation of European Christian norms and customs.[14] After Columbus, Spanish outposts were scattered throughout the Caribbean. The construction of forts and military strongholds took place irrespective of native consent and approval.

If non-European peoples converted to Christianity, paid for European travel expenses, and demonstrated prudence, then perhaps there was no reason to dispossess them of political authority. However, Mair's proposal was inapplicable to peoples of the New World because it adhered to a classical ethno-racial argument that geopolitically categorized the infidels of the Caribbean islands as brutish barbarians. Even if natives helped Europeans monetarily as a people, without formal kingship Christians could still take possession of these island barbarians through a superior rule in order

10 Mair, *In secundum Sententiarum* (1510), d. 44, q. 3, fol. 96r-96v. I will follow the Latin transcription of the question provided by Leturia in his appendix to "Maior y Vitoria ante la conquista," pp. 79–82.

11 See Carro, *La teología y los teólogos-juristas españoles ante la conquista de América, Segunda Edición* (Biblioteca de Autores Españoles, 1951), p. 289, n40.

12 Mair, *In secundum Sent.*, d. 44, q. 3, p. 80.

13 Leturia, "Maior y Vitoria ante la conquista," p. 70.

14 Mair, *In secundum Sent.*, d. 44, q. 3, p. 81.

to plant the faith.[15] Before the notion of savage natives gained currency in the Atlantic colonial world, there were barbarian infidels. Mair outlined a new colonializing perspective for a Eurocentric humanism independent of papalism.

Mair's judgment about the infidels of the New World was an empirically validated theoretical claim that deduced slavery from their barbarous nature. The sources of his ethno-racial argument derived from the Hellenistic Egyptian Ptolemy of Alexandria and Aristotle.[16] Both ancient thinkers adhered to a tripartite geopolitics whereby physical location and climate determined civilizational status in the global hierarchy of peoples. This remained an important feature of Iberian colonial expansion influencing the legal notions of its strongest partisans. Mair cited Ptolemy's second-century work on astrology, the *Tetrabiblos*, to classify entire blocs of peoples north and south of the equator as "wild beasts." The savage and burnt-skinned peoples of the south were comparable to the uncultivated peoples of the north hindered by the cold. Peoples of the middle region – conveniently in the Mediterranean locales of Italy, Spain, Greece, and Egypt – exhibited greater sociability and civilization than the rest of the world.[17]

Centuries before Ptolemy, Aristotle organized his tripartite geopolitics according to climatic conditions whereby extreme temperatures of hot and cold adversely affected the political nature of peoples within those respective regions. The *Politics* laid out a putatively ethnocentric worldview whereby Aristotle expanded his earlier division of Greeks and barbarians (non-Greeks) from Book One into a geopolitical context that relegated northern Europe and Asia to an inferior position.[18] Ptolemy of Alexandria would imbibe this geopolitical ethnocentrism left in the wake of Aristotle's famous student, Alexander of Macedon, and his successful military campaigns to spread Greek language and culture.

[15] Mair, *In secundum Sent.*, d. 44, q. 3, p. 81: "*Si erit alia policia quam regalis, illam insulam capiens mutare potest; et dignum est pro plantatione fidei, quod ipse regnum capiat.*"

[16] Mair, *In secundum Sent.*, d. 44, q. 3, p. 81: "*Citra ultraque equatorem et sub polis, vivunt homines ferini, ut Ptolomeus in quadrupertito dicit ... Primo Politicorum tertio et quarto dicit Philosophus: quod sunt alii natura servi alii liberi, manifestum est. Et in quibusdam determinatum est esse tale aliquid quibus ob ipsum prodest; et iustum est alium servire alium esse liberum. Et convenit alium imperare, alium parere illo imperio quod innatum est; quare et dominari. Propterea dicit Philosophus primo capite illius libri: quamobrem aiunt poete grecos barbaris dominari oportere, quia idem sit natura barbarous et servus.*"

[17] Benjamin Isaac, *The Invention of Racism in Classical Antiquity* (Princeton University Press, 2004), pp. 319–320.

[18] Aristotle, *The Politics*, Book 7, chap. 7, pp. 207–208.

Aristotle viewed natural slavery in his *Politics* as the result of climate rather than heredity.[19] Mair directly confirmed this point by linking classical tripartite geopolitics with Aristotelian natural slavery to establish a superior European right of conquering backward infidels across the Atlantic. Aristotle taught that some peoples inhabiting a specific region of the world were by nature free and disposed to govern political affairs whereas barbarian others were dependent on direction from a superior free society. Presupposing Aristotle's premise, Mair arrived at a fateful conclusion about the peoples across the Atlantic: "[T]he first to possess them, rightly rules over them, because they are by nature slaves, which is clear."[20]

The classical ethno-racial argument received positive demonstration from the early Spanish reports about non-industrious Taínos and warlike Caribs in the Indies. Mair further displayed his modern positivist inclinations by exploiting the category of "experience" (*experientia*) to confirm the geopolitical hierarchy of the ancients, albeit now in a Christian register that identified barbarian infidels as natural subjugates who "live like beasts."[21] Even more ominously, Aristotle had identified the natural slave with wild beasts, who could be hunted down justly in war if they resisted subjugation.[22] This linkage between the natural slave and untamed beast would influence international thought about English and Dutch colonial expansion in addition to Spanish thought.

The Christian political deployment of Aristotelian natural slavery to justify taking possession of people unfit to govern themselves acquired political clout among some of the strongest royalist and later imperialist partisans of Spanish conquest. In the next chapter, we consider the Spanish imperial courtier Juan Ginés de Sepúlveda, who strategically combined the ancient idea of natural subjugation with missionary war to advance a humanist argument for European Christian domination. Before the subject of lawful war attained central importance, political discussion focused intently on whether the Indians were natural subjugates who would benefit from forced incorporation into transatlantic Christendom. Those arguing against native self-governance

19 Isaac, *The Invention of Racism*, p. 73.

20 Mair, *In secundum Sent.*, d. 44, q. 3, p. 81: "*Quare primus eos occupans iuste eis imperat, quia natura sunt servi, ut patet.*"

21 Mair, *In secundum Sent.*, d. 44, q. 3, p. 81: "*Populus ille bestialiter vivit ... Et iam hoc experientia compertum est.*"

22 Aristotle, *The Politics*, Book 1, chap. 8, p. 45: "Hence expertise in war will also be in some sense a natural form of acquisitive expertise; for one part of it is expertise in hunting, which should be used with a view both to beasts and to those human beings who are naturally suited to be ruled and unwilling – this sort of war being by nature just."

turned to the *encomienda* as a spiritual, economic, and humanitarian solution for assimilating natives into a Castilian Catholic way of life.

The first major debate about the Indies unfolded at Burgos in 1512. It examined the legitimacy of the *encomienda* institution after the first Dominicans who arrived on Española in 1510 had leveled a critical indictment of Spanish colonizers and administrators the previous year. These Dominicans were disciplined friars from Salamanca. Led by Pedro de Córdoba and their chief preacher Antonio Montesino, they prayed and fasted for a year in response to the severely deteriorating state of the Taínos on the island. They decided, unanimously, to condemn and restrain the Spanish colonizers by withholding sacraments from *encomenderos*. The Dominican missionaries referred to the Taínos as "innocent peoples," and condemned in the strongest possible terms the "cruel tyranny" of the unjust wars and servitude Spaniards violently imposed upon them in order to "take and acquire gold every day."[23]

Public proponents of the *encomienda,* some of them Dominicans in high-ranking positions, relied on a variant of the Aristotelian political doctrine to justify native subjugation and compulsory labor. After all, the Spanish interpretation of natural subjugates was a fitting rationalization of the *encomienda.*[24] The Dominican friar Bernardo de Mesa, one of King Ferdinand's royal preachers, was the first to argue explicitly in Spain that the factors of terrain geography and island location determined the natural inferiority of the Caribbean peoples, as demonstrated by their vices.[25] Moreover, Mesa presented a moral opinion (*parecer*) before the royal court linking political subservience with the vices of idleness and idolatry. The friar proposed:

> [T]he Indians were granted to the king for their own good. Since idleness is the greatest evil they can commit, Your Highness must take great care and diligence to remove the degenerate harm of idleness by always commanding them to occupy themselves with spiritual and corporal activities. In truth, even though idleness is the stepmother of all the vices in every nation, much more is it so among the Indians, who are habituated into, and born from, the sin of idolatry and other sins, all of which are revived and increased by idleness.[26]

23 Las Casas, *Historia de las Indias*, III, cap. 4, ed. Agustín Millares Carlo (Fondo de cultura economica, 1986), pp. 441–442.

24 Pagden, *Fall of Natural Man*, pp. 36–37.

25 Zavala, *The Political Philosophy of the Conquest*, p. 49; Wey Gómez, *The Tropics of Empire*, p. 104.

26 Las Casas, *Historia de las Indias*, III, cap. 9, p. 460: "*[L]os indios eran dados al rey para su bien, y la ociosidad es el mayor mal que ellos pueden tener, que debía Su Alteza con gran estudio trabajar de les quitar el daño depravado de la ociosidad, mandándolos siempre ocupar en*

Idleness and idolatry were mutually reinforcing twin vices cited by chroniclers to substantiate Amerindian inferiority and reliance on Spanish rule. Native political liberty was a sham; alternatively, subjugation through forced labor was beneficial to Indians who needed their vices curbed and their work ethic developed by a superior Christian civilization.

The canon lawyer Palacios Rubios also briefly considered natural slavery in the *De insulis* defense of the Spanish civilizing mission, as noted in the previous chapter. However, as a theocratic jurist, Palacios Rubios was more inclined to rely on the canonistic tradition of missionary war rather than the classical geopolitical hierarchy attractive to other members of the royal court. In contrast, a court preacher and lawyer named Gregorio applied Aristotle's political doctrine to justify a despotic form of rule over the Indians, who were natural slaves in a qualified sense.[27] That qualification rested on a scholastic interpretation of habit – a stable disposition to act in a certain way – as a second nature. Such qualification did little to improve Gregorio's view of the Indians, who were "like animals that speak." Gregorio was rather forthright in his rejection of Dominican sympathizers like Córdoba and Montesino. For these outspoken Dominicans would have the Crown, according to Gregorio, "not make use of them [the Indians] by commanding them to serve Spanish Christians, through digging and extracting gold, because they were supposedly free persons." *Licenciado* Gregorio had identified the crux of the critical Dominican intervention: their staunch advocacy for native political freedom against Spanish claims of possession.[28] In direct contrast to the pro-Indian Dominicans, Gregorio and Mesa considered the Caribbean peoples natural subjugates who remained inescapably trapped in the vices of idleness and idolatry apart from a superior legal and religious culture to steer them.

The resulting opinion of the junta on the *encomienda* received formalization in the 1512 Law of Burgos, the "first comprehensive code of Indian legislation" constructed by Europeans.[29] The Crown made minimal attempts to improve native welfare and ultimately compromised by supporting a regulated forced labor policy. Perhaps its least abrasive contribution was to regulate hateful and derogatory speech directed at indigenous peoples.[30] Even

algunos ejercicios espirituales o corporales, que en la verdad, aunque la ociosidad sea madrastra de todas las virtudes en todas las naciones, mucho más lo es, [dice él,] en los indios, que eran habituados y criados en el pecado de la idolatría y en otros pecados, los cuales reverdecen y crecen con la ociosidad."

27 Gustavo Gutiérrez, *Las Casas: In Search of the Poor of Jesus Christ*, trans. Robert R. Barr (Orbis Books, 1993), pp. 280–281.

28 Las Casas, *Historia de las Indias*, III, cap. 12, pp. 471–472.

29 Hanke, *The Spanish Struggle for Justice*, pp. 23–24.

30 One such example punishable by fine was referring to Indians as "dogs."

so, the preamble to the Burgos code portrayed the Indians as inclined to a life of idleness and vice. It then stipulated thirty-five articles, most of which aimed at rooting out idleness and idolatry by forcing the natives to dig in the mines and to learn the Christian faith all under the supervision of *encomenderos*.[31] The extremely modest effort to secure the humane treatment of natives in the Law of Burgos was woefully insufficient to appease the Dominicans of Española. Pedro de Córdoba, Vice-Provincial on the island, returned to Spain briefly to challenge and amend the new regulation.

Although the New World Dominican condemnation of unjust war and forced labor drew retaliatory ire from the ranks of officials, colonists, and clergy, it drastically weighed on the conscience of the priest-*encomendero*, Bartolomé de las Casas. Having served a chaplain in the conquest of Cuba, Las Casas was materially rewarded for his efforts. But under the threat of excommunication from the Dominicans because of his personal encomienda, Las Casas resolved in 1514 to turn over his native subjects to another Spaniard and commit himself to a lifetime of irrepressible Indian advocacy.[32] Back in Spain in 1516, he published his first petition (*memorial*) identifying some fourteen "remedies" for the affair of the Indies.[33] Despite exhibiting naiveté in this initial attempt to alleviate the plight of the natives,[34] Las Casas opposed the colonial practices of dividing protectable land among Spaniards (*repartimiento*), the forcible seizure of natives from one island to work on others, and assigning native laborers as tributary subjects against their will (*encomienda*). This early work already expressed his lifelong dedication to defending "those Indians, who are human beings and free, and ought to be treated as free human beings."[35]

After the death of King Ferdinand, Las Casas's "remedies" earned him the title of "universal protector of all the Indians" (*procurador universal de todos los indios*) from Cardinal Jiménez de Cisneros, a shrewd public official and Franciscan reformer. Cisneros sent Las Casas back to the Indies in 1517, where he could implement colonial reforms under the supervision of three other friars who were members of the Jeronymite order. These Jeronymite friars, against the judgment of Las Casas, launched two inquiries into the affair

[31] Simpson, *The Encomienda in New Spain*, pp. 32–34.

[32] Gutiérrez, *Las Casas*, pp. 45–53.

[33] Las Casas, *Memorial de remedios* (1516), in *OC*, vol. 13, pp. 23–48.

[34] Adorno, *The Polemics of Possession*, pp. 63–69. Adorno summarizes the evolution of thought in Las Casas's Indian advocacy beginning with the 1516 *Memorial de remedios*, where he first recommended and later regretted using black slaves from Africa to restore Indian life.

[35] Las Casas, *Memorial de remedios* (1516), p. 28: "*[Y] se sepa cómo aquellos indios son hombres y libres y han de ser tratados como hombres y libres.*"

of the Indies that set the terms for a colonial policy upholding missionary war and the *encomienda*. As mentioned in Chapter 2, the Jeronymites and the chief justice official Alonso de Zuazo issued the cannibal questionnaire in 1519, which expanded the range of offenses punishable by war and enslavement to include, most prominently, idolatry. This rationalization for a war to eradicate idolatry and facilitate conversion came just in time as Hernán Cortés was making landfall in Mexico.

Two years before the cannibal questionnaire, the Jeronymites issued their first interrogatory on Española determining whether there was evidence of sufficient rational capacity and political agency among natives for them to live apart from the *encomienda* system controlled by Spaniards. These friars conducted their inquiry by interviewing twelve inhabitants of the island as witnesses. The following question, translated by Lewis Hanke, struck the heart of the whole affair:

> Does the witness know, believe, or has he heard it said, or observed, that these Indians, especially those of Española and women as well as men, are all of such knowledge and capacity that they should be given complete liberty? Would they be able to live *políticamente* as do the Spaniards? Would they know how to support themselves by their own efforts, each Indian mining gold or tilling the soil, or maintaining himself by other daily labor?[36]

The witnesses were nearly unanimous in their support of Spanish political possession and opposition to native political freedom. They drew from personal accounts about the alleged idleness and lack of industry among Indians. Only the witness Bernardo de Santo Domingo, one of the friars who was among the first group of Dominicans to arrive in Española with Montesino and Córdoba, defended the Indian capacity of self-governance and political liberty.[37] The Jeronymite inquiry, at its best, yielded freedom for a single Indian. Overall, it not only legitimized political subordination of native peoples through forced labor, but also precipitated a smallpox epidemic claiming about one-third of the local population because of forced assimilation.[38] The reality of labor shortage only increased the prospects for transplanting captured natives from other islands, black slaves from Africa, and the waging of new missionary wars against idolaters discovered on the continent.

Still, Las Casas and the Dominican sympathizers pressed on to eliminate the *encomienda* institution and affirm infidel political agency. The Indian

36 Hanke, *The Spanish Struggle for Justice*, pp. 42–43.

37 Bernardo de Santo Domingo even drafted an opinion (*parecer*) on the matter, see Las Casas, *Historia de las Indias*, III, cap. 94.

38 Simpson, *The Encomienda in New Spain*, p. 53.

cause received even greater theological authority from their Master General in Rome, Cajetan, who printed his commentary on Aquinas's *Summa* in 1517. The Dominicans on Española, whom Cajetan had personally sent in 1510, were now reporting to him in Rome the abuses of the Indians under the Spanish colonial system. According to Las Casas's narration of the event, a Spanish friar named Jerónimo de Peñafiel informed the Master General about the atrocities witnessed by Córdoba, which purportedly influenced Cajetan's commentary on the *Summa* as he was completing it.[39] The relevant commentary on Christian–infidel relations applicable to the affair of the Indies was contained in the *Secunda Secundae*, Question 66, Article 8. Aquinas's response to an objection in this article focused on the issue of dispossessing infidels of their property, heretics in particular, which had been a pastoral matter raised by St. Augustine during his time as bishop of Hippo.

In contrast to the tripartite geopolitical hierarchy, Cajetan introduced a tripartite legal categorization of infidels to bolster the dominium of peoples outside Christendom. The importance of Cajetan's legal categorization for Christian–infidel relations, and later international relations, was profound. Adopting the legal terminology of de facto and de iure authority – the same grammar of theocratic papalism – Cajetan began by distinguishing two traditional kinds of Christian–infidel political relations. The first category of infidels who were under Christian political authority in de iure and de facto senses included Jews, Muslims, and heretics within Christendom. The second category of unbelievers referred to those who had taken formerly Christian lands and were therefore under Christian jurisdiction in principle, although not in actuality. These latter inimical infidels, having declared war on the Church because of forced occupation and possession of Christian territories, belonged to the medieval context of war often cited by canonists during the Crusades.[40]

Cajetan's typology up to this point added nothing to the canonistic just war tradition and Christian–infidel relations. Nevertheless, it did clear the way for abandoning the traditional arguments for missionary war reliant on taking political possession of infidel lands to bring about conversion. The Dominican

39 Las Casas, *Historia de las Indias*, III, cap. 38. After hearing Peñafiel's report from Córdoba about the Indies, Cajetan reportedly asked, "And do you doubt your king is in hell?" (*Et tu dubitas regem tuum esse in inferno?*).

40 Cajetan, *Commentaria*, in *Sancti Thomae Aquinatis Opera omnia*, Leonine edition (Romae: 1886–1906), II-II, q. 66, a. 8, pp. 94–95. Consequently, neither Cajetan nor any of the other Spanish Dominicans denied the possibility of just wars against infidels who aggressively reject Christianity or attack Christian preachers. See his commentary on *ST*, II-II q. 10, a. 8, p. 90.

theologian then introduced a new distinction of infidels directly applicable to the Indies that categorically rejected imperial and papal claims of dominium based on right or factual possession. Beyond the previous two categories of infidels, other infidels had never been subject to Christian temporal powers – either in fact or in principle. Neither had they likely ever heard of the Gospel, which suggested Aquinas's category of pure unbelief, or negative unbelief.[41]

This categorical distinction, rooted in Thomistic axioms, assumed all non-aggressive infidels outside Latin Europe were free from Christian jurisdiction. It therefore supplied a principled affirmation of infidel political agency beyond European temporal claims. According to Cajetan: "Although they are infidels, the rulers of these peoples are legitimate rulers, whether governed by monarchical regime or by the state. They are not to be dispossessed of their political jurisdiction on account of their unbelief, since *dominium is from positive law, and unbelief is from divine law, which does not take away positive law*, as stated above in q. 10, a. 10."[42] Cajetan had creatively expanded the discourse of infidel rights to address the extra-European world.

Cajetan's commentary on the *Summa* question concerning infidel property and political rule rapidly spread among Dominican friars across Europe and the Atlantic during early the colonization period. The work even received attention from the Spanish conquistador-lawyer Fernández de Enciso, the outspoken theocratic defender of the Requirement and missionary war, as we saw in Chapter 2. Enciso's *Memorial*, composed around 1526, referred to "a doctor who wrote that the lands possessed by infidels – especially those in which the people there have never heard of the name of Jesus Christ – could not be abrogated without due cause. That is because jurisdiction and possession of the lands was from the law of nations, whereby they had acquired control and possession of the lands they occupied."[43] Cajetan and his *Summa* commentary were the obvious allusion here, a point further evidenced by Enciso's accompanying indictment of those Dominicans of Española who had

41 Aquinas, *ST* II-II, q. 10, a. 1. Negative unbelief contrasts with the positive unbelief of those who deliberately resist the truthfulness of the Christian faith. Domingo de Soto explicitly identified the connection between Aquinas's teaching on negative unbelief and Cajetan's third category of infidels. *De iustitia et iure* (Instituto de Estudios Politicos, 1967), lib. 5, q. 3, a. 5: "*Infideles autem tertii ordinis sunt, qui neque iure neque facto nobis subditi sunt: neque vero nobis infesti: quales sunt illi qui vel Christianum nomen non audierunt.*"

42 Cajetan, *Commentaria*, II-II, q. 66, a. 8, p. 94: "*Horum namque domini, quamvis infideles, legitimi domini sunt, sive regali sive politico regimine gubernentur: nec sunt propter infidelitatem a dominio suorum privati; cum dominium sit ex iure positivo, et infidelitas ex divino iure, quod non tollit ius positivum, ut superius in qu. 10, a. 10 habitum est.*"

43 *Colección de documentos inéditos*, Vol. 1 (1864), p. 446.

caused great harm to Spain because of their critical sermon attacking both the *encomiendas* and the *conquistas*.[44]

Without ever referencing the Indians of the New World explicitly, Cajetan's reference to positive law (or the law of nations) provided a critical theological counterpoint to both Mair's Eurocentric assertion of a superior right of conquest and the theocratic universalist conception of world order promoting religious war against infidels outside Europe. "I know of no law over their temporal matters," wrote Cajetan in his effort to chasten European political expansion. "No king, no emperor, not even the Roman Church," he continued, "can wage war to take possession of their lands or subjugate them under temporal authority, since there is no cause of just war."[45] By 1546, the year of Vitoria's death, the Salmantine theologian Melchor Cano, OP, in his *De dominio indorum* (*On the Sovereignty of the Indians*) referred to Cajetan's teaching as the "settled solution" for thinking about Christian–infidel relations in the New World.[46] Las Casas concluded that ignorance of Cajetan's principled teaching was a key factor leading to "the whole destruction of the Indies."[47]

Cajetan's account of infidel dominium cohered with his scholastic theological politics on Church and state. If he was a papalist in contrast to a conciliarist like Mair, or Jacques Almain, it was only in a qualified sense. Standard historical readings of Cajetan are minimal and treat his papalism almost exclusively within his continental European reformation context of combating both conciliarism and Lutheranism.[48] Yet from the standpoint of the Indies, a matter preoccupying Cajetan throughout his decade tenure as Master General of the Dominicans, his political thought appears in a new key. Cajetan's scholastic views on ecclesiastical and secular powers could affirm infidel political agency and the transcendent moral witness of the Church without adverting to theocratic universalism in either its papalist or imperialist modes. The Dominican theological commentator staked out a Thomistic *via*

44 Isacio Pérez Fernández, *El Derecho Hispano-Indiano* (Editorial San Esteban, 2001), pp. 117, 205.

45 Cajetan, *Commentaria*, II-II, q. 66, a. 8, p. 94: "*Contra hos nullus rex, nullus imperator, nec Ecclesia Romana potest movere bellum ad occupandas terras eorum aut subiiciendum eos temporaliter: quia nulla subest causa iusti belli.*"

46 Melchor Cano, *De dominio indorum*, in *Misión de España en América*, 1540–1560, ed. Luciano Pereña Vicente (CSIC, 1956), p. 126: "Pro certa explicatione suppono ex Caietano quod tripliciter sunt infideles."

47 Las Casas, *Doce dudas*, in *OC*, vol. 11.2, cap. 2, p. 40: "*La ignorancia deste principio ha causado principalmente toda la destrucción de las Indias.*"

48 Skinner, *Foundations of Modern Political Thought*, vol. 2, pp. 45–46; Francis Oakley, *The Watershed of Modern Politics* (Yale University Press, 2015), pp. 244–245.

media, later adopted by Vitoria, avoiding the extremes of theocratic papalism and the subordination of the Church to secular power or mere human consent.[49]

On the question of the authority of the Church, Cajetan wrote: "the pope's power is directly concerned with things spiritual absolutely for the supreme end of the human race." The exalted dignity of spiritual power over all other worldly manifestations, an argument that Vitoria explicitly shared with Cajetan, concerned "things temporal ordered to things spiritual (*in ordine ad spiritualia*)."[50] Later Jesuits like Francisco Suárez and Robert Bellarmine interpreted this middle position as the indirect theory of the Pope's spiritual power.[51] Accordingly, the Pope's power stemmed directly from Jesus Christ who handed the keys of the heavenly kingdom over to the Petrine ministry. Barring extreme cases of deposing or even slaying a heretical, tyrannical Pope, Cajetan's account of papal power admitted tremendous interventionist power over the baptized community in Christendom to the chagrin of conciliarists and Protestants. Nevertheless, outside Europe, Cajetan placed strict limits on the temporal claims of Christians over nonbelievers. Cajetan's view that unbelief was a false basis for popes and princes claiming the dispossession of infidel political power and property influenced Vitoria but also Hugo Grotius in his Dutch effort to discredit Portuguese monopoly on trade in the East Indies.[52]

Not all Catholic anti-conciliarists were extreme papalists, as seen in the fifteenth-century Spanish Dominican Cardinal Juan de Torquemada, whose rejection of worldwide papal rule over temporal affairs was a principal source for Vitoria's lecture on the Indians.[53] Although Torquemada was an important source for the Spanish Dominican repudiation of papal world dominium in temporal matters, his anti-conciliarism adhered to an imperial political theology affirming the Roman emperor as "lord of the world" reminiscent of its most literate medieval apologist, Dante Alighieri.[54] Torquemada defended imperial rule with an appeal to its natural and rational purpose: "[T]he

49 Vitoria, *On the Power of the Church* (Part I), q. 5, §1, p. 83.

50 Cajetan, "Apology," in *Conciliarism and Papalism*, p. 249; Vitoria, *On the Power of the Church* (Part I), q. 5, a. 8, p. 92; *On the American Indians*, q. 2, a. 2, pp. 261–263.

51 Rommen, *The State in Catholic Thought*, pp. 508–511.

52 Vitoria, *On the American Indians*, q. 1, a. 3, p. 246; Grotius, *Commentary on the Law of Prize*, chap. 12, pp. 312–314.

53 Vitoria, *On the American Indians*, q. 2, a. 2, p. 260, citing Torquemada's *Summa de ecclesia*. Also see Thomas Izbicki, "An Argument from Authority in the Indies Debate," *The Americas* 34, no. 3 (1978): 400–406.

54 James Muldoon, *Empire and Order* (St. Martin's Press, 1999), pp. 90–92. In Book 2 of *De monarchia* (1314), Dante praised the Roman *imperium* for advancing the greatest civilization

imperial principate, as far as it is due to men, is from natural law, which is called the law of nations. This conclusion is proved thus: what is fitting and expedient in men according to right reason is due to natural law or the law of nations, which is the same thing."[55] The fusing or collapsing of the law of nations into natural law would later signal the rise of political theology in the early modern international thought of the Spaniard Sepúlveda and the Oxford jurist Alberico Gentili, but also Hobbes. The Spanish scholastic theological reading of politics, in contrast, maintained and developed the important relationship between natural law and the law of nations (or positive human law) without conflating both concepts.

Cajetan offered a more compelling view of secular politics for the Spanish Dominicans than Torquemada or the conciliarists. The Master General dismissed outright any authoritative claims for empire from the Bible and natural law. Instead, he located imperial institutions strictly within the realm of positive law. Even so, this manner of imperial rule was certainly not universal dominium over the world. In another section of the *Summa* commentary, Cajetan argued: "No natural principle nor authority of Sacred Scripture forces all parts of the earth, nor all the nations of one part, to elect a single temporal prince, which is evident. Temporal principality naturally depends on the election of someone, unless he be a tyrant."[56] Rather than imagine the world under a single universal monarch like Dante or Juan de Torquemada, Cajetan appropriated the Aristotelian language of distinct, autonomous polities capable of defending their respective communities and punishing out of revenge.[57] These "self-sufficient" (*sibi sufficiens*) political communities each possess the rightful power for providing for the general welfare and declaring war through an elected ruler chosen by the people. There was a striking resemblance here in his scholastic political thought to the Italian jurist of autonomous city-republics, Baldus of Ubaldis (d. 1400), whose last teaching post was at the University of Padua, which coincidentally, was the place of Cajetan's first theological appointment almost a century later.[58]

on earth and its host of virtues. Nature and divine decree, Dante argued, rightly ordered the subjugation of all peoples under Rome's world empire.

55 Juan de Torquemada, "In Honor of the Roman Empire," in *Three Tracts on Empire*, eds. Thomas Izbicki and Cary Nederman (Thoemmes Press, 2000), pp. 119–120.

56 Cajetan, *Commentaria*, II-II, q. 40, a. 1, p. 314: "*[N]ec naturalis ratio nec auctoritas sacrae Scripturae cogit omnes quartas terrae, nec omnes nationes unius quartae, ad electionem unius principis temporalis, ut patet: et constat ex electione pendere naturaliter principatum temporalem alicuius, nisi sit tyrannicus.*"

57 Cajetan, *Commentaria*, II-II, q. 40, a. 1, p. 313.

58 Joseph Canning, *The Political Thought of Baldus de Ubaldis* (Cambridge University Press, 1987), chap. 3.

In the effort to distinguish ecclesiastical spiritual power from secular royal power amidst the conciliarism debate, Cajetan emphasized the integrity and independence of each sphere of power: "The reason for the difference between king and pope is that royal power is in the people first by natural law, and it is devolved to the king from the people. Papal power, however, is above nature; and, by divine law, it is first in only one person, not in the community, Christ having established the form of the supreme ecclesiastical government in only one person."[59] Since the papacy's power was strictly a matter of divine law, which did not take away positive law, Cajetan maintained a consistent outlook on the legitimacy of infidel dominium immune from Christian political claims. Remarkably, he did so by claiming that the original elective power of the people stemmed from natural right, which thereby granted an unimpeachable basis to all polities, Christian and infidel alike – be they democratic, aristocratic, or monarchical in form.[60]

That Cajetan identified a people's natural right of consent as the efficient cause of all political authority was a mainstay of early modern and modern scholastic political thought culminating in Suárez.[61] Cajetan's legacy and reception in the Indies context complicates a Eurocentric reading of the merely conciliarist roots of modern political ideas about sovereignty. For Spanish Dominicans Soto and Las Casas, the natural right of consent identified by Cajetan was nonnegotiable for thinking about the legitimate political power of non-European peoples. When Las Casas surveyed the Indies at the end of his prolific career, his argument against the tyranny of Francisco Pizarro in the Peruvian case turned on consent. The Protector of the Indians defended the restoration of Inca sovereignty on the basis that "the consent of the peoples and their rulers" – the "natural foundation and efficient cause" of every royal power – had been absent from the beginning of the Spanish conquest.[62]

Soto, with characteristic scholastic precision, summarized the political principle in this way: "[K]ings and princes are created by the people, who

59 Cajetan, *Apology*, p. 232.

60 Cajetan, *Commentaria*, II-II, q. 50, a. 1, *ad* 3, p. 375: "*[E]lectio regiminis non est pars regiminis, sed praevium ad omnem speciem regiminis, ad electionem siquidem populi spectat secundum naturale ius, an populare, an optimatum, an regale, sit futurum regimen.*"

61 Arthur Monahan, *From Personal Duties towards Personal Rights* (McGill-Queen's University Press, 1994), pp. 129, 142–145; Gabriel Bowe, *The Origin of Political Authority* (Clonmore & Reynolds, 1955), pp. 31–34.

62 Las Casas, *De thesauris*, in *OC*, 11.1, cap. 29, p. 318: "*Quia totius facultatis aut potestatis et jurisdictionis exercende atque adipscendi principatus eiusdem, de est Regibus nostris naturale fundamentum et efficiens causa, scilicet, consensus populorum et regum suorum.*"

have transferred their rule and power."[63] Soto included infidel peoples of the New World in the exercise of domestic political power. Later Catholic thinkers espousing transmission and translation theories of political authority were thoroughly indebted to Cajetan and the Spanish Dominicans. And although Cajetan did not formulate a conception of world order within the traditional genre of scholastic commentary, his appeal to natural law and positive law for thinking about Christian–infidel relations in an apostolic spirit gave his Spanish Dominican confreres the theological resources for developing one. The discourse of infidel rights was no longer constrained by a medieval canonistic concern with crusade and missionary warfare but applicable to those peoples outside Europe who had never heard of the Gospel.

INFIDEL RIGHTS, RESTITUTION, AND WORLD ORDER

The Dominican friars of Salamanca were embroiled in the affair of the Indies from the first moment of European contact with the native peoples across the Atlantic. Their original line of communication with the New World was none other than the Admiral Columbus. Several years before Columbus embarked on his first voyage in 1492, he met with the friars of the San Esteban priory in Salamanca to discuss his plan and gain the favor of the Catholic Monarchs. Diego de Deza (1443–1523), *Prima* Chair of theology at the university and prior of San Esteban, attended these meetings with Columbus, befriending the explorer and hosting him at the priory. The Dominicans of Salamanca were increasingly adept in the writings of their medieval teachers, Albert the Great and especially Thomas Aquinas, both of whom had theorized the spherical shape of the earth in scholastic treatises on place and motion.[64] This growth in scholastic theoretical knowledge was largely due to Deza, who made the study of Aquinas mandatory for Dominican theological formation. Taken by Columbus's proposal to circumnavigate a westward path to China, Deza petitioned the Crown to sponsor his first voyage. The Monarchs heeded the Dominican theologian's request and Columbus soon thereafter set sail. In 1504 and nearing the end of life, the Admiral graciously remembered that Deza was "the reason why Their Highnesses came to possess the Indies."[65] From the start, the affair of the

63 Soto, *De iustitia et iure*, lib. 1, q. 1, a. 3, p. 13: "*[R]eges ac principes à populo creati sunt, in quos suum transtulit imperium ac potestatem.*" Soto also cited here Justinian's *Digest* 1.4.1.

64 José Luis Espinel, *San Esteban de Salamanca: Historia y Guía* (Editorial San Esteban, 1995), p. 49.

65 Cited in Wey Gómez, *The Tropics of Empire*, p. 232.

Indies summoned the Order's conscience to reflect on the duty and manner of preaching the Gospel to all nations beyond the known world.

Amidst the Spanish Catholic Renaissance, there was a profound religious renewal privileging austerity to match the intellectual rejuvenation among the Order of Preachers. The first Dominican friars from Salamanca who arrived on Española during 1510 and 1511, fifteen in all, came from this climate of reform influenced by Deza and the Spanish Renaissance more broadly.[66] They were dedicated to sharing the Gospel in a manner consistent with the early apostles that involved silent contemplation, communal prayer, and attentive listening, all under the vow of poverty. On the island, their lives were even more ascetic than in Europe. The friars agreed on following stricter requirements reflecting the Order's earlier constitutions to develop greater discipline in the spiritual life, which included abstention from the outset from bread, wine, and oil. As the poor friars lived among the people at the Santo Domingo settlement, they attuned themselves spiritually to recognize both the extent of suffering among the innocent Taíno laborers and the undignified callousness of Spaniards.

No stranger to prophetic indictments and his complicit past, Las Casas recalled that certain Spaniards "were strictly concerned with getting rich off the blood of those poor" Indians who were farming and digging for gold on the island. Most other Spaniards did nothing in response to colonial dispossession and destruction of the natives. After observing intently what had devolved into the wretched affair of the Indies in less than two decades, Las Casas noted that the Dominicans "began to combine the concept of right [*el derecho*] with reality [*el hecho*]" in order "to address the ugliness and monstrosity of an injustice never before heard."[67] The result of their spiritual reflection on justice, seen from the perspective of the innocent and oppressed Indian, was an interrogation of the Spanish colonial soul through a series of existential questions: *Do the precepts of justice and charity not apply to them? Do they not have lawful jurisdiction over their lands? Have they offended us in any way?*

When the preacher Montesino ascended to the pulpit on the Fourth Sunday of Advent in 1511, he asked the congregation with the deadly gravity, "Tell me, by what right and with what justice do you hold these Indians in such cruel and horrible servitude? Are they not human beings? Do they not have rational souls? Are you not obligated to love them as yourselves?" (see Figure 3.1).[68] The underlying theological commitment of the Dominicans was

66 Ramón Hernández, "Primeros Dominicos del convento de San Esteban en América," *Ciencia Tomista* 113 (1986), p. 325.

67 Las Casas, *Historia de las Indias*, III, cap. 3, pp. 438–439.

68 Las Casas, *Historia de las Indias*, III, cap. 4, pp. 441–442.

FIGURE 3.1 "Statue of Antonio de Montesino in Dominican Republic." (Source: Getty Images/Christian Ender/Contributor)

that the Indians of the New World were rational human beings, especially deserving of love as innocent neighbors. They were equal participants in human nature sharing basic rights and political freedom just like Europeans.

This Dominican interrogatory in the court of Spanish conscience, theological to its core, opened a critical reflection on the subject of justice, more specifically rights, during the era of colonization overlapping with the reign of Charles I, King of Spain (1516–1556) and later Holy Roman Emperor.[69] While the 1517 Jeronymite interrogatory over native political agency was underway, Dominicans gathered for a theological junta at the University of Salamanca. Signed by thirteen theologians, the official conclusions of this important moment in the history of human dignity, unfortunately, were lost. Yet Las Casas remembered that its contents – delivered to him by the Dominican prior of San Esteban at the time, Juan Hurtado de Mendoza – defended the rational capacity of the Indians to receive the faith against heretical opponents.[70] Coincidently, this same Hurtado invited the exceedingly gifted teacher of theology, Francisco de Vitoria, to Salamanca in 1526. At the time,

[69] Gutiérrez, *Las Casas*, chap. 1.
[70] Las Casas, *Historia de las Indias*, III, cap. 99, p. 167.

Vitoria was teaching at the Dominican college of San Gregorio in Valladolid, a Castilian city that was the current seat of the Council of the Indies.

Vitoria entered a religious culture at San Esteban already deeply enmeshed in the Indies affair. The pioneer of the so-called School (Sp. *Escuela*) of Salamanca, Vitoria held the *Prima* Chair of Theology at the university for two decades (1526–1546) and trained an entire generation of theologians who would define the Spanish Second Scholastic. Among his most accomplished pupils and colleagues were Melchor Cano and Domingo Soto. Both succeeded him as *Prima* Chair. Both participated in the Council of Trent and intervened in important theological disputes concerning the doctrine of grace and the sacraments. During Vitoria's formative Parisian sojourn in theological studies, he began to garner respect and admiration for his sharp intelligence and open-mindedness from contemporary humanists like Erasmus of Rotterdam and Juan Luis Vives.[71] In Paris Vitoria dabbled in the theological *via moderna* of John Mair and others, though his commitment to the teaching of Aquinas developed under the tutelage of Peter of Crockaert. The Flemish Dominican Crockaert imparted a novel method of theological formation that principally adhered to the *Summa theologiae* rather than Lombard's *Sentences*. Vitoria assisted Crockaert by writing the prologue to his teacher's commentary on the *Secunda Secundae*, the moral theology part of the *Summa* discussing the cardinal and theological virtues in which justice figured most prominently. When Vitoria came to Salamanca after accepting Hurtado's invitation, he brought the new theological method of teaching clerics Aquinas's *Summa*.

Vitoria's writings were quite limited, consisting mostly of printed lectures delivered publicly and transcribed classroom notes on the *Summa* by students. Remembered among student disciples as a brilliant teacher, his theological reflection was responsive to current social and political challenges posed by reform and European expansion. He had the depth to raise new questions with careful subtleties while marshaling an array of traditional scholastic theological, philosophical, and legal sources to address them, Aquinas first among them.[72] Vitoria's legacy was immediately evident in his accomplished successor, Soto, whose most notable contribution in the realm of theology and law was an inventive treatise *On Justice and Right* (*De iustitia et iure*), dedicated to

71 Carlos G. Noreña, *Studies in Spanish Renaissance Thought* (Martinus Nijhoff, 1975), p. 47. For more on Vitoria's qualified humanism in context, see Santiago Piñón, Jr., *The Ivory Tower and the Sword: Francisco Vitoria Confronts the Emperor* (Eugene, OR: Pickwick Publications, 2016), chap. 5.

72 Juan Belda Plans, *La Escuela de Salamanca y la renovación de la teología en el siglo xvi* (Biblioteca de Autores Cristianos, 2000), pp. 312–313.

Emperor Charles V. Soto's momentous work extrapolated the second part of the *Summa* beyond the traditional genre of commentary by reflecting on contracts and commutative justice within an expanding mercantile economy and transatlantic setting. In this context, Soto observed, human desire goes unchecked and has introduced "new forms of deceit against what is just and lawful so that each person fills their insatiable avarice."[73]

Additionally, the practice of delivering *relectiones*, reinvigorated by Vitoria, exemplified Salmantine theological creativity and openness. These printed lectures on a current topic coinciding with the classroom (*aula*) teaching of the *Summa* for that semester usually took place during holidays and lasted about two hours. Vitoria and the first-generation *Prima* theologians of the Salamanca school, Cano (1546–1552) and Soto (1552–1560), delivered some thirty *relectiones* on various theological and social political subjects including the issue of almsgiving in the Spanish poor laws, King Henry VIII's divorce of Catherine of Aragon, and the topic of infidel rights and war in the Indies.

Because of the Dominican pastoral proximity to the New World at Salamanca, the Indies affair was never merely a peripheral matter in the thought and writings of the Spanish scholastic theologians of this "imperial" generation. Vitoria's two early *relectiones* addressing the subjects of civil and ecclesiastical powers made indirect and direct reference to the Indies, respectively. His *relectio* on civil power (1528) was an ingenious though somewhat immature work that employed Aristotelian metaphysical causes (final, efficient, and material) and biblical proof texts (e.g., Romans 13:1) to explain the natural and divine foundations of political agency through the commonwealth. Similar to Cajetan, Vitoria would argue, "public power is founded on natural right," the immediate Author of which is God.[74] That natural right resides in the commonwealth, or the people, implies a power to defend itself from harm, just as individuals do.[75] The natural right of self-defense, along with the power to direct and order its affairs for the conservation of the common good, makes a people self-sufficient or politically autonomous in a metaphysical sense. Scholastic philosophical commitment to the twofold purpose of civil power could facilitate a wider inclusion of diverse polities exhibiting lesser and greater social stratification and organization. I shall return to the implications of this topic for political agency in Chapter 6.

Infidel political agency was another theme in this lecture on civil power even if it remained undeveloped. With respect to infidel dominium, the

[73] Soto, *De iustitia et iure*, proemium.

[74] Vitoria, *On Civil Power*, in *Political Writings*, q. 1, a. 3, p. 10.

[75] Vitoria, *On Civil Power*, q. 1, a. 3, p. 11.

Salmantine theologian discounted heretical claims of ecclesiastical theocracy that located the titles to private property and public jurisdiction in the order of grace and papal power. Vitoria instead appealed to Scripture and its numerous passages confirming the legitimacy of infidel rulers from Pharaoh to Caesar. Like Cajetan, he made indirect reference to the Indies by dismissing the Christian charge of unbelief to justify dispossession of infidels: "[T]here can be no doubt at all that the pagans have legitimate rulers and masters … [N]either Christian sovereigns nor the Church may deprive infidels of their kingship or power on the grounds of their unbelief, unless they have committed some other injury."[76] From this passage, Cajetan's teaching on Christian–infidel relations was already in the background of Vitoria's thought. Additionally, Vitoria identified the crucial moral category of injury, which he would elaborate in future works as the only lawful basis for war.

Vitoria made no mention of the Indies in the 1528 lecture on civil power and only opposed the extreme hierocratic doctrines of papalism that denied the natural and rational basis of infidel dominium. However, he had already envisioned the unique contribution of theology to legal and political discourse with his introductory remark, "The office and calling of a theologian is so wide, that no argument or controversy on any subject can be considered foreign to his profession."[77] When Vitoria delivered his first *relectio* on ecclesiastical power four years later, he made a notable advancement to the scholastic theological discussion of political agency among infidels. It was his first theological work to explicitly mention the Indies, albeit briefly. That same year, Francisco Pizarro made his infamous seizure of the Inca ruler Atahualpa at the plaza of Cajamarca in Peru, assisted, incidentally, by a Dominican friar named Vicente de Valverde who most likely read the Requirement. Undoubtedly aware of the situation overseas, Vitoria's lecture opened a transatlantic horizon for discussing ecclesiastical power beyond all current ones focused on conciliarism and the Reformation in continental Europe.

Vitoria began his lecture by defining the Church as "the community of the faithful" and its power twofold according to its jurisdictional and sacramental aspects. Vitoria reflected on the theological significance of the Greek term *ekklesia* to emphasize those individuals "called together" into a community of faith sharing a single creed and baptism.[78] Vitoria isolated the baptismal identity marker, or the faithful incorporated into Christ through the waters

[76] Vitoria, *On Civil Power*, q. 1, a. 6, p. 18.
[77] Vitoria, *On Civil Power*, Prologue, p. 3.
[78] Vitoria, *On the Power of the Church* (Part I), in *Political Writings*, Introduction, p. 48.

of regeneration, to explore the theme of ecclesiastical power and its limits. Church politics for him was located in a middle position that avoided both theocratic papalism and the subordination of the Church to civil power.

According to the Spanish theologian, the Church has direct coercive power only over its baptized members and not over infidels outside the faith community. This power of the Church touches both the *true Body of Christ* in sacramental terms (the Eucharist and the powers of consecration) and the *mystical Body of Christ* in jurisdictional terms (the attainment of supernatural happiness among Christian peoples).[79] To clarify this position, Vitoria identified alternate underlying causes for both civil power and the spiritual power, the latter of which was superior. "The difference between civil power and ecclesiastical power," he says, "lies in the fact that civil power is derived from the commonwealth [*potestas civilis habet ortum a republica*], because it serves the natural purpose of the commonwealth … ecclesiastical power, on the other hand, exceeds not only the private authority of individuals, but that of the whole world [*totius mundi*]."[80] It is the Church's eminent concern with the ultimate happiness had in eternal life that makes its power impregnable against any individual or world power to the contrary, no matter how expansive its imperial ambition.

Despite having an authoritative spiritual reach transcending the global civil sphere, Vitoria also remained emphatic about ecclesiastical power's limitations. The relevance of this second point indicated a key contribution to Christian–infidel relations that set the terms for Dominican theological reflection on the Indies. Vitoria was well aware that the papal institution could presume the full breadth of ecclesiastical power in temporal affairs as it often claimed during the Middle Ages. He was unabashedly critical of the fictive Donation of Constantine, which had allegedly granted the Roman papacy the temporal power once held by Caesar.[81] In response to sycophantic popery, Vitoria taught that the Pope was not lord of the world (*Papa non est orbis dominus*). This controversial thesis in early modern Spain widened the prospects for recognizing infidel political agency:

> [T]he pope has no dominium in the lands of the infidel, since he has power only within the Church; as the Apostle said, what has he to do to judge them also who are without? (1 Cor 5:12). Unbelievers possess true dominium [*vere domini*], since the Apostle teaches that even the faithful must pay them tribute (Rom 13:6), and says that their power is ordained of God and that

79 Vitoria, *On the Power of the Church* (Part I), q. 2, a. 1, p. 58.
80 Vitoria, *On the Power of the Church* (Part I), q. 3, a. 2, p. 71.
81 Vitoria, *On the Power of the Church* (Part I), q. 5, a. 1, p. 85.

> their laws must be obeyed. But they do not have their dominium from the pope, since it is clear he would rather they did not have it – and indeed makes efforts to overthrow pagan empires.[82]

By constraining the overreaching claims of papal power, Vitoria creatively expanded the canon legal principle of immunity from judgment taken from St. Paul's teaching – originally meant to circumscribe ecclesiastical judgment of infidels in Latin Christendom – to include the dominium of infidels and their commonwealths outside Europe. Vitoria echoed Cajetan's Aristotelian designation of the civil commonwealth as a "self-sufficient" or "perfect" community in its own right. Therefore it "cannot be subject to anyone outside itself," such as the Pope, "otherwise it would not be self-sufficient [*non esset integra*]."[83]

Evidently, Vitoria's position on infidel dominium, like Cajetan, logically stemmed from his scholastic political theory. It was also directly applicable to the Indies context. Attentive to the boundaries of ecclesiastical power, Vitoria reiterated a truism of his first lecture that for infidels "temporal and civil power is integral (or suffices)."[84] Infidel polities therefore have an autonomous standing in world order, a point now indisputably clear since "all the power of secular princes comes from the community and commonwealth."[85] When Vitoria briefly referenced "the case of the islands recently discovered by the Spaniards" and the theocratic argument justifying the papal distribution of infidel lands, his opposition was resolute and clear.[86] The Alexandrine title, whatever it was, did not grant automatic political jurisdiction over infidels. This *relectio* on the power of the Church contained the scholastic principles for imagining a new world order no longer captive to theocratic papalism.

Vitoria's explicit attention to the Indies emboldened after the Spanish conquest of Peru in the 1530s, as seen in his *relectio* on ecclesiastical power. Astonishingly, the whole affair figured directly in his treatment of justice. This was *the* Dominican intellectual moment concerning the Indies. The friar Valverde, Pizarro's chaplain caught at the center of the preposterous capture

82 Vitoria, *On the Power of the Church* (Part I), q. 5, a. 1, p. 84.

83 Vitoria, *On the Power of the Church* (Part I), q. 5, a. 3, p. 87.

84 Vitoria, *On the Power of the Church* (Part I), q. 1, a. 1, p. 52: "*Apud paganos est integra potestas temporalis et civilis.*"

85 Vitoria, *On the Power of the Church* (Part I), q. 6, a. 3, pp. 103–104: "*[T]ota potestas principum saecularium est a communitate et respublica.*" See his reiteration of this claim, q. 6, a. 7, p. 107: "*[P]otestas principum est tota a republica.*"

86 Vitoria, *On the Power of the Church* (Part I), q. 5, a. 9, p. 100.

of Atahualpa that precipitated the downfall and looting of the Inca Empire, returned to Spain in 1534.[87] Members of Pizarro's company (or *peruleros*) were also returning to Spain with lucrative booty from Peru. As it happened, an internal strife within the Order of Preachers concerning the Indies affair was rapidly developing. High-profile Dominican missionaries to the New World from Salamanca such as Tómas Ortiz and Domingo de Betanzos were becoming outspoken supporters of the *encomienda* and missionary war, testifying before the Council of the Indies against native freedom. There they had a very sympathetic ear from its president, the former Dominican Master General after Cajetan, García de Loaysa. Ortiz had already delivered a *Memorial* to the Council in 1526 based on experience in which he described the Amerindians of the mainland continent as inveterate cannibals and brutes lacking all sense of justice.[88] Friar Betanzos, who had been instrumental to Las Casas's entrance into the Order of Preachers and one of the first Dominicans of Española, now stood in front of the Council in 1533 denying native capacity for freedom and self-rule because of their backward state.[89] These were authoritative, hardened opinions informing royal policy from members of the most prominent religious order in Spain. Under Loaysa's presidency over the Council in 1534, the statement of Betanzos contributed to an overturning of the King's short-lived but notable 1530 decree, which had suspended all previous declarations of enslaving Indians because of the "greed" of Spanish conquistadors and the loose application of the Carib category.[90] The peaceful method of evangelization espoused by Cajetan and Córdoba was losing its moral and legal force due to a few outspoken friars with close association to the Crown.

In November of 1534, with rising tension between Dominicans, Vitoria wrote to his Spanish provincial Miguel de Arcos. He expressed a scathing opinion of "the corrupt profits and affairs of the Indies," paying careful attention to the themes of innocence, injury, war, and restitution.[91] In the letter, Vitoria mentioned that his knowledge of the Indies came from eyewitness testimony of persons present at the conflict with the Inca Atahualpa and his people, none of whom had caused "the slightest injury" against

87 Ramón Hernández, "Interrelaciones de misioneros y teologos ante los problemas de América," in *La iglesia en América* (Editorial Deimos, 1992), p. 116.

88 Francisco López de Gómara, *Historia General de las Indias y vida de Hernán Cortés* (Biblioteca Ayacucho, 1979), cap. 217, p. 310.

89 Daniel Ulloa, *Los predicadores divididos* (El Colegio México, 1977), p. 102.

90 Richard Konetzke, *Colección de Documentos para la Historia de la Formación Social de Hispanoamérica, 1493–1810*, vol. 1 (CSIC, 1953), pp. 134–136.

91 Vitoria, "Letter to Miguel de Arcos, O.P." in *Political Writings*, Appendix A, pp. 331–333.

Spaniards. Vitoria began with a recognition that the Indians were true owners of their property before the conquistadors had seized it. He then proposed that war – which the Spaniards had no grounds for in this instance – could be the only justification for taking the property of people outside Spain's political jurisdiction. Although an extended conversation about the justice of waging and conducting war was possible, it could only happen after first addressing the "shocking" truth of what was happening in the Indies: pillaging, robbery, tyranny.

Deferring to the indigenous side of the affair, Vitoria concluded that they were most "certainly innocents" in the so-called war. The claim of innocence (*innocens*) provided Vitoria a salient moral and legal designation for esteeming the intrinsic worth of persons be they Europeans or Indians. As he indicated in his *aula* lectures on the *Summa*, "an innocent person is his very own good and alone he suffers, and therefore it is not lawful to kill him."[92] Importantly, this category of innocence upheld the fundamental dignity of infidels just as Christians.[93] Vitoria was also cognizant of the vitriol surrounding Spanish portrayals of the natives as bestial and irrational. After admitting the Indians were innocent victims and not the other way around, the Dominican theologian made a pointed remark against their cultured despisers: "[I]f the Indians are not men but monkeys, they are incapable of injury. But if they are men, and our neighbors, and as they claim vassals of the emperor, I cannot see how to excuse these conquistadors of utter impiety and tyranny."[94]

Regardless of whether Spain arguably possessed just titles to war in the Indies, a subject Vitoria explored later in the famous 1539 *relectio*, the conquest of Peru and other conquests "more vile" were glaring examples of widespread injustice and dispossession of entire native communities. Vitoria's opinion became more forceful at the end of the letter when he declared that the affair was no case of uncertain restitution. The matter was incontrovertibly clear: the Spaniards must restore the property and dominions of the dispossessed native peoples just as Salamanca would need restitution following an act of plundering.[95] Despite Vitoria's general tendency to focus more on the European side of the affair in contrast to Las Casas, here we can still detect the egalitarian impulse of his concept of justice.

92 Vitoria, *On Homicide and Commentary on* Summa Theologiae II-II Q. 64, trans. John P. Doyle (Milwaukee: Marquette University Press, 2008), with Latin facing, pp. 186–187: *"Sed innocens est bonum suiipsius et ipse dumtaxat patitur, et ideo non licet illum occidere."*

93 Vitoria, *On Law*, *ST*, I-II, 105.2, in *Political Writings*, p. 204.

94 Vitoria, "Letter to Arcos," p. 333.

95 Vitoria, "Letter to Arcos," p. 333.

Restitution – or reinstating what belongs to another – was a principal component for attaining justice in scholastic and canonistic literature. It provided the moral context for explicitly raising the Amerindian question (*la duda Indiana*) in the Spanish theological writings by placing the harmed individual at the center of analysis. The Dominican theologians benefited from their Order's preexisting reflection on restitution to strengthen their critical interventions against unjust colonial expansion and dispossession of the natives. As a moral act of commutative justice between individuals, restitution rectifies the wrong caused by theft, which is when someone unjustly takes something from another person who is the rightful possessor. Yet restitution entailed more than merely returning or restoring a material thing to its owner (*dominus*). In Aquinas's question on restitution in the *Summa*, the medieval Dominican identified the "injurious action" underlying the violation of an owner's will.[96]

The first Dominicans of Española, trained in Aquinas's moral thought, expressed this insight as early as 1517, the same year of the Jeronymite interrogatory and the theological junta at Salamanca on the rational agency of the Indians. Fray Pedro de Córdoba sent a letter to the newly crowned King Charles, which read: "In recent days we have preached straight out against them [the culprits], declaring to them the state of damnation in which they live and the obligation they have of making restitution not only for what temporal goods they have acquired in this manner, but also for the harms they have caused in the course of the acquisition."[97] Preaching went hand in hand with restitution, not violence. The sacrament of penance was also crucial to the act of restitution since it involved the perpetrator's free will to make amends according to his or her conscience. In addition, restitution for the Indians went beyond addressing their material losses to include their personal harms and sufferings. The language of rights later articulated by the Spanish Dominican theologians provided a novel means of explicating the precise nature of injury affecting the will of individual persons.

Aquinas's adherence to the classical Roman definition of justice – giving to each what is theirs (*ius suum cuique tribuere*) – left his reflection open to further juridical refinement.[98] The Dominican theological literature on

96 Aquinas, *ST* II-II, q. 62, a. 6.

97 Pedro de Córdoba, "Carta al Rey," in *Miguel Angel Medina, Una comunidad al servicio del indio* (Madrid: 1983), pp. 265–266: "Nosotros en los días pasados predicamos régiamente contra ellos, declarándoles el dañable estado en que vivian, y la obligación que tenian a restituir, no solamente lo que temporalmente adquiriesen por esta manera, más aun, los daños que por esta tal manera se hicieren."

98 Aquinas, *ST*, II-II, q. 57, a. 4, *ad* 1; q. 58, a. 1.

restitution was concerned with not only the agent of wrongdoing, but also the patient suffering harm. After all, justice was the specific cardinal virtue intersubjective in nature, which meant it directly pertained to one's relationship with another person. In seeking to redress an injustice, the chief aim of restitution was due compensation to the injured *dominus* whose will had been violated.[99] That Vitoria, Soto, and Las Casas as Dominicans chose to address the dominium and rights of infidels through a theological reflection on restitution was no mere coincidence, especially in light of Vitoria's letter to Arcos. Furthermore, Cajetan's definitive commentary on Question 66 had already made restitution a matter of obligation for those "unjust conquerors and occupants" who "commit great robbery" in the name of Christ against infidels outside of European Christian jurisdiction.[100]

Vitoria's classroom lectures on Question 62 of the *Secunda Secundae*, Soto's *Relectio de dominio*, and Chapter seven of Las Casas's first draft of *De unico vocationis modo* were all various treatments of restitution surfacing circa 1535. These works came on the trail of Pizarro's conquest of the Inca capital of Cuzco and Council of the Indies President Loaysa's rescinding of a royal ordinance prohibiting Indian enslavement through war. 1535 was also the year Julián Garcés, Dominican bishop of Tlaxcala, sent a letter to Pope Paul III condemning the shameless diabolical work of Spaniards in the Indies "whose greed is so great, that in order to swallow their fill ... swear that rational creatures made to God's image are beasts and asses."[101] Most striking, the incredible Dominican confluence of ideas about restitution turned on the subjective natural rights of all human beings made in the divine image, particularly *indios*, as the juridical benchmark for a new world order. In their strategic effort to combine theology and law within an early modern European colonial context, these Spanish Dominicans expanded the vocabulary of justice in an identifiably egalitarian mode. They recognized the moral and juridical status of infidels, in this case the Indians, as a rational people with political agency and as individual subjects capable of suffering injury.

Vitoria and Soto were scholastic theologians with juridical tendencies whereas Las Casas was a canon lawyer formed in Aquinas's theology after joining the Dominicans in 1522. The writing style and literary output of the Salmantine schoolmen and the bishop-canon lawyer was quite different but when it came to questions about natural law and commutative justice, there

99 Aquinas, *ST* II-II, q. 62, a. 6, *ad* 1.

100 Cajetan, *Commentaria*, II-II, q. 66, a. 8, p. 94.

101 A. Lobato Casado, "El obispo Garcés O.P. y la bula Sublimis Deus," in *Actas del primer congreso internacional sobre los dominicos y el nuevo mundo* (Editorial Demos, 1986), p. 786.

was a remarkable symbiosis of thought, especially with respect to the rights of infidels. They were innovative precursors to human rights language in their distinct articulations of subjective natural rights.[102] They understood these rights as private or public claims generating an incumbent justiciable action, or a subjective power immune from unlawful coercion, both of which pertained to the nature of the agent(s) in his or her own person vis-à-vis other persons or groups. Before considering the three respective works of Vitoria, Soto, and Las Casas outlining their theological conception of a new world order in which peoples and individuals outside Europe were endowed with moral worth and political recognition, let us further elaborate the *subjective* and *natural* features of their rights talk.

The juristic inflection characterizing the theology of these Spanish Dominicans was most evident in their subjective interpretation of the concept of right (Lt. *ius*, Sp. *derecho*) in these early works. Once the domain of medieval canon lawyers, later theologians of the fourteenth and fifteenth centuries like the "modern doctors" Jean Gerson and Conrad Summenhart drew attention to the idea of *ius* as *facultas*, a licit subjective power or license over something.[103] This view of *ius* contrasted with more objective senses of it as either a synonym for law or the Aristotelian-Thomistic "just thing" – the object of justice – which referred to a certain equality between external things and persons. Although the Spanish scholastic theologians appropriated the Thomistic notion of justice in key respects, they also reinterpreted *ius* to account for a more subjective meaning responsive to the "modern" theologians.

In this regard, Vitoria interpreted *ius* as "a *facultas* in using a thing according to the laws" and Soto defined it as "a just license in using a thing."[104] The Salmantine theologians located these definitions of right within a wider discussion of the nature of true dominium to account for restitution. Rather than

[102] Tierney, *The Idea of Natural Rights*, chap. 11; Maurico Beuchot, *Los fundamentos de derechos humanos en Bartolomé de las Casas* (Editorial Anthropos, 1994); David Lantigua, "Faith, Liberty, and the Defense of the Poor: Bishop Las Casas in the History of Human Rights," in *Christianity and Freedom*, vol. 1: *Historical Perspectives*, eds. Timothy Shah and Allen Hertzke (Cambridge University Press, 2016), pp. 176–209.

[103] Avelino Folgado, *Evolución historica del concepto del derecho subjetivo* (San Lorenzo de El Escorial, 1960), Primera parte, caps. 5–6; Tierney, *Idea of Natural Rights*, chaps. 9–10; Alejandro Guzmán Brito, *El derecho como facultad en la neoescolástica Española del siglo XVI* (Iustel, 2009), pp. 17–27.

[104] Vitoria, *Comentarios a la Secunda secundae de Santo Tomás*, ed. Vicente Beltrán de Heredia, 6 vols. (Biblioteca de teológos españoles, 1932–1952), 62.1, no. 9: "*quia est facultas utendi re secundum leges*"; Soto, *De dominio*, in *Relecciones y opúsculos*, I, trans. Jaime Brufau Prats (Editorial San Esteban, 1995), no. 6: "*licentia iusta utendi aliqua re.*"

focusing on the virtuous agent of justice, they considered the due compensation of a wronged *dominus*. In doing so, they explicated the moral category of injury, and attended to its obvious legal repercussions. Their analytical contribution identified restitution as a moral act responsive to all injury, and not merely theft of physical property. Vitoria captured the innovative point: "For this I am obliged to support restitution, by making amends for doing injury to someone in the thing to which he had any faculty. Thus whatever that faculty is, if I do injury to it, I am bound to restore it."[105]

Salmantine theological emphasis on the restoration of subjective right understood as a faculty or power over the use of a thing was indeed a juridical, perhaps "modern," shift in Aquinas's moral theology. Nevertheless, Aquinas's moral teachings remained central to the discussion. A strictly juridical treatment of right might have been able to account for someone's rightful possession of a faculty or power to something, but it did not account for the nature of the relationship between the possessor's right and the possessed thing. The Spanish Dominicans strengthened the moral theological basis of subjective right by specifically appropriating Aquinas's view on natural dominium belonging to all rational and free creatures made in the image of God.[106] In the discussion of injustice as theft, a topic overlapping with restitution, Aquinas identified the characteristic human dominium or "power of using" (*potestatem utendi*) the common things of the earth for creaturely conservation.[107] This power was a principal expression of the divine image communicated to all rational creatures possessing hands and ruling over animals. The ordained power of using things, or the dominium over externals, established by God in creation, reflected the original dominium of human freedom over actions. Subjective rights for the Spanish Dominican theologians were therefore rooted in natural dominium.

In a series of elucidating propositions, Vitoria presented his account of subjective right in his commentary on Aquinas's question on restitution.[108] After acknowledging a possible doubt about dominium over possessions

[105] Vitoria, *Comentarios*, 62.1, no. 8: "*Quia ad hoc quod ego tenear ad restitutionem, satis est quod faciam injuriam alicui in re ad quam ille habebat facultatem quamcumque; id est quaecumque esset illa facultas, si facio illi injuriam, teneor illi restituere.*"

[106] Jaime Brufau Prats, *La escuela de Salamanca ante el descubrimiento del Nuevo Mundo* (Editorial San Esteban, 1989), chap. 1; David M. Lantigua, "The Image of God, Christian Rights Talk, and the School of Salamanca," *Journal of Law and Religion*, 31.1 (February 2016): 19–41.

[107] Aquinas, *ST*, II-II, q. 66, a. 1.

[108] For various treatments of this pivotal explication of subjective right in Vitoria's commentary, see the following: Daniel Deckers, *Gerechtigkeit und Recht: Eine historisch-kritische Untersuchung der Gerechtigkeitslehre des Francisco de Vitoria, 1483–1546* (Verlag Herder,

following from the scholastic juristic teaching that in the beginning everything was held in common, he proceeded to argue for dominium "in the nature of things" (*in rerum natura*).[109] Without a basic conviction in natural dominium, there could be no genuine restitution of another's subjective right to a thing. According to the first and second propositions, divine sovereignty provided the unalterable foundation for natural dominium among humans. No power and no dominium existed apart from God, the Lord of all creation.

Vitoria's third and fourth propositions focused on dominium and right as a constituent of human uniqueness in the created natural order. Here the metaphysical account of Aquinas on the image of God and rational agency became definitive. Referring to the medieval master, Vitoria argued, "only the rational creature has self-ownership of actions [*dominium sui actus*]."[110] This capacity for self-directed action fundamentally distinguished humans from other animals as did the capacity to commit and suffer injury. Vitoria then turned to the image of God as an objective safeguard for natural dominium and subjective right. Citing the biblically authoritative text of Genesis 1:26–28, Vitoria claimed God "has given to all humankind dominium over all created things and all creatures."[111] The *ius*-dominium over all things, which God has communicated to everyone through the divine image, comes into sharper relief when humans are viewed as the summit and end of creation.[112] Humans exist for their own sake, then, and not for the sake of anyone or anything else.

By virtue of the fundamental *ius*-dominium, God and nature do not fail in providing the necessary means for human sustenance and conservation. The natural *ius*-dominium has both objective and subjective dimensions that reflect the twofold meaning of right as either law or faculty. First, there belongs to humanity a natural right by which persons necessarily conserve their livelihood.[113] This notion of *ius* has the character of natural law in the objective sense of fulfilling the aim of self-preservation, which corresponds

1991), pp. 144–193; Brett, *Liberty, Right and Nature*, pp. 126–132; Tierney, *Idea of Natural Rights*, pp. 258–265; Guzmán Brito, *El derecho como facultad*, pp. 62–78; Simona Langella, *Teología y ley natural: estudios sobre las lecciones de Francisco de Vitoria*, trans. Juan Montero Aparicio (Biblioteca de Autores Cristianos, 2011), pp. 144–152. (See Figure 3.2.)

109 Vitoria, *Comentarios*, 62.1, no. 9: "*His ergo preamissis, dubitatur an in rerum natura sit aliquis dominus alicujus rei. Posset enim quis hoc dubitare, postquam a principio mundi omnia erant communia … Ideo ergo quaeritur an sit aliquis dominus in rerum natura. Quia si diceretur quod nullus est dominus, jam nullum esset dominium, et ita nulla esset restitutio.*"

110 Vitoria, *Comentarios*, 62.1, no. 11.

111 Vitoria, *Comentarios*, 62.1, no. 12.

112 Vitoria, *Comentarios*, 62.1, no. 12: "*[H]omo sit finis omnium creaturaram, sequitur quod est dominus omnium.*"

113 Vitoria, *Comentarios*, 62.1, no. 13: "*[D]e jure naturali est quod conservet se in esse.*"

to Aquinas's discussion of natural inclinations.[114] Vitoria accounted for this meaning of natural *ius* as "what is right by necessity" in his earlier commentary on Question 57. Accordingly, the right of conservation is naturally self-evident "because there has never been a nation so barbarous that did not believe it is lawful for humans to use things."[115] Correlatively, then, the common objective natural right to conserve life logically entails everyone's subjective faculty or right of using (*ius utendi*) things for survival and sustenance.[116] Vitoria's account of *ius* therefore contains a dual meaning attentive to its objective and subjective dimensions. The object of natural *ius*-dominium is the preservation of life through the agent's subjective power or faculty of using created things.

God communicates *dominium rerum* and the right of use to everyone through the divine image with no exception whether it is at the level of individual or community. The fifth and sixth propositions outline Vitoria's assertion that humanity both in the Edenic state of integral or innocent nature and the postlapsarian state live according to the natural *ius*-dominium. Sin cannot abolish dominium neither does it denigrate humanity's God-given place to use the things of creation. Remarkably for Vitoria, "anyone can use and even waste anything as he pleases provided he does no injury to other men or himself."[117] This proviso to the *ius utendi* indicates its status as a subjective natural right permitting someone to do as one pleases (*pro libito*) within a framework of natural law that respects the basic precept of non-maleficence toward others. And while its language of using and wasting things may ring of possessive individualism or ecological anthropocentrism, it must be read in view of Vitoria's eye to the Indies, the very topic that concluded his propositions on *ius*-dominium.

The remaining propositions, seven through twelve, consider the division and appropriation of things at the level of communities or peoples from a biblical hermeneutic concerning the law of nations. Vitoria follows the common opinion of the jurists that *ius gentium* belongs to human law and that it is the juridical space for discussing the division of the earth by the first humans (*primi homines*) settling territory, establishing distinct political rule,

114 Aquinas, *ST*, I-II, q. 94, a. 2.

115 Vitoria, *Comentarios*, 62.1, no. 13: "*[Q]uia nulla fuit nec est gens tam barbara quae non credat esse licitum homini uti rebus.*"

116 Vitoria, *Comentarios*, 62.1, nos. 12–13: "*[C]onfirmatur ex diffinitione juris et dominii, quae est facultas utendi re; sed homo potest uti illis; ergo habet ius in illas*"; "*Cum ergo Deus omnia alia fecerit, dicendum est quod illa fecit propter hominis conservationem. Ergo habet ius utendi omnibus illis.*"

117 Vitoria, *Comentarios*, 62.1, no. 16: "*[Q]uia quicumque posset uti qualibet re et etiam abuti pro libito suo, dummodo non noceret aliis hominibus vel sibi.*"

FIGURE 3.2 "Statue of Francisco de Vitoria in front of Convento de San Esteban, Salamanca, Spain." (Source: photograph by David Lantigua)

and acquiring property rights.[118] Abraham and Lot supply the archetype for this original division of land into parts, or the biblical law of nations. According to Genesis 13:7–9, Abraham and his nephew went their separate ways across the land, to the left and the right, in order to eliminate strife between their people. "Therefore, the first humans would have been able from common consent to divide things among themselves."[119] Here lay the beginning of *ius gentium* in the biblical narrative.

The principle of consent served a key role in Vitoria's elaboration of the right of peoples. Abraham and Lot consented to each one having his respective land. However, this was not a formal agreement or stipulated treaty between them. Rather, it belonged to *ius gentium* in a virtual manner through a consensual understanding according to which each one first settled a land by effectively occupying it. Occupation could therefore be determined when "someone begins to take care of fixed lands and another person other lands."

118 *Digest*, 1.1.5.

119 Vitoria, *Comentarios*, 62.1, no. 21: "*Et ita primi homines potuissent ex communi consensu dividere inter se.*"

Additionally, "through the use of those things it happened that the former was content with the lands which he occupied, and the latter the other lands, so that the one did not occupy the other's lands."[120] The fact of occupation, or taking political control of land and its inhabitants, provided a strong justificatory rationale for Spanish expansion, as we saw in the previous chapter. Yet, when viewed from the perspective of the rights of first occupants over their inhabited lands, it could also be used to critique and oppose unlawful occupation, a common strategy for resisting expansionism in European colonial history.[121]

Vitoria made the qualified point, citing the *Digest* (41.1.3), that one could occupy a place and seize animals and fish as one wished unless there was already an original inhabitant, in which case permission was required to enter another's land and retain its goods.[122] Contrastingly, among Spanish theocratic partisans of colonialism the consent of infidel natives was ultimately irrelevant since they were forced under the Requirement between recognizing Spanish sovereignty and incurring war. Denying political rule among Indians, Spanish claims of sovereignty and control over the mineral deposits of the land went unchecked. More ominously still, the popular designation of natives as irrational barbarians, or natural slaves, as seen in Mair and later in Sepúlveda, turned them into fitting objects of possession by the first European takers, like the *ferae bestiae* of Roman law.

In the twelfth and final proposition, Vitoria considered the grounds for lawfully transferring *dominium rerum* from one party to another. This was crucial for determining when unlawful occupation and dispossession had taken place and the obligation of restoring the wronged. Barring situations of extreme necessity, in which case dominium reverted to God through the common possession of all things, Vitoria identified two sources for the alienation and transference of *dominium rerum*: one from the will of the possessor and the other from the authority of the prince or ruler. Tellingly, Vitoria's entire restitution discussion of *ius*-dominium terminated with attention to the Indies affair, which provided a corollary test case for the final proposition. In

120 Vitoria, *Comentarios*, 62.1, no. 23: "*Et forte sic facta fuit, non consensu certo et formali, sed quodam consensu intepretativo, ita quod incoeperint aliqui colere certas terras et alius alias; et ex usu illarum rerum factum est ut ille esset contentus terris quas occupaverat, et alius aliis, ita quod unus non occupabat terras alterius. Et hoc non aliquo consensu formali, sed virtuali.*"

121 Fitzmaurice, *Sovereignty, Property, and Empire*, p. 14.

122 Vitoria, *Comentarios*, 62.1, no. 26: "*Nunc etiam multa in rebus humanis sunt indivisa et quae non sunt appropriata; et ista sunt occupantis, et quilibet potest occupare illa pro libito suo, ut sunt ferae, aves, pisces, nisi alius primo occupaverit illa recludendo ea vel vetando quia sunt in terra sua.*"

neither sense did the infidels of the New World willingly submit and transfer their possessions to Christians:

> Christians are unable to occupy the lands of infidels if those infidels are considered true owners [*veri domini*] of those territories, and they are not [lands of] Christians. But if they have taken them by force, it is otherwise. Christians are able then to attack them, like in Africa, where Saracens have taken lands from Christians. It follows that because the division of things has occurred those lands belonged to those [other] infidels. And they, as well as their princes, are unwilling to give them to us. Since therefore those are true owners, if they themselves do not give them to us, it follows that we cannot retain and occupy their lands. Like the case of the Indians, certainly no one can seize lands from them. That is because no Christian ruler is superior to them. Neither is the pope superior to them in either temporal or spiritual matters, if they have not been baptized. For the pope only has power over those who are Christians or had been Christians such as heretics.[123]

Vitoria here reiterated his affirmation of infidel dominium from the previous *relectiones* on civil and ecclesiastical powers. Yet he did what Cajetan did not do by explicitly inserting the "Indians" into the abstract category of infidels outside Christian rule. The Salmantine theologian categorically rejected any kind of Christian civil and ecclesiastical jurisdiction over Amerindians and their lands that did not respect their voluntary consent. His commentary on Question 66, Article 8, reiterated this essential point by referring once again to the recently discovered "*insulani*" who were neither de iure, nor de facto under Christian jurisdiction. "[I]t is in no manner lawful to seize their goods or remove public authority because it denies the *dominium rerum* of those who are infidels."[124] Restitution always entailed that some injury had occurred demanding restoration of a right of possession. Locating the affair of the Indies within the penitential treatment of restitution strongly suggests that Vitoria was offering a critical indictment of current colonial practices rooted in ecclesial life. Both the Requirement and the forced labor system rested on the alleged temporal power of the Crown entrusted by the papacy to take possession of idolatrous or idle natives and their lands. Vitoria's dethronement of theocratic universalist claims of jurisdiction over Indians pointed to a new kind of discussion about war according to the parameters of *ius gentium* rather than punishing violations of natural law.

123 Vitoria, *Comentarios*, 62.1, no. 28.

124 Vitoria, *Comentarios*, 66.8, no. 6: "*De istis dico quod nullo modo licet de per se capere bona illorum, nec auctoritate publica, quia non amittunt dominium rerum ex eo quod sint infideles.*"

While Vitoria taught students theology from the *Secunda Secundae* of the *Summa* during the day in 1535, Soto taught them the Lombard's *Sentences* during the evening hours. Soto derived the topic of his 1535 *Relectio de dominio* from his lectures on the themes of restitution, penance, and salvation based on Book Four of the *Sentences* concerning the sacraments.[125] Like Vitoria, Soto reflected on the Indies affair in the context of restitution and through an extrapolation of subjective right according to the nature of things. The iconic starting point to Soto's *relectio*, or "rereading" of Scripture, was Genesis 1:28, where natural dominium received biblical warrant: "Subdue the earth and have dominion over the fish of the sea and over the birds of the air and over every living thing that moves upon the earth." More directly than Vitoria, Soto argued for the foundation of dominium in the image of God.[126] By grounding natural dominium in the divine image, just like Aquinas's *Summa*, Soto brought the metaphysical attributes of human beings to bear on restitution. What made humans owners of their actions, in principle, was the expression of their spiritual and moral powers through the intellect. This basic dominium of action (*dominus actionem*), or self-ownership, enabled the dominium of externals. Yet Soto provided a distinct view of subjective right in comparison with Vitoria.

In the simplest terms, Soto defined natural dominium in this early work as the human power to use a thing (*potestas utendi re*).[127] Soto's reference to the *potestas utendi* as the original mode of natural dominium over the earth resonated with Aquinas's ordained "power of using" the things of the earth to conserve life. For Aquinas, one of the chief distinguishing marks of human subjectivity among rational creatures made in the divine image is their capacity to use a thing for a specific purpose in attaining an end.[128] Soto followed and extended Aquinas by linking the subjective power or faculty of use with the right of using something for a specific act such as eating and drinking consumables for nourishment.[129] This teleological conception of power informed Soto's subjective reformulation of *ius* from Question 57 of the *Summa*. The Spanish theologian equated power (*potestas*), right (*ius*), and

125 Brufau Prats, "Introducción," pp. 81–82, in *Relecciones y opúsculos*, I.

126 Soto, *De dominio*, no. 11.

127 Soto, *De dominio*, nos. 11 and 14.

128 Aquinas, *ST*, I-II, q. 16, a. 2.

129 Soto, *De dominio*, nos. 2, 6–7. Offering a reading of the medieval Franciscan poverty disputes, Soto claimed that mendicants could lack true ownership, or power of alienability and selling, while using a right to consume food in the act of eating. For more on the importance of the Franciscan debate in the development of subjective rights, see Tierney, *Idea of Natural Rights*, Part 2.

what is just (*est quod justem*), albeit pithily in the *Relectio de dominio*.[130] The equivalence of these notions was precisely what supplied his definition of *ius* as "a just license in using a thing."

Like Vitoria, Soto adhered to the objective and subjective meanings of right based in natural dominium under God. For example, in the mature work *On Justice and Right*, Soto outlined its dual meaning: "The title of natural dominium that man has over the bounties of the earth is natural life, without which he is unable to be conserved. For this reason God and nature have given to man alone conjointly an appetite to preserve himself and also a right of using [the earth] for necessary sustenance."[131] The natural appetite or inclination toward the object of self-preservation remained inseparably linked to the subjective right of using the earth's bountiful goods. Relatedly, the fundamental common title of natural dominium also yielded the natural right of defending oneself and one's own goods.[132] Yet Soto went beyond his Salmantine predecessor's discussion of right by focusing on another constitutive element of dominium according to the divine image – the freedom of the will. Importantly, Soto placed free choice (*liberum arbitrium*) at the origin of the power to use or not use a thing as one pleases attributed to a human *dominus*.[133] He would later make his point even clearer in separate discussions about children and slaves by stating that freedom is the foundation of dominium.[134] Soto's expansive account of subjective right placed a greater accent on liberty than Vitoria. Even children and slaves as social and political inferiors can have a rightful claim, founded on a basic level of freedom and agency, to receive what is necessary for sustenance from their superiors.

In the case of infidel dominium regarding the Indies affair – a topic Soto treated near the end of his 1535 *relectio* – the right in question was not a subjective claim upon a superior, but a subjective freedom of independence and immunity from external coercion. This entailed respect for both infidel personal property (*dominium rerum*) and political rule (*dominium*

130 Soto, *De dominio*, no. 2: "*[P]otestas, ut diximus, idem est quod ius, ius autem idem est quod justum ut dicit Sanctus Thomas, Secunda Secundae, q. 57, a. 1.*"

131 Soto, *De iustitia et iure*, lib. 4, q. 1, a. 1: "*Titulus dominii naturalis quod homo habet in terra nascentia, est naturalis vita, quae sine illis conservari nequit, ratione cuius Deus et natura hominis dedit unam cum appetitu servandi se ius etiam utendi necessario alimentum.*" Cf. *De dominio*, no. 9.

132 Soto, *De dominio*, no. 16.

133 Soto, *De dominio*, nos. 10 and 17: "*Nullus est dominus alicuius rei nisi sit in potestate sua ea uti et non uti; sed solus homo inter creaturas habet hanc potestatem per liberum arbitrium*"; "*Ad verum dominium requiritur quod homo possit quomodocumque uti re pro libito.*"

134 Soto, *De iustitia et iure*, lib. 4, q. 1, a. 1 and q. 2, a. 2: "*[D]omini u fundetur in libertate*"; "*[F]undamentum dominii sit libertas.*"

iurisdictionis) according to natural law and the law of nations. Soto's *relectio* may have developed Vitoria's earlier rejection of papal worldwide dominium, but it was the first public lecture among the Salmantine theologians to deny the Roman title of emperor as lord of the world and its notion of universal empire. In the words of David Lupher, the *relectio* written by the confessor of Emperor Charles V "deserves to be considered a bold challenge to legitimacy of Spanish dominion in the Indies."[135] The defense of infidels as true owners in the context of restitution was crucial to this twofold repudiation of overreaching papal and imperial power currently justifying the Spanish possession of the Indies. Appropriating the Thomistic axiom to address infidel dominium under the third category like Cajetan, Soto declared:

> The Emperor has no right nor dominium over the lands of infidels, excepting those lands that once belonged to us like in Africa or by right of war if they invade us like the Turks. But in the case of the islanders who are recently discovered these two [causes] cease. From the fact that they are infidels, they do not lose their goods nor the political authority they possess. In the same way, they do not lose it on account of the most serious sins as Saint Thomas demonstrates in the *Secunda Secundae*, q. 10, a. 10. For, he says, the difference of jurisdictions and authority have been introduced by human law, but the distinction between believer and infidel is from divine law. But divine law, in that it is from grace, does not take away human law, which is conformed to natural reason. But this is not the place to settle this dispute. We are supposing that, if they have never been believers, they do not lose the right over their own goods solely because of their unbelief.[136]

The Thomistic political axiom operative in the Dominican theological response to the Indies strengthened the argument for infidel political agency by making positive human law (or the law of nations) – the result of natural reasoning among infidels – immune from the coercive jurisdiction of divine law and the Church. We will return to the law of nations as a creative juridical resource for the Spanish Dominicans in Chapter 6. Like Vitoria, Soto rejected claims about the papal foundations of worldwide dominium among Holy Roman Emperors as a "foundationless" fiction. For Christ never received a temporal title to rule over the world. Rather, following Cajetan's formulation, Christ "only had power in temporal things ordained to a spiritual end, namely, ordained to redemption." Soto cited the Gospel of John (18:33) where

135 David Lupher, *Romans in a New World: Classical Models in Sixteenth-Century Spanish America* (University of Michigan Press, 2003), p. 62. See also Anthony Pagden's revision of his earlier view in light of Lupher's critique, "Conquest and the Just War," in *Empire and Modern Political Thought*, ed. Sankar Muthu (Cambridge University Press, 2012), pp. 30–60.

136 Soto, *De dominio*, no. 32.

Christ told the Roman governor Pilate that his kingdom was not of this world. Soto ironically added: "It is astonishing that with Christ coming to preach poverty in the world, he himself would accept rule over the world (*dominium mundi*)."[137]

Scholastic political theory informed by Thomistic principles clearly undergirded Soto's disavowal of worldwide imperial rule.[138] Cajetan, as we have seen, precluded universal empire based on natural law and the idea of the commonwealth as a self-sufficient political community. Yet Soto's attentiveness to a pluralistic setting of different political jurisdictions according to the law of nations and his account of subjective natural right in view of the Indies affair brought a conception of world order forward unlike Cajetan. Natural law and the law of nations in its local instantiation among a distinct people for Soto provided an unimpeachable safeguard against worldwide imperialism, like the tyrannical kind historically associated with the ancient Romans, who ruled "by right of arms" (*ius erat in armis*) over unwilling nations with no other title than superior prowess.[139] Presuming the earlier discussion of subjective natural right, Soto indicated that *ius naturale* provided an independent basis for every commonwealth's civil power in the people.[140]

The *sine qua non* for election of a universal ruler would have to be the consent of the whole world (*consensum totius orbis*). Soto denied any historical precedent for such a claim. Even when Caesar Augustus issued his edict claiming universal Roman sovereignty, he could only have imagined those territories already subjugated by the empire. Certainly, the Emperor meant neither the Antipodes "nor the peoples recently discovered in Peru."[141] Given the diversity and independence of political powers across the globe, universal temporal dominium was simply an impractical proposition, a mere guise to expand empire tyrannically. The political and juridical elaboration of dominium from Aquinas's *Summa* by Soto and Vitoria in 1535 propelled infidel dominium to the center of the Indies affair and a case involving the restitution of infidel rights. Their emerging scholastic theological conception of world order shorn of overreaching imperial and papal claims of power over infidels was not a secularization of natural law and the law of nations. On the contrary, it stemmed from the biblical faith that all humanity, arranged in a world of independent polities, was in possession of the divine image and therefore exhibited rational agency and freedom of use.

137 Soto, *De dominio*, no. 33.
138 Pagden, *The Burdens of Empire*, p. 53.
139 Soto, *De dominio*, no. 30.
140 Soto, *De dominio*, no. 29: "*[N]am quaecumque respublica habet iure naturae potestatem sui.*"
141 Soto, *De dominio*, no. 31.

UNJUST WAR AND THE ETHIC OF EVANGELIZATION

Dominican theological focus on restitution in the Indies affair was inseparable from the spiritual task of evangelization. The restoration of justice and right for the native victims of unjust war entailed the proclamation of the true Gospel to liberate Spanish Christian oppressors from sin. Only by removing the obstacle of self-imposed tyranny and injustice would it be possible to pursue the true aim of Spanish presence in the New World: the conversion of the native peoples. In order to fulfill this singularly spiritual mission, theologians had to contend with the long-standing tradition and practice of missionary warfare. Once again, the Spanish Dominicans of Española under the Vice-Provincial leadership of Córdoba were a font of practical wisdom for the theologians in the effort to disjoin preaching from warfare.

In the 1517 letter directed to the newly crowned King Charles, Córdoba proposed a strategic intervention to address the plight of "the native Indians" (*los indios naturales*) who were subjected to the bondage of Castilian *encomenderos*. These Spaniards "have lived bad examples giving into luxuries, violence, blasphemies, and diverse cruelties" by diligently forcing the native laborers "to extract gold and cultivate other *haciendas*, working all day under burden, and suffering the burning heat of the sun." To bring a halt to the ongoing destruction of other native peoples encountered in new places, Córdoba proposed, "if among them there entered preachers alone [*predicadores solos*] without the force and violence of these evil Christian adventurers, I think that there could be established among them a church almost as great as it was in the beginning."[142] Fray Córdoba turned to the apostolic witness of the early Church as the singular model of evangelization in the New World. Sending "preachers alone" sufficed to fulfill the title over the Indies entrusted by the Pope to the Catholic Monarchs.[143]

When Cajetan treated the topic of infidel dominium and restitution in his *Summa* commentary on Question 66, Article 8, he presented the same model of peaceful evangelization as Córdoba. "Jesus Christ, *King of kings* (Rev 17:14, 19:16), who *has been given all power in heaven and on earth* (Mt 28:18), did not send armies and soldiers to take possession of the world, but sent holy preachers, *like sheep among wolves* (Mt 10:16; Lk 10:3)." Cajetan spoke plainly about the toxic linkage between evangelization and conquest: "We sin most gravely if the faith of Christ enlarged in this way ... We must send to these ones preachers leading good lives, who can convert them to God by word and

[142] Córdoba, "Carta al Rey," p. 264.

[143] Gutiérrez, *Las Casas*, p. 41.

example, and not those who oppress, rob, scandalize, and conquer."[144] The influence of the first Dominicans of Española on Cajetan's *Summa* commentary, as claimed by Las Casas, becomes more plausible in view of the "preachers alone" method outlined by Córdoba.

Peaceful evangelization was the only method of safeguarding the liberty of infidels capable of accepting or refusing the Gospel. Hugo Grotius's *De iure praedae* written for a very different context of European expansion nearly a century later, in the chapter also published as *Mare Liberum* (*The Free Sea*), recognized the moral impact of infidel rights articulated by Cajetan and the Spanish theologians on Castilian royal and Roman papal policy. According to the young humanist lawyer, the Dominicans rightly claimed, "the American Indians should be converted to the faith not through war but solely through preaching of the Word, and that the liberty taken from them on the pretext of conversion should be restored to them."[145] As Grotius observed, preaching and restitution went hand in hand for the pro-Indian Dominicans of the New World.

In the first public letter of Las Casas addressing the Council of the Indies in 1531, now a member of the Order of Preachers, the friar interpreted the title of Pope Alexander VI's *Inter caetera* in strictly spiritual terms for converting the infidel peoples of "this *Nuevo Mundo*." Like Cajetan, Las Casas invoked the apostolic example to be like sheep among wolves.[146] But the peaceful method of encountering gentiles established by Christ had not corresponded to the reality across the Atlantic. According to Las Casas, the first foot set in the Indies by Christians were "wars committed against all divine law and natural right" whereas the second foot brought to those Indians who escaped war was "tyrannical governance" and "wretched servitude" in order to dig for gold and fish for pearls (see Figure 3.3).[147] Las Casas devoted the rest of his long career propounding the "preachers alone" interpretation of the papal donation in opposition to the two colonial practices of missionary war and forced labor. Nearing the end of his life, he wrote in his *Doce dudas* (*Twelve Doubts*) that "the first entry and foot with which the Spaniards came to the Indies ... from

[144] Cajetan, *Commentaria*, II-II, q. 66, a. 8: "*Iesus Christus*, Rex regum, *cui* data est omnis potestas in caelo et in terra, *miserit ad capiendum possessionem mundi non milites armatae militiae, sed sanctos praedicatores*, sicut oves inter lupos ... *Unde gravissime peccaremus si fidem Christi Iesu per hanc viam ampliare contenderemus: nec essemus legitimi domini illorum, sed magna latrocinia committeremus, et teneremur ad restitutionem, utpote iniusti debellatores aut occupatores. Mittendi essent ad hos praedicatores boni viri, qui verbo et exemplo converterent eos ad Deum: et non qui eos opprimant, spolient, scandalizent, subiiciant.*"

[145] Grotius, *Commentary on the Law of Prize*, chap. 12, p. 314.

[146] Las Casas, "Carta al Consejo de Indias" (1531), in OC, vol. 13, p. 72.

[147] Las Casas, "Carta al Consejo de Indias," pp. 71–72.

FIGURE 3.3 "South American Indians Panning and Working Gold." (Source: Getty Images/Bettmann/Contributor)

their discovery in 1492 up until today – December of the year 1563 – was violent, odious, tyrannical and most cruel."[148] He then reiterated that "the singular cause and end" of Spanish presence in "the Indian world" (*orbe indiano*) was nothing else but the peaceful preaching of the faith to convert the native peoples.

The earliest draft of Las Casas's *The Only Way of Calling All Peoples to the True Religion* (*De unico vocationis modo omnium gentium ad veram religionem*), completed around 1535, was the first explicit condemnation of missionary warfare in defense of the apostolic method of peaceful evangelization. Although the first four chapters of *De unico modo* have been lost to history, the last three chapters remain. Las Casas introduced the remaining chapters of the treatise by focusing on the Great Commission of Christ, who taught the apostles the one and only way of teaching everyone the true religion and preaching the faith. The only way established by Christ and divine providence was in total conformity with natural reason through the persuasion of the intellect and human freedom by gently attracting the will. Preaching the faith as a missionary, like the teaching of knowledge as an orator, must attract the listener through kindness and gentleness.[149]

A method of persuasion that respects freedom, rather than a method of coercion imposing necessity, is the only way to teach knowledge in a manner proportionate to universal human nature. Correspondingly, only one way of preaching exists because "there is only one species of the rational creature individually dispersed throughout the whole world." In contrast, fear of

[148] Las Casas, *Doce dudas*, cap. 12, p. 74.
[149] Las Casas, *De unico vocationis modo*, in *OC*, vol. 2, cap. 5, §2, p. 24; §5, pp. 52–54.

violence and the threats of war completely undermine the sound and sane reception of the faith thereby "annulling the dignity of the rational creature."[150] The linkage of preaching with the coercive tactics of war undermines the free act of believing:

> If [the faith] is presented hastily, with sudden disturbance or with the clamor of weapons that inspires terrors, or with violent threats . . . it is evident that the human mind will become dismayed . . . consequently, reason will be clouded and understanding impossible . . . and there is neither conformity nor affinity whatsoever in this with the act of believing, but rather, the most detestable contradiction and incongruity.[151]

The friar marshalled an impressive list of authorities including Scripture, ancient philosophers, Church Fathers, medieval theologians, and canon lawyers to make his argument promoting the "preachers alone" policy of Spanish Dominicans in the New World against missionary warfare.

Remarkably, the last and final chapter seven of this work overlapped with the Salmantine theological treatment of restitution and subjective natural right according to commutative justice in 1535, and did so by giving exclusive attention to Cajetan's new category of infidels – those outside Christian European lands. The opening conclusion to the chapter on restitution began with recognition of the following injustice: "War declared against infidels of the third category, who have never known the faith or the Church . . . with the strict purpose of subjugating them under Christian rule through war in order to receive Christian religion, by preparing their souls and removing the impediments of faith, is a reckless, unjust, iniquitous, and tyrannical war."[152] To frame the discussion within the context of restitution, Las Casas presented missionary war as a violation of natural right and the law of nations. In this case, innocent nonbelievers outside of Christian political jurisdiction have become the victims of "infinite and irreparable harms like death, massacres, slaughters, plundering, enslavement, and similar calamities."[153] Christian aggressors must restore what rightfully belongs to infidels or risk eternal damnation.

150 Las Casas, *De unico vocationis modo*, cap. 1, §1, pp. 20–22.

151 Las Casas, *De unico vocationis modo*, cap. 5, §4, p. 48.

152 Las Casas, *De unico vocationis modo*, cap. 7, §1, p. 484: "*Bellum indictum infidelibus tertiae speciei . . . qui nihil unquam de fide aut Ecclesia intellexerunt nec quovis modo ipsam Ecclesiam offenderunt, ob hoc solum, ut imperio Christianorum per bellum subiectis ad suscipiendum fidem seu Christianam religionem ipsorum animi preparentur vel fidei tollantur impedimenta, est temerarium, iniustum, iniquum et tyrannicum.*"

153 Las Casas, *De unico vocationis modo*, cap. 7, §1, p. 486.

Las Casas relied on the scholastic-juristic heritage of the Dominicans to extrapolate *ius naturale* underlying infidel dominium. Like the Salmantine theologians, Las Casas entered his discussion of natural right from a juridically inflected Thomism open to both its objective and subjective meanings, and its plural sense. The definition of justice in Justinian's *Digest* – giving and conserving for each what is theirs – enabled Las Casas to accent "all the rights and all the goods" (*universa iura et bona cuncta*) of infidels affected by this kind of unjust war.[154] Las Casas combined Roman legal thought and Scripture to expound the juridical unity of the human race according to the objective and subjective dimensions of *ius naturale*:

> Among all human beings nature itself has established the right of kinship [*ius cognationis*]. Therefore, it is contrary to natural right and thus intrinsically wrong for one man to assault another, which is supported by Justinian's *Digest* (1.1.3). And indeed, this right of kinship among all human beings is so natural and confirmed by the precept of the Lord, which says: "Love one another as I have loved you (Mt 19:19, 22:39; Mk 12:31–33; Lk 10:27; Rom 13:9; Gal 5:14)." It can neither be renounced by pact nor by mutual consent … And with the aforementioned war this right is shattered, indeed, all rights are violated.[155]

Las Casas's reference to *ius cognationis* – a natural right of "blood" or kin relations existing between all persons irrespective of religious affiliation – clearly had precedent in ancient Roman thinking. According to Cicero's Stoic philosophical view, the objective right of kinship was an acknowledgment of natural equality and the privileged place of humanity alongside divine beings within the cosmos.[156] For Roman jurists, *ius cognationis* could have a more universal and cosmopolitan meaning, as Las Casas noted, referring to nature's establishment of a "certain kinship" among humans.[157] It could also denote the right of peace assumed between persons related by blood or patrilineal succession.[158] During the Middle Ages, *ius cognationis* expressed "the right and expectation of peaceful intercourse" but was widened in a spiritual sense to replace blood kinship with baptismal kinship.[159] The

154 Las Casas, *De unico vocationis modo*, cap. 7, §2, p. 496.

155 Las Casas, *De unico vocationis modo*, cap. 7, §2, p. 498.

156 Cicero, *The Laws*, trans. Niall Rudd (Oxford University Press, 1997), p. 105.

157 *Digest*, 1.1.3.

158 *Digest*, 1.1.12.

159 Charles Reid, Jr., "The Rights of Self-Defence and Justified Warfare in the Writings of the Twelfth- and Thirteenth-Century Canonists," in *Law as Profession and Practice in Medieval Europe: Essays in Honor of James Brundage*, eds. Melanie Eichbauer and Kenneth Pennington (Ashgate Publishing, 2011), p. 84.

unity of faith provided the true bond between peoples – water being thicker than blood. In the context of the crusades, *ius cognationis* became a justification for Christian wars against infidels. Commenting on Innocent IV, for example, Hostiensis appealed to the solidarity of Latin Christians bound together by faith in opposition to infidels.[160] Las Casas deliberately overturned this medieval Crusader interpretation of Christian hostility toward infidels by affirming, in Renaissance form, the solidarity of all rational creatures sharing a common human kinship and right of peaceful relations that the bond of faith protects, rather than undermines.

Although the Roman, indeed Ciceronian, dimensions of Las Casas's proclamation of universal humanity and natural right were on display in *De unico modo*, Aquinas provided the Christian theological rubric to elucidate a richer meaning of "what is each one's own" (*esse suum uniuscuiusque quod*).[161] According to the *Prima Pars* of the *Summa* cited by Las Casas, divine wisdom grants to each thing according to its nature and condition.[162] Otherwise put, every creature receives its natural due from God. In the case of human beings, it is in their nature to have hands and for animals to serve them. The possession of hands and ruling over animals in Aquinas was, as indicated earlier, a reference to the image of God and the ordained power of using the things of the earth out of human necessity. Although Las Casas did not explicitly invoke the image of God to ground dominium or right in *De unico modo* like Vitoria and Soto, he certainly had the Thomistic metaphysical implications in view. Only in his later works, considered in Chapter 6, did he directly appeal to the divine image in defense of infidel political sovereignty and the possession of lands and property.

Las Casas immediately followed the discussion of what is each one's natural due by employing Cicero's notion of "the right of human society" (*ius humanae societatis*), an idea that also surfaced in Paulus Vladimiri.[163] If anyone takes more than what is due by depriving another's property, then a violation of justice or right has occurred. The focus on the personal property of individuals under the heading of the right of human society was the perfect segue into the restitution of infidels under Cajetan's third category. In the aftermath of destruction across the Indies, restitution was the necessary path of salvation for Christian perpetrators:

160 Russell, *Just War in the Middle Ages*, p. 141.

161 Las Casas, *De unico vocationis modo*, cap. 7, §4, p. 524.

162 Aquinas, *ST*, I, q. 21, a. 1, *ad* 3; q. 22, a. 4, q. 19, a. 5, *ad* 3.

163 Cicero, *On Duties*, trans. Walter Miller (Harvard University Press, 2005), Book 1, 7, p. 22.

> The lands, provinces, kingdoms, honors, dignities, possessions, children, wives, goods, and whatever other goods can be counted theirs are owed to the third category of infidels against whom this war has taken place, according to their nature and condition as ordained to them by divine wisdom. . . . Those who cause this war, or participate in it in some other mode, violently usurp all the goods previously mentioned against the will of their individual owners [*invitis propriis dominis*], and thus a violation of the right of human society. In order to observe justice, it is necessarily required they do compensation and therefore obligated toward restitution. This obligation is necessary for salvation in that without restitution and complete satisfaction it is impossible to attain salvation.[164]

The universal right of kinship solidarity and the right of human society reflected the objective sense of *ius*, which upheld basic precepts of neighborly love and non-maleficence. Restoring the subjective claims of individual infidel owners dispossessed of their jurisdiction, property, and lands rested on these objective natural rights uniting all of humanity in a singular world order.

In perhaps his most famous expression concerning world order, the Dominican friar would write: "All humankind is one and all are alike with respect to their origin and nature."[165] This scholastic juristic conception of world order colored by humanism was neither an abstract individualism nor a parochial universalism. Rather, adhering to Cajetan's definitive category of infidels outside Christian political jurisdiction that included pagan and idolatrous "peoples" from the Tartars to the Turks, Christian republics must love the infidel nations of the world as they love themselves, bringing them to the faith by true doctrine and virtuous exemplars.[166] Cajetan's third category established a view of Christian–infidel relations no longer characterized by hostility and resistance to conversion but now in conformity with universal kinship and solidarity among peoples as neighbors. A world order of diverse neighbors had its normative foundation not only in natural *ius* and the law of nations, but also by the efficacious work of grace and salvation.

Crucially, then, if Christians violated the natural order of rights for infidels, their salvation was at stake. The language of subjective rights in a theological mode had the effect of raising the moral status of injured victims deprived of personal and public goods, ordained and secured by objective universal right

164 Las Casas, *De unico vocationis modo*, cap. 7, par. 4, p. 524.
165 Las Casas, *Apologética historia sumaria*, in *OC*, vols. 6–8, cap. 48, p. 537.
166 Las Casas, *Doce dudas*, cap. 4, p. 44.

and Gospel precepts of neighborly love. However, the concept of restitution could not sufficiently account for what Las Casas referred to as "infinite injuries and abuses."[167] Inspired by the spiritual insight of his Dominican confreres on Española and the scholastic thought of Aquinas expounded by the Salmantine theologians, Las Casas elaborated the subjective meaning of *ius* to account for not only the loss of material goods (or external things), but also injuries against incalculable goods like respect, freedom, and loved ones caused by violent colonial dispossession:

> Now, accordingly, those who cause the aforementioned war not only take away unjustly the goods of infidels and whatever things pertain to them like household items, which are less important. These are plainly called exterior things. They also take away their more precious things [*res sibi magis pretiosas*]; namely, wives, children, parents, lords, authorities, honors, servants, helpers, and every kind of freedom [*omnimodam libertatem*]. And this violence is done with the greatest injuries, offenses, and immeasurable harms. Consequently, they caused an inequality in justice in one mode or another with regard to external things and also actions and passions. Therefore, they are obliged to go beyond restitution in material things and make satisfaction for all the damages, injuries, and offenses the infidels received.[168]

No amount of restitution could ever restore the loss of a human being, or those "more precious things." Las Casas was at pains to describe the "immeasurable harms" against infidels caused by attacks on the dignity of the rational creature and the unquantifiable goods of life. His scholastic attention to the rectification of inequality or injustice with regard to actions and passions – harms that are transitory in reality but remain in their effect – enabled greater recognition of losing "more precious things."[169] Justice for the victims of unjust war remained unattainable by merely secular legal arrangements. Spanish perpetrators of violence were therefore required "to go beyond restitution" by doing satisfaction if they sought the reconciliation with God and neighbor necessary for salvation. In other words, restitution was but a preamble, albeit necessary, for satisfaction, which entailed humble acknowledgment of one's sins before the confessing community of faith. The sacrament of penance attentive to the forum of conscience and the free will of the perpetrator was oriented toward this more comprehensive notion (*in solidum*) of justice involving restitution and satisfaction.

167 Las Casas, *De unico vocationis modo*, cap. 7, §5, p. 542.

168 Las Casas, *De unico vocationis modo*, cap. 7, §5, pp. 536–538.

169 Citing Aquinas, *IV Sententiarum*, dist. 15, q. 1, a. 5, solutio 1. Cf. *ST*, II-II, q. 62, a. 1 *ad* 2 and q. 62, a. 6.

Following an episcopal meeting in Mexico City in 1546 joined by Franciscan clerics, Las Casas mandated all his clergy to abide by his "Twelve Rules for Confessors" (or *Confesionario*). This controversial work by the recently appointed bishop of Chiapa, New Spain, enforced the unprecedented royal decree known as the New Laws, which abolished private *encomiendas* and terminated wars to enslave Indians.[170] The "Twelve Rules for Confessors" was a chief contributing factor to the junta at Valladolid considered in the next chapter. It claimed, quite subversively, that all the Spanish incursions and wars in the New World had been unjust (Rule 7). The controversial confessional manual stipulated that *encomenderos* had to set their forced laborers free, conquistadors had to abandon further wars against Amerindians, and arms dealers (*mercaderes*) had to stop supplying the machinery of war (Rule 1). Failure to rectify these injustices meant excommunication by means of the priest withholding absolution in confession. If the Spanish perpetrators chose to comply and pursue justice, they would make a public legal pledge granting the priest power to oversee the restitution with the bishop providing a final safeguard to enforce the binding promise in ecclesiastical court (Rule 5). Payment of losses incurred, tears of repentance and seeking forgiveness from victims, even exchanging one's own freedom for a native in bondage, were all radical measures proposed by Las Casas to begin the long process of restoring the dominium and rights of infidels.

Restitution brought together the holistic pursuit of justice with the goal of salvation for both harmed innocent natives and ensnared European oppressors. Dominican preaching and administration of sacramental penance focused on the act of restitution in response to the gross injustices of forced labor and missionary war – tyrannical obstacles that stood in the way of salvation for Amerindians and Spaniards alike. When civil law failed to render justice to the Amerindians in the aftermath of aggressive wars and colonial dispossession, the Dominicans of Española, and later Bishop Las Casas, relied on preaching, penance, and the ecclesiastical court to preserve the liberating truth of the Gospel. The crisis of conscience stimulating the Law of Burgos and the enforcement of the 1542 New Laws, as well as the Valladolid junta, resulted from mendicant disciplinary measures expressing the transcendent spiritual authority of the Church over secular law and colonial powers.

The idea and practice of missionary war extending from the Crusades to the Reconquista, and now to the Indies, was a direct violation of the apostolic

170 For a splendid historical overview and translation of the "Twelve Rules for Confessors," see David Orique, OP, *To Heaven or to Hell: Bartolomé de Las Casas's* Confesionario (University of Pennsylvania Press, 2018).

ethic of peaceful evangelization. This spiritual and evangelical commitment was as much a statement about the proper method of preaching as it was an affirmation of the freedom of unbelievers to accept the Gospel freely and without violent coercion. Addressing the destruction of the Indies before the Crown, Las Casas put it summarily: "In order to receive our holy faith the freedom of the will is required among those who accept it. God left in the hand of each person the free choice to accept it or not. And since this is the end that God has assigned to the entire affair of the Indies, it remains established in the voluntary will of these peoples, and not in any force or violence done to them."[171]

The authentic manner and duty of preaching the Gospel in the Indies was the central Dominican concern over the whole affair and the inspiration underlying the Order's critical response to the scandalous pairing of evangelization with violence. Those Dominicans associated with the first community on Española, and the university and priory of San Esteban in Salamanca, inhabited this spiritual context. Vitoria was undoubtedly among them. In Vitoria's 1537 *Relectio de temperantia*, he warned about the odious combination of preaching and force by reminding his audience that the Christian religion at its best "grants the freedom of becoming Christian to anyone: it has never used violence, but always reasons and proofs with infidels."[172] The fragment of the *relectio* to which this passage belonged, discovered only in the twentieth century among archives of Miguel de Arcos, focused specifically on the Indies affair.[173]

Vitoria's two lectures on the Indies (*Relectio de Indis*) delivered in both January and June of 1539 centered on the moral question of war. In fact, the second lecture is not known typically as the *relectio posterior*, but instead, by its subject matter, *De iure belli* (On the Law of War). Nevertheless, two observations are worthy of consideration for our analysis of Vitoria's historic contribution to Christian–infidel relations. First, the second lecture's treatment of just war in more theoretical terms naturally follows from the prior lecture addressing the strictly unjust, and possibly just, titles by which the Spanish Crown could claim political rule in the Indies. Which is to say, Vitoria's discussion of possible just titles in the first lecture presumed the principles and norms elaborated in

[171] Las Casas, *Entre los remedios*, in *Tratados de Fray Bartolomé de las Casas*, II (Fondo de Cultura Económica, 1965), p. 745.

[172] Vitoria, *Fragmentum relectionis de temperantia* (*Appendix*), in *Relecciones jurídicas y teológicas*, Tomo II (Editorial San Esteban, 2017), p. 734.

[173] Pagden and Lawrance provide a translation of it in *Political Writings*, pp. 217–230.

the posterior lecture.[174] Second, a single "rereading" of a biblical passage for both lectures provides the theological hermeneutic of the *Relectiones de Indis*: Christ's Great Commission to preach the Gospel throughout the world (Mt 28:19). Inseparable from the apostolic mandate to teach all nations and baptize them in the name of the Trinity, Vitoria suggested, was the issue of religious coercion. The classic scholastic question in view here was whether it was permissible to baptize children of infidels against the wishes of their parents.[175]

It seems astonishing from such an entry point that Vitoria's Indies lecture did not provide a strict treatment of the apostolic method of evangelization similar to Las Casas's *De unico vocationis modo*, or Soto's later *Commentary on Book Four of the Sentences*. But that was neither the intent nor the audience of a university-wide lecture based on the classroom teaching of the second part of the *Summa* from previous years. For the genre of the *relectio*, concerned with a pressing moral and social issue, was neither theological treatise nor theological commentary. Its specific stated purpose was to place the affair of the Indies within the court of Spanish conscience by rejecting the common justifications for transatlantic rule and colonial dispossession of infidels and raising bona fide doubt about even lawful ones. It supplied reasons for doubt that could aid theologians and priests generating moral opinions (*pareceres*) on the Indies affair, which Vitoria himself officially provided in one instance on the subject of mass baptism across the Atlantic. Vitoria's questioning and doubt about the right by which Amerindians came under Spanish rule stemmed from knowledge "of the bloody massacres and of innocent individuals pillaged of their possessions and dominions."[176] His incisive criticism of the Peruvian case represented in his 1534 letter to Arcos already evinced a deep awareness of the injustice surrounding the Indies affair.

Beginning with the fact of injustice overseas in light of the Great Commission, Vitoria's *relectio* attempted to move the moral discussion of Christian–infidel relations surrounding the Indies "out of the province of lawyers" and secular power, and into the realm of ecclesiastical power and the moral authority of the Church. This effort was not some vie for clerical power but a clear acknowledgment of an egregious transcontinental problem beyond the control and even purview of royal jurisdiction and civil law. It demanded theological attention and Church intervention on behalf of

174 Consider Vitoria's opening statement to the posterior lecture, *On the Law of War*, in *Political Writings*, p. 295.

175 See, for example, Aquinas, *ST*, II-II, q. 10, a. 12; q. 68, a. 10.

176 Vitoria, *On the American Indians*, p. 238.

doubtful cases of individual conscience implicating Spaniards directly in the Indies affair. As the Dominicans of Española demonstrated nearly two decades earlier, the Church's moral teachings and spiritual power were the last bulwark of protecting justice on the Spanish side of the encounter. *De Indis* was consistent with the Dominican strategy of critically engaging the Amerindian question by placing evangelization and conversion of infidels at the center of the dispute. In addition, its focus on conscience's doubt regarding conquest, informed by the moral judgments of theologians and priests like Vitoria and his confreres, pointed to the work's wider relationship to restitution, rights, and the sacrament of penance. Vitoria set the terms of the theological inquiry plainly:

> Since these barbarians we speak of are not subjects [of the Spanish Crown] by human law . . . their affairs cannot be judged by human statutes, but only by divine ones, in which jurists are not sufficiently versed to form an opinion of their own. And as far as I am aware, no theologian . . . has ever been called upon to study this question and provide a solution. Yet since this is a case of conscience, it is the business of priests, that is to say, of the Church, to pass sentence upon it.[177]

Remarkably, Vitoria began here from the demonstrable premise that the Amerindians were not under the legal and political jurisdiction of the Crown. The divine and biblical support for his claim that Amerindians were not legitimately under Spanish rule rested on his earlier lecture addressing ecclesiastical power. The Pauline *foris* or "outsider" principle of canon law, derived from 1 Corinthians 5:12–13, respected both the spiritual immunity and political independence of infidels on theological grounds. The Apostle to the gentiles, St. Paul, had exhorted the Corinthian Christian community, "God will judge those outside." Therefore, civilian lawyers were categorically unsuited to opine the matter, simply speaking, because it was beyond their legal jurisdiction. The extra-European political context of Amerindian life demanded a supranational and supra-imperial imaginary for thinking about a new kind of world order comprised of independent political communities. Only a divine or theological hermeneutic grounded in natural law, the law of nations, and canon law could sufficiently address the problem of conscience among Spaniards, since the matter involved both universal rights claims and salvation for Europeans and non-Europeans.[178] The divine mandate to proclaim the Gospel to the whole world was a fitting ecclesiological context for

177 Vitoria, *On the American Indians*, p. 238.
178 Ruston, *Human Rights and the Image of God*, pp. 80–81.

engaging Christian–infidel relations outside the legitimate borders of Christendom. Vitoria's reflection on the Indies affair from an explicitly theological standpoint proved a milestone in the longue durée of international relations in the West. The *relectio* was a most skillful application of Roman law and canon law to the emergent genre of moral theology.

The first (*prior*) lecture of *Relectio de Indis* was broken into three parts, each of which concerned (1) the nature of infidel dominium; (2) the unjust titles of ruling over the Indies; and (3) the possible just titles for discussion. With respect to the unjust and just titles, it deserves mentioning that Vitoria's rationale for structuring his discussion of the Indies as a juxtaposition of a conflict in Spanish conscience. And what may seem to be a Eurocentric focus on the just and unjust titles of the Spaniards overlooks two things: his *relectio* began with a substantial treatment of infidel rights; and his audience were Spaniards whose souls were at risk. Vitoria's theological task, along with his Dominican confreres, was to render an authoritative moral judgment that could sufficiently treat the doubts of conscience among individual Spaniards involved in the colonial project. He appealed directly to Aristotle's agent of practical wisdom, or trustworthy experts and teachers to render a judgment on the matter.[179] Individuals judging their actions as good or bad according to their private conscience apart from the Church's wisdom in cases of doubt was not enough.[180] The conscience of a baptized believer develops within the Church community, which offers counsel and discernment regarding matters necessary for salvation.

What made the affair of the Indies such a challenging case for conscience was that there might be valid arguments on both sides of the issue, or so it seemed. For Vitoria, however, the arguments on each side did not have equal weight. The injustices perpetrated against infidels under false titles were strictly binding according to the moral weight of theological beliefs and authoritative Church teaching. In contrast, any alleged lawful titles were probable opinions at best. Vitoria considered eight of these altogether and some in greater detail and more accurately than others. Although these opinions might assuage an individual's conscience, they could not guarantee that the action was lawful in its entirety because of remaining doubts concerning particular matters that Vitoria never attempted to address fully.[181]

179 Aristotle, *Nicomachean Ethics*, trans. David Ross (Oxford University Press, 1998), Book 2, pp. 38–39.

180 Vitoria, *On the American Indians*, pp. 235–236.

181 See Vitoria's second and third propositions for resolving a doubtful case and his subsequent explanations, pp. 237–238.

Vitoria's *De Indis*, similar to chapters six and seven of Las Casas's *De unico modo*, identified and condemned the unjust wars across the Atlantic, albeit in a pointed and terse manner. Las Casas, importantly, never ruminated about the possibility of just causes for war from the Spanish colonial side whereas Soto remained apophatic in his judgment by only identifying unjust claims to war. Nevertheless, the critical edge of Vitoria's judgments should not be underestimated. The Salmantine theologian's identification of seven unjust titles by which Spaniards presumed transatlantic rule explicitly repudiated the regnant arguments of theocratic world order in its papalist and imperialist modes, as seen respectively in Palacios Rubios and Cortés, along with their underlying causes of war. Furthermore, the second part of the *relectio prior* on the unjust titles presupposed the theological arguments of the first part in which Vitoria succinctly defended the dominium and rights of infidels.

The incontrovertible thesis of the first part of *De Indis* rehashed Vitoria's previous thinking on the Indies from his *relectiones* and commentaries on the *Summa*: Amerindians possess true dominium (*veri domini*), a belief established by their rational creaturely status of being made in the image of God, and supported by the natural law and the law of nations. Vitoria addressed four possible critiques against native dominium over their lands and property before the arrival of the Spaniards. These arguments abrogating native dominium over public jurisdictions and private possessions defended familiar Christian positions legitimizing the causes of war against barbarians in extra-European lands. They did so under the conviction that barbarians were infidels, mortal sinners, mentally incompetent, and irrational.[182] All the relevant Spanish descriptions of the Amerindians to authorize conquest – idolaters, sodomites, cannibals, lazy, nonindustrious, beastly, backwards, natural subjugates – were associated with these colonial arguments that Vitoria tackled head on.

Vitoria was unyielding in his commitment to the image of God present in all peoples across the whole world, regardless of moral and social status. That image belonged to every individual of a rational nature. For "man is the image of God through his nature, that is through his rational powers."[183] Natural dominium, or mastery over one's actions through the intellect and free will, stemmed from the image of God. In a fundamental ontological sense, then, every individual made in the divine image, existing for his own sake, is true *dominus* of himself through his actions. Vitoria's patristic and scholastic account of the *imago Dei* did not morally exclude individuals exhibiting less

[182] Vitoria, *On the American Indians*, q. 1, a. 1, p. 240.

[183] Vitoria, *On the American Indians*, q. 1, a. 2, p. 242: "*[H]omo est imago Dei per naturam, scilicet per potentias rationales.*"

than optimal capabilities or even serious deficiencies in the exercise of reason. Small children, for example, possess the image of God even before the use of reason and are therefore owners of a sort.

The ramifications of Vitoria's ontological claim were not only moral, but also juridical. Precisely because children have natural dominium conferred by the divine image, they are capable of suffering injury (*iniuria*). Which is to say, they can have their rights violated. Vitoria expounded his juridical claims from the following ontological assertion: "[T]he child does not exist for another's sake, but for his own sake [*propter se*]."[184] Additionally, the severely mentally impaired could not be denied dominium either. When it came to the question of the Amerindians, Vitoria conceded popular reports about their seeming irrationality, attributing any apparent backwardness to lack of education. However, this was no bid to launch a civilizing mission. Vitoria considered these accusations only after first indicating that the Amerindians, "in truth, are not *amentes*, but have use of judgment," demonstrated by "a particular order in their affairs" at the societal level that included organized cities, laws, marriages, commerce, and rulers.[185] Regardless of how they might appear to European outsiders, Amerindians could not be subjects of colonial dispossession. They had true dominium over their public jurisdictions and private possessions, "just like Christians" (*sicut Christiani*).[186] In other words, they were full-fledged participants in a world order according to natural right and the law of nations.

The moral force of Vitoria's juridical claim here did not rest on the rights of children or the rights of the mentally impaired. For the Amerindian "barbarians" were neither nature's children nor nature's dependents. Rather, reliant on the theological and canon legal tradition, Vitoria included Amerindians within a world order under the familiar rubric of infidel rights. As he observed in the conclusion of the first part: "It would be harsh to deny to them [the Indians], who have never done us any injury, the rights we concede to Saracens and Jews, who have been continual enemies of the Christian religion. Yet we do not deny the right of ownership of the latter, unless it be in the case of Christians lands which they have conquered."[187] For the Spanish Dominican theologians, transatlantic international relations between Spaniards and Amerindians, the old and new worlds, drew upon preexisting

184 Vitoria, *On the American Indians*, q. 1, a. 5, p. 249: "*[P]uer non est propter alium, sed propter se, sicut est brutum.*"

185 Vitoria, *On the American Indians*, q. 1, a. 6, p. 250: "*[V]eritatem non sunt amentes, sed habent iudicium*"; "*[H]abent ordinem aliquem in suis rebus.*"

186 Vitoria, *On the American Indians*, q. 1, conclusion, p. 250.

187 Vitoria, *On the American Indians*, q. 1, conclusion, p. 251.

Christian–infidel relations back in Europe. The rights of the European infidel other provided the legal lens for imagining the transatlantic other in a manner that could supplant theocratic models of Christian–infidel relations.

For Vitoria, Aquinas's proof "that unbelief does not cancel either natural or human law" also gave sturdy theological support to the Spanish scholastic conviction "that is not lawful to take away the possessions of Saracens, Jews, or other unbelievers because they are infidels *per se*. To do so is theft or robbery, no less than it would be in the case of Christians."[188] Nevertheless, there were shortcomings to the traditional infidel categorization deployed in Latin Christian Europe. Strictly speaking, the traditional category of the infidel could only secure at most Amerindian claims to property (*dominium rerum*) against Spanish invaders since denial of infidel political authority had been the political norm in Latin Christendom. The European case of nonbaptized infidels in Christendom was not enough to establish native political independence (*dominium iurisdictionis*) abroad, which was the most contentious point over Spanish rule in the Indies. Pope Innocent IV had already conceived of such a possibility, but his opinion, as previously noted, circumscribed infidel dominium under papal power. This explains why Cajetan's third category of infidels – those who had never heard the faith – necessarily widened the scope of infidel rights to address the Indies affair. As Cajetan "elegantly deduces" for Vitoria, the charge of mortal sin or unbelief does not provide Christians with a lawful title to dispossess Amerindian infidels of either their goods or their lands.[189]

The theological and legal framework of Christian–infidel relations applied and expanded to a new world order followed from conviction in the Lord's Great Commission to spread the Gospel to all peoples. Vitoria's understated evangelical intervention in *De Indis* belonged to the fourth unjust title to rule and wage war in the Indies: that infidels persistently refuse to accept the faith of Christ. As we saw in Mair and the Spanish royalist supporters of theocratic world order, refusal to convert was taken to be an inimical form of resistance to faith indicative of idolatry or barbarism, and therefore a cause for colonial dispossession through war. Vitoria did not concede such a claim in the least. If infidels of the third category committed any sin at all in refusing to accept the Gospel (which, in itself, was *not* grounds for ruling over them), it could only be after they have received miraculous signs and compelling reasons to believe in the faith.

188 Vitoria, *On the American Indians*, q. 1, a. 3, p. 244.
189 Vitoria, *On the American Indians*, q. 1, a. 3, p. 246.

Turning to the facts on the ground as a Dominican insider, Vitoria described the whole affair with characteristic aplomb: "I have not heard of any miracles or signs, nor of any exemplary saintliness of life sufficient to convert them. On the contrary, I hear only of provocations, savage crimes, and multitudes of unholy acts." Some positive examples from certain friars and clergy notwithstanding, these efforts overall have been "thwarted by others with different aims."[190] Citing Aquinas, Gregory the Great, and canon law on the question of Christian–infidel relations back in the Old World, Vitoria strengthened his evangelical point that pagans and Jews cannot be forced to have faith. "Belief is a matter of will," he continued, "but fear considerably diminishes the freedom of will. To come to the mysteries and sacraments of Christ merely out of servile fear would be sacrilege."[191] Even if there were miracles performed by holy preachers, Spaniards could not advance war to punish Amerindians for committing the sin of positive unbelief, or any other mortal sins.

Like Las Casas, Vitoria could see that the mechanics of fear used in forced religion had tremendous political implications, which he later addressed in his sixth unjust title. By vitiating free and voluntary consent among Amerindians, the Spaniards had denied the true dominium of infidels. The fundamental assumption of the Requirement was utterly false and therefore invalid. The so-called "voluntary choice" of Amerindians accepting Spanish sovereignty was done out of fear and ignorance, which undermined any freedom of election. Describing the colonial strategy of the enforced Requirement without explicitly saying so, Vitoria notes that the Amerindians "do not realize what they are doing, perhaps, indeed, they do not even understand what it is the Spaniards are asking of them. Besides which, the request is made by armed men, who surround a fearful and defenseless crowd."[192]

Under the belief that infidels have dominium and rights, Vitoria rejected any conjured obligations or legal titles imposed by Spaniards on Amerindians to either accept the Christian religion, recognize papal power, or submit to foreign imperial power. In his posterior Indies lecture on just war, he categorically rejected difference of religion and imperial expansion as causes of war.[193] By November of 1539, the same year Vitoria delivered his *relectiones* on the Indies, the Dominican prior of San Esteban had received an imperial letter forbidding "certain religious teachers" from discussing the Spanish

190 Vitoria, *On the American Indians*, q. 2, a. 4, p. 271.

191 Vitoria, *On the American Indians*, q. 2, a. 4, p. 272.

192 Vitoria, *On the American Indians*, q. 2, a. 6, pp. 275–276.

193 Vitoria, *On the Law of War*, q. 1, a. 3, pp. 302–303.

"right" (*derecho*) to rule the Indies in their "*repeticiones*."[194] Additionally, Emperor Charles prohibited any questioning from the priory of the authoritative force and validity of the papal donations to the Crown. Without complete royal oversight, Charles averred, the teaching of the Dominican theologians might bring scandal and harm to both Spain and the papacy.

Vitoria never addressed the Indies again in another *relectio*, whereas Domingo de Soto continued to teach and write about the affair until his death in 1560. Soto was prior of San Esteban off and on during the decade of 1540, living long enough to moderate the junta at Valladolid and attend the Council of Trent. His earliest public discussion of the Indies in the *Relectio de dominio*, as we saw, indisputably rejected imperial claims to take possession of new lands based on worldwide Roman rule or the universal power of Christ – the expansionist logic of either imperialism and theocratic papalism. Soto's response to the Indies in this early lecture represented the peace ethic of evangelization in simplest form. He relied on the same interrogative – *by what right?* – of the first Dominicans of Española to address European imperial rule across the Atlantic:

> The Emperor in no way has rule over the whole world. Therefore, by what right do we obtain rule overseas? Truly, I do not know. We have, according to the Gospel: *Go and preach the Gospel to every creature* (Mk 16); whereby we have been given the right of preaching [*ius praedicandi*] over the earth and, consequently, the right of defending [*ius defendendi*] ourselves against whoever obstructs us from preaching. Wherefore, if we are not safe, we are able to defend ourselves from them at their expense. But to go beyond this by taking their goods and subjecting them to our rule, I do not see from where we have such a right.[195]

The apophatic answer of Soto was not a moot or inconsequential point. Soto recognized only two relevant rights for Christian relations with infidels overseas in this *relectio*: preaching and self-defense. Unlike Vitoria's ruminations about the right of war emerging from the law of nations, Soto confined his analysis of *ius* within the parameters of divine law and natural law. Notice his qualification of the natural right of defense, which of itself authorizes neither public war nor a right of conquest. Consistent with the scholastic-juristic tradition of private defense against an attacker as part of the natural law, Soto accepted a legitimate use of force proportionate to the aim of protecting

194 Luis G. Alonso Getino, *El maestro fr. Francisco de Vitoria* (Imprenta católica, 1930), p. 150. Ramón Hernández likens the repetitions to "re-readings" (*relectiones*). See his *Francisco de Vitoria: Vida y pensamiento internacionalista* (Biblioteca de Autores Cristianos: 1995), p. 135.

195 Soto, *De dominio*, no. 34.

the lives of preachers that may or may not lead to the unintended death of the attacker.[196] Yet, as he adamantly asserted, there was no right "to go beyond this" defense justifying transatlantic rule over infidels who had never heard of the Gospel.

Soto further tempered the prospects of warfare and aggression through divine law and its apostolic norm of peaceful evangelization. Here he resounded the Dominican missionary approach explicit in Las Casas, Cajetan, and Córdoba:

> Most importantly, when the Lord sent his disciples to preach (Lk 9; Mt 10), he did not send them as lions, but as sheep among wolves, not only without weapons, but also without staff, bag, bread, and money. He added: "Wherever they do not welcome you, as you are leaving that town shake the dust off your feet as testimony against them." (Lk 9:5) He did not say that we should preach to the unwilling themselves. Rather, upon leaving, we leave it to God's judgment. It is not my intention to say these things in order to condemn everything that has happened on these islands, for the judgments of God are deep. God may wish to convert such a number of peoples in a way unknown to us.[197]

The evangelical context of Christian–infidel relations placed additional measures on Spanish conduct in the Indies. Although Soto acknowledged that the defense of preachers was in accordance with natural law, he held the religious conduct of preachers to the higher standard of divine law. Missionaries were expected to follow the apostolic method of evangelization embodying meekness, voluntary poverty, and peacefulness. Relatedly, preaching should not take place against the will of listeners just as baptism should never be forced upon nonbelievers. This "shake the dust from your feet" doctrine, which left unwelcoming infidel communities to divine judgment and not human judgment, was a common argument in the Dominican effort to constrain Spanish aggression in the Indies.[198] This teaching, notably, proposed an exit strategy for inhabited lands to prevent ongoing colonial incursions. It also placed a constraint on the liberal use of self-defense against inhospitable peoples outside Europe.

Soto did not condemn outright the entirety of Spanish activities across the Atlantic. However, it would not be excessive to say he condemned most of what was happening, as many of his confreres did. Besides, as Vitoria pointed out, whatever authentically Christian examples there were among Spaniards

196 Aquinas, *ST*, II-II, q. 64, a. 7.
197 Soto, *De dominio*, no. 34.
198 Adorno, *Polemics of Possession*, p. 74.

were undermined by the scandalous behaviors of so many adventurers, *peruleros*, *encomenderos*, and conquistadors. Soto's position on the apostolic method of peaceful evangelization in the New World remained consistent throughout his life. As he mentioned in his treatise *De iustitia et iure*, there was indication that he prepared a work entitled *De ratione promulgandi Evangelium*, which was singularly dedicated to presenting a theological political treatment of preaching, justice, and Spanish rule over infidels of the Indies.[199] The treatise on the Indies has been lost unfortunately, leaving us only with fragments and arguments dispersed in his later writings to piece together his mature position.

A possible fragment of the missing work contained in the *Relectio an liceat civitates infidelium* gives some indication of Soto's position on the matter. This literary fragment, composed in 1554 on the heels of the Valladolid junta moderated by Soto himself, addressed the question of whether it was lawful to subjugate or conquer infidel peoples because of their idolatry. Soto followed the position of his Dominican confreres Las Casas and Vitoria in opposition to the canonistic teachings of Innocent IV, Palacios Rubios, and Sepúlveda, among others. Invoking the well-known verse of John 3:16, Soto reminded his listeners that God did not send his infant Son into the world to judge it, but to save it through him. Soto contrasted the task of preaching with punishment to emphasize his point: "The end of preaching the faith is the forgiveness and remission of sins. Thus to punish the offenses of infidels itself is diametrically opposed to this end. The Catholic faith has not handed us a power for punishing them."[200] On the contrary, the Pauline *foris* principle has restricted any alleged international right of punishing infidel outsiders. Christians cannot wage war against infidels, neither dispossessing them nor depriving them of their rights, under the pretext of punishing their sin of idolatry or any other sins. The Church only has the power to judge baptized members according to the law of the Gospel. Furthermore, no right or faculty exists in natural law or the law of nations by which foreigners can judge and punish people in another territory under its own distinct authorities. Not even the ancient Roman Empire possessed the right to punish by arms the Spartans in their own land.[201]

199 Soto, *De iustitia et iure*, lib. 4, q. 2, a. 2; q. 4, a. 2. Soto mentioned that he addressed in the lost work the question of both Christian princes and vassals (or public and private persons) waging war against infidels of Cajetan's third category, see lib. 5, q. 3, a. 5.

200 Soto, *An liceat civitates infidelium*, in *Relecciones y opúsculos*, p. 244: "*Finis praedicandae fidei est peccatorum condonatio et remissio. Huic autem ex diametro observatur infidelium crimina punire. Ergo fides catholica nullam nobis tradidit potestatem eadem puniendi.*"

201 Soto, *An liceat civitates infidelium*, p. 249.

FIGURE 3.4 "Domingo de Soto's *In quartum Sententiarum*, dist. 5, q. unica, a. 10." (Source: photograph of University of Salamanca manuscript by David Lantigua)

Soto's most detailed discussion available concerning the peace ethic of evangelization in the context of the Indies was in his *Commentary on Book Four of the Sentences* (*In quartum Sententiarum*) (see Figure 3.4). The relevant scholastic question to launch his *Sentences* commentary, like Vitoria's *Relectio de Indis*, was whether it is permissible to baptize Jewish children against the will of their parents. That Soto, like Vitoria, approached Christian–infidel relations through the question of forcible baptism and religious coercion only accentuates the evangelical and theological import of the affair of the Indies for them according to infidel rights. Soto, Vitoria, and Las Casas followed Aquinas in declaring forcible conversion of adults or their children an evil.[202] However, Soto and Las Casas condemned the practice in the strongest categorical moral terms: it was intrinsically evil (*per se malum* or *intrinsice mala*) and admitted no exceptions.[203] They adhered to the moral theological

202 Aquinas, *ST*, II-II, q. 10, a. 8 and a. 12.

203 Vitoria considered forcible baptism as evil *per accidens* and therefore lawful under proper rulers but difficult to implement in practice because of the bad results that stem from it. See "Lecture on the Evangelization of Unbelievers" in *Political Writings*, Appendix B, p. 344. Las Casas and Soto squarely condemned the practice as evil *per se*. Soto treated the matter in his

principle extrapolated from Scripture that evil cannot be done to achieve a good, even the supreme good of converting souls.

With greater depth than the earlier *Relectio de dominio*, Soto's *Sentences* commentary reaffirmed the right of preaching (*ius praedicandi*) granted by Christ in the context of the New World. Soto now had to qualify this right in several ways to avoid its abuse in justifying Spanish colonial aggression and conquest. Which is to say, the right of preaching entailed in Alexander VI's papal concession had to conform to both natural law and the divine law of the apostles, or nature and grace. As he extrapolated from Aquinas, "the divine law, which brings grace, does not destroy, but perfects, the right of nature."[204] Soto began with the Thomistic position that infidel children cannot be forced to convert against parental consent just as adults cannot be forced. Following Aquinas, Soto defended this position against religious coercion with three reasons. First, it is in accordance with natural right that parents have the authority to educate and instruct their children in customs and laws. To violate this right (*ius*) is an injurious act. Soto here acknowledged a right of immunity in religious matters. Second, forcible conversion will cause an injury to faith when children revert to the tradition of their parents. Last, the long-standing universal custom of the Church has prohibited the practice.[205]

The defense of preachers from unwarranted violence was still present in Soto's discussion. However, such injustices do not automatically license war, much less conquest, since that would most likely make the faith appear scandalous to nonbelievers. Soto acknowledged cases in which a foreign tyrant might physically obstruct preachers through violence or imprisonment of missionaries. In these situations, Christians can lawfully defend themselves and use force to repel attackers though must do so without bringing injury to the faith.[206] Presumably, one criterion for avoiding scandal would be to permit only a proportionate amount of force to protect the preachers and repel attackers. Put in the manner of his *Relectio de dominio*, it would mean not

Commentariorum … in quartum Sententiarum (Terranova, 1561–2), dist. 5, q. unica, a. 10, p. 308, col. 1: "*Vi autem baptizare infideles, qui in sua infidelitate permansuri creduntur, est sacrilegam iniuriam irrogare fidei; quod cum sit per se malum, pro tota salute mundi non est faciendum.*" Las Casas rejected forcible conversion in the context of condemning the encomienda as an intrinsically evil institution. See his "Carta a Fray Bartolomé de Miranda" (1555), in *OC*, vol. 13, p. 290.

204 Soto, *In quartum Sententiarum*, p. 310, col. 2: "*Divinum enim ius quod gratia tulit … ius naturae non destruit, sed perficit.*"

205 Soto, *In quartum Sententiarum*, p. 303, col. 1.

206 Soto, *In quartum Sententiarum*, p. 304, col. 1: "*Si quis eamdem praedicationem nobis impediret et cohiberet iure possemus eius violentiam, etiam armis propulsare, nisi ubi experimento comperiremus scandalum inde oboriri in iniuriam fidei.*"

going beyond the bounds of a just defense. Another criterion for preventing scandal to the faith, which also had roots in Soto's earlier *relectio*, was to deliver the Gospel only to those willing to receive it. The preaching of the faith could not be forced upon those unwilling to hear it, even among natives who might fiercely hinder it.[207] Any wars bringing hatred and scandal to the faith had to cease. These criteria for intervention and war to protect preachers outlined an important legacy for other Salmantine Dominicans such as Melchor Cano and Juan de la Peña.

Soto's articulation of the right of preaching abided by the order of nature and grace. Like Las Casas, he paired the supernatural act of preaching the Gospel with the natural act of teaching the truth to establish the harmonious relationship between faith and reason. For Soto, the right of preaching (*ius praedicandi*) rested on the natural right of teaching (*ius docendi*), the latter of which designated the freedom (*libertas*) and faculty (*facultas*) of teaching others by persuading them and getting them to understand the truth.[208] The Great Commission (Mt 28:19), literally, was a mandate to "teach all nations" (*docete omnes gentes*) about the saving work and commands of Christ.

In a subtle but important sense, Soto's position on the right of preaching contrasted here with Vitoria, which would have political ramifications. When Vitoria considered the second possible argument whereby Amerindians might justly come under the rule of Spaniards, he established the right of preaching on the classical *ius gentium* and not strictly the natural law. In particular, the Christian right of preaching presupposed "the right of traveling" (*ius peregrinandi*) and trading (*negotiandi*) under the law of nations. Although Vitoria did not appeal to a natural right of teaching infidels like Soto, he did conclude that Christians "must be able to teach them the truth if they are willing to listen, especially about matters to do with salvation and beatitude."[209] Vitoria's shift of legal domain from the law of nature to the law of nations allowed the violation of the right of preaching to provide a legitimate basis for authorizing a public act of war against infidels. Again, Vitoria only outlined one possible argument in the complex case of an individual's conscience, but it was nevertheless a notable difference between him and Soto. The right of traveling proved consequential for early modern international legal thought among the Protestant empires of commerce considered in the next chapter.

207 Soto, *In quartum Sententiarum*, p. 304 col. 2: "*Illos autem, qui nos audire nollent, compellere ut nos audirent, non possemus ut paulo inferius confirmabimus.*"

208 Soto, *In quartum Sententiarum*, p. 304, col. 1.

209 Vitoria, *On the American Indians*, q. 3, a. 2, p. 284.

Scripture, apostolic doctrine, and Church custom offered additional qualifications for properly exercising the right of preaching in accordance with Christian ethical norms. Soto's commentary interpreted the Great Commission of Christ to preach the Gospel in apostolic terms: not by force of violence, but by persuasive teaching.[210] Additionally, the concrete example of Christ from Scripture illustrated the model of persuasion as a work of love in contrast to acts of violence, injury, and fear. Soto would offer some seven arguments from Gospel teaching to establish the peaceful method of preaching supported by other Dominicans like Las Casas, Córdoba, and Cajetan. Evidently, the doctrine and practice of missionary warfare across the Atlantic was in the background. Missionaries must go out like sheep among wolves. If unbelievers reject these missionaries, they must depart from such towns and villages by shaking the dust from their feet and abandoning judgment to God. Soto prohibited the persistence of preaching by force, or the use of threats and terror, so that infidels hear or receive the Gospel. According to Soto and the Spanish Dominicans, this was the strategy of Muslim expansion across the world whereas unarmed Christians were to conquer the world with the power of truth alone.[211] Fighting to persuade infidels of the Gospel, in turn, dissuades listeners. Turning the right of preaching into an instrument of forcing the faith on others was wholly counterproductive.

The twofold order of nature and grace in Soto's mature discussion of the right of preaching adhered to the Thomistic dictum of grace perfecting nature, rather than denigrating it. Soto's *Sentences* commentary derived two telling conclusions from Aquinas's political axiom directly applicable to the Indies affair. Each conclusion outlining Soto's political judgment on the matter represented the common opinion among pro-Indian Dominicans. In response to the arguments of the theocratic papalists and royalists alike, Soto rejected the use of war and political subjugation to bring about infidel conversion. Remarkably, Soto defended his position here by reinterpreting the juridical significance of Aquinas's political axiom: since divine law cannot abolish human law, much less can it take away human freedom (*libertatem humanum*) grounded in nature. If infidels were subjugated on account of the faith, not only would it make the faith odious to them, it would also violate their "natural right of liberty."[212] On this basis, Jaime Brufau Prats has concluded

[210] Soto, *In quartum Sententiarum*, p. 305, col. 1: "*Non ait, vi ipsum obtrudite, sed docendo persuadete.*"

[211] Soto, *In quartum Sententiarum*, p. 306, cols. 1–2.

[212] Soto, *In quartum Sententiarum*, p. 308, col. 1: "*[I]us namque divinum, quod est ex gratia, non tollit humanum, quod est ex naturali ratione: ergo multo minus tollit libertatem humanum, ut possit quispiam ratione fidei in servitutem pertrahi: hoc enim esset eandem fidem exosam, et*

that Soto anticipated liberty in religious matters as a fundamental human right.[213]

The natural right of liberty among infidels derived from Aquinas provided an additional juridical basis for properly interpreting the title of Pope Alexander VI. When Soto considered the papal concession in his *Sentences* commentary, he revisited the natural and biblical norms discussed earlier to qualify the right of preaching granted by Christ. Preaching in "these countries and regions" conceded by the Pope had to conform strictly to the natural right of teaching and the apostolic ethic of evangelization. Soto's scholastic *quaestio* on the natural right of infidel parents over their children enabled him to strengthen his argument against a destructive misreading of the papal title as a donation of governable lands that supported colonial dispossession. He could give attention to the Amerindian side of the affair and not just the Spanish side. The teaching of the faith to all nations by "learned and honest men" therefore had to respect the fundamental natural right of those willing to listen. In extreme cases involving tyrants who violently impede Christian missionaries, it would be permissible to send along "some commander" for their guardianship though conducted with great care and prudence.[214] Exercising the natural right of defense in the case of protecting preachers or new converts from tyranny could neither dissolve infidel dominium, nor bring scandal to the faith.

The power that Jesus Christ conceded to the papacy, beginning with St. Peter, was for the redemption and salvation of the world. Hence, the Pope's entrustment of certain lands and territories to the Spanish Crown or whomever was for the strict spiritual purpose of converting outsiders of the Church. Native peoples of the New World could only come under the rule of the Spanish Crown in two ways: if, after becoming Christians without coercion, they voluntarily elected them as kings; or, after having already converted and transferred authority, they should apostatize and renounce Christ."[215] The Church did not possess the requisite power to claim coercive jurisdiction over whatever lands were "donated" by the papacy to Christian rulers. St. Paul's *foris* principle in canon law denied the existence of a power and right to punish infidel outsiders through war unless they invade the lands of Christians. Relatedly, the Church may have habitual (*habitu*) jurisdiction or power *in potentia* over the earth for the sake of spreading the faith, but this is not actual

execrabilem apud infideles facere, si eis diceremus, quod ad illam introducendam possumus illos contra naturale ius libertatis captivare."

213 Brufau Prats, *La escuela de Salamanca*, p. 114.

214 Soto, *In quartum Sententiarum*, p. 310, col. 1.

215 Castañeda Delgado, *La teocracía pontifical*, p. 477.

(*actu*) power bearing any coercive force unless a people have accepted the faith freely.[216] Here Soto was following his confrere Las Casas, who had succinctly shown at Valladolid that Amerindian infidels were potential (not actual) members of the Body of Christ, or the Church, and therefore not subject to Christian authorities.

If Jesus did not claim temporal dominium over the earth, then neither could the Pope. Soto argued that the papal grant of the "Occidental islands of the infidels" to the Catholic Monarchs could not concede dominium over their property and goods as if he possessed it himself.[217] The plain verity of this firm Dominican conviction denying papal power over infidels unwittingly advanced the public discussion of war in the Indies among colonialist partisans beyond a papal politics of natural law to an imperial politics of natural law. The junta at Valladolid provided the formal venue in which a scholastic theological conception of world order clashed with a new Spanish humanist one, thus outlining the ambivalent tone that later marked modern European international relations. Soto, Las Casas, and the Spanish Dominicans were at the center of the imperial controversy over the Indies, but they would now address the matter without their friend and guide, Vitoria.

[216] Soto, *In quartum Sententiarum*, p. 303, col. 2: "*Videtur enim Paul 1 Cor. 5 reclamare dicens:* Quid enim mihi de iis qui foris sunt iudicare? Nam eos, qui foris sunt Deus iudicabit. *Quasi dicat: Eorum iudicium, qui in Ecclesiae societatem non sunt recepti, Deo reservandum est. Unde colligit, quod licet Ecclesia in potentia, et habitu iurisdictionem habeat in omne orbem si fidem susceperit, actu tamen vim coactivam exercere non potest, nisi in eos, qui eam sua sponte susceperint.*"

[217] Soto, *In quartum Sententiarum*, p. 309, col. 2.

4

The Politics of Natural Law at Valladolid, 1550–1551

In the spring of 1550, the Holy Roman Emperor Charles V, King of Spain, ordered the immediate suspension of all *conquistas* across the Atlantic. A council of fourteen theologians, jurists, and officials of the royal court would gather at the chapel of the Dominican college of San Gregorio in Valladolid in Spain between 1550 and 1551 to evaluate the conduct of war and conquest in the Indies.[1] The crisis revealed in the imperial conscience two clearly opposed positions concerning proper evangelization thereby exposing the ambivalent core of infidel rights beginning with Pope Innocent IV during the Middle Ages. It was an acute moment of debate over the meaning of the Alexandrine papal bull, *Inter caetera*. Did the papal letter justify Spanish rule over the infidel peoples of the Indies? The contrasting positions were represented by two impressive figures of Renaissance Spain: the royal biographer and humanist translator, Juan Ginés de Sepúlveda (1490–1573), and the Dominican missionary and canon lawyer, Bishop Bartolomé de las Casas.

It would be remiss to read the Valladolid junta as a conflict between Sepúlveda's realism versus Las Casas's rationalism. These IR categories blunt the conceptual range of the religious legal culture of sixteenth-century Catholic Spain. Contrary to conventional history or popular accounts, like Jean-Claude Carrière's drama *La Controverse de Valladolid*, the debate was also not about the humanity of the Indians. Rather, the ideological struggle concerned infidel rights, the fruition of a centuries' long dispute about religious wars against infidels in Christendom and now in the Indies. The extent of Christian jurisdiction over unbelievers outside European territories was the defining political issue of the junta. Domingo de Soto, a council member

[1] For exclusive book-length treatments of the dispute, see, respectively, Lewis Hanke, *All Mankind is One* (Northern Illinois University Press, 1974) and Jean Dumont, *La Vraie controverse de Valladolid* (Criterion, 1995).

asked to summarize the contrasting positions of Sepúlveda and especially Las Casas, provided the state of the royal question as confessor to Emperor Charles: "Is it lawful for Your Highness to wage war against those Indians prior to the preaching of the faith in order to subjugate them to your Empire so that, once they are subjects, they can learn more easily and conveniently about their errors and the truth of Christianity through the teaching of the Gospel?"[2] Put more succinctly: Was the religious coercion of infidels by means of missionary war lawful? The Spanish theocratic universalists had been arguing in the affirmative following the logic of the Requirement. Sepúlveda shared their aims but developed an imperial humanist answer. Most Spanish Dominican theologians and missionaries in the New World were at complete odds with this violent method of evangelization.

The Valladolid responses to this contentious question brought into perspicuous view two incompatible doctrines concerning the lawful spread of Christianity and its moral norms. With deep roots in the Latin West, each doctrine, espoused respectively by Sepúlveda and Las Casas, relied on a different model of evangelization and understanding of ecclesiastical power. Las Casas, as we saw in the previous chapter, adhered to an apostolic ethic of peaceful evangelization, or the only way of teaching true religion through gentle persuasion. When he interpreted Pope Alexander's "concession" to the Crown and its right to preach (*derecho para predicar*), he was clear that it had to abide by "all the means proportionate and necessary for preaching," which excluded "war, theft, imprisoning, and killing."[3]

Sepúlveda, in contrast, recognized two different methods of bringing the Gospel to the Indies. One strategy was long, arduous and risky because it required a slow process of admonition and teaching. In what must have been a personal jab at Las Casas during the junta, Sepúlveda referred to a Dominican missionary who had been killed by natives on the Florida coast the previous year. Although never mentioning him by name, this would have been none other than Friar Luis Cáncer, a polyglot whose skills had directly assisted Las Casas during the 1530s in the peaceful evangelization of a hostile region of northern Guatemala later known as Verapaz (or "True

[2] Soto, *Sumario*, in *Relecciones y opúsculos*, p. 204: "*[S]i es lícito a Su Majestad hacer guerra a aquellos indios antes que se predique la fé, para sujetarlos a su Imperio y que, después de sujetados, puedan más fácil y cómodamente ser enseñados y alumbrados, por la doctrina Evangélica, del conocimiento de sus errores y de la verdad cristiana.*"

[3] Las Casas, *Aquí se contiene una disputa o controversia*, in *Tratados de Fray Bartolomé de las Casas*, I, rep. 12, p. 429: "*[S]olo tenemos derecho o precepto para les predicar, y para todos los medios de predicación y ley evangélica proporcionables y necesarios, dentro de los cuales no se contienen ni entra el guerrear, robar, captivar, y matar.*"

Peace").[4] Sepúlveda mentioned the tragic death of Las Casas's friend, ignoring the case of Verapaz, to make the searing point that such a risky method was ineffective because it lacked the necessary pairing of preachers with soldiers ready for war.[5] Alternatively, Sepúlveda advanced a preferable strategy easier, more efficient, and even advantageous to barbarians – the way of political subjugation through missionary warfare. According to this view, the papal "donation" licensed the conquest of barbarians first, followed then by preaching.

The proper method of evangelization was not the only difference between Sepúlveda and Las Casas. Each one interpreted natural law and the law of nations for divergent political purposes in the Indies. Natural law has always admitted of rival traditions, along with various definitions and meanings.[6] However, the tendency among IR scholars has been to treat natural law in ambivalent yet homogenous terms. In the English school, for example, Hedley Bull regarded the natural law with its attendant notion of universal society among Spanish late scholastics as a Janus-faced concept. On the one hand, the natural law generated "a weapon with which to combat conceptions of obligation that treated non-Christian or non-European peoples as devoid of rights." On the other, asserted unilaterally, it also provided "a rationale for forcing non-European peoples into commercial and diplomatic intercourse against their will."[7] Martin Wight also shared this ambivalence about natural law, qualifying his appreciation of the Spanish Dominicans with the proviso that theorists of rationalism did not endorse equal rights, but appropriate rights based on political trusteeship.[8]

Instead of thinking about natural law as a Janus-faced monolith, this chapter clarifies the contrasting politics of natural law at Valladolid among its key interlocutors. Sepúlveda turned the natural law and the law of nations into a comparative benchmark for identifying Amerindian irrationality and

4 For more on this important episode in Las Casas's life, see Benno Biermann, "Bartolomé de Las Casas and Verapaz," in *Bartolomé de Las Casas in History*, pp. 443–484.

5 Juan Ginés de Sepúlveda, *Aquí se contiene una disputa*, in *Tratados*, I, obj. 12, p. 327. Sepúlveda also rejected the Dominican plan to send preachers without soldiers to Florida, *Demócrates segundo*, ed. Angel Losada (CSIC, 1951), pp. 72–73.

6 For attention to divergent views of natural law in thinking about international relations, see William Bain, "Rival Traditions of Natural Law: Martin Wight and the Theory of International Society," *International History Review* 36, no. 5 (2014). With respect to divergent theological and philosophical views of natural law from the Middle Ages to the modern era, see Jean Porter, *Nature as Reason: A Thomistic Theory of the Natural Law* (Grand Rapids, MI: Eerdmans, 2005), chap. 1.

7 Bull, "The Emergence of a Universal International Society," in *The Expansion of International Society*, p. 120.

8 Wight, *International Theory*, p. 79.

justifying the politics of colonial dispossession in the spirit of the ancient Roman Empire. On this imperial-humanist view, natural law and the law of nations were reducible to a timeless code of precepts emanating from God and enshrined in a civilized society possessing the wisdom to judge, and the power to improve, lesser peoples. Las Casas, in sharp contrast, deployed natural law and the law of nations in a critical mode to explicate native political resistance toward Spanish aggression. For the Dominican friar, these universal laws were expressions of human reason present among diverse peoples but also potent sources for safeguarding subjective rights.

The junta at Valladolid was a defining moment in the history of Christian–infidel relations, and therefore international legal thought in the West. It did not establish a transatlantic treaty between different peoples, neither did it construct a mutually agreed upon arrangement of laws and institutions binding Europeans and non-Europeans. Nevertheless, amidst an intercontinental crisis of conscience culminating at the junta, Spanish theologians generated an inclusive, flexible, and reflexive regime of law based on common humanity and universal society to morally recognize the worth, and juridically protect the rights, of non-European individuals and peoples confronted with European colonialism. As we observed in the previous chapter, this crucible of conflict in the New World did not yield a formal or a conventional system establishing international law. Rather, what emerged was an enduring normative commitment to the idea and practice of world order with legal ramifications for protecting the subjective rights of non-European unbelievers from foreign and domestic tyranny. The Spanish contributions to international legal thought become more conspicuous in the context of the Valladolid junta, which retained an ambivalent legacy for early modern and modern discussions of European colonialism considered in the next chapter.

BISHOP LAS CASAS AND THE VALLADOLID JUNTA

Educated in theology, philosophy and letters at Alcalá and Bologna, respectively, Juan Ginés de Sepúlveda (1490–1573) imbibed a brand of humanism that attempted to retrieve a classical warrior ethic of Roman glory similar to Machiavelli and in contrast to Erasmianism. According to Machiavelli's realist humanism, effective politics utilized force to impose fear and motivate respect toward civil institutions and rulers, as the "armed prophets" Moses, Romulus, and Theseus had victoriously done in founding their societies.[9] Sepúlveda embraced this coercive model of politics by placing the Roman

9 Niccolò Machiavelli, *The Prince*, trans. Peter Bondanella (Oxford University Press, 2005), p. 22.

Empire at its center, yet he did so from his Spanish Catholic cultural and legal ambit. Consequently, he did not espouse pagan republicanism within an Italian city-state as did Machiavelli, but rather Christian colonialism within a transatlantic empire. Best known for his translation of Aristotle's *Politics* into Ciceronian Latin, Sepúlveda's expert knowledge of classical languages earned him the respect of popes, kings, and theologians. Emperor Charles appointed Sepúlveda as his official chronicler and chaplain. The Cordoban humanist would compose both a voluminous imperial biography of Charles and a Latin account of the Spanish conquest of the New World entitled *De orbe novo* in which the armed prophet Hernán Cortés represented the newfound glory of Spain's overseas empire.

In August of 1550, Sepúlveda delivered his basic arguments for missionary war and conquest of the Indies for about three hours before the royal council at Valladolid. He marshalled an authoritative list of theological sources including Scripture, Augustine, Gregory the Great, and Aquinas. Yet Pope Innocent IV provided him the most authoritative canon legal opinion on missionary war. Apparently, the jurists of the council were unanimously in favor of the canonistic opinion of the Crusade decretal *Quod super his*, which stipulated the standard causes of war against infidels.[10] This is a crucial point since standard treatments of Sepúlveda's defense overemphasize the doctrine of Aristotelian natural slavery to the exclusion of his canon legal arguments thus overlooking the justificatory role of the latter.[11]

According to Soto's *Sumario*, Sepúlveda identified four causes of war applicable to the case of the Indies, each of which rested on the difference of religion between Christianity and paganism.[12] (1) For the punishment of sins *contra natura*, or against natural law, like idolatry and cannibalism; (2) on the basis of inferiority, infidel barbarians must naturally submit to the superior rule of virtuous Christians; (3) for preventing injuries against the natives as seen in human sacrifice; (4) for removing obstacles and securing a path for Christian preaching to facilitate conversion. Each one of these causes was already contained in his earlier dialogical treatise on war entitled *Democrates secundus* (Sp. *Demócrates segundo*), or *Democrates alter, sive de justis belli causis apud Indos* (c. 1545). The causes were all reducible to a single overarching rationale for imperial expansion: the political enforcement of natural

[10] Angel Losada, *Juan Ginés de Sepúlveda* (CSIC, 1973), p. 209.

[11] See, for example, Brading, *The First America*, p. 1: "[T]he central issue at Valladolid was Sepúlveda's Aristotelian thesis that the natives of America were slaves by nature and hence unfit to govern themselves." In Hanke's *All Mankind is One* there is not a single mention of the canon legal dispute concerning the rights of infidels.

[12] Soto, *Sumario*, p. 205.

law on barbarian infidels by a superior civilization. Sepúlveda's traditional legal justification of punishing infidels through war had already been exploited by theocratic universalists like Palacios Rubios and Hernán Cortés. But it was Sepúlveda's reinterpretation of the right of war according to imperial humanism that laid an ideological path for legal and philosophical arguments used in early modern European expansion.

What made the Indians across the Atlantic appear as "barbarians" to Sepúlveda was their inability to live "according to natural reason" demonstrated by their "publicly-approved evil customs."[13] They were inferior peoples trapped in vices, which had become like second nature. They were still members of humanity, however. Belief in the shared humanity between Christians and barbarian infidels was presumed in the Alexandrine title of inculcating the faith to all peoples, which also sanctioned the natural law's universal jurisdiction over everyone. The humanity of the Indians was therefore never in question at Valladolid, despite Sepúlveda's earlier vituperative rhetoric about them as "*homunculi*," or halflings deprived of culture.[14] Such crude expressions, wedded to an Aristotelian doctrine of natural inferiority, was the key factor preventing the dialogue's approval for publication from the universities of Salamanca and Alcalá.[15] As a point of heresy, it would find a receptive audience neither among officials at Valladolid nor at the Council of Trent. Sepúlveda had to change strategies at Valladolid to overcome the suspicion of denying Indian humanity. Missionary warfare was a more convincing, traditional way to dispossess native sovereignty.

Sepúlveda had already acknowledged in his *Democrates secundus* that Christians and pagans possess a common humanity. Infidels "are called our fellows and brothers, and are sheep of the same shepherd, although not of the same flock. For there is '*the same Lord of all, generous to all who call on him*', '*who desires everyone to be saved and to come to the knowledge of the truth*'."[16] The Spanish humanist framed his arguments for conquest within the acceptable moral paradigm of theocratic world order attentive to the rights of infidels, despite the radical curtailment of those rights. Similar to Palacios Rubios, he disagreed with extreme hierocrats who believed that pagans were "not true and legitimate rulers and owners of their things by reason of their unbelief." Sepúlveda would say, beyond Palacios Rubios, that legitimate infidel rule, and not merely infidel possessions, remained in effect even after

13 Sepúlveda, *Aquí se contiene una disputa*, obj. 8, p. 311.
14 Sepúlveda, *Demócrates segundo*, p. 35.
15 Pereña, "La intervencíon de España en América," in *De bello contra insulanos* (CSIC, 1972), p. 49.
16 Sepúlveda, *Demócrates segundo*, p. 76. Romans 10:12 and 1 Timothy 2:4.

the coming of Christ. This permitted him to take a stance on European expansion quite distinct from theocratic papalism. St. Paul gave him biblical authorization for imperial rule in Romans 13, which expressed a new humanist horizon for colonialism: even pagans can have "imperial administration over the whole earth" (*imperio orbis terrarium administrabatur*).[17] The target of his Amerindian censures endorsing dispossession did not rest on paganism as such, but crimes associated with pagan unbelief. The crimes most relevant to the Indies, as evidenced in the Old Testament and politicized by Spanish reports, were the worship of idols and human sacrifice. Both sins were "contrary to the judgments of reason" and therefore violations of natural law.[18]

On imperial-humanist grounds, Sepúlveda claimed that weaker and inferior peoples marked by incivility must naturally submit to wiser and more humane civilizations, Christian or pagan. The Roman Empire did just that for the benefit of barbarians, as Western Christians had long observed. By means of good laws and virtues in accordance with eternal law and natural law, the *pax Romana* historically eradicated crude customs and corrected vices among barbarians.[19] This was the imperial civilizing blueprint for Spanish conquest of the Indies, the only means of facilitating the effective preaching of the Gospel in the lands donated by Pope Alexander VI. The papal donation was therefore "a mere confirmatory act" subsequent and subordinate to a superior sovereign's natural right of dominating barbarian idolaters.[20] That the papacy merely confirmed a universal natural power to enforce justice residing in a superior civilization independent of spiritual authority represented Sepúlveda's important step toward the secularization of natural law through imperial politics.[21]

The day after Sepúlveda spoke before the council, Bishop Las Casas spent the next five reading his grueling defense of the Indians. Gathered at the *junta* as official advisors were sympathetic Dominican theologians along with Soto from Salamanca and Valladolid, Melchor Cano and Bartolomé de Carranza (d. 1576). One can only surmise that Vitoria would have been directly involved. Unfortunately, he had fatally succumbed to an illness in 1546 so his final views on the matter will never be known. Cano, a theological force of

17 Sepúlveda, *Demócrates segundo*, p. 82.

18 Sepúlveda, *Demócrates segundo*, p. 42.

19 Sepúlveda, *Demócrates segundo*, pp. 31–32. See Lupher, *Romans in a New World*, pp. 112–122, for more on Sepúlveda's political use of the Roman imperial legacy.

20 Brading, *The First America*, p. 87.

21 Sepúlveda inhabited a Spanish imperial theocratic ambit already outlined by a jurist of the royal court, Miguel de Ulzurrun, who defended the Roman imperial title of Charles V over the whole world in 1525. See Lupher, *Romans in a New World*, pp. 46–49.

the Renaissance and humanism in his own right, now held the *Prima* Chair position of theology at Salamanca after Vitoria. Sepúlveda was greatly displeased with the strong Dominican theological presence as he indicated in a personal letter composed a few months before the first session of the junta. He feared that with none in Spain "more opposed" to the conquests than the Dominicans, the council's judgment might be unfairly biased.[22] Sepúlveda's concerns were reasonable considering that his *Democrates secundus* was a rebuttal to Spanish Dominican rejections of missionary war and the perpetuity of the *encomienda* system of forced labor.

The conflict between the outspoken Dominicans and the royal partisans of conquest precipitated the junta at Valladolid, which hurled the irrepressible personalities of Bishop Las Casas and Sepúlveda to the center of an intercontinental crisis. Valladolid was the result of Dominican persistence to undermine colonial dispossession in the New World by dissolving the *encomienda* system of forced labor and prohibiting missionary warfare. Their decades' long public advocacy for the natives beginning on Española with the 1511 sermon had already merited two significant victories within the Church and Crown thereby influencing royal law and papal policy. Pope Paul III's "new" decretal *Sublimis Deus* (1537), as the canon lawyer Las Casas often termed it, was a Roman ecclesiastical response to Dominican eyewitness testimony and letters concerning the violent exploitation of Amerindians in the name of religion.[23] Emperor Charles's promulgation of the New Laws of 1542, which placed native peoples under the direct protection of the Crown and terminated the perpetuity of the *encomienda* and the enslavement of Indians, was also result of Las Casas's tireless Dominican interventions at the Council of the Indies.[24]

The Dominican pursuit of restitution and remedies for the Indians was indeed significant and unmatched. At the core of the new royal and papal policies was greater recognition of the dignity and rights of non-Europeans inside and outside Christian jurisdiction. In the words of Pope Paul III, all the native peoples of the New World were fully capable of reaching "the invisible highest good" and seeing God "face to face" through the gift of faith. Christians were to bring the Gospel to the Indian nations by attracting them through good example and respecting their liberty and ownership of things. Any other means by force and subjugation of the Indians through war and

22 Francisco Castilla Urbano, "La consideración del indio en los escritos sepulvedianos posteriores a la Junta de Valladolid," *Cuadernos americanos*, 26.4 (2012), 57–58.

23 Parish, *Las Casas en México*, pp. 15–22.

24 Clayton, *Bartolomé de las Casas*, chap. 10.

bondage was the work of Satan. At Valladolid, Las Casas cited Paul III's letter to demonstrate how Sepúlveda's arguments have "gone totally astray," ignoring the apostolic method of preaching to the Indians and the freedom and property "that nature has granted them for their lawful use and enjoyment."[25] The Dominican Bernardino de Minaya, who went to Rome to inform the Pope of the atrocities in the Indies, had also won a brief from Paul III in 1537. This short letter entitled *Pastorale officium* promoted the Dominican practice of excommunicating any colonial Christian who enslaved the Indians and robbed them of their possessions.[26]

The New Laws of 1542 were the strongest royal measure ever taken against the *encomienda* system and its private beneficiaries during the early colonization period. The aim of the New Laws was to advance the "good treatment and protection of the Indians," starting with a full-scale reform of the Council of Indies to eliminate bribery and to always inquire judicially about any Spanish abuses.[27] The royal laws stipulated that there would be no future for the *encomiendas*. When the holders of *encomiendas* die, the Indians retain the status of "free vassals" before the Crown, meriting the exact treatment as Spaniards. Additionally, no longer would wars and exchanges be able to justify the replenishment of forced labor. The ordinances would now protect native inhabitants from labor services, including mining and pearl fishing, which were "against their will" (*contra su voluntad*).[28]

Despite these notable gains in justice for the Indians, enforceability and longevity were a different matter. The papal letter of *Sublimis Deus* may have kept its doctrinal course. However, Pope Paul III's brief on excommunication *Pastorale officium* became a quick target of imperial censure. The letter riskily aligned the papacy with Charles's now overturned 1530 antislavery law, which had prohibited "all of his subjects from daring to submit the Indians of the West and South to slavery, or depriving them of their goods."[29] In accordance with the system of royal patronage, the Emperor, fearing papal subterfuge, was able to get Paul III to revoke the brief. Additionally, Fr. Bernardino de Minaya was placed under arrest.[30]

The New Laws of 1542, which Las Casas had directly influenced through his native advocacy back in Spain, were an extraordinary achievement in

25 Las Casas, *In Defense of the Indians*, chap. 12, pp. 100–103.

26 Pope Paul III, *Pastorale officium* (1537), in *Las Casas en Mexico*, pp. 304–305.

27 Hanke, *The Spanish Struggle for Justice*, p. 91.

28 *Leyes nuevas de Indias* (1542), in *Teoría y leyes de la conquista*, Segunda Edición (Universidad de Sevilla, 2008), pp. 428–440.

29 Pope Paul III, *Pastorale officium*, p. 304.

30 Gutiérrez, *Las Casas*, pp. 308–310.

principle though not in practice. At the prospect of colonial rebellion, *encomenderos* and civil administrators alike immediately flouted the royal laws. Furthermore, the new ordinances did not provide extensive enough measures restricting conquest and war. Las Casas and Rodrigo de Ladrada, another Dominican friar who had assisted him with Cáncer in the evangelization of Verapaz, submitted a petition (or *memorial*) to Emperor Charles in 1543. They petitioned the Crown to make the prohibition of future conquests more explicit in order to avoid both further abuses of natives and scandal to the faith. The Dominicans pleaded for the Crown to recognize that all the *encomiendas, repartimientos*, and wars were unjust and destructive to the native peoples. Only attacked and aggrieved Indians had waged a just war (*justa guerra*) against Spanish Christians due to their suffering of oppression, theft, and death. Since justice was on the indigenous side, it demanded full restitution from the Spaniards.[31]

When Las Casas tried to implement the New Laws as Bishop of Chiapa from 1545 to 1547, he had to contend with opposition from private, civil, and ecclesiastical parties. He drafted his "Twelve Rules for Confessors" (*Confesionario*) during this time, which stipulated, just like the petition to the King, the abolition of the *encomiendas* and all wars of conquest, identifying both as unjust and contrary to reason. Specifically, the seventh rule of the *Confesionario* was unyielding in its indictment of the whole affair, and therefore extremely contentious: "[A]ll the things that have been done throughout the Indies with the entrance of the Spaniards into each province . . . have been contrary to natural law and the law of nations (*derecho natural y derecho de las gentes*) and also against divine law, and, therefore, is entirely unjust, iniquitous, tyrannical, and deserving of all eternal fire."[32] Consequently, every Indian, held captive by forced labor, had to be freed in order to begin the process of granting them full restitution.

With the sheer lack of colonial administrative enforcement of the New Laws, Las Casas turned to spiritual power through the sacrament of penance and the ecclesiastical court instead. The *Confesionario* was the singular New World manual for pursuing native restitution and it immediately caught the attention of royal partisans of conquest back in Spain. At the behest of Sepúlveda, the Council of the Indies confiscated all existing copies of the Las Casas's *Confesionario*. Sepúlveda even went to the Council of Castile in 1548 to charge Las Casas with high treason (*lèse majesté*) for challenging the legitimate rule of the Spanish Crown over the Indies. Concurrently, Las Casas

31 Las Casas, "Memorial al Emperador" (1543), in *OC*, vol. 13, pp. 144–145.

32 *Confesionario*, in *To Heaven or Hell*, pp. 85–86.

solicited the University of Salamanca to ban publication of Sepúlveda's *Democrates secundus*.[33] Thus the royal stage was set at Valladolid for the enigmatic confrontation between these two mortal adversaries and their diametrically opposed writings on the affair of the Indies, *Democrates secundus* and the *Confesionario*.

When Las Casas spoke during the first meeting of Valladolid in 1550, he directly addressed the imperial mission to civilize through subjugation contained in Sepúlveda's just war arguments from *Democrates secundus*. Yet Las Casas was not privy to the first session in which Sepúlveda presented his official position before the Council.[34] As a result, Las Casas spent several chapters at the beginning of his *Apologia* saying "Adios, Aristotle!" and the doctrine of enslaving barbarians.[35] A grand provocateur, Las Casas had already condemned the pagan philosopher to hellfire years earlier in his struggle against Spanish colonial sympathizers of Aristotelian natural slavery.[36] The mistaken impression resulting from commentators reading Las Casas has been that Valladolid focused on the question of the humanity of the Indians because the debate began there. Although Sepúlveda defended a geopolitical account of servitude similar to Mair, he did so with almost no emphasis on Aristotle and relied more on Aquinas's *Commentary on the Politics* and Gonzalo Fernández de Oviedo's *Historia General y Natural de las Indias*.[37] The definitive rhetorical strategy of Sepúlveda at Valladolid turned on the doctrine of missionary war and religious coercion that could justify subjugation of barbarian idolaters and their enslavement as a punishment for sins against the natural law.[38]

Even with the rhetorical shift in Sepúlveda's position at Valladolid, the imperial humanist's earlier writings contained far more documentary ammunition for conquest based on missionary war than natural slavery anyhow. Las Casas did not ignore this fact. In the spirit of *De unico vocationis modo*, the Dominican bishop directed most of his Valladolid defense of the Indians to anathematizing the doctrine of missionary war underlying the Spanish conquests, which he likened to the violent political expansion of Islam. Importantly, Las Casas still inhabited the Christian just war tradition even

33 Orique, *To Heaven or Hell*, pp. 43–44.

34 Soto, *Sumario*, p. 205.

35 Las Casas, *In Defense of the Indians*, chap. 3, p. 40. The Latin puts it: "*Valeat Aristoteles!*"

36 Las Casas, *Historia de las Indias*, III, cap. 149, p. 343: "*el Filósofo era gentil y está ardiendo en los infiernos.*"

37 Sepúlveda, *Apologia*, in *Obras completas*, III (Ayuntamiento de Pozoblanco, 1997) no. 4, p. 197; *Aquí se contiene una disputa*, obj. 8, p. 311.

38 Pagden, *Fall of Natural Man*, p. 112; Adorno, *Polemics of Possession*, p. 115.

as he attempted to purge it of the crusader heritage of missionary war.[39] In his repudiation of the injustice of the African slaving expeditions conducted by the Portuguese, he still maintained the permissibility of war against infidels in specific cases involving self-defense, protection of one's kingdoms and lands, and the malicious persecution of Christians without legitimate cause.[40]

The bishop-lawyer delivered before the council the same simple yet resounding message from his earlier treatise on peaceful evangelization: "To subjugate infidels by war in order that they may accept the faith is evil."[41] His interrogative indictment of Sepúlveda and the conquistadors was particularly ringing: "What does the Gospel have do with firearms?"[42] Las Casas availed himself of voluminous biblical teachings, writings of Church Fathers, scholastic theology, and ancient philosophy to construct the sixty-three chapters of his *Apologia*. Wherein he responded to Sepúlveda's misleading interpretations of Augustine, Gregory the Great, and Aquinas head on. He took special interest in refuting the errors of Aristotle on natural slavery and Pope Innocent IV on natural law, but also the recent egregious accounts of the natives provided by the Scottish theologian Mair and the Spanish chronicler Fernández de Oviedo.

Proficient in the *ius commune* tradition, Las Casas also had Roman and canonistic legal sources at his fingertips. His juridical defense of the Indians targeted Sepúlveda's imperial civilizing mission, "[N]ot even a truly wise man may force an ignorant barbarian to submit to him, especially by forfeiting that one's liberty, without doing injury. This the poor Indians suffer, with extreme injury, against all divine and human rights and against the natural law itself."[43] The bishop pressed further, declaring even more controversially:

> Since, therefore, every nation by the eternal law has a ruler or prince, it is wrong for one nation to attack another under pretext of being superior in wisdom or to overthrow other kingdoms ... Hence every nation, no matter how barbaric, has the right to defend itself against a more civilized one that wants to conquer it and take away its freedom. And, moreover, it can lawfully punish with death the more civilized as a savage and cruel aggressor against

39 For a concise overview of Las Casas's place within the Christian just war tradition, see Daniel R. Brunstetter's chapter in *Just War Thinkers: From Cicero to the 21st Century*, eds. Daniel Brunstetter and Cian O'Driscoll (Routledge, 2017), pp. 92–104.

40 For a translation of the relevant passage of Las Casas from *Historia de las Indias*, see Document 22 of *Bartolomé de las Casas and the Defense of Amerindian Rights: A Brief History with Documents*, eds. Lawrence A. Clayton and David M. Lantigua (University of Alabama Press, 2020).

41 Las Casas, *In Defense of the Indians*, chap. 51, pp. 319–320.

42 Las Casas, *In Defense of the Indians*, chap. 25, p. 173.

43 Las Casas, *In Defense of the Indians*, chap. 4, p. 46.

the law of nature. And this war is certainly more just than the one that, under the pretext of wisdom, is waged against them.[44]

Much like Vitoria, Las Casas was willing to concede barbarism here for the sake of argument, yet the descriptor had no effect on any barbarian's rightful claim of freedom and sovereignty guarded by natural law and the eternal law to resist "more civilized" aggressors. The justice of war was incontrovertibly on the side of the people defending their livelihood, not the allegedly superior culture expanding its rule. By appealing to natural law from the perspective of poor, innocent Indians, rather than imperial might, Las Casas offered a radical critique of any purported European right of war. If John Mair "were an Indian" (*si Indus esset*), Las Casas stingingly observed, he might recognize the injustice accurately.[45] The native right of resistance to foreign tyranny grounded in legal sources would occupy much of Las Casas's mature writings after Valladolid, a point we shall return to in Chapter 6. As practitioner and theorist, he therefore belongs to the annals of international legal and political thought (see Figure 4.1).[46]

Bishop Las Casas would never actually portray the natives as barbaric and vicious, but meek and amicable and capable of retaliation following Spanish aggression. His major three-volume work known as the *Apologética historia sumaria*, composed a couple of years after Valladolid, set out to demonstrate the rationality of political life and religious practices among various Amerindian societies against their European-cultured despisers. It did so on the Christian Stoic premise that "all humankind is one," regardless of cultural achievements, sharing in common reason whereby "everyone possesses his own knowledge, will, and free choice as formed to the image and likeness of God."[47] Natural reason's divine image also contains a religious component, which "dictates, moves, and impels humans to submit themselves to some superior who can make up for their defects and faults" by helping and healing them.[48] The religious and political lives of the Amerindians designated that they were fully capable of receiving the Gospel peacefully without colonial subjugation.

A critical claim of this proto-anthropological work, written to expand his arguments from Valladolid, was that New World native societies were

44 Las Casas, *In Defense of the Indians*, chap. 4, pp. 47–48.

45 Las Casas, *In Defense of the Indians*, chap. 53, p. 329.

46 The regrettable exclusion of Las Casas as political theorist from standard historical treatments of international legal thought was a concern of Lewis Hanke, Latin Americanist founder of the Hispanic Reading Room at the Library of Congress, *The Spanish Struggle for Justice*, p. 153.

47 Las Casas, *Apologética historia*, cap. 48, pp. 536–537.

48 Las Casas, *Apologética historia*, cap. 72, p. 639.

FIGURE 4.1 "Portrait of Bartolomé de las Casas." (Source: Getty Images/DEA PICTURE LIBRARY/Contributor)

"ordered creations of natural reason" rivaling classical cultures of the Old World.[49] Over 240 chapters of the *Apologética historia* were dedicated to showing how "Indian peoples" (*gentes Indianas*) fulfilled qualities of the Aristotelian political taxonomy. Las Casas argued that Amerindians such as

[49] Sabine MacCormack, *Religion in the Andes* (Princeton University Press, 1991), p. 211.

the Aztecs and Incas had surpassed classical pagan cultures of Europe "beyond comparison in their supreme use of judgment," especially in matters of religion.[50] Contrastingly, the ancient Romans, even more than the Egyptians and Greeks, publicly celebrated as gods objects "so inferior and vile and against all natural reason" and did so "presuming that they were wiser" than the other peoples they subjugated.[51] The Spanish Dominican bishop engaged here in a "tour de force of transvaluation," unseating the humanist civilizational appraisal of the Roman Empire and elevating the Indian peoples in its place.[52]

If the *Apologética historia sumaria* was a work of ethnographic history and comparative theology presenting the rational agency of Amerindian cultures over pagan Rome, the *Apologia* at Valladolid supplied the theological and juridical arguments for native resistance according to natural law, human law, and divine law. The *Apologia* began with a treatment of the barbarian category and its political deployment by Aristotle to denote the natural slave and uncivilized peoples. Las Casas did not deny the possibility that barbarians in the strict classical sense might exist, referring to fierce and cruel groups who, governed by neither law nor ruler, have no marriage, no trade, and no alliances. Even so, these extremely rare examples of "strangers to reason" who do not live in any organized manner through the common practices of the law of nations cannot be reduced to the unpropertied status of a natural chattel-like slave.[53] These groups, inhabiting a primitive-like state, were to be respected as naturally free members of universal society, and potential members of the Church. After all, they are "created in God's image. They are not so forsaken by divine providence that they are incapable of attaining Christ's kingdom. They are our brothers, redeemed by Christ's most precious blood, no less than the wisest and most learned men in the whole world."[54] Alternatively, there was nothing in principle excluding Christians from being considered barbarians, morally speaking, whenever they engaged in cruel and heinous activity. Like idolatry, the term barbarian had critical moral purchase for Las Casas, serving the reflexive aim of indicting Spanish abuses. Spanish colonial Christians who mistreated the Indians through brutal war and massacre were even "worse than barbarians."[55]

50 Las Casas, *Apologética historia*, cap. 193, p. 1263.

51 Las Casas, *Apologética historia*, cap. 118, p. 858; *In Defense of the Indians*, chap. 5.

52 Lupher, *Romans in a New World*, p. 138.

53 Las Casas, *In Defense of the Indians*, chap. 2.

54 Las Casas, *In Defense of the Indians*, chap. 3, p. 39.

55 Las Casas, *In Defense of the Indians*, chap. 5, p. 53.

But it was the theological account of the barbarian that could finally wrest the idea from its ancient political philosophical usage, used to justify imperial expansion. In the Christian theological sense, true barbarians were not those considered backwards or wild, but were those who simply did not acknowledge Christ as Lord. Departing from the classical philosophical view represented by Aristotle, and now Mair and Sepúlveda, Las Casas like Vitoria appropriated a theological interpretation of the barbarian as any infidel outside the Church.[56] This point was strategically important because of the preceding Christian legal tradition of infidel rights. Relatedly, the attempt to intervene politically in the affairs of barbarians or infidels because of their alleged incivility or idolatry required legitimate jurisdiction, which Christians simply lacked in the New World. The setting of limits and boundaries to Christian jurisdiction, whether of princes or popes, thereby opened a greater space for recognizing the negative and positive rights of infidels.

The nub of Sepúlveda's argument for conquest, as noted, was the traditional medieval canonistic cause of punishing infidels for infractions of the natural law. This rationale, considered at length in Chapter 2, legitimated widespread Spanish possession of the Indies. Sepúlveda was well aware of this homogenous cause of war when he defended the common canonistic opinion of Pope Innocent IV at Valladolid. "By this cause alone of not guarding the natural law or being idolaters," he argued, European civilizations possess the right to punish and conquer inferior peoples outside Christendom.[57] Two essential proofs supported Las Casas's counterargument to constrain this overreaching theocratic claim about Christian jurisdiction in the Indies. One proof was ecclesiological. It focused on Aquinas's teaching on the mystical Body of Christ to discriminate between actual and potential membership in the Church. The other proof was the canon legal principle of spiritual immunity derived from St. Paul's First Letter to the Corinthians (5:12–13), which restricted judgment of those outside (Lt. *foris*) the Church. Both proofs, like Soto's *Commentary on Book Four of the Sentences*, had clear implications for properly interpreting the Alexandrine bull and providing moral theological grounds for a world order that affirmed infidel liberty and rights.

In Chapter six of the *Apologia*, Las Casas moved through the various categorical distinctions of infidels outlined by Cajetan. The relevant category of unbelievers who had never accepted the faith or lived under Christian rulers were not actually subject to Christ and the authority of the Church. Therefore,

56 Las Casas, *In Defense of the Indians*, chap. 5.

57 Sepúlveda, *Aquí se contiene una disputa*, obj. 7, p. 311: "*Porque aquellos doctores dicen que por sola esta causa de no guardar la ley de natura o ser idólatras pueden ser debellados y punidos.*"

they could not be punished "for any crime at all, no matter how atrocious it may be."[58] Although Christ possessed all power in heaven and on earth (Matthew 28:18), this power could not negate the natural right of freedom, since grace must respect the order of nature. According to Aquinas's teaching on the mystical Body of Christ with its scholastic act-potency distinction, everything in creation was subject to Christ, but not in the same way. Only when an unbeliever willingly embraces the faith and receives baptism do they become effective or actual subjects (*in actu*) of Christ's power and jurisdiction through the Church. Otherwise, they only remain potential subjects (*in potentia*) of Christ and the Church with the freedom of will remaining intact fully.[59]

Infidels outside the Church are potentially under the power of Christ and therefore subject, like everyone else, to the complete power of Christ at the eschatological judgment.[60] Las Casas extrapolated this teaching on the mystical Body of Christ from Aquinas's *Summa* and presented a scholastic theological conception of world order according to which the Church has power over creation supernaturally from Christ, "who does not force anyone," and naturally, from "the freedom of the will, which cannot be forced either."[61] In other words, the Church has a universal power and jurisdiction that remains ineffective apart from the free consent among individual persons. The role of the Church in safeguarding world order must therefore respect infidels in their "the freedom of the will to convert if they wish."[62]

Like the Salmantine Dominican theologians and in direct contrast to Sepúlveda and theocratic universalists, Las Casas fundamentally denied the ecclesiological basis for a universal authority, imperial or papal, possessing the punitive power to enforce the natural law over the world. If the Church were to extend such jurisdiction over the affairs of infidels across the Atlantic, it would assume an unbecoming power that only Christ as Lord could claim. Yet Christ did not even exercise such power during his earthly mission. Instead, he reserved it for the final divine judgement, when all power over good and evil acts would be rewarded or punished accordingly.[63] In the meantime, the Church had to wait patiently for the conversion of unbelievers according to every individual's freedom.

58 Las Casas, *In Defense of the Indians*, chap. 6, p. 55.
59 Aquinas, *ST*, III, q. 8, a. 3 *ad* 1.
60 Aquinas, *ST*, III, q. 59, a. 4 *ad* 2.
61 Las Casas, *In Defense of the Indians*, chap. 6, pp. 60–61.
62 Las Casas, *Aquí se contiene una disputa*, rep. 6, p. 371.
63 Las Casas, *In Defense of the Indians*, chap. 6, p. 56.

The second proof undermining idolatry as a cause of war was the canon legal principle restricting punitive judgment only to those within the Church, and letting God judge those outside.[64] Chapters seven through ten of the *Apologia* at Valladolid echoed Vitoria's all-important Pauline *foris* principle for prohibiting wars against idolatry in the New World with the support of Scripture, Church Fathers, and Church customs. Las Casas summarized his point: "It is not the business of the Church to uproot idolatry by force or to punish idolaters."[65] To punish idolaters outside the Church's competence would not only be a usurpation of power, it would also set up an obstacle to the proclamation of the Gospel, most likely inciting riot, sedition, and hatred toward the Christian faith.[66] Christ had entrusted his disciples with the power to preach only with gentleness, kindness, and benevolence. The proclamation of the Gospel to unbelievers must entail the dispensing of mercy and forgiveness of sins, not the threat of punishment through fear of war and death.

Las Casas, following Vitoria, deliberately extended the medieval canon legal principle of outsider immunity to Cajetan's new category of infidels. The principle of infidel immunity from coercion by Christian authorities must have been an astonishing claim at Valladolid before a Council familiar with the Requirement and the key justifications for the *conquistas*:

> Therefore when unbelievers, no matter how idolatrous or sinful they may be, who have not embraced the faith, and especially those who have not heard anything about it, but have their own lands, kingdoms, and territories separate from Christian lands, commit crimes and sins outside the boundaries and territory of the entire Church, its jurisdiction does not extend to them. It clearly follows then, that the Church and its members do not have the right to punish them for idolatry or any criminal or heinous deed, as long as it is committed precisely within the limits of their domains or their unbelief, as is the case with our Indians and other similar peoples.[67]

64 Soto's *Sumario* captured the interrelatedness of both proofs in Las Casas's defense at Valladolid, p. 215: "The reason there is no power to punish their [infidels] idolatry is because they are not within the Church's judicial court. Where he [Las Casas] expounds the authority of St. Paul from 1 Cor 5, *For why should judge those who are outside? Is it not your business to judge those within? God will judge those outside*. According to which he noted that, although to Jesus Christ, in terms of his humanity, all men are subject to him in potency (*potentia*), but not in act (*actu*). Which is to say, Christ did not take complete power over the world in act as a man over all men with regard to God, but rather for the sake of preaching and teaching the faith."

65 Las Casas, *In Defense of the Indians*, chap. 7, p. 65.

66 Las Casas, *In Defense of the Indians*, chap. 8, p. 72.

67 Las Casas, *In Defense of the Indians*, chap. 9, p. 84.

The meaning of the Alexandrine bull received further clarification from these ecclesiological and canonistic proofs against missionary war. As a bishop-theologian trained in canon law, Las Casas accepted the authoritative force of *Inter caetera*, interpreting it as a papal act of conceding Spain the title of preaching the Gospel in the Indies and superior jurisdiction of Spain if and only if the natives consented though this position would evolve and mature in his thought. The concluding five chapters of his *Apologia* juxtaposed his reading of the papal bull to Sepúlveda's colonialist interpretation.[68] Following his Dominican theological counterparts, the bull's execution under the Crown strictly had to abide by an apostolic ethic of evangelization and an understanding of ecclesiastical power denuded of jurisdictional authority over infidels of Cajetan's third category. Moreover, Pope Paul III's *Sublimis Deus* (1537) provided an additional hermeneutic for the Alexandrine bull. Las Casas argued: "Paul III expressly forbids these detestable wars that are waged against the Indians under the pretext of religion. He commands that they be led to the faith not by the terror of war but by the word of God and by holy living."[69]

Aside from serving as guides for properly interpreting the Alexandrine bull, the ecclesiological and canon legal proofs undermining the missionary rationale of the *conquistas* were also theological principles to affirm the liberty and immunity of the native peoples in matters of religion. The *foris* principle in Latin Christendom had established a negative right of immunity from coercion or nonintervention by Christians in the spiritual affairs of outsiders. This observation enabled Las Casas to establish canon legal precedent back in Europe for applying to the political case of the Indies not unlike Vitoria. Although infidels are subject to the same civil laws as Christians in Europe, when it comes to "religion and spiritual matters, no matter whether they be Jews, Mohammedans, or idolaters, they are in no way subject to the Church nor to her members, that is, Christian rulers. And therefore when they celebrate and observe their rites they cannot be punished by Christian rulers, for [the latter] lack jurisdiction in this area ... as is noted by the doctors in canon law."[70] Later in the defense, Las Casas explicitly extended this canonistic principle to the "Indians," who "are subject neither to us nor to the Church, since they are pagans who have lawful and free sovereigns in their own kingdoms. Therefore we cannot impose any kind of law on them."[71] The

68 Las Casas, *In Defense of the Indians*, chaps. 59–64.

69 Las Casas, *In Defense of the Indians*, chap. 62, p. 360.

70 Las Casas, *In Defense of the Indians*, chap. 6, pp. 54–55.

71 Las Casas, *In Defense of the Indians*, chap. 51, p. 320.

foris principle was a chief constraint on theocratic world order of the papalist or imperialist expression, shifting from a principle of toleration in Christendom to a principle of political independence in the New World.

However, Las Casas's argument did not stop at the level of constraining judgment over the spiritual and political affairs of infidels. Religion and the worship of God were basic constituents of every society and community. Human beings were not merely rational political animals, but also rational religious creatures seeking aid from a divine agent in the face of weakness, vulnerability, and defect. This anthropological datum offered an additional argument accounting for the positive expression of religion on the political level. Las Casas was keenly aware of the central importance of religious practices for any people's flourishing, and this further reinforced infidel political autonomy and self-rule. Cicero and Aquinas were crucial for thinking through this anthropological dimension.[72]

Las Casas combined these philosophical and theological observations of humanity's natural religious orientation with canon law to yield the following general argument protecting infidel immunity in religious matters not strictly as a negative right, but a positive one for promoting human society even among idolaters:

> Because nature itself teaches that the whole human race must worship God and because divine worship is made up of ceremonies, it follows that, just as men cannot live without the true God or a false god believed to be true, they cannot live without the exercise of some ceremonies, especially since the common opinion among the gentiles has been that the entire welfare of a commonwealth is preserved in happiness by means of ceremonies and sacrifices. Therefore, if against their wills we should completely abolish their ceremonies, they would have, in addition to the great number of other resulting, only an apparent adherence to the Catholic faith and the Christian religion, and we would appear to be openly compelling them to embrace that faith – and this is forbidden.[73]

Religious worship, a basic requirement for any society's welfare, inevitably varied according to the knowledge, customs, and civil laws of each people. Yet, as both Cicero and Aquinas agreed, worship was also a facet of natural law, belonging to unbelievers as much as Christians. Las Casas's recognition of the universality of man's religious nature was the preeminent basis for his

72 *De unico vocationis modo*, cap. 5, §6, p. 64. Citing Cicero, *The Laws*, 105; *In Defense of the Indians*, chap. 35, p. 230. Citing *ST*, II-II, q. 85, a. 1.

73 Las Casas, *In Defense of the Indians*, chap. 7, pp. 69–70.

affirmation of "natural human equality."[74] The argument of Bishop Las Casas was indeed polemical and controversial on this point, yet it was even more radical. The crux of the debate at Valladolid reached its zenith when Las Casas concluded from man's religious nature that everyone, even pagans, had a right to protect their religion from attack by aggressors seeking to vanquish it. Immunity from coercion in religious matters received its politically subversive force from the adjoining right of a people to defend themselves against a foreign tyrant.

If the natural law accounted for the injuries suffered by infidel natives at the hands of Spanish invaders, then the law of nations established the infidel right of waging war against them. Religion and the offering of sacrifices was a matter of both the natural law and, in accordance with Roman jurists, the law of nations.[75] From this reading, Bishop Las Casas arrived at bold conclusion about religion among infidels: "[T]hey are bound, without doubt, to defend the worship of their gods and their religion by going forth with their armies against all who attempt to take those things from them or injure them or prevent their sacrifices – to fight, kill, capture, and exercise all the rights consequent on a just war according to the law of nations."[76] Despite the falsity of pagan religion, Las Casas still supposed that infidels could be in probable error because of their civil laws and long-standing customs, and would therefore consider lawful war against anyone "in their own defense and that of their gods."[77]

Astonishingly, idolaters, in this case those occupying the Indies, "have probable cause to defend their religion," and are "bound by natural right" to do so.[78] That is because "all of us are naturally bound to love and serve God more than ourselves and, consequently, to defend the honor of God and divine worship even unto death." Given the fundamental natural equality and common humanity, Las Casas could assert, "there is no difference in obligation with respect to the true God, as seen among the Christians, and those who

74 Cary J. Nederman, "Civil Religion – Metaphysical, Not Political: Nature, Faith, and Communal Order in European Thought, c.1150–c.1550," *Journal of the History of Ideas* 74.1 (2013): 18. See also *Worlds of Difference: European Discourses of Toleration, c. 1100–1550* (Pennsylvania State University Press, 2000), chap. 7.

75 Las Casas, *In Defense of the Indians*, chap. 35, p. 230. Citing *Digest*, 1.1.2.

76 Las Casas, *In Defense of the Indians*, chap. 38, p. 244.

77 Las Casas, *In Defense of the Indians*, chap. 44, p. 282. For more on Las Casas's treatment of the rationality and error operative in Amerindian religion, especially human sacrifice, see Lantigua, "Religion within the Limits of Natural Reason: the Case of Human Sacrifice," in *Bartolomé de las Casas, O.P.: History, Philosophy, and Theology in the Age of European Expansion*, eds. David Orique and Rady Roldán-Figueroa (Brill, 2018), pp. 280–309.

78 Las Casas, *Aquí se contiene una disputa*, rep. 11, p. 407.

do not know, yet hold and esteem some god as if it were the true one." The bishop relied on the scholastic theological tradition to argue that, especially in religious matters, even an erroneous conscience must bind. The significance of this claim regarding the religious rights of both believers and unbelievers was profound. He remarked further:

> So idolaters esteem and learn to make those idols the true God, by serving and adoring them as they should be serving and adoring the true God . . . they also know by natural reason the first principle of human agency, which belongs to *synderesis* – that they should obey, honor, and serve God; and infidels possess this principle in its entirety [*y lo tengán integro los infieles*]. It is because of this false estimation and binding of conscience that they are bound to defend their supreme god or gods they believe to be the true God, and their religion [*son obligados a defender su dios o sus dioses que tienen por verdadero Dios, y su religión*]. Just as we Christians should defend our true God and the Christian religion, lest we fall into mortal sin.[79]

At Valladolid, Bishop Las Casas expressed the underlying natural principle of human reason to honor a supreme being and the right of defending religion against violent persecution. With a universal normative basis in rational nature, Christians and non-Christians rightly protect their religion from extermination. The juridical egalitarianism in religious matters is difficult to overstate here. In a brilliant rhetorical maneuver, Las Casas turned to Cicero once again to strengthen his argument against the Latinist Sepúlveda. Cicero's oration *Pro Fonteio*, claimed Las Casas, contained a speech that affirmed the following point: "[A]ll men are bound by natural right to defend their God or gods taken to be the true God."[80]

The obligation to defend one's religion – whether it is the true religion or a false one believed to be true – stemmed from the same universal right, since everyone was "inclined naturally to love and serve God." The habitual knowledge of the natural law (in *synderesis*), whereby a person possessed a natural desire to know and love God, provided the ineradicable foundation for his recognition of religious rights for individual persons and peoples. As Gustavo Gutiérrez has argued, the bishop made an extraordinary theological claim in the Latin West by articulating – well before Protestant formulations – that individuals and peoples in error, even infidels, have rights against papal and civil tyranny.[81] Sepúlveda's objections to the bishop's *Apologia* at Valladolid further illustrated that the crux of the great controversy revolved around this

79 Las Casas, *Aquí se contiene una disputa*, rep. 11, pp. 407–409.
80 Las Casas, *Aquí se contiene una disputa*, rep. 11, p. 409.
81 Gutiérrez, *Las Casas*, pp. 205–206.

claim about the rights of infidels, especially in religious matters. The imperial humanist correctly accused Las Casas for teaching that the Amerindians "rightly defend their religion and idolatry" according to natural law and the law of nations.[82]

The twofold thesis of Bishop Las Casas at Valladolid represented precisely what was at stake for him in the affair of the Indies: all the *conquistas* waged by Spaniards were unjust whereas the Indians justly defended their religion from extermination. Remarkably, Las Casas had already made these claims several years before Valladolid. According to the heated textual exchange at Valladolid, his 1546 "Twelve Rules for Confessors" (*Doce reglas* or *Confesionario*) contained both arguments concerning the injustice of all the Spanish wars, and the rightness of infidel self-defense in matters of religion.[83] This only further explains why in a letter to King Philip II written a year before the Valladolid junta, Sepúlveda condemned the "scandalous and diabolical" *Confesionario* of Bishop Las Casas. Sepúlveda asserted, overconfidently, that Las Casas composed the *Confesionario* to refute his own dialogue on the justice of the conquests.[84] Sepúlveda conscientiously juxtaposed his *Democrates secundus* with the *Confesionario*, thereby positioning himself as an ally of the Crown's rule over Indies in contrast to the bishop and certain other "passionate friars" who opposed the Spanish right of political subjugation.

One of those opposing friars was none other than Melchor Cano, who had given his theological endorsement of Las Casas's *Confesionario*. Between 1548 and 1549, before serving as an imperial theologian at the Council of Trent, Cano, a theologian influenced by humanism, exchanged letters with Sepúlveda. Their letters concerned, among other things, the affair the Indies. Incidentally, the letters came just after the theological commissions at the universities of Salamanca and Alcalá rejected *Democrates secundus* for publication. Sepúlveda was bitter and insulted, insinuating that the decision was the biased result of a few corruptors. In response, Cano elevated Vitoria's

82 Sepúlveda, *Aquí se contiene una disputa*, obj. 11, p. 319.

83 Sepúlveda, *Aquí se contiene una disputa*, obj. 11, p. 319. Las Casas validated Sepúlveda's accusation that the *Confesionario* proposed both the injustice of the Spanish conquests and the rightness of Amerindians to defend their religion according to conscience, *Aquí se contiene una disputa*, rep. 11, p. 405. Although the first thesis remains in the *Confesionario* (seventh rule), there is no indication of the second thesis in the existing version of the work. The discrepancy suggests there was likely another edition of the work in circulation that contained this controversial claim and it did not remain in the final version published with the 1552 treatises.

84 Losada, *Juan Ginés de Sepúlveda*, p. 202.

"contrary view" on the Indies presented in the *Relectio de Indis* to reinforce the committee's rejection of *Democrates secundus*.[85]

Cano was already aware of Sepúlveda's opinions prior to the university commission on *Democrates secundus*. Before taking the *Prima* Chair at Salamanca, he inhabited the Aquinas Chair of theology at Alcalá where he delivered a university lecture *On the Sovereignty of the Indians* (*De dominio indorum*) in 1546. The contents of Cano's *relectio*, based on his classroom lectures on the *Summa*, was a deliberate response to the arguments of Sepúlveda's *Democrates secundus* shaped by Vitoria.[86] Cano countered Sepúlveda's principal justifications for war in the Indies owing to the "natural" inferiority of the Indians and the right of conquest by a superior civilization, as seen in case of the Roman Empire, or the punishment of crimes including idolatry and cannibalism committed against natural law.

Cano's alternative legal argument about the Indians consistent with the Thomistic political axiom began with the following claim derived from the Roman law of first occupant, a key resource for Salmantine counterarguments: "By the law of nations they first occupied those regions; therefore, they cannot be dispossessed because of mortal sin . . . or unbelief." Additionally, echoing Vitoria, although true dominium does pertain to children, the Indians do not qualify as simple-minded people on the level of immaturity: "They are not inept but have ordinary use of reason. They have their laws and are capable of receiving the teaching of the Gospel. Therefore, they have dominium over their political affairs (*dominium iurisdictionis*)."[87] Following the Dominican line of argument attentive to original occupation, the law of nations as positive human law undergirded the legitimate rule of unbelievers.

Against Sepúlveda's notion of a superior right to conquer lesser peoples, Cano was also adamant about natural egalitarianism. According to natural right (*ius naturale*), there are no slaves by nature. Neither can anyone be intrinsically subject to rule by another people, "For all are born equal." With respect to international politics, "no republic has the authority to overthrow another" due to an alleged superiority in wisdom.[88] Titles to conquest based on promoting the well-being or utility of barbarians were equally specious for

85 Lupher, *Romans in a New World*, p. 120.

86 Pereña, *Misión de España*, p. 72.

87 Cano, *De dominio indorum*, p. 102: "*Jure enim gentium illam partem primi occupabant qua non possunt privari ob peccatum mortale . . . neque ob infidelitatem [. . .]. Cum tamen illi non sint stulti, sed habent mediocrem usum rationis, quoniam leges suas habent et susceptibiles sunt evangelicae doctrinae, ergo habent dominium iurisdictionis.*"

88 Cano, *De dominio indorum*, p. 104: "*omnes enim nati sunt aequales*" and "*nulla respublica habet authoritatem alteram opprimere.*"

Cano. Relatedly, any arguments for war and conquest on account of the sins of the barbarians also lacked justification. The use of Augustine and Aquinas to justify the legality of Roman expansion was an abuse of historical interpretation. Imperial Rome, far from exemplifying justice, "invaded most places with avarice and ambition" just like they captured the silver and gold mines of Spain according to the First Book of Maccabees (8:3).[89] Similar to Vitoria, Cano concluded that if Europeans (e.g., the French) were not attacked for violating natural law in their own countries, then neither should Indians in theirs. European Christian relations among equal sovereignties was a pattern for ordering Christian–infidel relations in the New World.

Europeans had no legitimate jurisdiction through positive law or the law of nations to punish natural law violations in the Indies. Hence, there was no imperial power to subjugate other people on this ground since natural right guarded against a coercive civilizing mission. The reading of *Inter caetera* as a papal donation of lands and jurisdiction overseas had no validity. Citing the canon legal *foris* principle, Cano derived another crucial conclusion in agreement with his Dominican counterparts: "The Pope has no power over barbarians."[90] Without spiritual power over the affairs of infidels outside Christian jurisdiction, there can be no temporal power over them either. Cano's concise theological counterarguments to Sepúlveda's *Democrates secundus* clearly isolated and challenged two fundamental imperial-humanist justifications for war: a superior right to conquer the uncivilized and the punishment of sins against natural law. Let us consider Sepúlveda's legal arguments for conquest of the Indies more closely in order to appreciate his ideological legacy for European expansion.

DISPOSSESSING IDOLATERS

The natural slavery argument for conquest was never taken that literally within the legal culture of Catholic Spain. Its rhetorical force consisted in identifying those accidental qualities of a "second nature" to distinguish infidel barbarians from superior Europeans. Furthermore, when Spaniards raised the argument against the peoples of the New World, its purpose was to deny native self-rule and authorize the *encomienda* system of forced labor, not to justify chattel slavery. Alleged incivility and ineptitude among Amerindians were byproducts of either climatic conditions or entrenched barbaric practices. As it happened, the dominant theocratic conception of world order based on conflictual

[89] Cano, *De dominio indorum*, p. 110.
[90] Cano, *De dominio indorum*, p. 130.

Christian–infidel relations overshadowed the classical geopolitical explanatory paradigm thereby reducing the latter's justificatory importance. Nevertheless, geopolitical hierarchy remained important for Sepúlveda's imperial-humanist account of a European order of law with universal scope.

Although the junta at Burgos in 1512 boasted some partisans of natural slavery, Palacios Rubios and theocratic world order had the favor of the royal court. The Requirement became the legal protocol. For the theocratic royalist, the natural slavery argument was useful for designating "feeble" people utterly incapable of self-rule. But the more effective legal device for taking possession through political rule was the act of war contained in theocratic world order. A punitive act of war could imply the total right of conquest, which entailed not only taking possession of governable lands, but also the seizure of property and treasure, and the making of slaves. Vitoria and the Spanish Dominicans therefore did not introduce the discourse of war for addressing the Indies. Rather, read in historical political context, they significantly chastened the idea of war through appeals to justice and charity, as we will consider in Chapter 6.

Theocratic world order and its model of Christian–infidel relations in perpetual conflict was the authoritative discourse within which Sepúlveda deployed his new and distinct imperial-humanist arguments for the Spanish conquest of the Indies. Both his *Democrates primus* (1535) and the *Democrates secundus* were written as dialogues between the Italian humanist character Democrates and his Christian defense of war against the untutored Lutheran Leopoldus. Already in that first dialogue, Sepúlveda praised the glorious deeds of El Cid who waged a holy war of Reconquista against the Moors. All wars to subjugate infidel enemies of the Christian religion adhered to a just cause, similar to the three classic ones of avenging injury, recovering stolen goods, and punishing evildoers.[91]

When Sepúlveda explicitly considered war against infidels in *Democrates secundus*, he rehearsed the three traditional just causes identified by St. Isidore and codified in Gratian's *Decretum* before introducing other causes, founded on natural law and divine law.[92] The one "most applicable to those barbarians vulgarly called Indians" was an ancient dogma and it decreed that their "natural condition is such that they must obey others, and if they refuse superior rule and there is no other recourse, then they should be subjugated

91 *Demócrates primero*, in *Tratados Politicos de Juan Ginés de Sepúlveda*, Sp. trans. Angel Losada (Instituto de Estudios Politicos, 1963), p. 176.

92 Sepúlveda, *Demócrates segundo*, pp. 16–17, referring to self-defense, recovery of goods, and punishment of offenses.

by arms. Such a war is just according to the law of nature testified by the most eminent of philosophers."[93] Of course, Sepúlveda had Aristotle's *Politics* in sight. Scripture provided additional confirmation for convenience's sake.[94] Reliant on classical sources, Sepúlveda presented a classical philosophical account of nature whereby the imperfect must submit to the perfect, the weak to the strong, and the vicious to the virtuous. By grafting this hierarchical essentialism onto natural law and the law of nations, and therefore world order, it meant that all forms of dominium and right implied relationships of superiority to inferiority, domination and submission.

The political implications of Sepúlveda's natural right were simple enough: barbarian and inhumane peoples needed the example and authority of wise, virtuous princes to abandon their incivility. Democrates claimed in the second dialogue that Spaniards "by superior right" (*optimo iure*) and virtue rule over the barbarians of the New World just as "children are subject to adults, women are to men, the savage and inhuman to the mild-mannered, and the grossly intemperate to the continent and moderate."[95] Sepúlveda's eyewitness source for his argument about the natural inferiority of the Indians stemmed directly from Fernández de Oviedo. The chronicler's *Historia General y Natural de las Indias* had identified the Amerindians as a "people whose nature is idle and vicious, of little industry" and "vile and inclined to evil."[96] They were a monolithic category of people with "thick skulls" who possessed "bestial understanding."[97] The nature of the barbarian, largely determined by their inveterate evil customs, was completely subject to the articulation of humanity and right reason now defined by Sepúlveda's European cultural elitism.[98]

Above all, idolatry was the chief mark of inferiority among the peoples of the New World. Idolatry established a genus containing the associated sins and crimes of cannibalism and human sacrifice, popularly portrayed by Oviedo

93 Sepúlveda, *Demócrates segundo*, p. 19: "*[Q]uarum una est, et quae maxime convenit in istos Barbaros, Indos vulgo dictos, quorum mihi videris patrocinium suscepisse, ut armis, si non patet alia via, in ditionem redigantur, quorum ea conditio naturalis est, ut aliis parere debeant, si eorum imperium recusent. Hoc enim bellum iustum lege naturae Philosophorum maximi testantur.*"

94 Prv 11:29, where "the fool will be servant to the wise."

95 Sepúlveda, *Demócrates segundo*, p. 33: "*[O]ptimo iure Hispanos istis novi orbis, et insularum adiacentium barbaris imperitare, qui prudentia, ingenio, virtute omni, ac humanitate tam longe superantur ab Hispanis, quam pueri a perfecta aetate, mulieres a viris, saevi, et immanes a mitissimis, prodigiose intemperantes a continentibus et temperatis.*"

96 Fernández de Oviedo, *Historia General y Natural*, primera parte, lib. 3, cap. 6, p. 71.

97 Fernández de Oviedo, *Historia General y Natural*, primera parte, lib. 5, proemio, p. 125.

98 José Fernández-Santamaria, *The State, War and Peace: Spanish Political Thought in the Renaissance, 1516–1559* (Cambridge University Press, 1977), p. 190.

and Cortés. Punishment of idolatry therefore constituted the most important cause for war applicable to the Indies. The strength of Sepúlveda's arguments for conquest could not strictly rest on moral philosophical claims about cultural superiority but required authoritative grounding within the Latin Christian legal tradition. As Sepúlveda indicated at Valladolid: "[W]hoever worships idols violates the natural law to the greatest degree. Therefore, idolaters can rightly be punished by Christians through war so that, as subjects under our rule, they can be compelled to live according to the natural law and God shall neither be dishonored nor offended by their worship of idols."[99] The legal weight of this argument for wars of idolatry against infidels was formidable. First, it was common opinion within the missionary warfare doctrine of canon lawyers. It also overlapped with the traditional just cause of punishing the crimes of evildoers. Finally, it was the accepted doctrine and practice of the Spanish papalist-royalists, theorized in the *De insulis* of Palacios Rubios and practiced through the Requirement.

In *Democrates secundus* and at Valladolid, Sepúlveda explicitly referred to the theocratic universalist opinion contained in the *Quod super his* decretal commentary of Pope Innocent IV. Notably, this second cause for war against the Indians received the most extensive treatment in Sepúlveda's work. Considered among "the most learned men," the canonist pope taught that: "Christians, on account of the supreme Pontiff's authority, have a right of punishing and correcting pagans."[100] Christian rulers have the authority to attack pagans through war when pagans do not guard the universal natural law within their respective jurisdiction. The barbarians of the New World had failed exceedingly on this score, evident in the idolatrous acts of human sacrifice practiced by the Aztecs of Mexico and the Inca of Peru.

Sepúlveda made his single reference to the "modern" theologian Vitoria at this point. According to Sepúlveda, Vitoria (and Cano) had incorrectly read him by assuming that failure to live in accordance with natural law supposedly entailed crimes among individual members of the commonwealth. But this was an overstatement of Sepúlveda's claim. Rather, Sepúlveda had in mind communities that publicly approved customs and institutionalized conventions contrary to nature.[101] Applying the same universal law to European peoples would not justify intervention in France or England because they did not meet the criteria for widespread barbarism. When gross impunities

99 Sepúlveda, *Apologia*, no. 7, p. 201: "*Qui autem idola colunt ii maxime violant legem naturae. Iure igitur idolotrae bello possunt a Christianis coerceri, ut ipsorum imperio subiecti ex lege naturae vivere cogantur, neve per idolorum cultum ab ipsis Deus blasphemetur, et offendatur.*"

100 Sepúlveda, *Demócrates segundo*, p. 45.

101 Sepúlveda, *Demócrates segundo*, pp. 57–58.

against the natural law were backed by a whole society, it required intervention from superior people to correct such blatant violations of natural reason.

Innocent's decretal commentary also gave Sepúlveda support for his fourth cause for war applicable to the Indies – to secure an effective path for evangelization.[102] Again, there was precedent in the missionary warfare tradition for this cause with Christian sources accompanying Innocent IV that included Pope Gregory the Great, St. Bernard of Clairvaux, and now, apparently, Pope Alexander VI. One of Sepúlveda's most notable humanist patrons, Pope Clement VII (1523–1534), a son of the powerful Medici family of Florence, championed this cause before the imperial court with no reservation. *Inter Arcana* (1529), a letter of Pope Clement on the Indies addressed to Emperor Charles, was a complete endorsement of evangelization through political subjugation: "We trust that … you will compel and with all zeal cause the barbarian nations to come to the knowledge of God … not only by edicts and admonitions, but also by force and arms, if needful, in order that their souls may partake of the heavenly kingdom."[103]

The detour of conquest allowed for a more efficient preaching of the Gospel, clearing the path of obstacles like idolatry that stood in the way of receiving the truth. Pope Gregory the Great's supposed endorsement of the Roman exarch Gennadius to spread Christianity in Africa by means of war was a historical favorite of Sepúlveda.[104] The Christian origin of missionary war traced back to this letter justifying the imperial subjugation of barbarians. Once barbarians have been "deprived of the license to sin" and their "customs opposed to natural law uprooted," only then could the Christian religion readily spread among them.[105] Such a cause was not strictly Christian, however. Divine providence had ordained the ancient pagan Romans, as Saint Augustine observed, to bring the world under their imperial rule and thereby chasten the "grevious evils of many nations."[106] Sepúlveda craftily repurposed Augustine in the spirit of Dante's apology for Roman Empire.

102 Sepúlveda, *Demócrates segundo*, beginning on p. 64.

103 Pope Clement VII, *Intra Arcana* (1529). Cited in Lewis Hanke, "Pope Paul III and the American Indians," *Harvard Theological Review* 30.2 (1937): 77.

104 Sepúlveda, *Demócrates segundo*, 71; *Aquí se contiene una disputa*, obj. 4, p. 297; *Apologia*, no. 11, p. 206. Notably, Melchor Cano, by including history as a humanist source of theological reflection, disputed Sepúlveda's usage of Gennadius at Valladolid. See *De locis theologicis*, ed. Juan Belda Plans (Madrid: Biblioteca de Autores Cristianos, 2001), lib. 11, cap. 2.

105 Sepúlveda, *Del reino y los deberes del rey*, in *Tratados politicos de Juan Ginés de Sepúlveda*, p. 106

106 Augustine, *City of God*, trans. Harry Bettenson (London: Penguin Books, 2003) Book 5, chap. 13.

Even though Sepúlveda had to be cautious rhetorically about Aristotelian natural slavery at the Valladolid meeting, he could continue to maintain his strongest arguments for conquest according to the logic of religious coercion embedded in the missionary warfare tradition. Political superiority over barbarians and religious coercion of infidels were two aspects of the same right of the Spanish Crown to subjugate Indians by enforcing the norms of natural law. Sépulveda made the relevant point in his *Democrates secundus*, "[T]he barbarians can be reduced to our sovereignty with the same right [*eodem iure*] by which they can be forced to hear the Gospel. For whomever aims at an end with justice, that one by the same right can employ all things pertaining to the end."[107] Whereas Las Casas believed war and conquest were evil and disproportionate means to bring about the end of conversion, Sepúlveda came to the obverse conclusion by subscribing to the logic of religious coercion. The goal of bringing the faith and therefore salvation to the New World "could not be done suitably without subjugating the barbarians."[108]

During the second session of Valladolid in the spring of 1551, Sepúlveda delivered eleven objections to Las Casas's critique of missionary war. In response to the Spanish Dominicans who denied the punishment of idolatry as a lawful basis for war, Sepúlveda assured the Council of the following: "We do not approve of going to war with idolatrous Indians to kill and destroy them … but rather, it is done for the purpose of subjugating them and removing their idolatry and evil rites, and to eliminate obstacles to the preaching of the Gospel."[109] Sepúlveda was well-acquainted with the Latin Christian idea and practice of indirect religious coercion to advance Spain's civilizing mission. According to the medieval argument, indirect coercion by means of conquest was not a direct imposition of faith on the will, but an acceptable strategy employing fear and terror to compel the intransigent and free them from their evil habits.

The Innocentian doctrine of missionary war applied to the New World was, in fact, a logical extension of Augustinian arguments for indirect coercion.[110] Undoubtedly aware of this connection, Sepúlveda frequently cited Augustine's unsavory letter to Vincentius in 408 concerning the Donatist

107 Sepúlveda, *Demócrates segundo*, pp. 65–66; *Apologia*, no. 14, pp. 209–210.

108 Sepúlveda, *Demócrates segundo*, p. 66.

109 Sepúlveda, *Aquí se contiene una disputa*, obj. 1, p. 291: "*[N]osotros no decimos que a estos indios idólatras se les ha de hacer guerra para matarlos y destruirlos como a los de tierra de promisión, sino para sujetarlos y quitarlos la idolatría y malos ritos, y quitar los impedimentos de la predicación evangélica.*"

110 Castañeda Delgado, "Las doctrinas sobre la coacción y el 'Idearium' de las Casas," in OC, vol. 2, xvii-xlii.

controversy, along with other works.[111] In the letter, Augustine abandoned his earlier policy of persuading heretics, preferring instead the use of temporal power to suppress them. The Bishop of Hippo's instrumentalist logic was simple: the most efficient way to get someone to renounce his or her prejudice and seek the truth was to instill the fear of punishment under an imperial decree.[112] The proof for its effectiveness consisted in the numerous examples of heretics from Augustine's hometown who had returned to the Catholic fold. It was also evident in the case of pagan idolaters, many of whom were corrected after compelled to seek the true God by imperial laws forbidding their worship.[113]

The *ratio* of coercion in the case of heretics was different from that of pagans according to Augustine no doubt.[114] Whereas pagans were punished for their crimes, heretics were admonished to depart from error. Nevertheless, this distinct reasoning should not detract from what was perspicuously clear in the letter to Vincentius: the religious coercion enforced by imperial power against heretics and pagans used the same tactic of fear in service to the ultimate aim of getting them to embrace the truth. "Not that anyone can be good against his will," wrote Augustine, "but by fear of enduring what he does not want, he either gives up the hatred that stands in his way, or he is compelled to recognize the truth he did not know."[115] Augustine's instrumentalist logic of coercion was formally applicable to those inside and outside the Church under the same regime of law.

The teaching on religious coercion proposed that an individual's will can neither be forced to be good nor to accept the faith. Instead, the will must only be compelled by fear of punishment to stop committing evil and to consider the truth. Sepúlveda understood the singular logic of Augustine's strategy of religious coercion in both cases of compelling heretics back to the fold and getting pagans to abandon idolatry through imperial decrees.[116] It boiled down to efficiency and effectiveness, the anchoring principles of Sepúlveda's method of evangelization by means of conquest. Heretics and pagan idolaters could be coerced indirectly by imperial politics to get them to abandon their errors under the threat of capital punishment and dispossession of property, a practice initiated under Emperor Constantine. Conversion to the faith was

111 Sepúlveda, *Demócrates segundo*, p. 75: "*Epistolam saepe a nobis memoratum perlegas.*"

112 Augustine, "Letter 93 to Vincent," in *Saint Augustine Letters*, vol. 2, trans. Sister Wilfrid Parsons (Catholic University of America Press, 1953), pp. 72–74.

113 Augustine, "Letter 93," p. 82.

114 Augustine, "Letter 93," pp. 65–66.

115 Augustine, "Letter 93," p. 72.

116 Sepúlveda, *Apologia*, p. 204; *Aquí se contiene una disputa*, objs. 2–3.

therefore an *indirect* (and not intrinsically necessary) result of a *direct* punishment for a crime stipulated by imperial laws.

For Sepúlveda, Augustine's letter to Vincentius offered the missionary warfare rationale linking threats of violence with preaching: "[W]hen the use of terror is conjoined to beneficial instruction, so that not only the light of truth dispels the darkness of error, but also that the force of fear breaks the bonds of evil custom, we rejoice in the salvation of many."[117] Christians had the authority to compel unbelievers to enter (*cogite intrare*) the order of right reason by removing their idolatry or any other obstacle hindering the knowledge of virtue and superior wisdom.[118] In practice, Sepúlveda saw logical consistency between Constantine's imperial laws against idolaters and the missionary warfare of the Roman Gennadius to expand the Christian faith.[119] Indirect religious coercion thereby gave full authorization to the tributary labor of the New World *encomiendas* for civilizing and converting the natives after they were subdued through war.[120]

The paradigmatic example of armed evangelization available to the Spanish colonial imagination was conquistador, Hernán Cortés. His fight to spread the faith against Aztec idolaters was not for an individual republic but for an entirely new world on behalf of the Holy Roman Emperor. Sepúlveda's imperial narration of the conquest of Mexico in *De orbe novo* placed the traditional justification for religious coercion explicitly in the mouth of Cortés. In a speech before his soldiers in Veracruz, Cortés rallied them toward battle in hope of the salvation, fame, and riches that awaited them afterwards. The last aim of warfare though was the most pious of all and directly in service to their King and Emperor Charles:

> To propagate the Christian religion and the empire of the Spaniards over the length and width of the world. Once the most powerful nations have been subjugated to our power, and their worship of idols and barbarous customs have disappeared thanks to us (as it happened on the islands), they will be

[117] Sepúlveda, *Demócrates segundo*, p. 73: "*Cum igitur terrori utili doctrina salutaris adiungitur, ut non solum tenebras erroris lux veritatis expellat, verum etiam malae consuetudinis vincula vis timoris abrumpat, de multorum (ut dixi), salute laetamur.*"

[118] The infamous Christian political reference to religious compulsion – the wedding feast parable of Luke 14:23 – was a mainstay of early modern Protestant debates concerning conscience and religious toleration. Cited in Augustine's Letter 93 and *Demócrates segundo*, p. 70.

[119] Sepúlveda, *Aquí se contiene una disputa*, obj. 4, pp. 298–289: "*[A]sí estas guerras de Gennadio, como la ley de Constantino, se enderezaban principalmente a la emendación y salvación de los infieles.*"

[120] Sepúlveda, *Demócrates segundo*, pp. 122–123.

better disposed and receptive to learn and embrace Christian piety, not against their will, but through the teaching of the Gospel.[121]

From Emperors Constantine to Charles V, Sepúlveda viewed the imperial punishment of crimes as extending to those inside and outside the Church, within and beyond Europe. In contrast, the Spanish Dominicans adhered to the *foris* principle, applying it to Cajetan's third category of unbelievers outside Europe who were neither de facto, nor de iure under Christian rule. Where the Spanish Dominicans saw no civil statutes or positive laws of Spain applicable to punish external infidels residing in their respective kingdoms, Sepúlveda appealed to the universal jurisdiction of natural law enforceable through the expansive reach of imperial power. Idolaters, like heretics, could forfeit their property and goods according to earthly laws, as Augustine indicated.[122] The crucial qualification here for Sepúlveda was that dispossession was a judicial act on the part of public authority.

An imperial civilization like Spain, then, exceeding in virtue and religion, could publicly seize the lands and the possessions of barbarian idolaters wherever they encountered them because of offenses to God and nature. Returning to Augustine, although now using his work against the Donatist Petilianus, Sepúlveda claimed that the first native inhabitants of the Promised Land were expelled from it because they did not properly use it. Similarly, the dispossession of Pharaoh's treasure by the Hebrews was lawful after the Egyptians had offended the Lord with idols used to worship earthly creatures. For they made "ill-use of that gold."[123] Sepúlveda drew the conclusion from Augustine's anti-heresy writings that pagan idolaters, as a result of abusing their possessions, were subject to having their goods lawfully taken and appropriated by public Christian authorities. The idolatrous abuse of goods could be taken as an insult to God or a harm to the commonwealth, both of which were violations of natural law and the divine law undergirding it.

Sepúlveda's extension of the imperial rationale of dispossession to goods and lands abused anywhere in the world was consequential for European colonialism. Such attention to the abuse or ill-use of movables and immovables would be immensely significant in the evolving ideology of European

[121] Sepúlveda, *Historia del Nuevo Mundo*, Sp. trans. Antonio Ramírez de Verger (Allianza Editorial, 1987), lib. 5, p. 134: "[P]ropagar la religión cristiana y el imperio de los españoles a lo largo y ancho del orbe. Pues sometidas las naciones más poderosas a nuestro poder, una vez desaparecido el culto a los ídolos y sus costumbres salvajes gracias a vosotros, tal como sucedió en las islas, se vuelven más dispuestas y dóciles para aprender y abrazar, no en contra de su voluntad, la piedad cristiana mediante la doctrina del evangelio."

[122] Sepúlveda, *Demócrates segundo*, pp. 88–90.

[123] Sepúlveda, *Demócrates segundo*, p. 88.

expansion for different purposes. Anthony Pagden has observed that the Latinist imperial chronicler moved the ideology of European expansion and conquest closer to the discourse of humanist jurisprudence.[124] In the Spanish colonial context, the ill-use of goods associated with idols was a powerful justification to seize native treasures at sacred burial sites, teeming with precious stones and metals. It might also entail the disuse of land rich in mineral deposits that remained underexploited. Distinctly, in the English colonization of North America, dispossession was not viewed as a punishment of idolatry carried out by public authority. Rather, as we will consider next chapter, with improperly utilized land considered more objectionable to the English, native dispossession resulted from an individual settler's effective cultivation of otherwise wasted space. Abuse and ill-use of things and land, taken out of Augustine's original Roman imperial context, were cues of dispossession refashioned by Sepúlveda and deployed in a humanist manner for an extra-European world.

Sepúlveda also provided the juridical imaginary for executing universal natural law through warfare conducted by imperial power. He claimed that pagan idolaters "find themselves in a similar situation to those who have committed a crime punishable by the seizure of goods, which has still not yet been sanctioned under a sentence from a judge. They are able to use their goods until they are condemned and stripped of them. In crimes of this stature, war is a punishment. The public declaration of war is itself like a judge's sentence."[125] Pagan idolaters were the unwitting fugitives of Sepúlveda's imperial world order, doing as they pleased with their ill-used goods until European imperial power brought the natural law and the law of nations forcefully down on them as punishment.

Overall, Sepúlveda's imperial humanist commitments could avoid the charge of denying infidel dominium because his argument for dispossession was not based on an exclusive claim about the Church's spiritual power over infidels. Even Aristotle and Plato were believers of a sort, acknowledging a single philosophical god. Sepúlveda did entertain the possibility that there could be "some town found" in the New World "that was civilized and humane, lacking idolatry and inclined by nature to venerate the one true God."[126] Yet his aggressive imperial political aims made these prospects highly dubious, or nonexistent. Nevertheless, infidels can and did hold dominium

[124] Pagden, *Spanish Imperialism and the Political Imagination: Studies in European and Spanish-American Social and Political Theory, 1513–1830* (Yale University Press, 1990), p. 28.
[125] Sepúlveda, *Demócrates segundo*, p. 90.
[126] Sepúlveda, *Demócrates segundo*, p. 44.

truly; they also exhibited virtue extravagantly even without true religion, as Augustine himself acknowledged of the ancient Romans.[127] Dominium therefore was not founded on grace and charity, but on the wisdom and virtue of civilized nations, Christian or pagan. Barbarian idolaters, not infidels as such, were the legitimate targets of dispossession in Sepúlveda's scheme. Within Renaissance political thought in a colonial context, the Spanish humanist had initiated a dissolution of the theological and canonistic rubric of Christian–infidel relations that preserved the immunity, and therefore legal boundary, of those outside the Church. In its place was no longer the missionary warfare doctrine executed through a theocratic papalist politics of natural law, but an emergent secularizing humanist doctrine of subjugating barbarians through the imperial politics of Christian or pagan civilizations.

THE IMPERIAL POLITICS OF NATURAL LAW

The idea and politics of natural law in Sepúlveda's arguments for conquest of the Indies, and war more generally, had many similarities with theocratic papalism. Perpetual wars against infidels, purportedly waged by Christian authorities to punish gross violations of natural law, were "just and holy" for advancing the Gospel and bringing civilization to foreign lands.[128] Yet Sepúlveda recognized more acutely than Palacios Rubios that missionary warfare was parasitic on secular political authority for its success. Religious coercion could be indirect only because the enforcement of natural law through imperial politics was direct. It was of no consequence to the Spanish humanist that canon law traditionally categorized indirect coercion as an imperfect form of justice based on fear and considered its use only in moderation to avoid scandalizing the faith.

The imperial politics of natural law undergirding Sepúlveda's conception of world order represented a marked departure from theocratic papalism by moving in a decidedly modern, even secular, direction. Humanism in its militant expression was Sepúlveda's intellectual repository for thinking about world order a century prior to the civilian jurist Alberico Gentili. Competing views on world order in Catholic Spain during the middle of the sixteenth century, considered in previous chapters, included the Thomistic brand of scholasticism of the Dominican theologians and the

127 Sepúlveda, *Demócrates segundo*, p. 33, where he cited Augustine's Letter 138 to Marcellinus: "God has shown in the most wealthy and famous empire of the Romans, how great civic virtues are, even without true religion."

128 Fernández-Santamaria, *The State, War and Peace*, p. 168.

theocratic papalism of the royalists. Strikingly, Sepúlveda's imperial humanist rationales for world order gained greater traction outside Spain in a Europe shaped by the Westphalian imaginary. In this wider context, Sepúlveda provided ideological foundations for subsequent European justifications for colonial expansion among humanist jurists and naturalist philosophers of the seventeenth century. More broadly, his imperial humanist account of natural law and the law of nations anticipated the parochial European universalism embedded in modern international relations.

Critical legal and postcolonial scholars regard Vitoria as the definitive Spanish precursor of colonial international law for defending European expansion through war without reliance on papal power.[129] These claims about Vitoria's alleged secularization of natural law and the law of nations, aside from ignoring his scholastic theological and political commitments, also skirt the ideological importance of Sepúlveda for subsequent European colonial thinking. In a pivotal shift, Sepúlveda transmuted a medieval papalist doctrine of war as a punishment for sins against the natural law into a thoroughly secular political idiom no longer dependent on the Church or the Pope for its execution. Whereas Vitoria and the Spanish theologians rejected a European right of war to punish infidels for their sins on the basis of the canonistic *foris* principle, Sepúlveda embraced punitive war wholeheartedly and placed it at the center of the imperial right of expansion. In addition, his discourse of dispossession also turned on native abuse, misuse, and uselessness of their goods.

Sepúlveda tellingly wrote in his first dialogue that Aristotle, not the Pope, was the "best" interpreter of natural law.[130] *Democrates primus*, as José Fernández-Santamaria has effectively shown, was a brilliant Renaissance display of the "secularization of wisdom" in which Aristotle and the Old Covenant, the natural law and the Decalogue, fused together in the common pursuit of moral, notably martial, virtues.[131] The work also contained theoretical claims about the natural law and the law of nations that were wholly relevant to the case of the Indies later treated in *Democrates secundus*.

[129] Anghie, *Imperialism, Sovereignty, and the Making of International Law*, pp. 17–18: "Vitoria ... in the course of refuting the conventional basis for Spanish title creates a new system of international law which essentially displaces divine law and its administrator, the Pope, and replaces it with natural law administered by a secular sovereign." Also see Brett Bowden, "The Colonial Origins of International Law: European Expansion and the Classical Standard of Civilization," *Journal of the History of International Law* 7 (2005): 9–10, who essentially follows Anghie's thesis.

[130] Sepúlveda, *Demócrates primero*, p. 199.

[131] Fernández-Santamaria, *The State, War and Peace*, pp. 172–188.

Sepúlveda's first dialogue, an argument for the compatibility of war and the Christian religion, capitalized on the Christian states of life – the active and contemplative lives – in order to bring wisdom down from its contemplative heights through prudence and make it the normative basis for civic affairs through the active life. Importantly, Jesus gave sanction to the active life (*vita activa*) of moral virtue shared by all rational peoples since he came to fulfill and not abolish the commandments of the Law, which stipulated the classic moral precepts of the natural law.[132] The Gospel mandates of Jesus therefore only supplied mere additions, or "counsels" of perfection, for those dedicated to spiritual contemplation (*vita contemplativa*) of a Kingdom not of this world.[133] So although the contemplative life of religious perfection possessed a superior quality, the active life of moral virtue was necessary for maintaining the "natural society of humankind" (*sociedad natural de los hombres*) because of its accord with natural law.[134] Relatedly, theology may be a nobler discipline, as Aristotle observed, yet it was not a necessary one.[135] (See Figure 4.2.)

The nascent modern claim here was that theology and revelation merely confirmed what philosophy and reason already grasped about the natural law and naturally acquired virtue. With the task of a philosopher like Aristotle "to declare wisely and appropriately what is contained in nature," and its associated virtues and customs, Sepúlveda registered a new secularized politics of natural law and practical ethics anticipating later neo-Stoic humanist arguments for European expansion.[136] Against the early Lutheran distaste of Aristotle and scholasticism, Sepúlveda's Democrates reminded Leopoldus that Christian theologians throughout the centuries have studied philosophers like Aristotle and Plato in detail.[137] For Sepúlveda, revelation may have a privileged access to knowledge of the natural law, but in terms of moral precepts, Aristotelianism was on par with the Christian religion. "Christians are no different from Peripatetics" when treating virtues and vices judged by reason because both consider it an error to depart from nature and right reason.[138] As a result, Innocent IV, Nicholas V, and Alexander VI – the reputed papal authorities on wars for European Christian expansion – were redundant or ancillary to the philosophical task of interpreting the natural law among

132 Sepúlveda, *Demócrates primero*, pp. 148–150.

133 Sepúlveda, *Demócrates primero*, p. 161.

134 Sepúlveda, *Demócrates primero*, p. 159.

135 Sepúlveda, *Demócrates primero*, p. 160.

136 Sepúlveda, *Demócrates primero*, p. 198: "*Pues misión del filósofo es declarar sabia y propiamente lo que contiene la naturaleza y lo que, por el contrario, desecha.*"

137 Sepúlveda, *Demócrates primero*, pp. 194–197.

138 Sepúlveda, *Demócrates primero*, pp. 188–189, 201.

FIGURE 4.2 "Juan Ginés de Sepúlveda, 1490–1573." (Source: Getty Images/ Universal History Archive/Contributor)

superior peoples. Aristotle was the ancient philosophical expert on natural law. The Roman Empire, whether pagan or Christian in character, was its enforcer.

Sepúlveda's account of the natural law also typified the early modern inclination to devise a universal moral standard for resolving conflict across political and confessional divides. As a timeless moral code evident to all rational people, the natural law emanates directly from the eternal law on high, which is its "immortal head and source."[139] Sepúlveda would employ Augustine's definition of the eternal law as "the will of God that commands the protection of the natural order and prohibits its disturbance" to sanction natural law's binding authority.[140] In terms of content, the natural law provided a list of moral precepts commanding and prohibiting certain actions, expressed most succinctly in the unchanging Decalogue. These precepts "are to be guarded and obligate all men for all times."[141] The importance of the Decalogue in Sepúlveda's account notwithstanding, Aristotle's idea of natural justice from the *Nicomachean Ethics*, or "that which everywhere has the same force," offers the philosophical definition of natural law required for its universal applicability across cultures.[142] Based on this permanent and universal natural law authorized by God, civilized societies have a criterion accessible through wisdom for measuring just and unjust laws within their borders and beyond.

The natural law provided Sepúlveda's imperial humanist world order with an absolute and unchanging standard by which superior peoples could attempt to civilize the world in their image. What made people superior was the presence of virtue, the enabling factor of prudential judgment regarding good and evil actions.[143] And although Aristotle was the philosophical expert on natural law, the Roman jurists took natural law a step further by politicizing it through the law of nations. On Sepúlveda's profitable humanist reading, the Roman jurists held that not all peoples, simply speaking, used the law of nations, but in particular those peoples who were "*humanae*," or civilized, because they demonstrated superior prudence and wisdom.[144] The Spanish imperial Latinist exposed and exploited a menacing qualification in Ulpian's juristic definition of *ius gentium*: it was the law used by "civilized peoples"

139 Sepúlveda, *Demócrates primero*, p. 150.

140 Sepúlveda, *Demócrates primero*, p. 150, referring to Book 1 of Augustine's *De libero arbitrio*.

141 Sepúlveda, *Demócrates primero*, p. 149.

142 Sepúlveda, *Demócrates primero*, pp. 151–152.

143 Sepúlveda, *Demócrates primero*, pp. 152–153.

144 Sepúlveda, *Demócrates primero*, p. 153: "*Por lo cual, los jurisconsultos, al definir el Derecho de gentes, no dicen simplemente que es aquel del que se sirven todas las gentes, sino que añaden 'las gentes prudentes'.*"

(*gentes humanae*).[145] The law of nations was therefore a practicable instrument of elite cultures for protecting the universal precepts of natural law.

In view of Sepúlveda's geopolitical commitments, there can be little doubt he categorized among the civilized peoples those inhabiting the "temperate" European regions of Spain, Italy, and Greece for superiority in natural virtue, customs, and reason.[146] He thereby constructed a Eurocentric law of nations with coercive power to subjugate through war unwilling and uncivilized peoples around the world. He followed the classical hierarchy that placed the peoples of Asia and Africa at the bottom of civilization. But Sepúlveda did not leave it solely to geopolitical locale or civil law for legitimately authorizing the punishment of sins *contra natura*. The sanction of punishment, as noted before, had to originate from the eternal law of God.[147] Sepúlveda was intractably theocratic, but in an overt humanist sense because even pagans like the ancient Romans could carry out this divine task of punishing and correcting lesser peoples. St. Paul's letter to the Romans provided Sepúlveda with the biblical proof text supporting all political authority, exemplified in the coercive power of Caesar, as proceeding from God.[148]

In a work dedicated to Philip II, *On the Rule and Duties of the King*, Sepúlveda summarized his long-standing position on the imperial politics of natural law:

> Among all nations there exists great difference: some are more civilized and wise whereas others in their lives and customs depart from reason and the natural law, and are considered barbaric and uncivilized [*que en su vida y costumbres públicas se apartan de la razón y Ley natural, por bárbaras e incivilizadas*]. The condition of the latter is such that on account of their barbarity they should obey the rule of those more civilized and cultured according to natural right so that they may be governed by better laws and institutions. If they refuse to submit to this superior rule that is just and beneficent for them, they can be forced by natural right [*por Derecho natural pueden ser obligadas*] ... With this right the Romans, a most civilized and virtuous people, subjugated barbarians under their *dominio*, as St. Augustine affirmed when he said, "God conceded to the Romans the greatest sovereignty in order to subdue the great evils of many nations." You see that it was not only lawful according to Christian laws, but also by natural right.[149]

145 Ulpian's definition in the *Digest*, 1.1.1.4: "*Ius gentium est, quo gentes humanae utuntur.*"
146 Sepúlveda, *Del reino*, p. 117.
147 Sepúlveda, *Demócrates segundo*, p. 42.
148 Romans 13:1. Cited in Sepúlveda, *Demócrates segundo*, p. 82.
149 Sepúlveda, *Del reino*, pp. 34–35.

Beyond classical geopolitical hierarchy with its multiple climatic differences, Sepúlveda presented world order in strictly dualistic terms: there were simply those fit to rule, and others required to submit to the wiser. The virtuous and barbarians; the civilized and mere mortals. According to the metaphysical principle of hierarchical perfection determinative of his idea of world order, native acquiescence could be taken as fulfilling a natural desire for betterment from a higher civilization. Since superior authority was a natural right established by God and the hierarchy of nature, it was also taken as beneficial to imperial subjects, even when it involved war. The civilizing mission of Sepúlveda's imperial humanism was in full view: the stuff of improvement in this political scheme was not land, but people, no matter how low they were on the scale of humanity determined by European culture.

Turning to Sepúlveda's discussion of benevolent imperialism, the subject of war and the relationship between natural law and law of nations warrants attention. Sepúlveda had done something incredibly important in the European ideological history justifying foreign conquest. War in the Christian legal tradition belonged to the intermediate juridical space between natural law and civil law known as the law of nations. This Christian juristic perspective had the advantage of recognizing war as the result of sinful humanity and an historical accident rather than a natural dimension of human coexistence. However, by identifying the law of nations as a right of superior peoples to enforce natural law, Sepúlveda virtually conflated natural law and the law of nations. More specifically, he presented the law of nations as the practical side of his hierarchical essentialist natural law theory. The universal reach of the natural law and law of nations made them "common" and therefore beneficial to "less civilized peoples." The law of nations contained the precepts of the Decalogue, the moral reference point for all the laws of nature. These unchanging moral precepts were in essence divine because they stemmed from the eternal law.[150] They provided the universal measure among imperial civilizations to judge the customs and laws of lesser peoples.

The political significance of the Bible came to bear especially when Sepúlveda defended the naturalness of war. As we saw in the previous chapter, among the Spanish Dominican theologians the patriarch Abraham and his nephew Lot were the narrative reference point for the biblical law of nations in Genesis 13 when they each consented to dividing the land and going in different directions. Sepúlveda took up Genesis 14 for a very different purpose to address the first instance of war recorded in the biblical narrative. After Lot had been taken captive by an alliance of eastern kings, Abraham mustered

[150] Sepúlveda, *Del reino*, p. 54.

a modest army of clansmen and overtook his enemies through war. Upon his return from the successful campaign, he received a divine blessing from the gentile priest-king, Melchizedek.

The Spanish Dominicans would have accounted for Abraham's skirmishes as resulting from the biblical law of nations. Sepúlveda read the matter differently. Since the Hebrews had yet to receive the written Law from Moses (or the Decalogue), Abraham must have acted strictly according to natural law. The conclusion was evident: natural law and divine law clearly authorized war, which was "a most desirable thing" and "most beneficial to the whole human race."[151] The romanticizing of war dismissed the recognition of war made by the Spanish theologians, even just war aimed at peace, as unavoidably brutal and horrible. An important corollary here might have been that the declaration of war, which now belonged to natural law and divine law and not exclusively the law of nations, need not require public authority. Yet Sepúlveda followed the common opinion of Christian just war thinking by denying the authority of the private individual to take up arms and avenge himself.[152] The norms of self-defense, not war, governed private cases. Later humanist-minded jurists, like the eclectic Grotius considered in the next chapter, would characteristically depart from this common Christian legal opinion by arguing for the lawfulness of private war on the high seas and in the wilderness to enforce natural law and the law of nations.

The Pentateuch was replete with examples of wars waged by the Israelites under the provocation of God. Following Palacios Rubios and the biblical basis of the Requirement, Sepúlveda saw in Deuteronomy 20 perhaps the strongest evidence confirming the twofold authorization of war by God and nature. After citing the terms of peace outlined in verses 10 through 14 – to surrender or be conquered – Sepúlveda extrapolated from Deuteronomy the total and unrestricted right of war, namely conquest: "Whomever conducts a just war, by the custom of peoples and by divine and natural law, has permission to kill their enemies, submit them to slavery, dispossess them of their goods, destroy their towns and cities, lay waste their lands, and carry out all manner of evil against their enemies to attain victory, provided that all these things are done with good intention and with an eye to peace."[153]

By grounding war in natural and divine law, Sepúlveda could then turn to the New World and judge the affair on virtually the same terms as the biblical conquest of the Promised Land under the guise of benevolent imperialism.

[151] Sepúlveda, *Demócrates primero*, p. 169.

[152] Sepúlveda, *Demócrates primero*, p. 171; *Demócrates segundo*, pp. 18–19, 31.

[153] Sepúlveda, *Del reino*, p. 113.

The law or right of conquest was permanent and unchanging from the perspective of the eternal law of God. In the discussion of war across the Atlantic from *Democrates secundus*, Sepúlveda explicitly stated that the acts of killing enemies, submitting them to slavery, and seizing their possessions were all part of attaining peace through a just war in conformity with natural law and the law of nations. It was both a decree of nature and common consensus among civilized peoples. Before the arrival of civilized Christianity, anyhow, barbarians occupied a state enfolded in war.[154]

The apparent "naturalness of the war" in the case of the Indies only dictated its harmony with justice and reason, which was of benefit to the Spanish victors but "much more advantageous to the conquered barbarians."[155] Conquest was allegedly suited to make better societies on both sides of war. Sepúlveda's humanism was clearest in asserting imperial benevolence on behalf of improving barbarian life. When Spaniards arrived in the Indies, they should offer the Requirement terms of peace to the natives, giving them some time to deliberate about accepting the rule of the Crown and the great benefits derived from superior law and true religion. If the idolatrous natives resisted, the Spaniards could appeal to the superior right of enforcing natural law or humanitarian emancipation when the peoples in question publicly practiced human sacrifice. It was essentially no different for the Portuguese who had seized barbarian Africans against their will. For "humane servitude" was far more beneficial than "savage liberty."[156]

Native submission to the Requirement mandate would facilitate their becoming a subject people as stipulated by Deuteronomy 20.[157] The *encomienda* system, a legitimate form of tributary labor according to its proponents, provided the means for improving native barbarians. Over time, the contributions of European customs and religion through the labor arrangement under imperial subjugation would make them "more civilized," thereby permitting them to handle "more liberty" in the political sense.[158] Acquiescent Indians would be subjects of the Crown and not anyone's personal property in order to avoid stirring rebellion and instability.[159] To allay critics, including the Dominicans, Sepúlveda maintained the Spanish purity of intention in the right of ruling over the natives by defending their right over possessions, which slaves technically lacked. In a personal letter addressed to a relative, Sepúlveda

154 Sepúlveda, *Demócrates segundo*, 95, 35.
155 Sepúlveda, *Demócrates segundo*, 29.
156 Sepúlveda, *Del reino*, 108.
157 Sepúlveda, *Demócrates segundo*, 29–30.
158 Sepúlveda, *Demócrates segundo*, 120.
159 Fernández-Santamaria, *The State, War and Peace*, 212.

clarified his position regarding the beneficent treatment of the *indios* by Spaniards:

> I do not maintain that the barbarians should be reduced to slavery, but only that they should be brought under our command. Nor do I hold that we should dispossess them of their goods, but instead only to subjugate them without committing any acts of injustice against them. Nor should we abuse our authority, but rather keep it noble, courteous, and beneficial for them. Therefore, we must first uproot their pagan customs and then, with affability, compel them to accept the natural law, and with this magnificent preparation to receive the teaching of Christ, bring them to the Christian religion with apostolic meekness and words of charity.[160]

The Spanish imparting of laws, customs, and religion on the Indians for their benefit indicated a fundamental absence of culture and civilization among them. Sepúlveda creatively interpreted the political meaning of *nullius* as vacant to align with his imperial humanist agenda. Roman civilian jurists and medieval canon lawyers had traditionally recognized unoccupied land (*terra*) or an unclaimed thing (*res*) as possessions of the first taker or occupant according to the law of nations.[161] As treated in Chapters 3 and 6, the Spanish Dominicans began to apply this legal concept to strengthen infidel rights in the New World. For Sepúlveda's colonial arguments, the traditional Roman explanation of first taker was inadequate to actual circumstances. After all, Columbus's diaries indicated early on that there were "innumerable peoples" present in the regions of the Indies.

The locus of Spanish imperial claims of possession and occupation would not revolve around unoccupied or vacant land, but instead, the vacuity or emptiness of barbarian peoples themselves. Sepúlveda argued, "It was not because those regions belonged to no one [*nullius*], but because the mortals themselves who held those regions were unoccupied [*vacui*] by the empire of Christians and civilized peoples. On that account they had relinquished dominion to Spanish occupation according to the law of nations."[162] The papal donation of Alexander VI confirmed what natural law and the law of nations already authorized. Occupation was not merely a physical act of taking unclaimed land or things but had evolved into an imperial act of politically

160 Sepúlveda, "Carta 53," in *Epistolario de Juan Ginés de Sepúlveda*, ed. Angel Losada (Ediciones Cultura Hispanica, 1966), 193.

161 *Institutes*, 2.1.12; *Digest*, 41.1.1, 3.

162 Sepúlveda, *Demócrates segundo*, p. 83: "*Non igitur, quod Regiones illae nullius essent, sed quoniam ipsi mortales, qui regiones tenebant vacui erant ab imperio Christianorum, et humanarum gentium, idcirco in Hispanorum occupantiam ditionem iure gentium concessere.*"

possessing an uncivilized people comparable to wild beasts. Barbarians were the objects of *res nullius* for civilized European empires.

Spanish imperial possession was an unseating of any prior jurisdiction over a region held by barbarians in the face of an encroaching superior culture bringing natural law and true religion. The law of nations became an ideological instrument for this new civilizing practice of empire. It was the political handmaid of a universal code of natural law, which sanctioned war in the strongest possible sense. Sepúlveda's characterization of the way of life among barbarians in terms of emptiness and vacuity was a rhetorically forceful early modern humanist revision of the Roman legal idea of *res nullius*, which now denoted a people's lack of cultural artifice, the absence of an alphabet, the dearth of historical memory, and the need of written laws.[163] The "inhabitants of the New World," wrote Sepúlveda, "undoubtedly the most barbarous of all mortals," were "completely ignorant" in the use of writing and money.[164] Consequently, they could not have written law, or positive law, the rational basis for any civil order. The absence of positive law further illustrated the rational impoverishment of Indians, an argument strategically deployed later by English colonial thinkers in North America. No contest existed between the uncultured Indian mortals and the civilized Spaniards. Taking possession of the Indies in the manner Sepúlveda outlined was synonymous with the expulsion of indigeneity through the imposition of European culture and law.

In addition to law, culture, and religion, European civilization also improved the peoples of the Indies by bringing movable goods. Sepúlveda imagined a beneficial imperial network of mutual exchange between barbarians and Europeans, even in the aftermath of violent war. The resulting evils from waging wars in the Indies were small before the benefits accrued. What made the regions of the New World so desirable and attractive to Spaniards, aside from prospective conversion of its inhabitants, was the mineral wealth contained in the soil and the seized unlawful treasures. Once the Spanish Crown claimed possession, the soil's precious deposits transferred over and were subject to fuller exploitation and use.

Dispossession of precious metals was advantageous even for the natives, who had assigned little value to gold and silver. Sepúlveda noted that outside the idolatrous function of gold, the metal was useless to natives who had failed to establish monetary currency through law and voluntary consent. Besides, in exchange for precious metals, the Spaniards generously brought them iron and bronze, which were far more useful and necessary. Spaniards also

163 Sepúlveda, *Demócrates segundo*, pp. 35, 79.

164 Sepúlveda, *Del reino*, pp. 35, 64.

exported horses, mules, hogs, oxen, goats, and sheep to the Indies all for the benefit of the natives. Lastly, due to the vacuity of the native peoples, they were poised to receive immensely from European civilization and religion, which contributed to the development of culture, laws, written language, and social institutions.[165]

Often relegated to a mere footnote in the history of international legal thought, the Latin chronicler Sepúlveda equipped later humanist jurists with the secular political device of the law of nations practiced by imperial civilizations situated in the European geopolitical space. His secular transmutation of authority over European expansion from the pope to Aristotle, from the Church to empire, was a significant ideological moment in the colonial history of international thought. After Sepúlveda, the imperial politics of natural law and the European law of nations no longer demanded, in theory, a necessary relationship with the Church and the papacy for justifying colonial dispossession and punitive war against infidel barbarians. His focus on the civilizational improvement of the vacuous life of barbarian people through a novel interpretation of the Roman law of occupation and the possession of their useless or abused goods by virtue of a superior European culture paved the way for wider colonial justifications along a Westphalian axis independent of papal power during the seventeenth century and beyond. His use of classical and biblical history, and especially contemporary Spanish reports of the New World, only added rhetorical force to the growing humanist jurisprudence of international thought. It was therefore the imperial historian Juan Ginés de Sepúlveda, not the Spanish Dominican theologians, who strategically constructed the humanist ideological bridge linking the ancient and early modern legal grammar of European empires. With no official conclusion ever reached, the Valladolid junta remained an ambivalent legacy for the new empires of commerce.

165 Sepúlveda, *Demócrates segundo*, pp. 78–79.

PART II

GOD, EMPIRES, AND INTERNATIONAL SOCIETY

5

From Infidels to Savages: Empires of Commerce and Natural Rights

An extraordinary transformation occurred in international legal thought outside Spain over the course of early modern European expansion. As civilian jurists overshadowed theologians in addressing extra-European relations, and the Pope's authority over natural law migrated to secular powers, the ambivalent legal category of the infidel widely dissipated from an international European scene marked by Protestantism and humanism. By 1749, the German philosopher Christian Wolff in his grand treatise on the law of nations argued for no restriction on entering treaties "with a nation devoted to any other religion" because of a natural duty toward humanity as such.[1] Historian Jennifer Pitts has incisively observed that soon thereafter Emer de Vattel, inspired by Wolff, would refer to any special treatment on making alliances with infidels as "superfluous."[2] These international legal thinkers no longer saw the relevance of the infidel category for relations with peoples outside Europe. Non-Europeans were humans rather than infidels. If there was any legal dissonance between Europeans and non-Europeans, it was based more on propensity to violence rather than difference of religion.[3] Natural law and the law of nations, which pertained to all humanity and made no distinction among infidels, provided the modern rubric for world order in European international thought. Church law and the papacy belonged to a bygone medieval era of Christian–infidel relations.

How did European thinking about interactions with peoples of the Indies move from Christian–infidel relations to an identifiably modern form of international relations? This chapter explores the preceding question. It

[1] Christian Wolff, *The Law of Nations Treated According to Scientific Method*, trans. Joseph Drake (Liberty Fund, 2017), chap. 4, §429.

[2] Pitts, *Boundaries of the International*, 20.

[3] Pitts, *Boundaries of the International*, 88.

considers the growing ideological displacement of the canonistic legal category of infidel, and the associated crime of idolatry, during the seventeenth century in the political context of the Indies, East but especially West. In Spain and colonial Latin America, the Christian–infidel distinction under a theocratic world order persisted under the authority of the papal grant to establish a civilizing empire of evangelization, as articulated by the legal writings of the seventeenth-century Spanish administrator and judge, Juan de Solórzano Pereira (d. 1654).[4] When the idea of infidel rights surfaced at all in seventeenth-century international legal thought on the Indies among non-Iberian empires, it was often ascribed to the Spanish Dominicans, Vitoria most of all. Reaching a brief apex in Hugo Grotius, the usage of the infidel category in the global Indies discussion pointed to the lawfulness of establishing alliances, in war but often commercial, with non-Europeans. It also brought greater recognition of natural rights for the peoples of the Indies. Yet the language of infidel rights only had, at best, ancillary importance for an emergent mode of international relations detached from a Roman Church that had long enshrined this medieval idea in canon law, custom, and scholastic theology. Its influence would remain mostly implicit, intractably ambivalent, and largely compromised by a European civilizational paradigm. This is evident in John Locke's international thought, whose discussion concludes this chapter.

Conversely, this chapter also addresses normative ideas about the savage that developed in the infidel's wake and gestures at some important consequences of the shift for subsequent international legal thought. Modern international relations, indicative of Westphalian Europe, accommodated the idea of the savage to address extra-European peoples encountered in colonial contexts. Consider Vattel's identification of the American Indians: They were savages occupied with hunting, fishing, and gathering who "made no actual and constant use" of the land.[5] For a critical Enlightenment thinker like Kant, it was the idea of the savage rather than the infidel idolater that he deployed in his description of not only Native Americans, but also in a reflexive way similar to Las Casas against Europeans who unjustly conquer and exploit foreign subjects.[6]

4 Muldoon, *The Americas in the Spanish World Order*, chaps. 5–7.

5 Vattel, *The Law of Nations*, Book 1, chap. 18, p. 216.

6 Kant, *Toward Perpetual Peace*, pp. 78–79: "The main difference between the European and American savages is that while many of the latter have been entirely eaten by their enemies, the former know how to put their conquered to better use than to consume them, and prefer to increase the numbers of their subjects and hence also the number of tools at their disposal for even more extensive wars."

Beginning with the Spanish, the term "savage" was polysemous in the Indies context, denoting serenely simple people or ferocious wild beasts. Nevertheless, whether it was Columbus's rendering of meek Taíno islanders or Cortés's reference to barbarously recalcitrant Chichimecas, both Spanish descriptions portrayed the savages of the New World as uncivilized humans. Even the most socially stratified and culturally sophisticated peoples like the Aztecs were considered savage and barbarian because of their practices of human sacrifice and cannibalism.[7] This negative stereotype extended to European Protestant colonists. In the English colonial context of North America, following internecine conflict, native inhabitants were often designated treacherous savages, not infidel idolaters.[8] When the representative Westphalian thinker Hobbes joined the Virginia Company in 1622, two years before the Company's dissolution, it was during the immediate aftermath of the Powhatan uprising against the English colonists. Hobbes's first impression of the Native Americans, whom he later characterized as poor savages in a bellicose state of nature lacking civil society, belonged to this reactionary political climate.[9] The English political concept of the savage came to mean a wild, uncivilized human being in the state of nature, which was observable among the inhabitants of the New World.

That the Spanish legal obsession with idolatry in colonization never captivated the English suggested a different kind of European cultural encounter with native polities and groups on the Eastern seaboard of North America. The social and political tensions between the English and Native Americans involved growing disputes about cultivable land more than moveable goods like precious metals. Nevertheless, the popular Spanish portrayal of natives as backward barbarians and nonindustrious persisted under a European yardstick of civilization under the measure of natural law and the law of nations. Although idolatry failed to gain rhetorical traction in legal arguments for dispossessing Native Americans, there were other markers of incivility: apparent resistance to commerce, inhospitable treatment, and the lack of private property and agricultural industry. These criteria determined a genuinely political society and title to land. "Planting" civilized colonies thus became the distinctively English mode of settling America alongside, or at the expense of, native inhabitants, but also in competition with other Europeans. For the

7 Benjamin Keen, *The Aztec Image in Western Thought* (Rutgers University Press, 1990), p. 172.

8 Wilcomb Washburn, "The Moral and Legal Justifications for Dispossessing the Indians," in *Seventeenth-Century America: Essays in Colonial History*, ed. James Morton Smith (University of North Carolina Press, 1959), pp. 20–22; Francis Jennings, *The Invasion of America: Indians, Colonialism, and the Cant of Conquest* (University of North Carolina Press, 1975), pp. 77–78.

9 Hobbes, *On the Citizen*, chap. 1, p. 30.

English colonists, the waging of wars against idolaters was an antiquated, brutish practice of Romish Christians and Spanish conquistadors.

Aside from specific departures from the preexisting rubric of Christian–infidel relations, the chapter also identifies ideological continuities of Spanish international thought on influential figures who were responsive to Dutch, but especially English, commerce and settlement in the global Indies mostly during the seventeenth century. Chief arguments for undermining Iberian control of the Indies were already contained in the Spanish legal debates about the New World. Resistance to Spanish colonial abuses and the rejection of worldwide papal dominium were two of the clearest Dominican contributions seized by European imperial competitors to vilify Spain and deny exclusive Iberian title overseas. Las Casas's *Very Brief Account of the Destruction of the Indies*, in English translation and print by 1583, was a potent ideological weapon against Spain's colonial activities and part of a larger so-called "Black Legend."[10] Vitoria's denial of the Pope's universal temporal power assumed in the Alexandrine donation provided irrefutably clear and advantageous arguments for other European powers like the English and the Dutch. Hugo Grotius called it "the opinion of all men of sound judgment" in his *Mare liberum*, a work translated into English as *The Free Sea* in 1609 by the great supporter of colonization, Richard Hakluyt the younger.[11] Even French Catholic rulers, like Francis I, who sought to civilize and convert natives in North America to the same faith as Spain, challenged papal justification of Iberian control over the global Indies.[12]

Infidel rights, the discrediting of Iberian expansion, and the repudiation of papal worldwide dominium, were not the only Spanish legacies for wider European international thought deployed in and through Protestant imperial powers. Treatments of Spanish contributions to early modern international thought often restrict attention to the Dominican theologians affiliated with the School of Salamanca, Vitoria most prominent among them. This is due, in large part, to early modern jurists who appropriated and cited his work. Vitoria's discussion of the right of traveling, the violent denial of which might establish a valid cause for war after all other possible avenues were exhausted, was highly influential for the new commercial environs. As the theologian pondered for conscience's sake, "if the barbarians deny the Spaniards what is theirs by the law of nations, they commit an injury against

[10] Keen, *Essays in the Intellectual History of Latin America* (Westview Press, 1998), p. 81.

[11] Grotius, *The Free Sea (Mare liberum)*, ed. David Armitage (Liberty Fund, 2004), chap. 6, p. 38.

[12] Pagden, *Lords of all the World* (Yale University Press, 1995), p. 33; Muldoon, *The Americas in the Spanish World Order*, p.97.

them. Hence, if war is necessary to obtain their right, they may lawfully go to war."[13] Yet the appropriation of Vitoria's possible title according to a right of travel in a new context would stretch his meaning to accent instead the enforceability of freedom in navigation and trade.[14] Protestant international thought tended to downplay and ignore the argumentative thrust of infidel rights in his *relectio*.

A key task of this chapter is to explore the wider Spanish contributions to international legal thought through the analytic lens of Valladolid and its divergent ethics of evangelization and politics of natural law. The Valladolid frame of evangelizing non-Europeans turns our attention to the colonial periphery and thereby disrupts the standard Westphalian focus on a system of states lacking a higher arbiter in Europe. In addition to locating Spanish Dominican thought in historical context, Valladolid enables us to consider the importance of Sepúlveda's imperial humanism, and other important sixteenth-century interlocutors like Jesuit theologian José de Acosta (1540–1600) and humanist jurist Fernando Vázquez de Menchaca (1512–1569) in the conversation about Spanish ideological continuity with early modern Protestant international thought. Even if Sepúlveda's overzealous Catholic arguments for war and conquest lacked explicit support from Protestant imperial ventures, aspects of his thought, in addition to the Spanish Dominicans and their Spanish diffusers, overlapped remarkably with evolving ideas about international relations among English and Dutch colonial partisans. Of specific importance were Sepúlveda's imperial-humanist arguments for a right of punishment to dispossess barbarian peoples and the European civilizational improvement of the Indies through the political enforcement of the law of nations and the natural law.

By focusing on Valladolid, a conflicted legacy comes into view showing how scholastic theology and imperial humanism each contributed to an emergent Protestant, humanist, and naturalist jurisprudence at the root of modern international relations. The ideological kernel of this new international legal thought over the Indies entailed a moral commitment to the fundamental unity of humankind, ordained by divine providence (not the papacy), which held the promise of establishing international society through commercial relations safeguarded by specific rights of trade and settlement in accordance with natural law and human reason. Christianity could not but thrive in such

13 Vitoria, *On the American Indians*, q. 3, a. 1, p. 282.

14 Kingsbury and Adam Roberts, "Introduction: Grotian Thought in International Relations," in *Hugo Grotius and International Relations*, eds. Hedley Bull, Benedict Kingsbury, and Adam Roberts (Oxford University Press, 2002), p. 45.

an interconnected world of commerce carried out by just merchants and industrious laborers in search of commodities and land.[15] The Bible was still important to this European colonial endeavor though it functioned as a divine confirmation of what the natural law and law of nations, read through Roman legal and Stoic commitments, already prescribed. It was also read increasingly in historical terms, alongside classical Greco-Roman sources and New World chronicles. The Westphalian character of this nascent international society free from papal meddling only reinforced the authoritative importance among international theorists of a universal law accessible to all human beings and conducive to global commerce with resort to war as needed.

Altogether, a unique confluence of Spanish Catholic sources entered the stream of Protestant colonial thinking on the Indies. Certain themes considered in this chapter help identify areas of both continuity and innovation. First, the discursive Protestant shift from preaching by means of war to trading and commerce by force of arms. Second, the application of the right of punishment against enemies of the human race, rather than enemies of the faith, in an international state of nature. Lastly, the appeal to European civilization over and against natural savages in the argument for the rightful possession of vacant (*nullius*) land, not people. Although the uncivilized savages of the Americas might formally possess natural rights, these were rights now circumscribed by the political power of civilized European peoples rather than the Catholic papacy. The target of dispossession under Roman legal vocabulary wedded to Christian humanism moved away from Spanish focus on idols as abused and ill-used goods to vacant and underused land. As we will explore, idolatry was not the primary sin against natural law in the English colonial context, but rather, nonindustriousness, which left the land idle and waste. Neither native savages nor failed settlers could escape the guilt of violating the law of nature when land went unexploited.

CHRISTIAN COMMERCE BY FORCE OF ARMS

The Dutch chased the Portuguese from almost all their settlements in the East Indies; and several other nations planted colonies in America. The Spaniards considered these new-discovered countries as the *subject of conquest*; while others, more refined in their views, found them to be the proper *subjects of commerce*, and upon this principle directed their proceedings. Hence several nations have conducted themselves with so much wisdom, that they have given *a kind of sovereignty to companies of merchants*,

[15] I argue on these grounds that there was a distinctive Protestant ideology of empire with positive characteristics beyond a mere anti-papalism in contrast to Armitage, *The Ideological Origins of the British Empire* (Cambridge University Press, 2000), pp. 63, 66.

who governing these far-distant countries only with a view to trade, have made a great accessary power, without embarrassing the principal state.[16]

A striking feature of other early modern European seaborne empires, especially the English in North America, was the absence of a comparable Valladolid junta.[17] Indeed, there were notable English "apostles to the Indians" advocating justice for land claims on their behalf such as Puritans John Eliot and Roger Williams. However, the public significance of a clearly defined debate about infidel rights involving Native Americans reaching the royal court never happened in the British case or elsewhere. A few points may get at this important transnational difference of European legal history.

Arguments for conquest were less feasible in a political context markedly different from the Spaniards. The English Crown often exercised a less direct role over colonial affairs conducted by chartered companies in comparison with the jealous Catholic monarchy and its claim over Indian vassals. Another important factor lessening royal oversight was the existence of considerably smaller and less socially stratified native populations in North America unlike the native empires of Latin America. Perhaps the strongest reason was that very early on English colonists identified commercial trade and occupation of vacant space (*vacuum domicilium*) as overarching Protestant rationales for European presence in the New World thus eroding the title of evangelization and the incorporation of new Christian subjects through war. Without the papal title of spreading the Gospel and the political dispute over claiming jurisdiction over natives primarily through war and conquest, the ethics of evangelization and the language of infidel rights became less germane. Nevertheless, even though Protestant colonial thinkers were able to surmount the ideological impasse of Valladolid between Las Casas and Sepúlveda to meet a rapidly changing international society, they did not escape the ambivalent legacy of infidel rights exposed at Valladolid. Rather, it persisted in a concealed way since recognition of infidel natural rights for native peoples did not preclude superior European legal claims of dispossession.

During the second half of the sixteenth century and the seventeenth century, European imperial powers under the impulses of the Reformation and Renaissance ignored papal authority in the resolution of international disputes for new commercial ventures outside Europe. The vast open sea wrapping

16 Montesquieu, *The Spirit of the Laws*, vol. 2, trans. Thomas Nugent (Colonial Press, 1900), Book 21, chap. 21, p. 367.

17 Brading, *The First America*, p. 1: "Where, in all the long centuries of European imperialism, was there a scene to equal the public debate staged at Valladolid between Juan Ginés de Sepúlveda and Las Casas?"

around the southern tip of Africa to the East Indies and the expansive continental lands of the West Indies, both precipitated by fifteenth-century Portuguese and Spanish kingdoms, were also engines of colonialism for the ascendant seaborne powers of the English Crown and the Dutch United Provinces. In the words of Adam Smith, the discovery of new land and sea passage in the global Indies were "the two greatest and most important events recorded in the history of mankind."[18] These contentious geopolitical spaces on sea and land, which admitted no higher arbiter with sovereign authority, generated unprecedented legal reflection about universal norms ordering human relations where the commercial stakes between Europeans were extremely high and encounters with non-Europeans unavoidable.

Montesquieu approvingly observed that there was a new political actor on the international circuit during the seventeenth century with "a kind of sovereignty": the joint-stock company chartered and patented by commercial empires. English and Dutch merchants under the authorization of their governments established the Virginia Company (1606), the Massachusetts Bay Company (1629), and the Dutch West India Company (1621) in North America and the British Royal African Company (1660) dedicated to acquiring gold and trading African slaves. Large-scale company sovereigns that took on even stronger imperial features included the British (1600) and Dutch East India Companies (1602), both of which lasted nearly two centuries.[19] These sovereign companies organized by individual shareholders and merchants were extra-European hybrid agents of colonial expansion, resembling states in the administration of law, collecting taxes, providing protection, regulating economic and civil life, establishing diplomatic relations, waging war, inflicting punishment, and making claims to jurisdiction over land and sea.[20] Profit-centered investors underwrote these merchant empires, which typically received a monopoly over trade and commerce in regions of the global Indies designated by the English Crown and Dutch Republic.

Commerce as a fundamental reason of state characterized the international legal thought among seaborne empires during this mercantile period of European expansion on the eve of Westphalia.[21] The Roman *Digest*, which garnered supreme authority among humanist-minded jurists, was especially useful for establishing the temporal linkage between commerce and the many

[18] Adam Smith, *The Wealth of Nations* (Modern Library, 2000), Book 4, chap. 7, pt. 3, p. 675.

[19] J. C. Sharman, *Empires of the Weak* (Princeton University Press, 2019), chap. 2.

[20] Philip J. Stern, *The Company-State* (Oxford University Press, 2011), pp. 3–6.

[21] Armitage, *Foundations of Modern International Thought* (Cambridge University Press, 2013), p. 53.

political jurisdictions in the law of nations.[22] When Grotius, already the official Latin chronicler for the United Provinces, wrote his legal defense of the Dutch East India Company's (VOC) seizure of the Portuguese cargo ship *Santa Catarina* that occurred in 1603 on the Straight of Singapore, he identified the dual emergence of commerce and the sovereign state. According to Grotius's historical narration informed by classical jurists and historians and poets, these two transformations moved humans out of the realm of common ownership and into private possession under a sovereign ruler through the fixing of boundaries.[23] The shared beginnings of political sovereignty and commerce give one compelling reason why Grotius promoted divisible sovereignty in practice, which could extend the right of states to company actors like the VOC.

By the end of the sixteenth and beginning of the seventeenth centuries, the European idea of commerce between states inside and outside Europe rested on a strong Christian philosophical commitment to ancient Stoicism. The Italian-born Protestant convert and Oxford Professor of Civil Law, Alberico Gentili (1552–1608), articulated the universal bond of humanity in a Ciceronian spirit: "[W]e are members of a great body [*membra summus corporis magni*]. And in truth the world is one body."[24] This great body, or great society, including the whole world, indicated not only a moral unity for Gentili and other thinkers imbibing the wisdom of Stoic humanism. It also expressed a juridical unity of the world contained in the natural law and law of nations. "The New World," Gentili forcefully proposed, "is joined to our own."[25] Commerce allowed for greater latitude in European interactions with infidels. Nevertheless, this did not always mean that treaties with infidels were simply acceptable. Gentili believed infidels could not be trusted; therefore, one could maintain peace but not an official alliance with them.[26] Grotius's view, in contrast, was far more conducive to modern international law and the eighteenth-century arguments of Wolff and Vattel when he argued, "the right of making alliances is common to all men, and admits of no exception on the account of religion."[27]

Early modern empires of commerce supplanted any title of evangelization by political subjugation in the Indies transmitted by the papacy to the Spanish

22 *Digest*, 1.1.5.

23 Grotius, *Commentary on the Law of Prize*, chap. 12, pp. 319–320.

24 Alberico Gentili, *De iure belli libri tres*, vol. 2, trans. John C. Rolfe (Clarendon Press, 1933), Book 1, chap. 15, p. 67.

25 Gentili, *De iure belli*, Book 1, chap. 19, p. 89.

26 Alberico Gentili, *De iure belli*, Book 3, chap. 19, pp. 401–402.

27 Grotius, *The Rights of War and Peace*, ed. Richard Tuck (Liberty Fund, 2005), Book 2, chap. 15, pp. 827–828.

Crown with its conquistadors and chaplains. This did not mean the English and Dutch colonial thinkers were disinterested in preaching Christianity. Rather, they viewed evangelization as a byproduct of the subjective enforceable rights of trading, merchandizing, and settling unoccupied land. Therefore, religion would not, could not, be the exclusive purpose for European presence in the Indies. Contrary to the Spanish Dominicans, in the new European discourse of global commerce, there was scant motive to send religious preachers alone to uncharted lands. That was because saving souls and making profit were not antithetical aims. Both pursuits were mutually supportive for establishing a great society of humankind according to a neo-Stoic Christian view of world order.

In his early work, Grotius was optimistic about trading's prospect to prepare the path of Christianity. He mentioned the case of the Dutch establishing a Christian–infidel alliance with the Malaysian King of Johore against the Portuguese, similar to the alliance of Francis I with Ottoman Sultan Suleiman against Holy Roman Emperor Charles V.[28] Akin to Paulus Vladimiri, the Dutch jurist derived an ethic of the neighbor from the Good Samaritan parable to support the protection and the defense of "every human being," irrespective of religion. Grotius further argued that such conduct by Christians in service to equitable trading would inspire the conversion of peoples unlike failed Iberian Catholic attempts: "The Indian peoples must be shown what it means to be a Christian, in order that they may not believe all Christians to be as the Spaniards are. Let those peoples look upon religion stripped of false symbols, commerce devoid of fraud, arms unattended by injuries. Let them marvel at the faith which forbids that that even infidels should be neglected. In achieving these ends, we shall be preparing men for God."[29] For Protestant empires of commerce, the good example of armed Christian companies of merchants and settlers were the trailblazers for spreading Christianity, not austere mendicant preachers and certainly not conquistadors. Civility and upright moral conduct were the seeds for introducing a form of Christianity denuded of its violent crusader heritage.

Contemporaneous with the Dutch affair in the East Indies that occupied the young Grotius, the English were in the initial phase of colonizing North America. The English colonists had a remarkably similar perspective as the Dutch on the connection between commerce and the Christian religion in order to distinguish themselves from Spaniards. The original royal charter of

[28] Peter Borschberg, "Hugo Grotius, East India Trade and the King of Johor," *Journal of Southeast Asian Studies* 30.2 (1999): 225–248.

[29] Grotius, *Commentary on the Law of Prize*, chap. 13, pp. 434–435.

the Virginia Company in 1606 tasked its petitioners, among them Richard Hakluyt the younger, to bring Christianity and human civility to "the infidels and savages living in those parts."[30] Hakluyt's *Discourse of Western Planting* (1584) already paid tribute to planting religion and colonies together under the company, which would not take the form of conquest practiced by Spaniards. Neither would the English foolishly send preachers unaccompanied by soldiers and a company for protection as the Spanish Dominicans had done in Florida, "where they were miserablye massacred by the Savages."[31] Establishing a European colonial settlement first, or planting near natives, would supply the best method of civilizing non-Europeans. Here was the English Protestant prerequisite for the conversion of infidels and savages.

In addition to a refutation of Pope Alexander VI's "most unreasonable and injurious donation," Hakluyt's *Discourse* joined many English Elizabethan propagandists by relying on Las Casas's scathing accounts of Spanish brutality in the New World, where "hellhounds and wolves" have undermined conversion.[32] The English planting of colonies abroad would not only provide a safe haven for European Protestants fleeing persecution, it could also protect the natives from Spanish tyranny.[33] Hakluyt's promotion of empire according to a transatlantic exchange of commodities rather than the backbreaking labor of seizing precious metals featured merchants and trading companies as principal agents of English colonization.[34] Providence was assuredly on the side of English commercial expansion. Hakluyt defended traffic among merchants as the divinely authorized and natural means of establishing a mutually beneficial exchange of commodities between peoples dependent on one another's goods.[35]

From the English and Dutch colonial perspectives, the Iberian Catholic powers had failed to engage infidel peoples with civility and humanity, the true marks of Christian commerce. Alberico Gentili presented a critique of the Spanish conquests on this score: The Spaniards were not interested in

30 "The charter that created the Virginia companies" (April 10, 1606), in *New American World: A Documentary History of North America to 1612*, vol. 5, ed. David B. Quinn (Arno Press, 1979), p. 192.

31 Richard Hakluyt, *Discourse of Western Planting* (1584), in *New American World*, vol. 3, pp. 72–73.

32 Hakluyt, *Discourse of Western Planting*, pp. 107, 116. For more on Elizabethan anti-papal colonial arguments that still invoked religious justifications, sometimes even conquest, for English expansion, see Ken MacMillan, *Sovereignty and Possession in the English New World* (Cambridge University Press, 2006), chap. 2.

33 Hakluyt, *Discourse of Western Planting*, p. 120.

34 Elliott, *Empires of the Atlantic World*, pp. 26–27.

35 Armitage, *Ideological Origins*, p. 71.

lawful commerce in the New World, but political rule and subjugation of the people.[36] This transnational difference with Spanish conquest may help explain why the language of infidel rights took on a different valence in the Dutch and English colonial deployments. For the Spanish Dominicans infidel rights underscored the independent political agency of natives, our focus in Chapter 6. Yet for the Protestant seaborne empires infidel rights largely served the purpose of protecting open trade relations between Christians and non-Europeans, and safeguarding claims to property according to natural law.

Grotius's twelfth chapter of *De jure praedae*, first published as the standalone work *Mare liberum*, contained his most extensive treatment of infidel rights owing to the Dominican theologians, Cajetan and Vitoria. It provided a clear illustration of the strategic use of infidel rights within an evolving discourse of global commerce. Although Grotius opened the chapter with a notable discussion of infidel rights, the chapter's wider argument was about the justice of the Dutch East India Company to wage private war against the Portuguese for hindering free trade – a subjective right of every individual and republic. Grotius began with a reflection on the divinely ordained nature of human sociability and commercial exchange to accentuate the gravity of Portuguese injustice:

> For God has not willed that nature shall supply every region with all the necessities of life; and furthermore, He has granted pre-eminence in different arts to different nations. Why are these things so, if not because it was His Will that human friendships should be fostered by mutual needs and resources, lest individuals, in deeming themselves self-sufficient, might thereby be rendered unsociable? In the existing state of affairs, it has come to pass, in accordance with the design of Divine Justice, that one nation supplies the needs of another, so that in this way whatever has been produced in any region is regarded as a product native to all regions. [...] Consequently, anyone who abolishes this system of exchange, abolishes also the highly prized fellowship in which humanity is united. He destroys the opportunities for mutual benefactions. In short, he does violence to nature herself.[37]

The doctrine of providential commerce articulated by Grotius held that the inhabitants of the world should unite in fellowship through a mutually beneficial exchange of goods "to offset the scarcity with the plenty that lay elsewhere."[38] From this standpoint, property and commerce were not only

36 Gentili, *De iure belli*, Book 1, chap. 18, p. 89.

37 Grotius, *Commentary on the Law of Prize*, chap. 12, pp. 302–303.

38 Ileana Porras, "Appropriating Nature: Commerce, Property, and the Commodification of Nature in the Law of Nations," *Leiden Journal of International Law* 27 (2014): 643.

permissible according to natural law and the law of nations, but also divinely sanctioned. Neither the Pope nor the Iberian powers could stand in the way of a universal right to engage in commerce, or the freedom to trade, since God and nature have authorized it so. Grotius's textual support for what he called the "sacrosanct law of hospitality" relied principally on Roman Stoics and civil jurists, as well as Vitoria's deployment of it as a basis for a just title.[39] Gentili's *De iure belli* (1598) also argued that the denial of passage, travel, and trade, admitting certain exceptions, was a justifiable cause of war. Due to nature's bestowal of freedom to travel, to take away "such privileges inflicts a wound on human society."[40] As the classical Stoics demonstrated for both Gentili and Grotius, the unequal distribution of commodities across the world made it necessary for everyone to engage in commerce and fellowship for mutual advantage. Resisting commerce, except under highly qualified circumstances, was a denial of humanity.

Of course, the chief subjects that Grotius specifically had in mind for the Dutch interaction were the infidel peoples of the East Indies, not the native inhabitants of the West. Nevertheless, Grotius thought it fit to incorporate the Dominican New World position on the rights of infidels. He provided a lengthy citation of Cajetan's commentary on Question 66 concerning the third category of infidels, which served two purposes for him.[41] First, it established the political sovereignty of the rational peoples of the East Indies, regardless of their unbelief. As a result, these peoples possessed the freedom to trade with the Portuguese or the Dutch, or whomever, as they wished. Second, since the pope had no temporal power over infidels, there could be no exclusive Portuguese right of trading from the Church. The English translation held a similar view, as expressed in Hakluyt's edition of this section in which he indicated that the infidel peoples of the East Indies were simply "free and in their own power."[42] The other great promoter of English colonization, Samuel Purchas (1575–1626), would also appropriate the Dominican view on infidel rights like Grotius to address the context of North America.

Purchas's *Hakluytus Posthumus, or Purchas His Pilgrimes* (1625) was a theological work that located England in a sacred history formed by a nationalist and cosmopolitan outlook opposed to papal theocracy.[43] Its historical reflection on the spiritual and economic significance of the

39 Grotius, *Commentary on the Law of Prize*, chap. 12, pp. 304–305.

40 Gentili, *De iure belli*, Book 1, chap. 19, p. 88.

41 Grotius, *Commentary on the Law of Prize*, chap. 12, pp. 308–314.

42 Grotius, *The Free Sea*, chap. 4, p. 20.

43 Armitage, *Ideological Origins*, pp. 84–85.

Virginia colony, in part, was to demonstrate that the planting of "another England in America" would not resemble barbaric Spanish attempts. The Dominican theologians were particularly important for Purchas's treatment "Of the proprietie which Infidels have in their Lands and Goods." Although infidels were strangers and foreigners to the Church, they were made after the divine image and retain an "immortall reasonable spirit."[44] Infidel property and political rule stem from nature and God, not grace. "The Gospel is not a sword to take away the earth, but to destroy hell."[45] Purchas cited Vitoria's *relectiones* on ecclesiastical power and the Amerindians, but also Cajetan's commentary, to strengthen his theological support of infidel rights. He then presented in his own words Aquinas's classic doctrine from the *Summa*, Question 10, Article 10: "Nor can Infidelitie which concerneth Divine Law, yea in matters supernaturall, take away the right which Positive or Naturall Law hath given."[46] This Dominican view on infidel rights, in contrast to certain notable exceptions like Sir Edward Coke, represented the common opinion among English colonial thinkers favoring the way of trade and settlement. Coke's extreme English common law reading of infidels as perpetual enemies undermined the possibility, in principle, of establishing the trade and even alliances with hospitable non-Christians crucial to commercial expansion.[47]

The *Hakluytus* would include Las Casas's *Very Brief Account*, followed by Purchas's own summary of what happened at the Valladolid junta to support the Spanish Dominicans.[48] He shared their criticism of the excesses of papal temporal power contrasting the latter with the proper method of evangelization: "[N]or can a pretended Vicar challenge justly, what his Lord never claimed, what hee also disclaimed: nor did hee send Souldiers but Preachers, to convert the World to the Faith truly Catholike." This critique should not be taken however as Purchas's promotion of the Spanish Dominican preachers-only method of evangelization. Purchas then added the characteristically Protestant hue on evangelization in a commercial setting comparable to Grotius when he referred to the figure of King Solomon, "who sent Ships of Merchandise and not of Warre to Ophir."[49] Solomon, King

44 Samuel Purchas, *Hakluytus Posthumus or Purchas His Pilgrimes*, vol. 1 (Macmillan Company, 1905), Book 1, chap. 1, §5, p. 40.

45 Purchas, *Hakluytus Posthumus*, Book 1, chap. 1, §5, p. 39.

46 Purchas, *Hakluytus Posthumus*, Book 1, chap. 1, §5, p. 43.

47 Pagden, *Lords of All the World*, 94–5; Richard Tuck, "Alliances with Infidels in the European Imperial Expansion," in *Empire and Modern Political Thought*, pp. 61–83.

48 Purchas, *Hakluytus Posthumus*, vol. 18, Book 8, chap. 4, pp. 85–180.

49 Purchas, *Hakluytus Posthumus*, Book 1, chap. 1, §5, p. 43.

David's son, was the moral exemplar for Purchas's alternative model of spreading the Gospel through commerce and making discoveries by freely traversing land and sea. Purchas began his sacred history in *Hakluytus Posthumus* with the figure of Solomon, who "passed all the Kings of the Earth with Riches and Wisdome."[50] Turning to the tropological sense of the biblical story, or its morally significant meaning to inspire good conduct, King Solomon represented a wise guide and teacher on "the lawfulnesse of Navigation to remote regions" in a manner unlike the campaigns of Alexander the Great and the Spanish conquistadors.[51] The English endeavor in the New World had to be understood instead in broadly Stoic cosmopolitan yet Christian evangelical terms. God, as Acts 17:26 reiterates, "hath made all the Nations one bloud ... and fellow members one of another." According to Purchas's economic doctrine of providence, this implied:

> [T]hat there should still remaine mutuall Necessitie, the Mother of mutuall Commerce, that one should not be hungry, and another drunken, but the superfluitie of one Countrey, should supply the necessities of another, in exchange for such things, which are here also necessary, and there abound; that thus the whole World might bee as one Body of mankind, the Nations as so many members, the superabundance in each, concocted, distributed, retained or expelled by merchandising (as by the Naturall bodily Offices and Faculties in nourishment) whereby not without mutuall gaine One may releeve others Wants.[52]

The aim of a mutual commerce that brought about greater equilibrium in the distribution of commodities, natural and artificial, was not merely material but spiritual. The best means left of spreading Christianity in this "last age" ushered in through Protestant Europe was navigation and commerce, not violent conquest. Purchas surmised, if God could turn German barbarians into Roman Catholics, then surely God "can of Merchants allured with Gold, make, or at least send with them, Preachers of his Sonne."[53] Contrary to papal assertions, the Iberian empires did not have a monopoly on trade in the global Indies; neither did they have one on salvation.

An important statement representative of the seventeenth-century Protestant view on European commercial expansion in the West Indies came from the early promotional tract, A *true declaration of the state of Virginia*, anonymously written on behalf of the same Company's colony in

50 Purchas, *Hakluytus Posthumus*, Book 1, chap. 1, p. 5.
51 Purchas, *Hakluytus Posthumus*, Book 1, chap. 1, §2, pp. 9–10.
52 Purchas, *Hakluytus Posthumus*, Book 1, chap. 1, §2, pp. 10–11.
53 Purchas, *Hakluytus Posthumus*, Book 1, chap. 1, §2, pp. 13–14.

1610. The tract inhabited a discourse of legal humanism, of which Hakluyt and Purchas also belonged.[54] It argued for an English title to Virginia based on historical precedent and the denial of papal claims to temporal power. Of special note was the tract's initial framing of English colonization in evangelical terms to outline the distinctive approach of the Virginia Company toward its relations with the native peoples of North America. Since the primary end of English presence in Virginia was "to plant religion," much was at stake in considering the proper means of achieving that end.

The tract began with a theological question posed by the Great Commission, "whether it not be a determined truth, that the Gospel should be preached, to all the world, before the end of the world?" It then proposed three possible ways or methods of preaching the Gospel to all nations. Read through the optic of Valladolid, the tract clearly outlined the two sides of debate between Las Casas and Sepúlveda on the ethics of evangelization. The first method of evangelization was apostolic, reliant on divine grace and exemplifying simplicity without the aid of temporal powers. Las Casas's only way of peaceful evangelization, which might lead to conversion of infidels or the martyrdom of Christians, typified this apostolic method of sending preachers alone. In contrast, there was a second method, aggressively imperialistic in practice, conducted by a prince through conquest so that preachers might follow with the faith. Sepúlveda's argument for evangelization by political subjugation was the obvious allusion.[55]

According to the Virginia Company, neither of Valladolid's options were tenable for interacting with Native Americans. An apostolic method risking martyrdom was vanity before the ignorant peoples comprising North America. Like Sepúlveda at Valladolid, and Hakluyt's *Discourse*, the tract mentioned the case of Florida, where Las Casas's friend Luis Cáncer suffered death as a preacher unaccompanied by weapons. The native peoples "did devour the Preachers of the word without speaking any word."[56] Evidently, for the Company, the apostolic age with its miracles had expired. Alternatively, the method of imperial conquest, rooted in ambition and violence, used religion only as a cover. Furthermore, the conquest argument had been disputed already by "the divines of Salamanca," namely, Spanish Dominicans like Vitoria and Soto. The Virginia Company then enlisted a third option eminently suitable to its aim in contrast to the merely apostolic

54 Fitzmaurice, *Humanism and America* (Cambridge University Press, 2007), p. 150.

55 *A true declaration of the state of Virginia* (1610), in *New American World*, vol. 5, p. 249.

56 *A true declaration of the state of Virginia*, p. 250.

and merely imperial: a mixed "way of merchandizing and trade."[57] Both the discoveries carried out by merchants, and the use of temporal means of defense to secure commerce with natives, offered a combined method that best encapsulated the Christian purpose of the trading company.

The important theological source here for the Virginia Company's identification of three methods for propagating Christianity – peaceful evangelization, imperial conquest, and commercial trade – was the Spanish theologian explicitly mentioned in the tract, the Jesuit José de Acosta. As a member of the burgeoning global missionary order of the Society of Jesus, Acosta spent over a decade in the New World. He wrote key works on Amerindian cultures that left an indelible mark on colonial international thinking about European expansion across the Atlantic, especially for Englishmen like Purchas but also John Locke.[58] In fact, Locke possessed a translated copy of Acosta's *Natural and Moral History of the Indies* (1604), which was one of the few works he actually cited in the *Second Treatise of Government* (1689). Locke also had a Latin text that contained Acosta's treatise on the proper method of evangelizing the Amerindians called *De procuranda indorum salute*, first published in 1588.[59] Since *De procuranda* would have been the direct source for the Virginia Company's promotional tract outlining the three methods of evangelization, it deserves further consideration here.

As seen in the previous chapter, Valladolid had sharply distinguished two opposed and incompatible methods of evangelization, and associated politics of natural law for thinking about infidel dominium. However, the Spanish Crown of Acosta at the end of the sixteenth century had opted for exploration, trade, and settlement rather than conquest and indigenous alliances as the lawful means of bringing Christianity to the peoples of the New World.[60] Acosta conceded the importance of Las Casas's position on the apostolic method of evangelization by affirming that recent Jesuits had conducted themselves accordingly in the East among the peoples of India, Japan, and China.[61] Following the Spanish Dominicans, Acosta also rejected Sepúlveda's

57 *A true declaration of the state of Virginia*, pp. 249–250.

58 For the best treatment of Acosta's influence on English colonial international thought, see Fitzmaurice, *Sovereignty, Property and Empire*, pp. 73–84.

59 John Harrison and Peter Laslett, *The Library of John Locke* (Oxford Bibliographical Society, 1965).

60 "Ordinances of New Discoveries" (1573), in *New Iberian World*, 1:368: "Explorers by land and sea are not to engage in any form of war and conquest, nor support one group of Indians against another, nor become involved in contention with the local people, nor do them any harm, nor take away any of their property, unless it be in the way of barter, with the agreement of the owners."

61 José de Acosta, *De procuranda indorum salute* (CSIC, 1984), lib. 2, cap. 8, p. 306.

now outdated method of evangelization by conquest principally on the canon legal grounds of the Pauline *foris* principle defended by Spanish Dominicans, which prohibited political judgment of infidel outsiders.[62] If such an expansive justification for war were granted to a political power, no sooner would the whole world devolve into calamities filled with discord and murder.[63] Just war must therefore proceed either from an injury against oneself or one's goods, a violation of the universal law of nations. Acosta rejected wars for the sake of attaining glory, acquiring riches, expanding empire, or simply spreading religion. Only defensive war was legitimate, not offensive wars.

Acosta's position on war in the case of the West Indies might give the impression of being synonymous with Vitoria. However, Acosta made an additional cultural judgment about Amerindian population in the conglomerate that was more akin to Sepúlveda's imperial humanism than Vitoria's theological scholasticism. Acosta enlisted the ancient category of the barbarian according to a hierarchical classification now informed by his transatlantic travels and missionary studies. His larger study *Natural and Moral History of the Indies* claimed that, despite having originated from the less uncivilized continent of barbarians in Asia, the simple hunters who came to occupy the Americas had forgotten their roots and lived according to the most primitive laws of natural instinct. Historical amnesia among the natives was how "there came to be an infinite amount of savagery in the New World."[64] Although there were some native peoples who possessed political organization and religion, like the Aztecs of Mexico and the Inca of Peru, they "were still removed from right reason and the general customs of the human race."[65] Acosta's humanist novelty lay in his progressive history of civilization, which placed the peoples of the Americas at the bottom of a ladder and in the category of barbarian savagery. This threefold civilizational scale of humanity broken up geopolitically – civilized Europeans, barbarian Asians, and native savages – bore a strong and notable influence on early modern European thinking about the New World but also modern international law among positivists well into the nineteenth and twentieth centuries.[66]

62 Acosta, *De procuranda*, lib. 2, cap. 3, p. 264.

63 Acosta, *De procuranda*, lib. 2, cap. 4, p. 272: "*Etenim si tantum licentiae reipublicae in rempublicam tribuas, nihil aliud agas quam ut brevi universum terrarum orbe perturbes et discordia ac caedibus impleas.*"

64 Acosta, *Natural and Moral History of the Indies*, trans. Frances M. López-Morillas (Duke University Press, 2002), Book 1, chap. 24, pp. 71–72.

65 Acosta, *De procuranda*, proemio, p. 64: "*Multum tamen etiam hi a recta ratione et consuetudine generis humani absunt.*"

66 On the similar threefold classification of American anthropologist, Lewis Henry Morgan, who influenced numerous international lawyers, see Neff, *Justice among Nations*, p. 311.

Whereas Vitoria formally adhered to an egalitarian notion of the law of nations that included Christian and infidels alike, Acosta followed Sepúlveda in applying a civilizational rubric onto the peoples of the West Indies thereby excluding all of them from the law of cultured, European nations because they lacked a formal alphabet and written law. Most natives of the Americas, he ventured in *De procuranda*, from Brazil to Florida, were "human savages similar to beasts" because of their crude customs and lack of government. In the New World, Acosta further opined, "there are infinite herds" of people comparable to Aristotle's natural slave.[67] Just as Sepúlveda had observed, without a written script native peoples were inept in terms of exercising reason. Ill-treatment of foreigners and missionaries, or any violation of the basic norm of hospitality, provided a litmus test for demonstrating widespread Amerindian barbarism. From the European colonial gaze, the natives of America failed to live according to universal norms accessible to reason: "In the presence of visitors and foreigners, they do not observe the law of nations, while among themselves they do not even know the laws of nature." Acosta continued his vituperations by suggesting that to presume native rationality and political freedom would amount to "entering into an alliance with wild boars and crocodiles."[68] With natural law and the law of nations providing a benchmark for measuring civilizational status, the savage peoples of America were humans by nature, yet hardly distinguishable in practice from *ferae bestiae*.

Acosta's fundamental denigration of Amerindian rationality and their alleged ignorance of natural law and abeyance of the law of nations led him to devise another method of evangelization applicable to the barbarism in the West Indies.[69] This "new way of evangelizing" (*novo evangelizandi*), as Acosta termed it, provided the ideological thrust of *De procuranda* later appropriated by the Virginia Company and other English colonial thinkers. It helped delineate a third way for Protestant empires of commerce that consolidated the ambivalent character of infidel rights for subsequent colonial deployments. On the one hand, Acosta rejected Sepúlveda's flagrant method of violent evangelization by political subjugation because it was unjust on Christian terms. On the other, the peaceful evangelization practiced by the

67 Acosta, *De procuranda*, proemio, p. 66: "*In hac sunt homines sylvestres feris similes.*"

68 Acosta, *De procuranda*, lib. 2, cap. 8, p. 306: "*In hospites et externos nullum gentium ius observantes cum ne inter se quidem naturae leges sciant. Quamobrem qui horum se rationi et arbitrio commisserit, poterit his cum apris et crocodilis amicitiam inire.*"

69 Brading, *The First America*, p. 188: "The purpose of this division of all humanity outside Christendom into three classes lay not in its utility for anthropological research but rather in affording a yardstick by which to measure what reliance should be placed on force of arms in the preaching of the Christian gospel."

early apostles and used by Jesuits for barbarians in the East Indies was also unsuitable for breaking the hardened customs of New World savages. The apostolic method relied on miraculous examples and the witness of martyrs. By Acosta's estimate, and that of the Dominican theologians, Spaniards had little or nothing to show the natives in the way of exemplary behavior. Yet in contrast to the Dominicans, Acosta denied the powerful witness of martyrs in the New World. The virtue of someone like fray Cáncer dying for Christ off the west coast of Florida would go unrecognized to native savages who would have seen him as nothing more than delectable food.[70]

In an artful intellectual maneuver, Acosta combined defensive war with a coercive method of evangelizing the "monstrous humans" of the Americas. The "new evangelization" could overcome the doctrinal impasse of Valladolid between Las Casas's impossible apostolic ideal and Sepúlveda's unlawful perversion of it. Pairing weapons and evangelization to secure a safe path for preachers had precedent in Innocent IV and the canon legal tradition. In practice, Acosta argued for joint expeditions to new lands comprised of armed soldiers and missionaries. The former could offer necessary provisions for long and dangerous journeys and the latter could bring salvation to any soul still captive to Satan. Although Soto and Vitoria supported the option of protecting preachers from imminent harm by tyrannical infidels, martyrdom remained a viable, indeed heroic, option for the Dominicans. They strictly presumed that the use of defensive force would remain proportionate to the threat against preachers and not scandalize the faith. Soto never explicitly justified a defensive war, much less conquest, and Vitoria only considered it as a possibility for analyzing problematic cases of conscience, as part of the penitential business of priests. These traditional scholastic criteria testified to the rationality of infidels who would consider a warlike religion forced upon them repulsive. For Acosta, however, there was little concern of bringing scandal to the faith because savage barbarians were currently incapable of recognizing true religion. As the Spanish Jesuit interpreted the matter, preaching had to be partly humane and partly violent in order to discipline, however slowly, the savageness (*feritate*) of the natives.[71]

Acosta's new evangelical method provided explanatory power for the Virginia Company's planting of religion. However, the pairing of preachers

[70] Acosta, *De procuranda*, lib. 2, cap. 8, p. 308.

[71] Acosta, *De procuranda*, lib. 2, cap. 12, pp. 338–340: "*Ut enim barbari, velut mixta humana et ferina natura, constat ut moribus non tam homines, quam hominum monstra videantur, sic quae cum illis instituenda est consuetudo, partim humana et liberalis, partim subhorrida et ferox sit, necesse est usque dum nativa illa sua feritate deposita, paulatim mansuescere incipiant et ad disciplinam humanitatemque traduci.*"

and protective soldiers still belonged to an uncouth Spanish Catholic model of colonization that imposed royal jurisdiction over native peoples. For English Protestants, armed merchants and settlers acting through sovereign-like companies were far more apt to extend commercial empires than either conquistadors or unguarded preachers. On this score, Acosta's response to the question, "By what right can Christians enter the lands of barbarians?", which immediately followed his discussion of the new method of evangelization, was especially useful for the Protestant deployment of subjective right in a commercial context.

Acosta began with Vitoria's first possible title over the Indies grounded in a right of traveling (*ius peregrinandi*). Aside from the customary practice of hospitality among nearly all peoples, Acosta went beyond Vitoria by grounding travel in an "innate desire to learn and experience new things," which grants to everyone the right (*ius cuique*) to visit even the most remote regions, as they please, so that they may see and observe the world.[72] Acosta articulated the individual right to travel and navigate freely within a global imaginary of commerce informed by his transatlantic experience and economic doctrine providence. This interpretation, far more than Vitoria's, was conducive to the evolving colonial justifications of new seaborne empires.

Commercial exchange through maritime travel, whereby what was abundant somewhere could be transferred to where it was in demand elsewhere, belonged to the order of divine providence for Acosta. The common Author of human nature made it so that everyone could associate with each other for the welfare of all. Just as everyone in human industry had a proper function, the whole world also formed a solidarity, so that certain commodities bountiful in one place and others in another region could be useful to foreigners. Drawing on personal experience, Acosta concluded: "I am not sure one could find any region more prosperous in gold and silver than this Peru."[73] Commercial exchange suited to European acquisition of precious metals was woven into the order of creation.

The world of commerce linking European Christians with foreign peoples of the Indies testified to not only providence, but also salvation. In the *Natural and Moral History of the Indies*, Acosta expounded on the greatness of divine wisdom:

> [God has] enriched the most remote parts of the world, inhabited by the most uncivilized people, and has placed there the greatest number of mines that

[72] Acosta, *De procuranda*, lib. 2, cap. 13, pp. 340–342: "*[C]erte innatus amor nova discendi atque experiendi, ius cuique facit ut remotissima quaeque, si libeat, oculis atque animo lustret.*"

[73] Acosta, *De procuranda*, lib. 2, cap. 13, pp. 342–324.

> ever existed, in order to invite men to seek out and possess those lands and coincidentally communicate their religion and the worship of the true God to men who do not know it . . . Hence we see that the lands in the Indies that are richest in mines and wealth have been those most advanced in the Christian religion in our time; and thus the Lord takes advantage of our desires to serve his sovereign ends.[74]

Commerce went beyond merely material commodities. European Christians could offer salvation in exchange for mineral deposits. The Virginia Company adopted a similar idea of spiritual-material commerce whereby Europeans buy from natives "the pearls of the earth, and sell to them the pearls of heaven."[75] Purchas, in his description of the Virginia colony's natural endowments, similarly advanced: "God in wisedome having enriched the Savage Countries, that those riches might be attractives for Christian suters, which there may sowe spirituals and reape temporals."[76]

The Virginia Company's promotional tract was not merely about establishing amicable trade relations with infidels, which had support from the law of nations and the Bible. It was also an apology for colonial settlement and inhabiting land, a matter of increased importance as the English discovered tobacco from the Native Americans. According to the Virginia Company, the English could possess land lawfully in the colony near natives because of sufficient space and vacancy, in addition to defending themselves from injuries. Strikingly, land was like a commodity open to transaction and commercial exchange. The English recounted how the natives sold them "land to inherit and inhabit" for copper.[77] Here and too often repeated elsewhere in North America during the seventeenth century, the English mistook natives for selling land as a tradeable commodity, which allegedly gave Europeans exclusive right over bounded territory no longer shared with the original inhabitants.[78]

The Christian legal humanist interpretation of global commerce, justiciable through the enforcement of the rights of trading and possessing unoccupied land, allowed for greater latitude in thinking about European expansion beyond the traditional evangelical parameters of Valladolid set by canon law, philosophy, and scholastic theology. Infidels and the question of trading and establishing alliances with them remained relevant. And so did the question of

74 Acosta, *Natural and Moral History*, Book 4, chap. 2, p. 164.

75 *A true declaration of the state of Virginia*, p. 250.

76 Purchas, *Hakluytus Posthumus*, vol. 20, Book 9, chap. 20, p. 232.

77 *A true declaration of the state of Virginia*, 250; Purchas, *Hakluytus Posthumus*, Book 9, chap. 20, p. 228.

78 William Cronon, *Changes in the Land* (Hill & Wang, 2003), p. 67.

what infidels rightly possessed according to natural law. However, the new global mercantile setting and associated economic doctrine of providence gave greater urgency to obstacles presented to trade and commerce rather than obstacles to evangelization, such as idolatry. To prohibit commerce with peaceable travelers was a violation of nature and the law of nations, or an injury to humankind, and therefore a punishable deed. As we will see, Grotius and Gentili were instrumental to this ideological evolution justifying European expansion by moving the discussion away from waging wars to punish infidels, considered enemies of religion, to waging wars to punish enemies of common humanity, who were like savage beasts.

INDIVIDUAL PUNISHMENT IN THE STATE OF NATURE

The broadly legal humanism of Gentili and Grotius would engage the pressing international matters of European commercial powers by turning principally to the *Corpus iuris civilis* of the Roman Empire, along with history, classical philosophy and poetry, to fill the content of universal reason.[79] As Gentili remarked, Justinian's Roman law was a perennial source of justice outlasting the empire itself because it was "not merely the law of the state, but also that of the nations and of nature."[80] The Spanish humanist Sepúlveda, considered in the previous chapter, had already presented the providential role of the Roman Empire for enforcing the natural law upon barbarians through the law of nations. Grotius similarly recognized the divine purpose of Justinian's *Institutes*, which contained the natural law and precepts of the law of nations.[81]

These epochal early modern Protestant jurists effected an emancipation of the natural law and the law of nations from the long-standing grip of popes, canonists, and theologians. In this regard, Gentili and Grotius followed the humanist ideological path paved by Sepúlveda, yet expanded it to a new situation of global commerce in which neither papal grants nor missionary war carried the legal weight of their colonial arguments. Their politics of universal law could justify the empowerment of imperial states and their

79 Grotius, "Prolegomena," 1756: "In investigating this law, I have benefited from the testimony of philosophers, historians, poets, and, lastly, orators. One should not naively believe whatever they say, since they are often loyal to a particular party, program, or cause; but what is affirmed by many people at different times and places to be obvious must be presumed to rest on some universal reason. In the issues we are considering, this reason can only be either a correct deduction from the principles of our nature, or some general agreement. The former means that it is a law of nature, the latter that it is a law of nations."

80 Gentili, *De iure belli*, Book 1, chap. 3, p. 17.

81 Grotius, "Defense of Chapter V of the *Mare liberum*," in *The Free Sea*, p. 105.

private citizens to enforce international norms between Europeans and non-Europeans, but also between rival European powers. Enforceable norms with universal jurisdiction were a practical requirement amidst the breakdown of European Christian unity through interconfessional strife and the growing awareness of profitable trade routes and interactions with native peoples in lands known and unknown.[82]

Gentili and Grotius, like the Spanish Dominican theologians, articulated universal subjective rights within a natural law framework. But it was their preeminent concern with commerce, rather than salvation, that structured their early modern privatized notions of justice. What was traditionally a facet of Roman private law offered a creative blueprint for them according to a neo-Stoic practical ethics.[83] These Protestant jurists of Roman law approached subjective rights from a Ciceronian view that identified the "innate force" of natural law, which was implanted in the individual agent seeking self-preservation through vengeance if necessary.[84] The subjective force of individual empowerments and claims of corrective (or commutative) justice applied to individuals themselves or between individual commonwealths. Roman private law expressed the prominent place of the individual for reimagining world order in a Protestant international key without the overarching authority of the Holy Roman Empire or the papacy. Grotius's earliest ruminations on it were illustrative: "nations in their relation to the whole of mankind occupy the position of private individuals."[85] Although there was some continuity here with the restitution tradition of commutative justice seen among scholastic theologians, the sacrament of penance was no longer the pastoral impetus framing these questions for the Protestant natural lawyers. Consequently, the importance of ecclesial identity for thinking through matters of commutative justice in colonial context was overshadowed by attention to a historicized international state of nature.

The powerful presence of sovereign-like companies advancing empires of commerce reconstituted this new discourse of subjective rights, natural law, and the law of nations to take full measure of the juridical importance of the private individual under consideration – the primary agent of free trade and colonial settlement in those contentious spaces outside conventional

82 Tamar Herzog, *A Short History of European Law* (Harvard University Press, 2018), p. 160.

83 Benedict Kingsbury and Benjamin Straumann, "Introduction: The Roman Foundations of the Law of Nations," in *The Roman Foundations of the Law of Nations: Alberico Gentili and the Justice of Empire*, eds. Kingsbury and Straumann (Oxford University Press, 2010), pp. 3–4.

84 In reference to Cicero's *De inventione*, II, 22. Gentili, *De iure belli*, Book 1, chap. 13, p. 59; Grotius, *Commentary on the Law of Prize*, chap. 8, pp. 133–134.

85 Grotius, *Commentary on the Law of Prize*, chap. 12, p. 330; *The Free Sea*, chap. 5, p. 31.

European geopolitical sovereignty. These prepolitical or extra-political spaces on sea and land lacked recourse to a common judge or political superior. Therefore, the prospect of confronting unruly individuals or groups who did not respect natural kinship and the law of nations, like pirates on the seas and savages in the wild, loomed large in Europe's legal imaginary of the Indies. To address this concern about hostile threats to natural sociability and universal kinship, both Gentili and Grotius identified a natural right of punishment originating from the individual as the proper safeguard on sea and in the wilderness to protect one's life, property, and freedom of traveling across the Indies or trading and settling there. Self-preservation had its adjoining right of punishment.

The clearest commercial setting for asserting a right of punishment was on the high seas, a space by nature open to everyone and not the possession of anyone. Gentili and Grotius adhered to the traditional teaching on war as a matter of public judicial recourse through the sovereign state. However, in confronting extra-political commercial spaces on the sea and wilderness, they supplied new arguments for war as a private matter where individuals enforced natural right. The existence of these extra-political situations pointed to the normative primacy of the individual in a prepolitical state for adjudicating war between sovereign powers that have no higher authority on earth. As Grotius argued for the VOC and its forced seizure of the Portuguese carrack in Singapore:

> For it is not the result of compact that one state has power over another, but rather by the force of nature, which allows every individual to seek his own right. Therefore, the existence of such a right is a preliminary requisite. This is the significance of the universally accepted doctrine that one state is made subject to another by transgressing. For whosoever wages war justly must become to that extent the judge of his adversary . . . turning back of necessity to the system in force under the law of nature, which permitted each individual to be the judge of his own cause.[86]

Private wars between individuals were indicative of life prior to the establishment of sovereign states. By extension, private wars have legal force in locales without public recourse or beyond the traditional geopolitical confines of the sovereign state. The example of Julius Caesar chasing down and punishing pirates on the waters after a Roman proconsul refused to indict them illustrated for Grotius that the law of nations was still enforceable in circumstances where written laws did not apply.[87]

86 Grotius, *Commentary on the Law of Prize*, chap. 2, p. 48.

87 Grotius, *Commentary on the Law of Prize*, chap. 8, p. 141; "Defense of Chapter V," p. 129; Grotius, *The Rights of War and Peace*, Book 2, chap. 20, p. 970.

Piracy, specifically, was a gross affront to the natural unity of humankind and the law of hospitality underlying commercial exchange. Gentili described piracy as contrary to the "league of human society" and "a violation of the common law of humanity." Accordingly, every single person could wage war against these enemies of human fellowship, which also included wars protecting allies. Gentili's indignant language toward pirates was thoroughgoing and exacting in its empowerment of the individual in search of vengeance not unlike Caesar's pursuit: "[S]ince we may also be injured as individuals by those violators of nature, war will be made against them by individuals. And no rights will be due to these men who have broken all human and divine laws and who, though joined with us through the similarity of nature, have disgraced this union with abominable stains."[88] In this section, Gentili referred explicitly to the Salmantine opposition to an international right of punishing violators of natural law represented by the Spanish canon lawyer Diego de Covarrubias. A student of both Vitoria and Soto at Salamanca, Covarrubias defended the Dominican theological position that the emperor and the pope lacked the necessary temporal jurisdiction to carry out a punitive war against infidel idolaters on the basis of sins.[89] It was not without reason then that elsewhere in Gentili's treatise, he told theologians to "keep silence" about the matter of war, which was not under their disciplinary domain.[90]

The natural right of punishment for violating the common law of humanity, as seen in the case of pirates, provided a commercial context for a legal reinterpretation of the individual enforcement of justice through private war on the seas. Indeed, part of the force of Grotius's argument against the Portuguese was the latter's pirate-like behavior of robbing the Dutch of profit in the East Indies and hindering their freedom of trade. When turning to land as a legal space, Gentili and Grotius invoked the category of the uncivilized barbarian to denote those who "drive away strangers" and thereby violate the universal norm of hospitality.[91] Gentili was somewhat measured in his analysis, recognizing instances a specific people have cause to restrict commerce and trading to preserve the good of society. Cases might include the prohibition of trading a certain commodity considered detrimental to the people, or the limiting of commerce on the frontiers of a society to avoid influencing its

88 Gentili, *De iure belli*, Book 1, chap. 25, p. 124.

89 Diego de Covarrubias y Leyva, "In Regulam Peccatum," in *Textos Juridico-Politicos* (Instituto de Estudios Politicos, 1957), p. 95.

90 Gentili, *De iure belli*, Book 1, chap. 12, p. 57.

91 Gentili, *De iure belli*, Book 1, chap. 19, p. 89; Grotius, *The Rights of War and Peace*, Book 2, chap. 2, p. 447.

inner life. These kinds of exception notwithstanding, interference with the freedom of commerce was a clear justification for retaliatory war.

Grotius's mature work *On the Rights of War and Peace* (1625) maintained his earlier position that public and private wars were legitimate to enforce free commerce, the denial of which constituted a glaring violation of the natural law and the law of nations. In accordance with the doctrine of providential commerce, the liberty applicable to persons traveling or passing through a land also extended to the free trading of goods and merchandize. Citing the ancient historian Plutarch, Grotius wrote that without commercial intercourse "human life would have been wild and savage," since it brings relief of one's another wants and establishes friendships.[92] Commercial exchange was the singular natural bond holding humanity together in friendship and solidarity and a necessary component of every civilization.

Due to the providential importance of trade, Gentili and Grotius spoke plainly about enforcement of it by means of arms and wars against anyone who posed an obstacle to it – pirates, uncivilized barbarians, and monopolizing seaborne powers like the Portuguese and Spanish. Such enforcement, as noted, pertained to individuals and not merely states. Yet Grotius went even further than Gentili by explicitly arguing for private wars in current geopolitical spaces lacking judicial recourse, which included barren lands, the wilderness, islands, oceans, and any locale where the people had no established government.[93] The Ciceronian influence on Grotius's idea about a prepolitical and extra-political subjective natural right was indelibly present here.[94] Cicero's *De inventione* identified vengeance as part of the natural law, an innate force (*innata vis*), which had both defensive and punitive meanings. Vengeance, according to Cicero, referred to either the defensive repulsion of violence toward oneself and others, or the infliction of punishment for wrongdoing. Although scholastic theologians from Aquinas to Vitoria similarly placed vengeance in the natural law, they restricted its meaning among individuals to acts of self-defense using proportionate force, not the meting of punishment.[95] For the scholastics, the latter was only consequent of public authority possessing civil jurisdiction. Grotius radically departed from the scholastic jurisdictional view. His detailed account of individuals exacting punitive violence in a state of nature was precisely what opened the possibility of private acts of war.

92 Grotius, *The Rights of War and Peace*, Book 2, chap. 2, pp. 443–444.
93 Grotius, *Commentary on the Law of Prize*, chap. 2, p. 49; chap. 8, p. 131–132.
94 Straumann, *Roman Law in the State of Nature* (Cambridge University Press, 2015), chap. 9.
95 Aquinas, *ST*, II-II, q. 64, a. 7.

As evident from the Spanish missionary wars against idolatrous natives, the category of punishment could expand the range of offenses against natural law. It could also widen the infliction of penalties though war to include conquest, seizing property of offenders and their inheritors, making slaves, and even destroying enemies. Punishment provided a highly interventionist rationale in European engagements with foreign peoples. To allay the abuse of punitive intervention, Grotius recognized that not every offense was punishable but only grievous violations of natural law and the law of nations.[96] What made an offense particularly egregious and sinful was its intrinsic wrongness, and its injury against the whole of human society. Both the nature of the evil itself and the extent of violating many individuals comprising the universal human community elevated these offenses.

With respect to offenses, Grotius certainly had in mind the Portuguese restriction on trading, which converted "the common right of all mankind into a private possession."[97] But the Dutch jurist did not stop at the Portuguese offense when he returned to the subject of punitive war in his later work. Classical civilization afforded numerous historical examples of grave unnatural offenses among barbarians punishable by war: in addition to the practice of piracy, there were records of inhumanity toward parents and the elderly, brutality toward foreigners, and the eating of human flesh. Even offenses that injure others indirectly such as suicide and bestiality were also included. Greek and Roman historians used these jarring examples to describe uncivilized barbarians. On this point, Grotius acknowledged his indebtedness to Aristotle and Isocrates, whose category of barbarian seemed to make war natural and just "against men who are like beasts."[98]

Perhaps to address the shifting colonial situation of the Dutch toward annexation and settlement in the Indies, Grotius aligned himself in *On the Rights of War and Peace* with the preceding canon legal opinion of Pope Innocent IV, which taught: "[W]ar is lawful against those who offend against nature."[99] As if establishing the terms of the Valladolid debate, Grotius contraposed Innocent's teaching, and therefore Palacios Rubios and Sepúlveda implicitly, to the opinion of Vitoria and other Jesuit theologians and jurists, all of whom were Spanish. Whereas Vitoria would assert "that the power of punishing is properly an effect of civil jurisdiction," Grotius's Innocentian opinion held that punishment redressed violations of nature

96 Grotius, *The Rights of War and Peace*, Book 2, chap. 20, pp. 1018, 1021.

97 Grotius, *Commentary on the Law of Prize*, chap. 12, pp. 366–367.

98 Grotius, *The Rights of War and Peace*, Book 2, chap. 20, pp. 1022–1024.

99 Grotius, *The Rights of War and Peace*, Book 2, chap. 20, pp. 1024–1025. For more on the Dutch colonial context of this teaching, see Tuck, *The Rights of War and Peace*, pp. 103–104.

and therefore proceeded from the law of nature. Yet Grotius went further than Innocent and Sepúlveda by concluding that the subjective individual power of punishment originated from a prepolitical state of nature.

Pope Innocent associated the power of punishment with the jurisdictional authority of the sword though he was unclear about its exact form among the earliest humans. In contrast, Grotius defended a prepolitical natural right of punishment, "which was both before the foundation of governments, and even is now still in force in those places, where men live in tribes or families, and are not incorporated into states." The emerging idea about a state of nature – both a legal fiction and an historical fact – had been absent from the theocratic papalism of Innocent IV and imperial humanism of Sepúlveda. Natural law's enforcement was now free of the Church since private individuals already possessed executive power in the state of nature. Grotius argued instead for the transference of a universal right of punishment from ecclesiastical power to secular power: just as bishops oversaw the universal Church, so too could kings take "care of human society in general" beyond domestic affairs.[100]

Gentili arrived at the same conclusion of Grotius and Sepúlveda on the right of punishing violations of natural law though he mistakenly included Vitoria in this category.[101] Gentili's position, which anticipated Grotius, held the following: "[T]he cause of the Spaniards is just when they make war upon the Indians, who practiced abominable lewdness even with beasts, and who ate human flesh, slaying men for that purpose. For such sins are against the nature of the human race [*contra naturam humani generis*], and the same is true of other sins recognized as such by all except haply by brutes and brutish men."[102] Despite the mischaracterization of Vitoria's opinion, which, in fact, had restricted Christian political judgment and punishment of non-Europeans, Gentili's reliance on the Salmantine theologian was most evident and accurate when he dismissed difference of religion as a cause for war.[103] Notably, Gentili also defended non-compulsion to the Christian faith relying on canonistic and patristic sources.

Gentili clearly departed from the Spanish Dominicans when he addressed the case of atheism. His humanism was thoroughgoing with respect to the ubiquity of natural religion as rational belief in a higher power. In this sense, he was similar to Sepúlveda. The main difference between them, however, was that whereas Sepúlveda permitted punishing infidels for their idolatry,

100 Grotius, *The Rights of War and Peace*, Book 2, chap. 20, p. 1028.

101 Pagden, *Burdens of Empire*, pp. 88–89.

102 Gentili, *De iure belli*, Book 1, chap. 25, p. 122.

103 Gentili, *De iure belli*, Book 1, chap. 9, p. 39.

Gentili did not. Strictly speaking for Gentili, not all infidels were excused from punishment: "[I]f there should by any who are atheists, destitute of any religious belief, either good or bad, it would seem just to war upon them as we would upon wild beasts (*feras*) . . . And such a war is a war of vengeance, to avenge our common nature."[104] Extending punitive war against infidel atheists deemed savage beasts was an innovative juridical claim of Gentili's humanism. Citing Cicero, Gentili claimed that those things agreed upon by all peoples, such as belief in a god, belonged to the natural law.[105] Therefore, an atheist could be considered a worse violator of the natural law than an idolater.

Although Grotius did not classify idolatry, or human sacrifice, as a lawful cause for war, he did affirm with Gentili that atheism provided legitimate grounds for punishment.[106] Religion, whether honoring a single god or many, stemmed from natural reason and belonged to the law of nations. For European humanism in an international context, the absence of even the most primitive belief in divine agency was an indication of savagery. Grotius was not blind to the overzealous application of this expansionist rationale promoting ambition and greed under the pretense of civilizing barbarian peoples.[107] Yet he and Gentili followed Sepúlveda and paradigmatic classical Greek thinkers in presenting war against savage barbarians as naturally just. Since savage barbarians did not live according to the natural law or the law of nations, they were subject to punishment by superior European civilizations committed to protecting humanity's bond.

In the manner of Sepúlveda, both Gentili and Grotius claimed the law of nations as the political instrument for enforcing right against the uncivilized and punishing breaches of the natural law. For Gentili and Grotius, the natural law and the law of nations were virtually conflated or tracked so closely that war attained the quality of being something natural against the enemies of humankind. Grotius, however, presented a more nuanced perspective trying to establish the role of consent in the law of nations. In the early work of *De iure praedae*, specifically the twelfth chapter that became *Mare liberum*, Grotius cited the Spanish humanist jurist Fernando Vázquez de Menchaca, who argued for the freedom of the seas and the natural right of commerce.[108]

Steeped in the discipline of *humanae litterae*, Vázquez de Menchaca relied on Greek and Roman authors as the paradigm and point of reference for all

104 Gentili, *De iure belli*, Book 1, chap. 25, p. 125.
105 Gentili, *De iure belli*, Book 1, chap. 1, p. 8.
106 Grotius, *The Rights of War and Peace*, Book 2, chap. 20, pp. 1033, 1040.
107 Grotius, *The Rights of War and Peace*, Book 2, chap. 20, p. 1026.
108 Grotius, *The Free Sea*, chap. 7, pp. 39–49.

cultural activity.[109] Justinian's *Digest* was the principal source for thinking about the law of nations in his *Controversiarum illustrium* (1564). Vázquez made a traditional civilian juridical distinction going back to fourteenth-century Italian jurist Bartolus of Sassoferrato between a primary (or primordial) and secondary law of nations.[110] Vázquez referred to the primary law of nations as the "natural law of nations" or "natural law *simpliciter*" because its permanent and self-evident status originated with God at the beginning of the human race. In contrast, the secondary law of nations did not belong to the first age of creation but was established by civil law and usage in temporal history. Over the slippage of time, it can be found among those civilized nations ruled by customs and laws that do not conduct themselves as wild savages.[111]

Grotius utilized Vázquez's twofold distinction of the law of nations in his early work to establish the dual basis of the universal precepts of the law of nations in both natural instinct and custom:

> For Vázquez argues that the law of nature, since it proceeds from Divine Providence, is immutable; and that the primary law of nations (which is regarded as different from the secondary or positive law of nations, the latter being susceptible to change whereas the former is immutable) constitutes a part of that natural law. For if there are certain customs incompatible with the primary law of nations, they are customs not proper to human beings (in the opinion of that same jurist), but to *wild beasts*; neither do they represent law and usage, but rather, corruption and abuse.[112]

Those customs in conformity with the primary law of nations belonged to the secondary law of nations. From Vázquez, Grotius concluded that freedom of navigation and trade belonged to the primary law of nations and therefore possessed a naturally binding and unchanging status under divine authorization. One could infer that the Portuguese were acting like wild beasts by

109 Salvador Rus Rufino, "Fernando Vázquez de Menchaca," in *Great Christian Jurists in Spanish History*, eds. Rafael Domingo and Javier Martínez Torrón (Cambridge University Press, 2018), p. 162.

110 For more on the civilian aspects of Vázquez's thought informing Grotius, see Brett, *Changes of State*, chap. 3, esp. pp. 69–70, 77–79.

111 Fernando Vázquez de Menchaca, *Controversiarum illustrium aliarumque usu frequentium libri tres*, eds. Fidel Rodríguez Alcalde and Calixto Valverde y Valverde (Talleres Tipográficas Cuesta, 1931–1934), tom. 4, lib. 2, cap. 89, pp. 423–424: "*Istud jus gentium naturale appellatur jus naturale simpliciter, et etiam appellatur jus gentium primaevum, hoc est, cum ipso humano genere simul proditum . . . Jus autem gentium secundarium est, quod non simul cum ipso genere humano proditum fuit, sed labentibus temporibus a plerisque earum gentium, quae moribus et legibus reguntur, nec ritu aut more ferarum silvestrem vitam agunt.*"

112 Grotius, *Commentary on the Law of Prize*, chap. 12, p. 346.

monopolizing free trade and ignoring the universal axioms and precepts contained in the law of nations.

In the mature thought of *On the Rights of War and Peace*, Grotius no longer made use of the civilian jurist language of primary/secondary law of nations.[113] The self-evident deduction from natural principles was nothing else but natural law whereas the voluntary general agreement among civilized peoples belonged to the law of nations. And both stemmed from universal reason.[114] Additionally, Roman law provided the repository of wisdom for thinking about the universal norms and precepts from the standpoint of civilized societies with the power to punish violators of universal reason, even among Europeans like the Portuguese. The practicable force of natural law and the law of nations pertained foremost to sovereign princes, but also trading companies like the VOC, each of which was, in juridical terms, a private individual occupying an international state of nature.

Although Grotius's legal scope focused on European competition to trade in the East Indies, his adherence to a humanist view of the law of nations with enforceable universal precepts had much wider application. Vázquez provided Grotius with a conceptual framework identifying the binding force of the law of nations in spaces where civil law did not apply, in particular, the liberty of navigation on the high seas.[115] Apparently, Vázquez began to conceive an international state of nature yet without the explicit political associations seen among the Westphalian thinkers. Notably, his law of nations was captive to the humanist reading of it as a law observed by peoples governed by upright customs and laws. Vázquez acknowledged the Roman character of the law of nations, which originated from the civil law of the Roman people and similar societies before spreading elsewhere. Following Sepúlveda's line of argument, the law of nations certainly did not extend to uncivilized peoples lacking proper customs, as Spaniards discovered in the "innumerable" examples from the New World.[116] Yet this humanist interpretation of the law of nations in parochial terms did not translate for Vázquez into a tool of

[113] For another earlier view of Grotius where he holds that the binding precepts of the law of nations were established either by God in the "minds of men" or consent and long-standing usage among civilized nations, see Grotius, "Defense of Chapter V," pp. 105–106.

[114] Grotius, *The Rights of War and Peace*, "Prolegomena," 1756.

[115] Citing Vázquez de Menchaca, *Controversiarum illustrium*, tom. 4, lib. 2, cap. 89, pp. 427–428, in Grotius, *Commentary on the Law of Prize*, chap. 12, p. 348: "In dealing with such foreign entities, the common law of nations, either in its primary or in its secondary phase, must be consulted and applied … the law of nations has precisely the same effect that it has always had, since the beginning of the world."

[116] Vázquez de Menchaca, *Controversiarum illustrium*, tom. 2, lib. 2, cap. 20, p. 28: "*Ius autem gentium negavit totum mundi orbem amplexum fuisse, nam primum excepit eas gentes, quae*

European expansion like Sepúlveda. Largely partial to critical arguments of the Spanish Dominicans about the New World, especially those of his esteemed colleague at Salamanca, Domingo de Soto, Vázquez rejected Pope Innocent's "suspect" doctrine permitting expansionary wars and dispossession on the basis of punishing natural law violations.[117]

The international right of punishing offenses against nature for Grotius and Gentili extended to both Europeans and non-Europeans, Christians and savage barbarians. Nevertheless, the cards were stacked heavily against non-Europeans who lacked the benefits of civilization and letters. From this geopolitical standpoint of a European conception of the law of nations, the idea of the natural slave took on greater colonial connotations. Gentili's neo-Stoic humanism restricted him from believing that there was a natural slavery pitting peoples against each other in war by metaphysical necessity. Rather, he espoused the standard Christian view from Augustine to Aquinas that slavery was a consequence of sin, and in conformity with natural reason as a form of punishment. Like Sepúlveda, Gentili identified the conflict between enemies on the basis of education or custom, which was a kind of second nature. For this reason, war with the Ottoman Turks, considered infidel enemies who were always plotting against Christians and seizing their possessions, was something "almost natural."[118] Both infidel Turks and atheists were comparable to beasts inclined to being punished and subjugated by Christians through war because of their hardened customs and malformation. The Aristotelian doctrine of natural slavery remained in so much as it referred to those trapped in such inveterate sins and wickedness.[119] Evidently, for Gentili, Indians of the New World were of a naturally brutish character and thereby subject to punishment and rule by civilized Europeans.

Grotius also followed theologians like Aquinas and the Spanish Dominicans in promoting the punishment of malefactors who reduce themselves to the level of beasts by the violent misuse of their wills.[120] Yet Grotius's reinterpretation of the teaching according to the international state of nature in his early career had a very different application, more conformable to an Aristotelian doctrine of natural slavery that denied a basic level of dignity

sive legibus et moribus honestis reguntur, quas innumeras esse apparvit, postquam nos Hispani novum orbem Indorum reclusimus ac invenimus."

117 Vázquez de Menchaca, *Controversiarum illustrium*, tom. 2, lib. 2, cap. 24, p. 81.

118 Gentili, *De iure belli*, Book 1, chap. 12, pp. 55–56. Vitoria, while avoiding the language of natural slavery, similarly viewed war with Saracen Muslims as a perennial or permanent facet of the law of nations. See *On the Law of War*, q. 3, a. 3, p. 318.

119 Gentili, *De iure belli*, Book 3, chap. 9, p. 330.

120 Aquinas, *ST*, II-II, q. 64, a. 2, *ad* 3.

pertaining to the image of God. "Men of deplorable wickedness," Grotius wrote in *De iure praedae*, "stripped, as it were, of all likeness to God or humanity – are thrust down into a lower order and assigned to the service of the virtuous, changing in a sense from persons into things, a process which constitutes the origin of slavery in the natural order, too; and therefore, it is permissible to destroy such men, either in order that they may be prevented from doing harm or in order that they be useful as examples."[121] Punitive power for the scholastic theologians inhered in the political authority of the state whereas for Grotius it extended to any prepolitical or extra-political state of nature among individuals. The legal importance of neo-Stoicism to justify an international right of punishing the deplorable cannot be gainsaid. Since individuals are citizens of the world, "the private avenger has in view the good of the whole human race, just as when he slays a serpent; and this goal corresponds exactly to that common good toward which ... all punishments are directed in nature's plan."[122]

Avenging the universal human community through wars against pirates, atheists, wild beasts, cannibals, unwelcoming hostiles, and all manner of savage barbarians provided early modern international legal thought immense latitude beyond the confines of Europe. Like Sepúlveda's imperial humanist world order, this neo-Stoic humanist world order advanced a right of punishment in the global Indies. However, Gentili and Grotius did not require the public authority of the Roman Empire or the Roman papacy to execute the punishment of savage barbarians. Private individuals, although having transferred such power to the state as citizens, were still equipped with the innate force to do so on the open seas and in the wilderness. John Locke, for whom the state of nature like Hobbes was empirically verifiable among the natives of the Americas, came to embrace this "very strange doctrine" contrary to the dominant Christian teaching on just war in his *Second Treatise of Government*.[123]

Locke's natural right of punishment and Hobbes's natural right to all things (*ius in omnia*) were necessary constituents for securing individual self-preservation. Any savage who threatened the preservation of one's life and goods in the state of nature could be vanquished like a beast according to the violent force of right. Locke's library had the complete works of Cicero, a fact attested by his resounding Stoic sympathy for individual punishment and

121 Grotius, *Commentary on the Law of Prize*, chap. 8, p. 135.

122 Grotius, *Commentary on the Law of Prize*, chap. 8, p. 139, referring to the Stoic philosopher Seneca's *On the Happy Life*.

123 Locke, *Second Treatise*, chap. 2, §§9, 13. Locke would have been familiar with Grotius's *De jure belli ac pacis* and *Mare liberum* as part of his colonial library collection.

sociability in a manner unlike Hobbes. Locke's state of nature grounded the "power to punish the crime" and to prevent it from happening again in the right of "preserving all mankind." When an individual has renounced reason by attacking a single person, that one has "declared war against all mankind; and therefore may be destroyed as a lion or a tiger, one of those wild, savage beasts with whom men can have no society or security."[124] Hence everyone in the state of nature has the power to kill an aggressive brute. Locke may not have identified the Indians as savages per se in the *Second Treatise*, yet this did not prevent him from using the example of Indians ignoring the civil laws of the three major non-Iberian commercial powers present in colonial North America – the English, the Dutch, and the French – to demonstrate the importance of a universal natural right of punishment.[125] That his library contained writings from John Smith, Acosta, and Purchas, all of whom described Native Americans as savage beasts subject to discipline and violent punishment, showed he was well aware of the inference. In fact, as we will see shortly, his argument for English colonial dispossession of land relied on such an inference between natives and savages.

Initially, the term savage did not carry normative power as a derogatory designation in the English colonial context of North America. Richard Hakluyt's use of it often echoed Columbus's wild and simple peoples disposed to receive the Gospel.[126] However, this less truculent meaning was strained by violent interactions between increasing English settlers and defensive Native Americans crystallizing in the Virginia massacre of 1622 (see Figure 5.1). Purchas's *Hakluytus Posthumus* signaled an important shift in English colonial legal thought that would clearly resonate with Locke's later deployment of the natural right of punishment in the *Second Treatise*.

Purchas, over the course of writing *Hakluytus Posthumus*, moved from a general account of infidels, who have natural rights, to the specific case of savages, who forfeited natural rights because of treachery. Although infidel rights were there in *Hakluytus*, Acosta's barbarian classification also informed Purchas's description of the Native Americans as descendants from Asia. If they inhabited the land of America at all, they roamed over it rather than

124 Locke, *Second Treatise*, chap. 2, §11.

125 Locke, *Second Treatise*, chap. 2, §9: "I doubt not but this will seem a very strange doctrine to some men: but, before they condemn it, I desire them to resolve me by what right any prince or state can put to death or punish an alien for any crime he commits in their country ... Those who have the supreme power of making laws in England, France, or Holland, are to an Indian but like the rest of the world, men without authority: and therefore, if by the law of nature every man hath not a power to punish offenses against it, as he soberly judges the case to require, I see not how the magistrates of any community can punish an alien of another country."

126 Jennings, *The Invasion of America*, pp. 75–76.

FIGURE 5.1 "Native inhabitants of Virginia." (Source: Getty Images/Leemage/Contributor)

dwelling on and settling it.[127] When Purchas turned to the Virginia plantation in the aftermath of the 1622 attack, he relied on the dehumanizing accounts of the natives to assert superior European rights over the forfeited natural rights of treacherous murderers. Purchas began his chapter on the Virginia colony reiterating the doctrine whereby it was unlawful for Christians simply to dispossess the good and lands of infidels.[128] However, he then proceeded to describe the inhabitants of the region. The Native Americans, whose land was rich, were only human in appearance yet ignorant of civility and religion. According to Purchas, they were captive to Satan's tyranny because of their wickedness and idleness, and "more brutish than the beasts they hunt, more wild and unmanly then that unmanned wild Countrey, which they range rather than inhabite."[129] The English were there "not to make Savages and wild degenerate men of Christians," as happened among the Spanish colonizers, "but Christians of those Savage, wild, degenerate men."[130]

[127] Purchas, *Hakluytus Posthumus*, Book 1, chap. 1, §8, pp. 80–82.

[128] Purchas, *Hakluytus Posthumus*, Book 9, chap. 20, p. 220.

[129] Purchas, *Hakluytus Posthumus*, Book 9, chap. 20, p. 231.

[130] Purchas, *Hakluytus Posthumus*, Book 9, chap. 20, p. 222.

In order to avoid unjust possession or theft of the land of Virginia, Purchas addressed two enforceable claims in conformity with nature and divine revelation applicable to the circumstances: the right to replenish the earth and the right of merchandizing or trading. The right to replenish the earth and subdue it was a biblical mandate given to rational creatures made in the divine image (Genesis 1:28).[131] Despite sin's pervasive presence, infidels still possessed this natural right in a fallen state. But that also meant the English had a "right of Plantation" of their colony in a land with vacant space and room of habitation. Purchas's descriptions of the wild natives as having "no settled possession in any parts" and as murderers generated both a "better right" of the English and a forfeited right of the "unnaturall Naturalls."[132] The adjoining right of merchandize had biblical support from King Solomon, as Purchas noted earlier in the work. This commercial right spoke to the divine wisdom of mutually beneficial commodity exchange. Purchas rested his judgment of the Virginia case on an alleged original harmony between the English and the Powhatans, who by natural law permitted cohabitation and commerce. All of that was now in question after the Virginia massacre, a most disloyal act of treachery against the English since the Powhatan chief had ceded the land in exchange for copper.

Purchas offered an exceedingly interventionist proposal for punishing Native Americans who violated natural law:

> If they since have declined, they have lost their owne Naturall, and given us another Nationall Right; their transgression of the Law of Nature, which tieth Men to Men in the rights of Natures commons, exposing them (as a forfeited bond) to the chastisement of that common Law of mankind; and also on our parts to the severitie of the Law of Nations, which tyeth Nation to Nation. And if they bee not worthy of the name of a Nation, being wilde and Savage; yet as Slaves, bordering rebells, excommunicates and out-lawes lyable to the punishments of Law, and not to the priviledges; So it is with these Barbarians, Borderers, and Out-lawes of Humanity.[133]

The rightful dispossession of savages in North America by Europeans had the earliest and most articulate defense from Purchas's legal humanism. English Puritans of the Northeast would strategically formulate similar arguments for dispossessing Native American peoples such as the Narragansetts and

131 On the importance of this passage in early colonial English justifications for land appropriation, see Peter Harrison, "'Fill the Earth and Subdue It': Biblical Warrants for Colonization in Seventeenth Century England," *Journal of Religious History* 29.1 (2005): 3–24.

132 Purchas, *Hakluytus Posthumus*, Book 9, chap. 20, pp. 222–223.

133 Purchas, *Hakluytus Posthumus*, Book 9, chap. 20, p. 224.

Mohegans. Yet English colonial thinkers increasingly turned their legal concerns to the question of settling land and not merely trade and commercial exchange. This reflected the general tendency of seventeenth-century colonial discourse to address settlement over trade. The works of Gentili and Grotius signaled an important shift in the discourse. However, it was Locke's proto-liberal international thought that most clearly typified the ambivalence of infidel rights for the English colonial setting of North America. Universal natural rights for savage Americans were entirely compatible with civilizational hierarchy and superior European claims of legal dispossession. Importantly for the English, dispossession did not concern political jurisdiction over an infidel people but rather private ownership of land underutilized by savages.

EUROPEAN CIVILIZATION AND LAND OWNERSHIP

Alberico Gentili's argument about the freedom of traders and travelers extended to settlers as well, so long as they conducted commerce lawfully in foreign lands.[134] With respect to settlement, Protestant natural lawyers like Gentili and Grotius argued that vacant land (*terra nullius*) was open to the first occupant. On this point, Gentili proposed: "The seizure of vacant places is regarded as a law of nature. So it was when the world was young."[135] Remarkably, Gentili identified occupation of land by first taker not with the law of nations, as it had been for the Roman jurists and the Spanish scholastics, but instead with natural law. When Justinian's *Digest* located the title of first occupant in natural reason, it was for the seizure of unclaimed things like animals, not land and places as Gentili proposed.[136] *Terra nullius* was for Gentili as much part of the natural law as *res nullius*.

The shift to the law of nature was evident already in the humanism of Thomas More's *Utopia* (1516), which had justified war against anyone who left land idle and waste and hindered others from using and possessing it.[137] But Gentili was imagining neither utopia nor a primeval time long gone. He posed an ominous question that would cast a shadow over modern international relations, "Are there today unoccupied lands on the earth?" Turning to his

[134] Gentili, *De iure belli*, Book 2, chap. 22, p. 263.

[135] Gentili, *De iure belli*, Book 1, chap. 17, p. 80.

[136] *Digest*, 41.1.3.

[137] Thomas More, *Utopia*, eds. George Logan and Robert M. Adams (Cambridge University Press, 1989), Book 2, p. 56: "The Utopians says it's perfectly justifiable to make war on people who leave their land idle and waste yet forbid the use and possession of it to others who, by the law of nature, ought to be supported from it."

colonial context, he further asked: "Under the rule of Spain is not almost the entire New World vacant (*vacuus*)?"[138] The implication raised in the latter question would signal an evolving justification for claiming possession of land in North America against either natives or Spaniards. After the argumentative mode of Sepúlveda, Gentili deployed the Old Testament to confirm natural law's conformity with divine law on the matter of seizing vacant lands. In the words of the Prophet Isaiah: "The creator of the heavens, who is God/ The designer and maker of the earth who established it,/ Not as an empty waste did he create it, but designing it to be lived in."[139] Wasted land was a violation of both divine command and natural law.

Since Gentili had virtually equated the law of nations with natural law and divine law, it was a logical step to establish the law of first occupant on the authority of God and nature accordingly. The inclusion of the Roman law of first occupant under the domain of natural law was characteristic of early English colonial justifications from both the Virginia Company and the Massachusetts Bay Company. When the poet and preacher John Donne delivered his sermon to a demoralized Virginia Company on the verge of collapse following the violent native retaliation of 1622, he reminded its members, among them Hobbes, of various colonial legal justifications for "not only Commerce, and Trade, but Plantations in lands, not formerly our own." Donne's first argument for settlement of land, established by "the Law of Nature and Nations," concerned "Land never inhabited, by any, or utterly derelicted and immemorially abandoned by the former inhabitants."[140] Similarly, the New England Puritan John Cotton claimed that the English Crown and planters "take possession of the void places of the country by the law of nature, (for *Vacuum Domicilium cedit occupanti*) or ... by way of purchase, and free consent."[141] The royal patent for the colony did not license murder and robbery of the Indians, but authorized the English taking of land either left vacant or sold by the Indians.

Grotius was also important to the discussion of occupation although he added more nuance than Gentili. He attended more to egalitarian dimensions like Vitoria by applying the case of lawful occupation to European lands. "If there be any waste or barren Land within our Dominions," he proposed, "that

[138] Gentili, *De iure belli*, Book 1, chap. 17, p. 81.

[139] Isaiah 45:18.

[140] John Donne, "A Sermon Preached to the Honourable Company of the Virginian Plantation (1622)," in *The Sermons of John Donne*, vol. 4, eds. Evelyn Simpson and George Potter (University of California Press, 1959), p. 274.

[141] John Cotton, *John Cotton's Answer to Roger Williams*, in *The Complete Writings of Roger Williams*, vol. 2, ed. Lewis Diman (Russell & Russell, 1963), p. 46.

also is to be given to Strangers, at their Request, or may be lawfully possessed by them."[142] Of course, this axiom pertained to lands within but also beyond Europe. Contemporaneous with English colonial settlements, the Dutch West India Company in 1621 had a charter to occupy unsettled parts of North America. In this historical context, Grotius introduced an additional qualification here to the law of first occupant: the primary indicator of barren or vacant land open to occupation depended on its lack of cultivation and unboundedness. This nascent agricultural criterion would have tremendous consequences for English colonial legal justifications, evident among the Puritans, the English Virginians, and especially Locke. However, Grotius was also attentive to the possibility that original inhabitants might still reside there. In such a case, although the uncultivated land did not constitute the property of the original inhabitants, and therefore was free for occupation, the sovereignty and jurisdiction of the original inhabitants over it remained intact.[143] This recognition of native jurisdictional authority at least provided a space for acknowledging the role of native consent in the establishment of property, a most contested feature of English colonization in North America.

Grotius spelled out the basic agricultural criterion further in his "Defense of Chapter V of the *Mare Liberum*" (c. 1615), an unpublished reply to William Welwod's modest argument for greater political control of seawater. Strikingly, the idea of subjective right as "a moral faculty over a thing," and not an objective norm of justice, was already present in Grotius's reply anticipating his later work *On the Rights of War and Peace.*[144] As Grotius indicated at the outset, commerce and the associated freedom of trading required arms to enforce subjective right. The relevant point about taking possession or occupying land, an immovable, demanded a specific power of standing over or sitting on the land. For Grotius, this further entailed acts of bounding, fencing off, and marking the land, none of which could be said of the sea, something common and free to all.[145] Cultivation of land, or matters of the soil, was for the purpose of bearing and producing fruit. In anticipation of Locke's theory of property, Grotius recognized that yielding goods on a wide scale demanded human labor and industry.[146]

Although Grotius was not specifically concerned with the case of the West Indies, he supplied to later thinkers in embryonic form what some scholars consider both the labor theory of property and the agricultural argument for

142 Grotius, *The Rights of War and Peace*, Book 2, chap. 2, p. 448.
143 Fitzmaurice, *Sovereignty, Property and Empire*, p. 97.
144 Grotius, "Defense of Chapter V," p. 107.
145 Grotius, "Defense of Chapter V," p. 110.
146 Grotius, "Defense of Chapter V," p.116.

European expansion.[147] The evolving early modern Protestant humanist view on the natural law of occupation would supply an acute justification for land appropriation in the English colonial context of North America. Purchas, for example, attached the criterion of effectively using land to the natural right of replenishing and subduing the earth. Because the natives were vagabonds and roamers, they scarcely counted as inhabitants.[148] Without exploitative use of land, they could not prohibit the English from exercising their God-given natural right to do so. The land remained largely untapped and therefore uninhabited by nomadic people who overlooked its potential "to feed and sustaine a hundredth, perhaps a thousand times as much people by due husbandry."[149] English colonists simply had a "better right" to the land than the original idle savages of Virginia. In the eyes of God, European Christians have "a juster use" of the earth than infidels because they neither waste nor abuse it.[150] Whereas Sepúlveda argued for the right of war against idolatry to make conversion more effective, Purchas articulated a natural right of occupation through a better use of the land than idle natives. Both Spanish and English arguments represented here operated under a logic of efficiency.

John Donne's other rationale for occupation was also instructive for the Virginia Company. By the power of nature, the English could contravene any prior claims of native inhabitants who did "not in some measure fill the Land, so as to bring forth her increase for the use of men."[151] In a similar plantation sermon delivered by John Cotton to the Massachusetts Bay Company (1630) just before departure, the Puritan preached that the right of taking possession was a principle of nature. For "in a vacant soyle, hee that taketh possession of it, and bestoweth culture and husbandry upon it, his Right it is."[152] Cotton's sermonizing carried tremendous argumentative weight beyond Grotius in a colonial setting: land in America remained vacant until its natural appropriation through agricultural use and labor. The biblical example of Abraham supported the natural right of claiming something through cultivation. When Abraham complained to King Abimelech that royal servants had unjustly seized a well from him, he did not plead his right on the ground of divine election because that would have been "frivolous" to an infidel ruler. Instead,

147 Barbara Arniel, *John Locke and America* (Clarendon Press, 1996), pp. 51–52; Keene, *Beyond the Anarchical Society*, 102; Georg Cavallar, *Imperfect Cosmopolis* (University of Wales Press, 2011), p. 27.

148 Purchas, *Hakluytus Posthumus*, Book 9, chap. 20, pp. 222–223.

149 Purchas, *Hakluytus Posthumus*, Book 1, chap. 1, §8, p. 82.

150 Purchas, *Hakluytus Posthumus*, Book 1, chap. 1, §5, p. 38.

151 Donne, "A Sermon Preached," p. 11.

152 Cotton, *God's Promise to His Plantations* (London, 1634), p. 5.

Abraham informed the king that he had *built* the well himself.[153] Therefore, Abraham's natural right stemmed from "his owne industry and culture in digging the well."[154] Like Purchas, Cotton associated the natural right of claiming underutilized soil with the biblical mandate to replenish the earth and subdue it. Relatedly, trading also had divine warrant from Jesus in the New Testament, when the Lord compared the Christian to a merchant in search of pearls.[155] Thus the newfound Massachusetts colony, or company, would be the fitting prelude to the church of North America, just as the Macedonian colony of Philippi had been for the earliest Christians.[156]

The same year as the Virginia massacre, Plymouth Plantation deacon and colonist Robert Cushman articulated his *Reasons and Considerations* (1622) for the English settlement of North America. Cushman invoked biblical justifications for European planting to convert heathens and take possession of empty lands. His description of the natives' uncivilized manner of life and their relationship to the land illustrated a common rhetorical strategy for legal dispossession:

> [T]heir land is spacious and void, and there are few and do but run over the grass, as do also the foxes and wild beasts. They are not industrious, neither have art, science, skill or faculty to use either the land or the commodities of it, but all spoils, rots, and is marred for want of manuring, gathering, ordering, etc. As the ancient patriarchs therefore removed from straiter places into more roomy, where the land lay idle and waste, and none used it, though there dwelt inhabitants by them (as Genesis 13:6,11,12 and 34:21), so it is lawful now to take land which none useth, and make use of it.[157]

Although the division of land between Abraham and Lot was a traditional scholastic-canonistic reference to mutual consent in the biblical law of nations, Deacon Cushman reinterpreted Genesis 13 to emphasize the importance of using wasted space instead. Without the proper use and cultivation of the earth to establish native occupation in the first place, the legal requirement of native consent for English land appropriation grew more tenuous.

153 Genesis 21:25 and 30.

154 Cotton, *God's Promise to His Plantations*, p. 5.

155 Cotton, *God's Promise to His Plantations*, p. 8.

156 Acts 16:12. For more on the significance of the biblical reference in Cotton and the founding of Boston, see the Introduction to Mark Peterson, *The City-State of Boston* (Princeton University Press, 2019).

157 Robert Cushman, "Reasons and Considerations Touching on the Lawfulness of Removing out of England into the Parts of America (1622)," in *The Puritans in America: A Narrative Anthology*, eds. Andrew Delbanco and Alan Heimert (Cambridge, MA: Harvard University Press, 2009), pp. 43–44.

Cushman's reasons contributed to a wider English colonial imagination that portrayed the Indians as poor savages on a continent rich with natural bounty yet squandered by their apparent nonindustriousness and disuse of land. Settlers would often remark about the sharp contrast they observed between the land's natural wealth and the poverty of the natives. The reality, however, was rather different insomuch as natives of North America, in addition to being hunters, were also planters and fishers who had taught the English settlers certain techniques of agriculture for growing grains.[158] After all, the Powhatans and Wampanoags had virtually saved the first colonists in Virginia and New England, respectively, from starvation by bringing them not only hunted game but also grown crop amidst seasonal changes. These events have been the subject of national memory and American legend in the stories of Pocahontas at Jamestown and the first European Thanksgiving at Plymouth. Indians of the Northeast who developed agriculture beyond hunting to withstand seasonal scarcities comprised about 80 per cent of the native population.[159]

European colonial claims for land in North America based on Scripture and the natural law of occupation had important English objectors. Most notably, the unconventional Puritan Roger Williams rebutted Cotton's argument about vacant land in the Northeast by reinterpreting the native use of land among the Narragansett peoples (see Figure 5.2). Native American hunting all over the region, and their practice of burning underbrush to facilitate this activity, was comparable to the protected gaming lands and forests of English aristocrats back in Europe.[160] In direct response to the colonial argument for lawful occupation, Williams also observed: "The natives are very exact and punctual in the bounds of their lands, belonging to this or that prince or people (even to a river, brook) etc."[161] Native Americans had sovereign claims over land shared among themselves, even if the land served a different ecological purpose than colonists concerned with maximum utilization to yield harvests and products for a larger number of people engaged in transatlantic commerce.

Although not attaining the public stature of Valladolid, Williams's defense of the native right to land and self-rule, along with his rejection of religious coercion, against Cotton and other Puritan divines was extraordinary.[162]

158 Washburn, "The Moral and Legal Justifications," p. 23.

159 Cronon, *Changes in the Land*, p. 42.

160 Cotton, *John Cotton's Answer to Roger Williams*, pp. 46–47.

161 Williams, *A Key into the Language of America*, in *The Complete Writings*, vol. 1, chap. 16, p. 120.

162 For a creative and illuminating comparison of Valladolid and the Puritan debates about the natives, see Alicia Mayer, "Controversial Cases on Humanitarian Doctrines: Bartolomé de las

FIGURE 5.2 "Roger Williams Lands in the New World." (Source: Getty Images Stock Montage/Contributor)

Having spent countless hours among the Narragansett people of the Northeast learning their language and preaching to them, Williams recognized the political context of indigenous forms of property. The native right to property was not based on individual ownership, but rather, on sovereign rights of the chief (or sachem) that demarcated the politically and ecologically bounded space for the indigenous community.[163] Relatedly, "purchasing" land was more a diplomatic exchange granting shared access to a bounded region through usufructuary than a commercial exchange establishing exclusive ownership of it.

When it came to the Massachusetts Court, English settlers strictly defined native property over land according to a European criterion of agricultural advancement, again citing the Genesis imperative to replenish and subdue the earth.[164] Conveniently, the European definition of lawful possession of land

Casas's Intellectual Legacy among New England Puritans," in *Bartolomé de las Casas, O.P.*, pp. 167–193.

163 Cronon, *Changes in the Land*, p. 60.

164 Cronon, *Changes in the Land*, pp. 62–63.

categorically denied recognition of native land tenure in its communal and distinct ecological dimensions, which shifted based on seasonal use. Williams decried the logic of Puritan colonial arguments, fearing that, "in this wilderness . . . God Land will be (as now it is) as great a God with us English as God Gold was with the Spaniards."[165] In a manner like Montesino's condemnation of gold idolatry on Española a century before, Williams was a voice crying out like John the Baptist in the wilderness of North America warning against the idol of land ownership.

Recognition of indigenous forms of property was inseparable from the question of native sovereignty for Williams. The enigmatic Puritan described the Narragansett people led by Chief Miantonomo as a monarchical form of government.[166] Similar to the Spanish Dominicans, Williams located the origin of civil power in the people themselves whose consent established the form of government. Yet Williams's Erastian Puritan commitments were on full display when he then argued that the power of the people to establish the sovereign ruler also entailed the sovereign's governance of the church. In sharp contrast to the Dominican theologians who distinguished the origins of secular power from ecclesiastical power, Williams viewed the people as the source of both. Astonishingly, he maintained an unyielding commitment to political liberty even for the "wildest Indians in America." He observed diverse forms of government in America originating from the native peoples, and this had radical implications for ecclesiastical power: "[T]heir civil and earthly governments be as lawful and true as any governments in the world, and therefore consequently their governors are keepers of the Church or both Tables, (if any Church of Christ should arise amongst them)."[167] Williams was undoubtedly the first European defender, in theory, of an authentically Native American church.

The charitable and radical effort of Williams to recognize and describe Native American modes of sovereignty and property would never attract wide hearing from English colonial legal discussions about land settlement. Agricultural arguments for land dispossession counteracted Williams's diplomatic and treaty-based approach to resolving property disputes with natives.[168] At the center of the colonial agricultural argument was the powerful political ideology of the state of nature, which classified Indians as a savage people

165 Williams, *The Letters of Roger Williams*, in *The Complete Writings*, vol. 6, p. 319.

166 Williams, *Key into the Language of America*, chap. 22, p. 163.

167 Williams, *The Bloody Tenent of Persecution*, in *The Complete Writings*, vol. 3, chap. 92, pp. 249–250.

168 James Tully, *An Approach to Political Philosophy: Locke in Contexts* (Cambridge University Press, 1993), p. 169.

whose vacant land was subject to lawful English possession. Beginning with Hobbes's formulation shaped by his experiences with the Virginia Company, the state of nature was a mode of life characterized by untrammeled liberty and natural right yet without positive law and civilization. Again, surveying North America, Hobbes observed that outside family and tribe, the savages "have no government at all."[169] With the exception of "the two great empires of Peru and Mexico," Locke described most Native Americans as peoples without any government or possessing at best "a very moderate sovereignty" in specific chiefs or generals during times of war.[170]

Locke's explicit empirical source concerning the state of nature, and perhaps that of Hobbes at the Virginia Company, was Acosta's *Natural and Moral History of the Indies*. Acosta had indeed identified a certain political form among the native peoples of Peru and Mexico, but these polities had emerged "from savage and fugitive men." Yet most native inhabitants of the American continents still lived in a savage state marked by freedom. Which is to say, they "had no kings or any form of government but lived in free groups like the Indians of Florida nowadays and the Chiriguanos and Brazilians and many other tribes, who do not have regular kings but in accordance with the occasions that arise in war and peace choose their chiefs as they like."[171] Acosta's portrayal of savage natives of America free of government and political order was the primary episteme informing Locke's state of nature and the Indians occupying it. Locke may have avoided Acosta's derogatory terminology of the savage in the *Second Treatise* but he fully endorsed the Jesuit's account of their uncivilized way of life.

Remarkably, almost a century before Hobbes, Vázquez de Menchaca had theorized a prepolitical state of nature exited through a mutual pact forming civil authority among individual persons. One of the striking features of Vázquez's humanist thought, in contrast to the Spanish Dominicans, was his view of political life as an artificial construction rather than a rational outgrowth of natural inclinations and natural law.[172] A natural state of equality and liberty was ultimately unsustainable without government and the development of civilization. This made Vázquez's political theory more amenable to Hobbes's radical claims about natural liberty as the uninhibited right to all things equally pertaining to everyone in a state of nature without the law and justice of the sovereign. Kant would follow Hobbes's hostile portrayal of the

[169] Hobbes, *Leviathan*, Part 1, chap. 13, p. 85.
[170] Locke, *Second Treatise*, chap. 8, §§102–108; *First Treatise*, chap. 11, §144.
[171] Acosta, *Natural and Moral History of the Indies*, Book 1, chap. 25, pp. 73–74.
[172] Brett, *Liberty, Right and Nature*, chap. 5.

state of nature made up of savage individuals possessing a brutish and wild freedom.[173] Even Locke's state of nature, which retained justice as a right of punishment to protect one's life and property, assumed the presence of wild liberty and equality according to the natural law.

Vázquez's ruminations about a prepolitical state of natural liberty and equality had an historical basis like the Westphalian thinkers. Vázquez anticipated Hobbes, Locke, and Kant by illustrating his point about the pitfalls of natural equality with the paradigmatic early modern colonial example: "For this has been proven to us by our conquests of Indian regions of the New World, where they are all wild savages, with no manner of cities or buildings or agriculture. This is the result of the equality of humans, which produces lazy, idle humans whose hands do very little work."[174] His 1564 opus of legal humanism provided an iconic and fateful theorization of a prepolitical natural state that conveniently mapped onto popular Spanish chronicles of New World natives portrayed as uncivilized and nonindustrious. The Indians in the conglomerate were wild savages who did not abide by the primary law of nations and had never known the secondary law of nations because of the absence of civilization. Vázquez applied the distinctively humanist criteria of city life and agriculture to distinguish European civilization from a wild state of natural equality and liberty. A century later, Hobbes's *De cive* frontispiece, discussed in Chapter 1, registered this exact juxtaposition of free Native American savages and civilized English rule.

Grotius, as we have seen, would expand the agricultural criterion intimated by Vázquez to establish propertied possession through cultivation of the soil. The shift from an ancient primeval community to a more "commodious" one whereby people acquired things and divided lands occurred through labor and industry.[175] However, Grotius did not make the additional inference as did Vázquez that those inhabitants of a natural state lacking agriculture and private property, which was the result of labor, were intractably lazy and wild savages. The language of savagery for Grotius was restricted to the discussion of punishing individuals whose customs and practices violated natural law and the law of nations. Grotius's adherence to natural sociability was simply too strong. He appeared to esteem those who lived in a state of

[173] Kant, "Idea for a Universal History from a Cosmopolitan Perspective," in *Toward Perpetual Peace*, pp. 8–10.

[174] Vázquez de Menchaca, *Controversiarum illustrium*, tom. 1, lib. 1, praefatio, p. 16: "*[Q]uam rem probe experti sunt nostri Indorum regionibus novi orbis subactis, ubi omnia sunt sylvestria et fera infecta, nulla forma urbium aut aedificiorum aut agriculturae ex hominum aequalitate, quae efficit homines pigros ignavos manusque ad labores minime moventes.*"

[175] Grotius, *The Rights of War and Peace*, Book 2, chap. 2, pp. 426–427.

innocence, or "primitive simplicity," proximate to the Garden of Eden. In this innocent state, everyone has a common right to use and consume those things of the untilled earth needed for survival. Rather than characterizing this earliest state of life in terms of laziness or perpetual war, Grotius saw it as one marked by a life of common use and friendship. In addition to the Jewish sect of the Essenes, the first Christians described in the Book of Acts and certain religious orders like the mendicants embodied this commendable way of life. Notably, the other laudable example mentioned by Grotius were some groups of Native Americans.[176]

Grotius viewed the shift from common use to private property as rational but not always necessary for social life thereby adding an important qualification to his account of the right of occupation. On this point, he received inspiration from theological arguments claiming that property was not present in the primeval state of Paradise because of the absence of sin. Like the scholastic theologians, Grotius retained the normative significance of common possession, as practiced among Native Americans and religious orders, who do so "without great inconvenience" to themselves. The natural principle of community inhered in the common equal right of occupation for everyone, which does not stipulate private property for this or that individual. The normative legal implications followed for Grotius: "[N]ecessity, which reduces everything to the natural law, because the mother of positive law should yield to necessity, makes common again things formerly owned."[177] To strengthen his argument, Grotius explicitly referred to Aquinas and his scholastic commentators, who offered the classic case of an impoverished person lawfully using another's property for sustenance due to extreme necessity.[178] Although an undeveloped aspect of Grotius's legal thought, the natural principle of the commons as a constraint on positive law signaled an important contribution of scholastic theology in an international setting.

Colonial legal arguments for English land ownership in North America also promoted the normative significance of the commons. Yet they often did so according to a European civilizational paradigm that rendered a universal natural right of using what was originally common as inferior to an individual civil-political right of private property. Take the example of the important lawyer and first governor of the Massachusetts Bay Colony, John Winthrop (1588–1649), who constructed an early colonial agricultural argument about land ownership for the new "city on a hill." In *Reasons to Be Considered for . . .*

176 Grotius, *The Rights of War and Peace*, Book 2, chap. 2, pp. 421–422.
177 Grotius, "Defense of Chapter V," pp. 85–86.
178 Aquinas, *ST*, II-II, q. 66, a. 7.

the Intended Plantation in New England (1629), Winthrop offered responses to various objections raised against the Company's colonization project. Winthrop began with a pertinent social question about migration informed by the biblical account of human dominion: If the sovereign Lord commands humans to "*replenish the earth and subdue it* ... why then should we stand here striving for places of habitation (many men spending as much labor and cost to recover or keep sometimes an acre or two of land as would procure them many hundred as good or better in another country), and in the mean time suffer a whole continent, as fruitful and convenient for the use of men, to lie waste without any improvement."[179] English settlers not only had legal permission to inhabit vacant land in North America, they were under a theological imperative to improve it for the glory of God. Labor and subjugation of the land was primed to yield far greater benefits for Europeans and natives.

In response to the objection that the original inhabitants of North America already possessed the land – a claim defended by New England interlocutor Williams – Winthrop's brief tract attempted to craftily resolve the issue by identifying a "double right to the earth" in natural right and civil right. This twofold right could simultaneously acknowledge a basic native claim of use for sustenance alongside a specific European right of land ownership. On the one hand, the natives of New England were apparently content, as the first humans had been, with common use of the land and taking from natural bounty what was necessary for survival. Since the natives neither enclose the land, nor settle it with habitation, nor improve it by taming cattle, they "have no other but a natural right to those countries."[180] On the other hand, the English could claim what was their own by enclosing and cultivating and subduing what remained underutilized. Crucially, English industry and labor conferred a civil-political right of individual appropriation of land. In addition to bringing Christianity, Winthrop believed the English had benefited the natives by imparting them with technological knowledge to improve upon the land.

Winthrop outlined in crude terms the savage native's universal natural right of using the earth circumscribed by the English settler's civil right of owning specific parcels of it. This manner of English legal argument would reflect the core ambivalence of infidel rights going back to the Middle Ages, maintaining

179 John Winthrop, *Reasons to Be Considered for ... the Intended Planation of New England*, in *The Puritans in America*, p. 72.

180 Winthrop, *Reasons to Be Considered*, p. 73.

both the natural rights of non-Christians and the superiority of European Christian civilization to delimit those natural rights. The Indians of North America had a rightful claim to property acquired from the commons of nature, yet the lack of organized political society and agricultural civilization meant that they had no individual claim like the English to appropriate the land. John Locke provided a paradigmatic articulation of this ambivalent legacy of infidel rights in the seventeenth-century mercantile colonial setting.

Historians of political thought have been widely attentive to Locke's colonial interests in North America, noting, for example, the Englishman's vast landholdings in the Carolina colony and his role as Secretary to its Lords Proprietors.[181] My concluding treatment of Locke will not rehearse this literature but rather isolates the ambivalent presence of infidel rights in his international thought. The idea of toleration in Locke is an obvious starting point for entering the topic of infidel rights. Locke wrote his famous *Letter Concerning Toleration* (1689) in Latin first during his exile in Holland amidst the revocation of the Edict of Nantes and the growing confessional disputes within Crown and society back in England. His letter precipitated an epistolary debate with Jonas Proast, whose Augustinian arguments – an "old engine in new varnish" as Locke would say – favored the state's indirect coercion of heretics to consider religious truth and renounce religious error.[182] Strikingly, the translated letter of toleration defending liberty of conscience as "every man's natural right" deployed, albeit implicitly, traditional canonistic and scholastic theological principles in a new Protestant key.

Locke's famous letter directly opposed the dominium founded on grace doctrine because of its intolerant political claims not only within single commonwealths but also between peoples. In words reminiscent of Dominican theologians against missionary war from a century earlier, Locke wrote:

> Nobody therefore … neither single persons, nor churches, nay, nor even commonwealths, have any just title to invade the civil rights and worldly goods of each other, upon pretence of religion. Those that are of another opinion, would do well to consider with themselves how pernicious a seed of discord and war, how powerful a provocation to endless hatreds, rapines, and slaughters, they thereby furnish unto mankind. No peace and security, no, not so much as common friendship, can ever be established or preserved

181 Arniel, *John Locke and America*; Tully, *An Approach to Political Philosophy*, chap. 5; Armitage, *Foundations of Modern International Thought*, chaps. 5–7; Sarah Irving, *Natural Science and the Origins of the British Empire* (Routledge, 2016), chap. 5; Onur Ulas Ince, *Colonial Capitalism and the Dilemmas of Liberalism* (Oxford University Press, 2018), chap. 2.

182 Adam Wolfson, *Persecution or Toleration* (Lexington Books, 2010), p. 40.

> amongst men, as long as this opinion prevails, "that dominion is founded in grace, and that religion is to be propagated by force of arms."[183]

Locke based his argument for toleration not merely on philosophical claims of fallibilism, as modern Enlightenment readers are so wont to point out, but also on Scripture and the apostolic tradition in order to reject the practice of converting infidels by force. Echoing Cajetan and the Spanish Dominicans, Locke appealed to the example and method of Jesus Christ, the Prince of Peace, "who sent out his soldiers to the subduing of nations, and gathering them into his church, not armed with sword, or other instruments of force, but prepared with the Gospel of peace, and with the exemplary holiness and conversation."[184] By inference, Locke also took aim at theocratic universalism when he invoked the Pauline *foris* principle restricting the political judgment of idolatry among Jews, Muslims, and pagans. The civil rights and property of infidels remain free from dispossession on the part of either the church, or the commonwealth.[185] In an unprecedented rhetorical spin on medieval canon law, Locke extended the nonjudgment of infidel outsiders to Christian communities themselves, since Calvinists, Lutherans, and Catholics all represented "different religions" of Christianity. If Jews and pagans could lawfully keep their property under Christian rulers, then why not Christians of other sects?

Locke's latitudinarian Protestant reading of the *foris* principle in Reformation Europe was cognizant of the doctrine's application toward American Indians, just as the Dominicans had taken the example of tolerating Jews in Western Europe for natives of the New World. This transatlantic application of a canonistic principle that could eliminate idolatry as a legal cause of war and dispossession only strengthened Locke's defense of infidel rights. Since the peoples of America and Europe belong to the common body of humankind, "neither pagans there, nor any dissenting Christians here, can with any right be deprived of their worldly goods by the predominating faction of a court-church." Locke went so far to claim that even nonbelieving Indians under a Christian magistrate in North America were immune from bodily punishment or dispossession of goods. He argued: "If they are persuaded that

[183] Locke, *A Letter Concerning Toleration*, ed. Ian Shapiro, p. 226.

[184] Locke, *Letter Concerning Toleration*, p. 217.

[185] Locke, *Letter Concerning Toleration*, p. 249: "Nay, if we may openly speak the truth, and as becomes one man to another, neither pagan, nor Mahometan, nor Jew, ought to be excluded from the civil rights of the commonwealth, because of his religion. The Gospel commands no such thing. The church, "which judgeth not those that are without," 1 Cor. 5.11, "wants it not. And the commonwealth, which embraces indifferently all men that are honest, peaceable, and industrious, requires it not."

they please God in observing the rites of their own country ... they are to be left unto God and themselves."[186] These words were not mere lip service but highlighted Locke's political commitment to tolerating Indian worship according to the liberty of conscience, as seen in the *Fundamental Constitutions* of Carolina that he helped draft.[187] Needless to say, his ideas on toleration and conscience were of considerable importance among the founders of the American republic envisioning the new Constitution's first freedom.

Native Americans certainly had natural rights in Locke's judgment, especially in the inward spiritual matters of religion and conscience. When Locke turned to the discussion of property in the fifth chapter of the *Second Treatise*, however, he severely curtailed native rights under European civilizational norms. It is important to note that Locke did not explicitly call natives savages here as Purchas had in the narrative of Virginia. Locke reserved the term of savagery in the *Second Treatise* generally for those who descended to the level of beasts in the state of nature and merited punishment by death. The natives of America, like all human beings, undoubtedly bore the divine image and possessed the law of reason. Nevertheless, their savage way of life could be inferred easily from their occupation of the state of nature in a manner fitting the descriptions of Acosta and Purchas.

A chief assumption of Locke's view on property in the *Second Treatise* was that the natives did not exhibit the full potential of reason under the divine mandate to subdue the earth through industrious labor. This was evident because of their deficient mode of property, along with the absence of money, sufficiently organized political life, and positive civil laws.[188] Locke relied on the crucial normative civilizational distinction between the state of nature and civil-political society to advance a more sophisticated version of Winthrop's twofold right in America: the poor Indians' natural right of property to gathered fruit or hunted deer for self-preservation and the industrious Englishman's individual right of land ownership for enlarging his possessions. For Locke, the natural rights of natives to their goods in America and the vast accumulation of land and money by European settlers were entirely compatible and just according to a protoliberal conception of world order.

Locke looked at the vast, untilled land in North America through a European gaze and saw a state of nature inhabited by "wild Indians." His

186 Locke, *Letter Concerning Toleration*, pp. 237–238.

187 Armitage, *Foundations of Modern International Thought*, p. 128.

188 Nagamitsu Miura, *John Locke and the Native Americans* (Cambridge Scholars Publishing, 2013), chap. 1.

telling assertion that "in the beginning all the world was America" captured the seventeenth-century English colonial mindset. The Bible was instructive for portraying this early historical stage of humanity descending from Adam. Against the Adamic paternal dominion claimed by absolute monarchy, Locke invoked the classic Christian legal doctrine that God gave the earth equally to humankind. In the *First Treatise*, he identified the right coincident with humanity in the beginning similar to America: "Every man had a right to the creatures by the same title Adam had, viz. by the right everyone had to take care of and provide for their subsistence: and thus men had a right in common."[189] Everyone could claim property over things of the earth in the state of nature as part of the original law of nature. The Indians of America indeed possessed property because they appropriated things from the land and from the great common of nature, the ocean. Their natural title to claim these goods of the earth derived from their proper labor, thereby making it their own without consent on the part of anyone else. Locke's innovation here was to revise the Roman law of occupation according to a labor theory of property.[190] Labor, importantly, "put a distinction between them and common: that added something to them more than nature, the common mother of all, had done; and so they became his private right."[191] What Locke had in mind about native labor, specifically, were its basic forms associated with hunter-gatherer societies, such as collecting acorns, picking fruit, and hunting and catching wildlife.

Locke's protoliberal labor theory of property was remarkably adept in identifying a right to private ownership even in the state of nature prior to social contract where every free man was "absolute lord of his person and possessions," an empire unto himself.[192] Locke therefore qualified the conventional colonial arguments of Winthrop and Cushman by recognizing an individual claim of property ownership among the natives who exhibited labor by seizing things from the common of nature. Yet Locke continued to maintain the agricultural criterion to designate a deficient mode of property among Native Americans in comparison to Europeans. Native labor for Locke pertained to taking fruit and animals from nature's common provisions. The mode of occupation acquired through native labor extended only to the unclaimed things of the earth, or *res nullius*.

189 Locke, *First Treatise*, chap. 9, §87; cf. §§37, 92.

190 Fitzmaurice, *Sovereignty, Property and Empire*, pp. 114–122.

191 Locke, *Second Treatise*, chap. 5, §28.

192 Locke, *Second Treatise*, chap. 9, §123.

The right in common to use the things of the earth was indicative of an early stage of humanity, like America, prior to the emergence of civilized society. The uncivilized manner of native life received further support in Locke from Acosta's description of them as peoples without money and organized government. Exiting the state of nature was not the result of property per se, but followed from the consent entailed in using money, erecting a government, and establishing positive law. The form of property required to accomplish the civilized departure from the state of nature was not the possession of nature's spontaneous products, as seen among the Indians, but the possession of an immoveable good – land. Only the English colonists could demonstrate this distinctively European mode of property through land ownership. The wild Indians of America possessed things from the earth as property, but they were still tenants in common when it came to land because they did not enclose and cultivate the earth. God's gift of the earth to humanity was for the greatest conveniences of life and for supreme enjoyment, which could not be attained if the earth remained uncultivated.[193]

Locke clearly discriminated two modes of property, and therefore a twofold right – one Native American, another European – in the vast wilderness of North America where no higher arbiter of government presided over all the land:

> The chief matter of property being now *not* the fruits of the earth, and the beasts that subsist on it, *but the earth itself*; as that which takes in, and carries with it all the rest; I think it is plain, that property in that too is acquired as the former. As much land as man tills, plants, improves, cultivates, and can use the product of, so much his property. He by his labor does enclose it from the common. Nor will it invalidate his right, to say everybody else has an equal title to it, and therefore he cannot appropriate, he cannot enclose, without consent of his fellow-commoners, all mankind. God, when he gave the world in common to all mankind, commanded man also to labor, and the penury of his condition required it of him. God and his reason commanded him to subdue the earth, i.e. improve it for the benefit of life, and therein lay out something upon it that was his own, his labor.[194]

Locke's specification of a twofold property right in the state of nature to either "the things" (*res*) that subsist on the earth or "the earth" (*terra*) itself rested on a European civilizational norm of improvement that could justify extensive land appropriation in North America. The novelty of Locke's idea of occupation as labor was to locate wholly within natural law the exclusive right to

[193] Locke, *Second Treatise*, chap. 5, §§26, 34.
[194] Locke, *Second Treatise*, chap. 5, §32. Emphasis mine.

vacant earth and underutilized land. *Terra nullius* in America was therefore no longer about specific peoples politically occupying lands according to the law of nations but about private individuals improving the earth itself in the state of nature.

The language of improvement in Locke's theory of property, politics, and knowledge was indicative of a larger project of empire marked by an English colonial interpretation of the Bible, humanism, and the new science of Francis Bacon.[195] The *New Organon* (1620) of Bacon, another important possession of Locke's library, had revolutionized modern scientific knowledge in practical terms by reorienting the aim of knowledge to the benefit and relief of the human condition.[196] Applied to Locke's colonial thinking on property in America, the native right of using the things that subsist on the earth, simply speaking, was woefully inadequate to yield, on the one hand, the greater conveniences and enjoyments of life, and, on the other, the greatest benefit for everyone.

Two factors obviated native claims of effective land occupation in America for Locke: the wastefulness of the land and the poverty of the natives. Locke saw the land of America as a squandered gift from God. In effect, it was a common waste, yet rich and teeming with boundless potential for growth. Locke echoed the arguments of Purchas, Cotton, and Cushman, all of whom believed that the Indians did not properly use the land to exploit its maximum potential. The benefit the Indians had received from underutilized land amounted to very little. Native extent of labor in terms of seizing the spontaneous products of the earth was not conducive to the preservation of the "one society" or the "one body" of humankind.[197] In contrast to Indian property, the English mode of land ownership was better suited to improve and benefit humankind as a whole and not just a particular family or tribal community. As Locke interpreted: "[H]e who appropriates land to himself by his labor, does not lessen, but increases the common stock of mankind." He continued further by drawing the normative comparison: "for the provisions serving to the support of human life, produced by one acre of enclosed and cultivated land, are (to speak much within compass) ten times more than those which are yielded by an acre of land of an equal richness lying waste in common."[198]

From this civilizational standpoint, Locke powerfully transmuted the colonial discourse of the Indies regarding native offenses against the natural law

195 Irving, *Natural Science and the Origins of the British Empire*, pp. 114–115.

196 Charles Taylor, *Sources of the Self* (Harvard University Press, 1989), pp. 213–214.

197 Locke, *Second Treatise*, chap. 9, §128.

198 Locke, *Second Treatise*, chap. 5, §37.

from idolatry to underutilization of the earth. Waste of the earth and its natural products were considered a violation of the common law of nature and liable to punishment. Therefore, any hindrance of the English who need no consent from effectively subduing the earth by tilling it would amount to theft and a violation of an individual right just as it would if natives refused to let the English take what was sufficient from the common of nature. Government was required precisely for settling disputes about property in a civilized state where consent mattered, especially over land ownership. The supreme end of forming political society was the preservation and enjoyment of property as Locke reiterated throughout the *Second Treatise*. Since the Native Americans lacked organized government, following Acosta's description, their form of property was limited to the fruits and beasts of the earth rather than the earth itself. Although the Indians were endowed with reason, according to which their labor in hunting animals made it their own, they could hardly count as part of "the civilized part of mankind" in the absence of positive civil laws, the correlate of government, to further determine private property rights.[199]

Locke's comparison of Indians and the English on property, hinging on the presence or absence of land ownership, was not only concerned with the issue of agricultural technology aimed at improving the earth and benefiting humankind. It also took into consideration the material conditions contrasting Indian and European ways of life. On this score, Bacon offered an influential English colonial interpretation of the New World praising the advantages of European civilization:

> [L]et anyone reflect how great is the difference between the life of men in any of the most civilized provinces of Europe and in the most savage and barbarous region of New India; and he will judge that they differ so much that deservedly it may be said that "a man is a God to man," not only for help and benefit, but also in the contrast between their conditions. And this is due not to soil, climate, or bodily qualities, but to Arts.[200]

The Baconian hierarchy of civilization did not admit the classical geopolitical difference of climate or heredity, but of ignorance in the arts, mechanical and literary. Less a Renaissance account of elitist virtue like Sepúlveda, Locke's empiricist theory of knowledge made a startling observation similar to Bacon when he spoke of "the whole great Continent of *America* . . . whose Ignorance is useful arts, and want of the greatest part of the conveniences of life, in a country that abounded with all sorts of natural plenty" (see Figure 5.3). In

199 Locke, *Second Treatise*, chap. 5, §30.
200 Francis Bacon, *The New Organon* (Cambridge University Press, 2000), chap. 129, p. 100.

FIGURE 5.3 "American Progress by John Gast." (Source: Getty Images/Fotosearch/Stringer)

particular, it was the ignorance of using iron that Locke believed was constitutive of native backwardness and therefore savagery. For were iron's usage "lost among us," he continued, "we should in a few Ages be unavoidably reduced to the wants and ignorance of ancient savage *Americans*, whose natural endowments and provisions come no way short of the most flourishing and polite nations."[201] The improvement of knowledge through the mechanical arts of civilization was a prerequisite for improving the earth. And this made every bit of difference between poor savage Americans and industrious European settlers.

In the Baconian spirit of relieving and ameliorating the human condition, Locke's *Second Treatise* strengthened the argument for English land ownership with its promise of generating conveniences of life beyond the material wants of native modes of property. The absence of the greater conveniences of life among the peoples of America was a palpable demonstration of their poverty despite the abundant bounty of the land. The natives simply did not

[201] Locke, *An Essay Concerning Human Understanding* (Hackett Publishing, 1996), Book 4, chap. 12, p. 297.

improve the land whereas the English did. Making explicit contrast of European and Indian ways of life was a frequent rhetorical tactic of the *Second Treatise*. Locke wondered if a cultivated acre in Devon in England was even more beneficial for the conveniences of life than a thousand acres in the "wild woods and uncultivated waste of America" for its "needy and wretched inhabitants."[202] It was extremely inefficient to let nature determine the products of the earth when reason and God have commanded the subjugation and cultivation of land through industry and arts. According to a strictly Indian form of labor through seizing nature's goods, commodities were limited to acorns, some fruits, water, leaves, and skins. In contrast, English labor and industry could yield bread, wine, and clothing, all of which were far more enjoyable and valuable commodities that improved the overall quality of life. Without land ownership and cultivation, the Indians "have not one-hundredth part of the conveniences we enjoy: and a king of a large and fruitful territory there feeds, lodges, and is clad worse than a day-laborer in England."[203]

A crucial economic dimension of civilized life starkly accented the difference between a native sachem and an English wage laborer in Locke's judgment. Whereas the English laborer could sell his own labor on the market to earn wages, the native sachem had no monetary system to produce the greater conveniences of life through hard industry. According to Locke's description, aside from the absence of land ownership and organized government, the natives lacked money, which added valuation to nature's products and land beyond necessity. For this reason, the degree of Indian industry and their form of labor was inescapably restricted to a life of want and very limited possessions. Locke apparently did acknowledge pre-monetary trade among the Indians whereby they exchanged perishables for durables such as shells, pebbles, and diamonds.[204] This description accorded with Roger Williams when he identified the importance of white shells (*wampum*) and dark shells (*suckauhock*) displayed on strings around the neck for Indian trading of corn, furs, fish, and venison not only among themselves, but also with the English.[205] Although Williams saw this as Indian money and coin, Locke did not. In Locke's view, the native exchange of shells was not money in the complete sense because it did not have the overall effect of transforming the desires of Indians to enlarge their possessions. The whole world was America

202 Locke, *Second Treatise*, chap. 5, §37.
203 Locke, *Second Treatise*, chap. 5, §§41–42.
204 Tully, *An Approach to Political Philosophy*, p. 160.
205 Williams, *Key into the Language of America*, chap. 26, pp. 173–178.

in the beginning precisely because "no such thing as money was anywhere known" there.[206]

Acosta's descriptions also provided Locke with resources for portraying the Americans as an uncivilized people not only lacking positive law and organized government, but also a monetary economy. This did not mean that the natives had no value or esteem for gold and silver. Their sacred temples, religious objects, and rulers were often adorned with these fine metals. The native Floridians, however, among the most savage barbarians according to Acosta, had no appreciation whatsoever for the metal's value. As Acosta definitively concluded in his *Natural and Moral History of the Indies*: "It has not been found that the Indians used gold or silver or any other metal for money, nor to establish the price of things."[207] Acosta, like Sepúlveda, presented the natives in monolithic terms as peoples without the voluntary pact and positive law needed to establish metal as a form of currency.

Locke strategically incorporated this sixteenth-century Spanish characterization of moneyless natives, along with influential English colonial descriptions, to reinforce the deficient mode of native property. However, there was a crucial ideological difference between Acosta and Locke on this point about money. Acosta, a Jesuit theologian in conversation with the Spanish Dominicans on the affair of the Indies, was at least cognizant of the destructive desires of European greed in the New World. Speaking about the natives, Acosta wrote: "[T]he truth is that their greed for it was not as immoderate as ours, nor did they idolize gold and silver as much (even though they were idolaters) as some bad Christians, who have committed so many excesses for the sake of gold and silver."[208] While Acosta did make this notable point about idolatry's avaricious effect on Spanish activity in the Indies, he never made the additional reflexive claim, as the Dominicans did, about European savagery toward the natives.[209]

The moral category of idolatry, evidently, could still serve for Acosta a prophetic function in his modest effort to curb vicious desires among Christians. For Locke, the civilizational difference between Native Americans and European colonists crystallized in an ideological point about human desire: natives had limited desire for possession whereas the English had unlimited desire to accumulate possessions.[210] This did not mean Locke favored the gross consumerism and throwaway culture of late advanced

206 Locke, *Second Treatise*, chap. 5, §49.

207 Acosta, *Natural and Moral History of the Indies*, Book 4, chap. 3, p. 165.

208 Acosta, *Natural and Moral History of the Indies*, Book 4, chap. 2, p. 163.

209 MacCormack, *Religion in the Andes*, pp. 266–267.

210 Tully, *An Approach to Political Philosophy*, p. 157.

capitalism. Leo Strauss powerfully articulated the ideological point of contrast in Locke, for whom "the terrors of the natural law no longer strike the covetous, but the waster."[211] Money's nonperishable and inconsumable status made it something immune from wastefulness. Hence it was detachable from the moral constraints of a natural law no longer focused on eradicating the root of all idolatry and evil according to the Bible – greed. For this reason, Locke was able to make an astonishingly troublesome assertion that money can be "hoarded up without injury to anyone."[212]

Importantly, Locke never said one could hoard material goods and land at the expense of those in dire need. In the *First Treatise*, Locke considered it sinful for anyone to "let his brother perish for want of affording him relief out of his plenty. As justice gives every man a title to the product of his honest industry . . . so charity gives every man a title so much out of another's plenty as will keep him from extreme want, where he has no means to subsist otherwise."[213] Letting food rot and perish, and leaving usable land vacant, were forms of waste that obstructed the common welfare of humanity even in the state of nature. In the case of North America where the land was vastly empty and native inhabitants use only what they need, the introduction of money could incentivize land ownership and utilization thereby benefiting humanity through world commerce.

Money, in contrast to organized government and civil laws, could exist in the state of nature alongside land ownership according to Locke. The use of money, which in the state of nature illustrated tacit consent over the value assigned to gold and silver, for example, permitted unequal possession of the earth before political society emerged to regulate property among individual citizens. Indian shells might function similarly yet *wampum* did not terminate in land ownership – the civilized European form of property. Money, which could store the value of labor beyond material wants by making beneficial improvement to the land, was a prerequisite necessary for individual land ownership. Yet this unequal taking possession of land by individuals still adhered to the moral prohibition on waste. On Locke's terms, the desire for money would make no sense for a settler family owning thousands of acres of cultivable land and cattle "in the middle of the inland parts of America" with "no hopes of commerce with other parts of the world."[214] Neither for that matter would it be advantageous to have money on an island lacking

211 Leo Strauss, *Natural Right and History* (University of Chicago Press, 1953), p. 237.

212 Locke, *Second Treatise*, chap. 5, §50.

213 Locke, *First Treatise*, chap. 4, §42.

214 Locke, *Second Treatise*, chap. 5, §48.

commercial relations with the rest of the world. In both cases of either secluded land or a deserted island, the appropriate natural and rational behavior would be to use only what was required for attaining basic conveniences of life. Yet in a colonial context of trade and commerce, monetization was "the necessary condition for economic progress" that natives lacked and the English brought to America.[215] Money was the engine of commercial world order facilitated by European expansion.

An eighteenth-century dispute between the Mohegan people and English colonists in Connecticut that involved the English Crown relied on several key aspects of Locke's arguments about money and commerce and Acosta's description of the natives to justify European land ownership through improvement.[216] The clergyman John Bulkley acknowledged a modicum of native claims to property, even in land, but it was entirely restricted to necessary goods and nothing more. Before the arrival of the English, Mohegan way of life was simply debased, poor and barbarous, and disconnected from "communication with other parts of the world."[217] Locke and Acosta gave Bulkley's argument additional support for locating the Mohegans in the state of nature due to the absence of civil society and government. Yet even if they did exhibit political society, as some English critics like Williams and others argued, Bulkley maintained that they still lacked a monetary system to generate new desires beyond natural sustenance. It was only upon the encounter with the English, "by conversation and commerce," that the Mohegans "were made sensible" about the value of money and the selling and partitioning of land as a commodity through purchases and treaties.[218] The bottom line for Bulkley was that the English in North America had "an undoubted right to enter upon and impropriate all such parts of it as lay waste or unimproved by the natives and this without any consideration or allowance made to them for it."[219] Bulkley's main argument, just as Locke's in the fifth chapter on property in the *Second Treatise*, was to defend English land appropriation without native consent.[220]

Monetization was what facilitated the unlimited enlargement of British desire to have more than one needed by the accumulation of wealth and the finer enjoyments of life. The privatization of land ownership in conjunction

215 Ince, *Colonial Capitalism*, p. 65.

216 Craig Yirush, *Settlers, Liberty, and Empire* (Cambridge University Press, 2011), chap. 4; Fitzmaurice, *Sovereignty, Property and Empire*, pp. 173–183.

217 John Bulkley, "Preface," in Roger Wolcott, *Poetical Meditations* (London, 1725), p. xxxvii.

218 Bulkley, "Preface," pp. xl–xli.

219 Bulkley, "Preface," p. liv.

220 Tully, *An Approach to Political Philosophy*, p. 145.

with money would inevitably bring about an unequal society of haves and have-nots. Yet this was not an injustice for Locke because it benefitted humankind when connected by global commerce. Locke finally envisioned English society getting rich through commerce instead of conquest: "[I]n our present circumstances, nobody is vain enough to entertain a thought of our reaping the profits of the world by swords [...]. Commerce therefore is the only way left to us, either for riches or subsistence, for this the advantages of our situation, as well as the industry and inclination of our people, bold and skillful at sea, do naturally fit us: By this the nation of England has been hitherto supported."[221] Wealth, or riches, refer specifically to the greater conveniences of life that England has on par with, if not more than, other European states.

Wealth inequality through money and unequal possession of land was perfectly compatible with Locke's idea of universal natural rights. His twofold natural right to the goods of the earth and the earth itself, contrasting the inferior Native American versus the superior English claims of property, was a highly effective argument preserving the ambivalent legacy of infidel rights. However, he executed it in a Protestant commercial context shaped by legal humanism and natural philosophy. Locating the natives in the state of nature without a higher arbiter of organized government, without civil laws, and without money, was constitutive of the English logic of dispossession in North America. Acosta's description of the so-called savages of the New World along the terms first outlined by Sepúlveda explicitly informed the colonial thinking of Locke, Purchas, and Bulkley.

During the seventeenth century, a Eurocentric natural law justified English colonial expansion principally under the civilizational norm of improving the land and secondarily the punishment of offenses against nature. World commerce conducted by Protestant imperial powers belonged to the unimpeachable order of divine providence. The next and final chapter returns to the unique contributions of the Spanish Dominicans in the broader context of international thought. In contrast to legal humanism and protoliberalism, yet sharing some important but distinct features with eighteenth-century Enlightenment moral cosmopolitanism, the scholastic theologians employed not only the natural law but also the law of nations to strengthen the role of consent underlying native political agency. They would also constrain the excesses of European expansion by identifying the scope and limits of intervention.

221 Locke, "Some Considerations of the Consequences of Lowering the Interest, and Raising the Value of Money," in *Locke on Money*, vol. 1, ed. Patrick Hyde Kelly (Oxford University Press, 1991), pp. 222–223.

6

The Scholastic Law of Nations, Native Occupation, and Human Solidarity

Genealogies of European international thought that trace continuity between sixteenth-century Spanish Dominican theologians and seventeenth-century Protestant natural lawyers and philosophers must be attentive to the ambivalent legacy of infidel rights culminating at Valladolid for at least three reasons: First, it foregrounds the important religious and theological dimensions of Europe's interactions with new worlds through the ethics of evangelization. Second, it underscores the distinctively Protestant character of seventeenth-century empires of commerce like the English and Dutch seeking to contrast their mercantile approach from either conquest or apostolic preaching. Finally, it widens the scope of Spanish contributions to early modern and modern international thought by including theocratic royalist-papalism as well as imperial and legal forms of humanism.

This final chapter considers extant normative resources of the Spanish theologians for thinking about the law of nations in the colonial history of international society beyond the conceptual parameters of Westphalia. To that end, the chapter complicates homogenizing IR typologies that identify Spanish scholasticism with either modern rationalism or moral cosmopolitanism thus overlooking its distinctive contributions. Chapters 3 and 4 addressed subjective natural rights as a key dimension of natural law discourse in the Spanish Dominicans' defense of Amerindians. Violations of the subjective rights of original inhabitants of the New World by Europeans required restitution as a prerequisite to salvation. Yet there is more to consider in the Spanish theological conception of world order and its contribution to international thought. This final chapter explores the constructive meaning of *ius gentium*, or the law of nations, in the early modern colonial context. When exploring *ius gentium* among the Spanish theologians, I use the term "right of peoples" to designate its subjective dimension attentive to both native political agency and a supranational commitment to solidarity and justice between individuals and peoples. The right of peoples captures the normative force of *ius gentium* as both a political instrument of a people's collective self-determination and a universal moral norm protecting innocent members of a world order.

Among the Spanish theologians, these two aspects of the law of nations – independent political agency and interdependent solidarity among peoples – could sometimes be in direct conflict with each other when considering cases of lawful intervention. However, it was precisely by yielding a productive tension, grounded in a theological political doctrine of subjective natural rights, that they made an enduring ethical contribution to international thought. One way of reading Vitoria's *Relectio de Indis* can be to observe the tension at work between independent native polities and lawful European intervention and war in his outlining the strictly unjust and probable just titles for Spanish rule over natives endowed with rights. Vitoria privileged infidel rights discourse and political agency according to natural law and the law of nations before considering the possibility of just war in the Indies. The law of nations for Vitoria signals a nexus of independence and interdependence that "both legitimates division between properties and peoples and at the same time limits the claims they can make to exclude other members of the universal human society."[1] Vitoria and the Spanish theologians can provide a richer critical moral lens for international thought than the conventional Westphalian focus on the tension between political autonomy and universal obligation and interconnection, as seen in Emer de Vattel.[2]

The English School of IR gets at a similar tension by distinguishing the noninterventionism governing a *pluralist* order of independent states from the interventionist rationales organizing a *solidarist* order of interdependent states. And although this pluralist-solidarist debate in the English School has brought greater focus to the normative basis of international society by addressing rules of armed conflict and humanitarian intervention, it has done so in a rather restrictive manner determined by twentieth-century international politics.[3] By presupposing a decolonized world of sovereign nation-states, contemporary IR reflection on international society tends to marginalize indigenous modes of political agency. Paul Keal, in turn, has provided an important corrective to the standard notion of an international society expanding from Europe outward, which passes over the lasting historical effects of colonial domination on

1 Brett, *Changes of State*, pp. 13–14.

2 On the usefulness of Vattel's normative vision, see Jennifer Pitts, "Intervention and Sovereign Equality: Legacies of Vattel," in *Just and Unjust Military Intervention*, pp. 132–153.

3 For a solidarist defense of humanitarian intervention attentive to pluralist arguments in the English School, see Nicholas Wheeler, *Saving Strangers* (Oxford University Press, 2000).

indigenous peoples. Beyond the parameters of war waged by sovereign states, indigenous political agency promotes a view of self-determination not strictly about "statehood but control over decisions within institutional structures of states."[4]

The issue of humanitarian intervention and war today, as for the early modern Spanish theologians, remains relevant to the ethics of international society. Nevertheless, conflict and lawful intervention is secondary to the fundamental normative concern with the origin of political agency in the people, a key resource of thinking about indigenous self-determination outside the conceptual confines of the Westphalian political imaginary and decolonized nation-states. Self-determination, as demonstrated by international lawyers, often concerns contemporary political and ecological controversies involving the scope of democratic participation, cultural integrity, land usage, and control over natural resources among indigenous peoples.[5] In this chapter, we will focus primarily on the issue of native occupation and independent political agency in the Indies before turning to the ancillary topic of lawful intervention.

The Spanish theologians considered here provide normative resources for extrapolating indigenous political agency by giving attention to the people as a theological political concept. Although a "people" is not self-sufficient in an atomistic sense, as Oliver O'Donovan has argued, it is the largest coordinated agent that can put various cultural features and habits of communication into the service of the common good. Practically speaking, this coordinated agency receives fuller realization through defined boundaries and the emergence of political authority, whose purpose is to defend the common good of the people and maintain juridical order.[6] The patriarchs, the common experience of Egyptian bondage, and the Law of Moses, all reveal that Israel was already a people before entering the Promised Land, after which its identity enhanced through territory and kingship.

This chapter considers the theological and ecclesiological commitments that informed the Spanish scholastic-juristic interpretation of the law of nations as a right of peoples, which accounts for rational agency and political recognition residing in a unified people before taking on a discrete form of governance. When intellectual historians typically address the contributions of the Spanish theologians, they focus on their creative use of Roman legal

4 Keal, *European Conquest*, p. 132. See also James Anaya, chap. 3 of *Indigenous Peoples in International Law* (Oxford University Press, 1996).

5 James Anaya, *Indigenous Peoples in International Law*, chap. 4; Mattias Åhrén, *Indigenous Peoples' Status in the International Legal System* (Oxford University Press, 2018), chap. 9.

6 O'Donovan, *Ways of Judgment*, chap. 9.

vocabulary such as dominium, *imperium*, *res nullius*, *ius gentium*, and just war.[7] Important indeed, yet these notions cannot be treated apart from the theological concepts and canonistic principles interacting with them that expanded their traditional range of meaning. We have seen this already in their usage of the divine image (*imago Dei*), sacramental penance and restitution, the canonistic *foris* principle, and the nature-grace Thomistic political axiom for thinking through infidel rights. By translating biblical and canon legal teachings into political categories, the Spanish Dominicans strengthened native political agency and the worldwide protection of the innocent according to natural law and the law of nations. Additionally, ideas about consent and resistance, the mystical body of Christ (*corpus mysticum*), and neighbor love were foundational to their conception of world order even as it accommodated their respective and sometimes divergent political judgments.

THE SPANISH SCHOLASTIC-JURISTIC LAW OF NATIONS

For the Spanish theologians, the law of nations in a transatlantic colonial context simultaneously conferred political recognition to independent infidel communities and the moral interdependence of those communities in an expanding international society inspired by the universal proclamation of the Gospel. Universal norms of justice and solidarity set the parameters for interaction and, in some restricted cases, intervention between peoples. The concept of the law of nations provided them a constructive space for making political judgments about the Indies to address the contingencies of history in a sinful world made up of diverse peoples. In particular, the long-standing practices and institutions of political rule, division of property, war, and slavery came under the purview of the law of nations. Although these paradigmatic ancient practices of the law of nations were in common usage across the world, it did not mean their expression was the same among peoples and throughout history. Nevertheless, the variability of the law of nations' public and private expression in a world that included Christians and infidels, Europeans and non-Europeans alike, was a testament to shared human rationality, not civilizational hierarchy.

7 Benton and Straumann, "Acquiring Empire by Law: From Roman Doctrine to Early Modern Practice," pp. 18–25; Martti Koskenniemi, "Empire and International Law: The Real Spanish Contribution," *University of Toronto Law Journal* 61, no. 1 (2011): 1–36; Andrew Fitzmaurice, "The Problem of Eurocentrism in the Thought of Francisco de Vitoria," in *At the Origins of Modernity: Francisco de Vitoria and the Discovery of International Law*, eds. José María Beneyto and Justo Cordi Varela (Springer, 2017), pp. 77–93.

The scholastic-juristic law of nations was not an imperial tool for punishing violations of natural law by a superior culture. Neither did it justify the aggressive political enforcement of universal precepts on allegedly backward, inferior societies. It was instead a law of division separating jurisdictions and properties, and a law of solidarity uniting individuals and peoples. Like the natural law, it provided a critical hermeneutic for affirming native rationality and scrutinizing European Christian interactions with non-European infidels when applied to the Indies. At the core of the law of nations was an original right of consent deriving from natural law – the bedrock of scholastic thinking about political agency. Let us consider more in depth the unique influence of theology and canon law on the law of nations in the Spanish Dominican efforts at excavating a normative basis of order for international society.

Natural rationality and positivity were central features of the scholastic-juristic view on the law of nations. The Roman jurist Ulpian had distinguished the law of nations from what nature taught all animals, or natural law, by drawing attention to a law that was distinctively species-bound involving human relations (*inter se*).[8] In addition, Gaius established the law of nations on the basis of natural reason.[9] For Christian theologians, this begged the question of the relationship between natural law and the law of nations. The scholastic difficulty of reconciling the intermediate and ambivalent place of the law of nations as a temporal instantiation between natural law's strict rationality and civil law's strict positivity was a tension going back to Aquinas that generated creative reflection on the concept.

Aquinas's discussion of *ius gentium* was minimal, somewhat elusive, although authoritative for the Spanish Dominican theologians. The medieval friar aligned the Spanish scholastics with St. Isidore of Seville, who identified the law of nations as part of positive human law.[10] Yet more specific than either Isidore's *Etymologies* or Gratian's *Decretum*, Aquinas categorized the law of nations, along with civil law, as two kinds of positive human law. Nevertheless, the positivity of the law of nations did not detract from its important linkage to reason and natural law even if the precise meaning of the linkage remained unclear to subsequent commentators. Aquinas's law of nations tracked the natural law more closely than civil law did. This rational dimension of the law of nations established a crucial scholastic point expanding Gauis's Roman legal meaning: "The law of nations is indeed, in some way, natural to man, in

8 *Digest*, 1.1.3–4.

9 *Digest*, 1.1.9.

10 Isidore, *Etymologies*, V.vi; Gratian, D. 1, c. 9; Vitoria, *Comentarios*, 57.3, no. 2; Soto, *De iustitia et iure*, lib. 1, q. 5, a. 4.

so far as he is a rational being, because it is derived from natural law by way of a conclusion that is not very remote from its premises. Wherefore humans easily consented to this."[11] The exact meaning of the derivation from natural law was a point of distinction among the Spanish theologians.

According to Aquinas, the law of nations ultimately accounted for those practices without which humans would find it difficult to live together as rational social beings.[12] Yet how could two very different kinds of practice like private property and slavery both be said to derive from natural law when neither of them existed during the pristine age of natural law at the beginning of creation? Here lay one point of ambiguity for Thomistic commentators. Aquinas did offer more perspective through his treatment of natural inclinations, which provided a kind of teleological map of the natural law and the general human tendency toward the goods of life, marital union, society, and religious truth.[13] From this standpoint of the natural inclination to sociability, then, private property and slavery "derive" from natural law insomuch as there is "human agreement" about division of property or "some resultant utility" from slavery that sustains human life together.[14] Aquinas adhered to a tension affirming the rational character of the law of nations by its proximity to natural law as a derived conclusion without abandoning its positivity expressed through human consent. The Spanish theologians expanded their discourse of the law of nations from this Thomistic conceptual frame.

In contrast to Hobbes and the early modern humanist jurists, Aquinas's treatment of the law of the nations, albeit undeveloped in his thought, enabled the Spanish theologians to distinguish the law of nations from both natural law and civil law so that it was not collapsible into either one of the latter. It was incumbent on the Spanish Dominicans, however, to go beyond Aquinas by extrapolating the rational and positive character of the law of nations, thus demarcating their scholastic theological view generally from Renaissance imperial forms of legal humanism. They did so by emphasizing the general or universal character of the law of nations over legal humanism's parochial account that received its testimony, according to Grotius, from "the most ancient usage of civilized nations and by the authority of the wisest men."[15] Because of the universality of the law of nations, the Spanish theologians heavily stressed its proximity to natural law and natural right. Whereas Ulpian and early modern humanist jurists referred to *ius gentium* as the law of

[11] Aquinas, *ST*, I-II, q. 95, a. 4, *ad* 1.
[12] Aquinas, *ST*, I-II, q. 95, a. 4; q. 95, a. 2.
[13] Aquinas, *ST*, I-II, q. 94, a. 2.
[14] Aquinas, ST, II-II, q. 57, a. 3 *corpus* and *ad* 2.
[15] Grotius, "Defense of Chapter V," p. 105.

civilized peoples, a point seized by Sepúlveda, Vitoria saw it as a law established from "the common consent of *all* peoples and nations."[16] Accordingly, the law of nations included all rational agents created in the divine image and admitted the universal authority of the whole world instead of a specific geopolitical gaze determined by European civilization.

Soto's commentary on justice and right from the *Summa* also referred to the universal scope of the law "common to all peoples" (*commune omnibus gentibus*).[17] He shared with Vitoria a universal view of the law of nations in contrast to the provincial version of legal humanism. However, Soto did not appeal to the binding sanction of the world community or universal consent among all peoples as seen in Vitoria's discussion of *ius gentium*.[18] Commenting as a scholastic "moral philosopher," Soto provided his own interpretation to clarify the Roman juristic meaning of the law of nations as a "right that peoples universally (*ius quod gentes universae*), by virtue of possessing reason, have established for themselves."[19] The definitions of Ulpian and Gaius were under consideration in Soto's effort to locate natural reason as the universal basis of the law of nations, which "is observed in equal manner among everyone (*id apud omnes peraequale custodit*)."

Soto did not see localized human agreement at some discrete place – a distinct feature of civil law – as necessary for the establishment of the law of nations. Rather, the law of nations is what reason itself teaches each person.[20] Even though human consent and positivity explained the origin of independent polities in the law of nations, this did not require a formal gathering of peoples since through natural reason all peoples know it.[21] Vitoria, for his part, did not conflate the law of nations with civil law, either. This was demonstrated by his preference to speak of a "virtual consent," instead of a formal one, among peoples of the world established by fact rather than spoken word.[22] Vitoria's attention to positivity, though unclear at times, anticipated further elaboration from Spanish thinkers like Las Casas and Suárez on the role of ancient usage and custom in establishing the law of nations.

16 Vitoria, *Comentarios*, 57.3, no. 3: "*[E]x communi consensu omnium gentium et nationum.*" Emphasis mine.

17 Soto, *De iustitia et iure*, lib. 3, q. 1, a. 3. Similarly, see Francisco Suárez, *De legibus*, eds. L. Pereña, V. Abril, P. Suñer (CSIC, 1973), lib. 2, cap. 20, no. 1.

18 Brett, *Changes of State*, p. 85.

19 Soto, *De iustitia et iure*, lib. 3, q. 1, a. 3.

20 Soto, *De iustitia et iure*, lib. 3, q. 1, a. 3: "*[I]us gentium non requiritur hominum conventus in unum locum: quoniam ratio id singulos per se docet.*"

21 Soto, *De iustitia et iure*, lib. 3, q. 1, a. 3.

22 Vitoria, *Comentarios*, 57.3, no. 5; 62.1, no. 23.

In order to maintain both the linkage to, and distinction from, natural law, as outlined by Aquinas, Vitoria and Soto understood the law of nations as derived from natural law but not in a strictly necessary way. An important difference between Vitoria and Soto concerned the mode of derivation from the natural law. For Aquinas, the law of nations derived from natural law as a conclusion from natural premises, or a specification of natural principles.[23] Technically speaking, the law of nations was a discursive interpretation of natural principles indicative of humans as social animals seeking some beneficial result under contingent situations. Vitoria and Soto also concurred on this point. However, they had distinct ways of understanding the derived conclusion characteristic of the law of nations. Whereas Soto saw the rational conclusions of the law of nations as an illation from the natural law, Vitoria saw them as protective of the natural law. This subtle difference had important political implications for the law of nations and the reception, particularly of Vitoria, among later international thinkers.

Vitoria's *Summa* commentary on the law of nations question valorized Aquinas's categorization of it under positive law rather than natural law. Vitoria proposed that rationally established human enactments ordered toward social peace and concord provided the chief content of the law of nations.[24] By emphasizing positivity in the law of nations, even in a virtual sense, Vitoria could simultaneously affirm its widespread binding force and near permanence. Respectively, it is "always illicit to violate the law of nations because it is contrary to common consent" and it would take the whole world to overturn its norms, a sheer impossibility.[25] The close connection to natural law remained crucial for the law of nations thereby revealing its political dimension most clearly. Vitoria's prominent example from both the commentary and his early lecture on civil power, which would also factor into the *Relectio de Indis*, was the immunity of ambassadors.[26] Without the free admission of ambassadors between nations threatened by war, there would be less opportunity to attain peace, which was from natural law and of benefit to all peoples. In this regard, Vitoria concluded that the "law of nations comes so close to natural law that it would not be possible to preserve the natural law without the law of nations."[27] Or, taking the example of division of property,

23 Aquinas, *ST*, I-II, q. 95, a. 2.
24 Vitoria, *Comentarios*, 57.3, no. 1.
25 Vitoria, *Comentarios*, 57.3, nos. 3 and 5.
26 Vitoria, *On Civil Power*, q. 3, a. 4, p. 40.
27 Vitoria, *Comentarios*, 57.3, nos. 3 and 4: "*[N]am jus gentium ita accedit ad jus naturale ut non possit servari jus naturale sine hoc jure gentium*"; "*Nihilominus tamen jus gentium est necessarium ad conservationem juris naturalis.*"

the right of peoples is "necessary for the preservation of the natural law" in this case to avoid greater discord and war between people. As a rational conclusion benefiting the good of humanity, the law of nations took on an even stronger protective function with respect to natural law in Vitoria's analysis of the Indies affair.

When considering the first and most well-known possible title justifying a claim to Spanish rule in the Indies, Vitoria extrapolated from the law of nations an inviolable right of traveling (*ius peregrinandi*) to the lands of foreign peoples without detriment and harm to either party involved. Vitoria began with a striking interpretation of Gaius's law of nations as that "which *is or derives from* natural law."[28] Vitoria evidently brought the law of nations closest to natural law in this definition to address a concrete historical case. Scholars have therefore observed an inconsistency or confusion here and elsewhere regarding Vitoria's apparently conflicted groundings of the law of nations in either natural law, human enactments, consent of the whole world or consent of a greater part of it.[29] While these groundings were not necessarily at total odds, it was also far from clear how they overlapped for Vitoria. The pertinent issue of *De Indis* in our discussion was the political relevance of the law of nations, or the binding force of its rights and duties on peoples of the world.

Often overlooked by critics, Vitoria's first just title reiterated at least ten times the no-harm principle required for the Spanish to claim a right of traveling in the Indies without native hindrance. Any Spanish violation of the no-harm principle not only undermined the possible title, it also put justice and war squarely on the side of the innocent native occupants. Diplomatic immunity, the right of trading (*ius negotiandi*), and the right of preaching (*ius praedicandi*) were all concomitants of Vitoria's right to travel, which drew authoritative support from principles and precepts of Roman law and the Bible. Among later international thinkers, this probable title, especially refracted through Acosta's "new" method of evangelization, gave seeming endorsement of European colonial expansion through its political deployment of the law of nations to generate a just cause for war in the Indies. Vitoria did not cast the law of nations in a parochial humanist fashion like Sepúlveda, who had justified widespread Spanish dominion over the Indies. Far from it. Nevertheless, Vitoria's articulation of the right to travel as a derived conclusion safeguarding precepts of natural law and divine law, all

28 Vitoria, *On the American Indians*, q. 3, a. 1, p. 278. Emphasis mine.

29 Bernice Hamilton, *Political Thought in Sixteenth-Century Spain* (Oxford University Press, 1963), p. 116; Tierney, "Vitoria and Suárez on Ius Gentium, Natural Law, and Custom," in *The Nature of Customary Law*, eds. Amanda Perreau-Saussine and James B. Murphy (Cambridge University Press, 2007), p. 114; Neff, *Justice among Nations*, pp. 152–153.

of which were binding on the whole world, made it susceptible to interpretive overreach by European colonial partisans steeped in neo-Stoic Christian legal humanism.

The Roman legal principle of natural kinship and the biblical injunctions to welcome the stranger and love the neighbor gave Vitoria's right of traveling a secure foundation among all nations establishing both its universal inviolability and universal enforceability under appropriate circumstances. Similar to civilian jurists, Vitoria considered the binding force of duties and rights in the law of nations even when there was no clear derivation from natural law. Vitoria was open to establishing the law of nations not on an explicit grounding of natural law but on positive enactment alone, or rather, "consent of the greater part of the world, especially when it is for the common good of all (*consensus maioris partis totius orbis, maxime pro bono communi omnium*)."[30] Notably, the kinds of enactment accomplished by custom and fact that Vitoria mentions here include the host of relevant enforceable norms central to the subjective rights discourse of Gentili and Grotius: the inviolability of ambassadors, the common property of the sea, and prohibition of driving out strangers from one's land. Even when not manifestly derived from the natural law per se, these norms, along with the norm of enslaving prisoners of war instead of killing them, still had the force of law from consent as something beneficial to all peoples.

Unlike early modern humanist jurists such as Gentili and Grotius, Vitoria's scholastic political commitment to the jurisdictional view of punishment excluded the Innocentian doctrine of punishing violations of natural law as a cause for war against Europeans and non-Europeans. But his articulation of the law of nations in a New World context of just war with characteristic emphasis on protecting the natural law and promoting the common good of all peoples had undeniable colonial consequences. It was an argument that could be manipulated to assert an international right of punishing enemies of the human race for the sake of preserving the good of international society. Even Vitoria had to concede that there was truth in Innocent IV's doctrine of punishing sins against natural law when he proposed a fifth possible title to defend innocent natives from the tyranny of human sacrificial violence even if they did not request it.[31] In some cases, like human sacrifice, the punishable violation of natural law and the defensive protection of natural right were nearly synonymous.

Read outside of the wider corpus of his writings and historical context, and solely in view of his appropriation by later international thinkers, Vitoria's

30 Vitoria, *On the American Indians*, q. 3, a. 1, p. 281.
31 Vitoria, *On the American Indians*, q. 3, a. 5, p. 288.

right of traveling can appear as a highly interventionist justification for war under the universal cover of the law of nations promoting solidarity among all peoples. Yet by placing Vitoria's discussion of the law of nations in context and alongside his Dominican confreres Soto and Las Casas, we can better detect the commonality and distinct nuances in the scholastic-juristic law of nations for world order. Although he certainly did not conceive his *relectio* in terms of a new discipline of international law, Vitoria's account of *ius gentium* was still important to subsequent international legal thought. If not least because, as Annabel Brett has identified, he introduced a new source of positivity – the consensus of the whole world.[32] Yet Vitoria also lacked clarity and precision in certain ways. And his confreres and students would continue to rectify the new normative discourse of world order he had powerfully outlined. Soto engaged in a richer philosophical discussion of the law of nations than Vitoria, making important distinctions to explain its proximity to natural law and the discrepancy among some of its practices. Las Casas, as a canon lawyer and Dominican formed in the scholastic theology of Aquinas, provided a surprisingly humanist-inflected account of the law of nations attentive to *ius commune* and ethnographic history. Their contributions, to which we now turn, remain, unfortunately, mostly minimal in the broader history of international legal thought.

Soto's moral theological commentary on Aquinas, *De iustitia et iure*, presented a philosophical account of the law of nations consistent with his wider discussion of dominium and natural right considered in Chapter 3. The most in depth treatment on the law of nations from Soto came from Books 1 (q. 5, a. 4) and 3 (q. 1, a. 3), each of which corresponded to Aquinas's *Summa* discussion of the topic in I-II (q. 95, a. 4) and II-II (q. 57, a. 3). The important feature of Soto's treatment of *ius gentium* was the teleological or rational purposive dimension of *ius*, like dominium, among individuals and peoples.[33] The "right" of peoples refers to a certain kind of commensuration of one thing to another although not in an intrinsically necessary manner like natural right, but as "ordained to a determined end and deliberated through specific circumstances."[34] Whereas natural *ius* for Soto obtained among all living beings, *ius gentium*, in line with the Roman and medieval jurists,

32 Brett, *Changes of State*, p. 13.

33 Brett, *Changes of State*, p. 23. However, I think Brett tends to overstate the individual reasoner knowing *ius gentium* apart from a communal process of discernment and deliberation characteristic of humans as social beings. Cf. *De iustitia et iure*, lib. 3, q. 1, a. 3: "*[N]am dispersim universae gentes ratione naturali id iuris per docentur.*"

34 Soto, *De iustitia et iure*, lib. 3, q. 1, a. 3: "*[S]ed in ordine ad certum finem et per certas circunstantias consideratum.*"

belonged characteristically to human beings as rational creatures. The derived conclusion from natural law, then, follows like a reasoned consideration about how to achieve a certain end set by natural principles such as the desire for peace, tranquility, and sociability.[35] This process of ratiocination concerning natural principles can pertain to individuals but also collectively among peoples.

What Soto provided in contrast to Vitoria was a way of explaining derivation without reducing the law of nations to its political role of protecting natural law. Soto's key contribution turned on the illative or inferential process of reasoning expressive of humans as social creatures. Rather than formulating the law of nations as a strictly logical deduction terminating in precepts, Soto allowed for greater flexibility and variability over time and different places as reasoned conclusions about certain ends stemming from natural principles. Whereas natural right flows as a necessary consequence from the absolute nature of a thing (*absoluta rerum natura*) itself, to which the natural right of liberty inheres, the right of peoples identifies what is fitting to the nature of a thing as ordered to some end.[36] Soto used several examples to illustrate the inferential reasoning process that does not follow an absolute logical deduction for the right of a people: division of goods or property, slavery, and commercial contracts and exchanges.

Each of the aforementioned practices under the law of nations was a reasoned conclusion concerning various natural principles that overlapped with a Thomistic index of natural inclinations. In the case of humanity in a fallen state, people reasoned that it would be more convenient to divide possessions in order to attain social peace and to cultivate the fields of the earth. Soto adopted the standard Aristotelian-Thomistic rationale for property, or division of goods, which identified its purposes of curing laziness and eliminating social conflict.[37] The law of slavery, distinctly, resulted from a judgment that it was a fitting way in rather brutal circumstances "to liberate an enemy in war from death" so as to not frustrate the preservation of life. Furthermore, due to human sociability, people devised the buying and selling of things through contracts for helping one another in the attainment of useful things.[38]

These standard examples did not offer an exhaustive list of laws and customs and their explanations under *ius gentium*. Instead, Soto gave an account of

35 Soto, *De iustitia et iure*, lib. 1, q. 5, a. 4: "*Dicitur enim ius gentium quicquid mortales ex principiis naturalibus per modum conclusionis ratiocinati sunt.*"

36 Soto, *De iustitia et iure*, lib. 3, q. 1, a. 3.

37 Aquinas, *ST*, II-II, q. 66, a. 2.

38 Soto, *De iustitia et iure*, lib. 1, q. 5, a. 4.

how inferential reasoning among individuals and peoples generally operated. Importantly, the illative conclusions of *ius gentium* from natural principles were not strict conclusions like secondary precepts of the natural law in which reason moved from a basic principle of "no harm" to the specific precept of "do not kill." Instead, "the division of owned things," Soto argued, "does not strictly follow from the necessity of cultivating fields or to possess them in peace . . . but because it is most fitting and expedient for achieving that end."[39] Because of inferential reasoning among distinct groups, Soto could conceive of communal forms that did not find divided property purposive or convenient in the attainment of social order and peace. His own mendicant religious order was a case in point. Vitoria even entertained the possibility that the whole world could hold possessions in common but only do so free of discord and war with great difficulty.[40] Vitoria too wanted to show that *ius gentium* was not a strict and necessary deduction of the natural law, and therefore equivalent to natural law.

With great stress on the important relationship between the law of nations and natural law, Soto had to address a certain quandary. If the Thomistic position was that the first principles of natural law (I-II, 94.5) and its secondary precepts associated with the Decalogue were indispensable (I-II, 100.8), did the same follow for the law of nations? Here Soto made an important distinction among respective practices, which demonstrated flexibility and change in his account of the law of nations. Certain practices like division of things and political authority seemed to be more in accord with natural law as derivations because of their great convenience. For Soto, divided property was a clear example of a non-derogable practice, except under special circumstances like religious orders.[41] However, since slavery was against natural freedom according to standard Christian teaching and ancient Stoicism, it was something dispensable. Christians in conflict testified to this fact when they refused to enslave one another after wars.

39 Soto, *De iustitia et iure*, lib. 3, q. 1, a. 3: "*Haud enim necessitate colendi agros vel pacifice eorum possessionis consequitur tam necessario dominiorum divisio . . . sed quia est illi fini congruentissimum atque expedientissimum.*"

40 Vitoria, *Comentarios*, 57.3, no. 4: "*Posset quidem orbis subsistere si possessiones essent in communi, ut est in religionibus; tamen esset cum magna difficultate ne homines in discordias et bella prorrumperent.*"

41 Soto, *De iustitia et iure*, lib. 3, q. 1, a. 3. Vázquez de Menchaca seems to draw the conclusion that Soto's distinction between immutable and mutable aspects of the *ius gentium* was a scholastic appropriation of the civilian distinction between primary and secondary law of nations, a point inadvertently confirmed by Las Casas's similar scholastic yet civilian approach to the law of nations. See *Controversiarum illustrium*, tom. 4, lib. 2, cap. 89, pp. 424–425.

Due to the singular aim of Las Casas's theological and juridical writings in defense of Amerindian immunity from Spanish colonial dispossession for nearly five decades, the law of nations, like the natural law, took on a decisive political character. Immersed in the *ius commune* tradition to a greater extent than his theological confreres at the Salamanca, Las Casas would still fully inhabit the scholastic *doctrina* of Aquinas. At the end of his career and back in Spain, Las Casas communicated in a transatlantic letter to young friars back in his old bishopric of Chiapa that he affirmed no propositions concerning the Indies without proofs from principles based in Aquinas's teachings, citing Soto's *De iustitia et iure* as a source.[42] This may sound like mere lip service to the premiere theological authority for a religious order overseeing the inquisitorial procedure, but the clear evolution and maturation of Las Casas's thinking in conversation with Thomistic thought vindicates the general thrust of his claim.

As we observed in Chapter 4, the law of nations was a powerful resource aiding Las Casas's apologia for the Indians at Valladolid against Sepúlveda's imperial humanism. The law of nations afforded the Dominican bishop a powerful means of averring a native right of war against Spanish aggressors in order to defend their religion, even when it was idolatrous. More controversially, the law of nations had the authoritative force of the natural law in these matters. In 1552, the year after the Valladolid junta concluded, Las Casas published eight Spanish treatises in Seville, two of which contained his famous (or infamous) *Brevísima relación de la destrucción de las Indias* (*Very Brief Account*) and the allegedly treasonous *Aquí se contienen unos avisos y reglas para los confesores* (*Confesionario*). Both works appealed to natural law and the law of nations to condemn the injustice of Spanish wars in the Indies. Two other lesser-known writings in this corpus of writings, the *Tratado Comprobatorio* and *Principia quaedam*, each provided an account of the law of nations that identify Las Casas's place within the scholastic theological ambit of world order and his unique contribution of native political agency for international thought. What emerged from his advocacy and work was a unique and surprising scholastic theological brand of legal humanism with historical ethnographic narration as the normative font of jurisprudential reasoning.[43] Yet his scholastic-humanist bent ran diametrically counter to

[42] Las Casas, "Carta a los dominicos de Chiapa y Guatemala (1564)," in OC, vol. 13, p. 355.

[43] For an excellent presentation on the scholastic-humanist dimensions of Las Casas's thought, which contrasts his "*humanismo indígena*" from broader European humanism, see Mauricio Beuchot, *Filosofía y política en Bartolomé de las Casas* (San Esteban Editorial, 2013).

Sepúlveda's imperial humanism and was distinct from the Protestant natural lawyers considered in the previous chapter.

Las Casas embraced the universality of the law of nations similar to the Dominican theologians at Salamanca. The natural law and the law of nations were inclusive of Christians and infidels. Although reliant on the *ius commune* for thinking about the law of nations, Las Casas also appropriated Aquinas to bring greater philosophical nuance to bear on the concept, as seen in his *Tratado Comprobatorio*. This work presented a juridical commentary on the Alexandrine bull of 1493 to delimit papal and Spanish royal jurisdiction and affirm the lawful political rule of native peoples. After citing the canonistic *foris* principle restricting Christian political authority from punishing native practices, Las Casas treated the law "common to all peoples" undergirding the independence of each polity.[44]

Aquinas's discussion of *ius gentium* in the *Summa* provided Las Casas with a speculative account for "the authority of the law of nations *derived from* law or natural right" (*por auctoridad del derecho de las gentes derivado de la ley o derecho natural*). Las Casas followed his confreres in identifying the close proximity of the law of nations to natural law doing so with the creative sensibility of a jurist. The derived conclusion considered here was the choice of a ruler by the people – the voluntary basis of independent political jurisdictions under the law of nations. This theme of political consent would occupy the brunt of his legal writings until his death in 1566:

> Because peoples, by the light of natural reason, knew that doing this (electing a ruler) was something convenient and necessary, and because of it they agreed and consented to choose and submit themselves to such distinguished persons for their own common welfare. And that was how all peoples began to use it because they so easily adopted it. For this reason, it is said that such a usage and custom is the right of peoples [*derecho de las gentes*]. The right of peoples is nothing other than a certain use reasonable and advantageous for the good and benefit of peoples, which can be easily grasped by the light of nature, and whereby everyone consents to it as something that is convenient ... without which they would not be able to live among themselves. And therefore it is said that the right of peoples is natural to man because it is derived from reason and the natural law [*la razón y ley natural*], and has the force and vigor of natural right [*derecho natural*], because it is from those common conclusions that are derived simply from natural right,

44 Las Casas, *Tratado Comprobatorio*, in *Tratados*, II, p. 1073: "*[L]as cosas que son de derecho de las gentes son comunes a todos las naciones.*"

like its principles. This is what St. Thomas teaches in the *Summa*, I-II 95.4, c, ad 1 and II-II 57.3.[45]

At least two features here of Las Casas's interpretation of Aquinas to address the case of native peoples in the Indies were striking. First, the derivation of the law of nations from the natural law turned on the subjective force of natural right (*derecho natural*), which accentuated his vernacular usage of "*derecho de las gentes*." This right of peoples stemmed from shared reasoning on natural principles – as outlined by Aquinas's human inclinations in I-II, 94.2 – deemed necessary and conducive to human welfare.[46] The second feature, which expressed Las Casas's juridical contribution, was the key role he gave to the positive character of the right of peoples. He creatively bridged the rationality and positivity of the law of nations in a manner clearer than Vitoria by integrating consent, usage, and custom within a natural law framework.

Francisco Suárez, portrayed by historical commentators as the most important Spanish contributor to international legal thought, echoed the integrative view of Las Casas.[47] The seventeenth-century work *On Law and God the Lawgiver* (1613) formulated an authoritative interpretation of *ius gentium* as "the law which all the various peoples and nations ought to observe in their relations with each other (*inter se*)."[48] This normative recognition of an obligatory law *between* peoples rather than merely *among* peoples signaled a notable innovation for international thought. Furthermore, Suárez, with his remarkable clarity, also brought the scholastic aspects of the law of nations, rationality and positivity, closer together. Suárez followed Soto's interpretation of the law of nations as an inferred conclusion in harmony with nature but not in a strictly necessary, or self-evident, way. Nevertheless, since the law of nations derives from the free will of men (*ex arbitrio hominum*) and is constituted by them (*ab hominibus constituto*), it rightly belongs to human positive law instead of natural law.[49] It therefore takes universal expression through custom (*consuetudo*), a kind of law "introduced by the habitual conduct of nations."[50]

Suárez identified freedom and consent as constitutive of the positive law of nations, which denoted the voluntary acceptance of a custom among peoples

45 Las Casas, *Tratado Comprobatorio*, p. 1071.

46 Las Casas, *Tratado Comprobatorio*, p. 1081.

47 Consider Neff's esteem for Suárez in *Justice among Nations*, p. 158, whom he considered clearer and more detailed than both Vitoria and Grotius.

48 Suárez, *De legibus*, lib. 2, cap. 19, no. 8.

49 Suárez, *De legibus*, lib. 2, cap. 19, no. 3.

50 Suárez, *De legibus*, lib. 2, cap. 19, no. 9.

by long usage.[51] The same constellation of ideas attentive to natural reason and positivity operated in Las Casas's account of the law of nations. Emphasis on the positivity of the law of nations was particularly strong in the most scholastic of Las Casas's legal writings, *Principia quaedam* ("Certain Principles"). This concluding work to the 1552 Sevillian treatises, as José Cardenas has keenly observed, provided legal axioms to all the preceding seven treatises on the Indies comparable to the Roman *regulae* of Justinian's *Digest* and the *De regulis iuris* of medieval canon law.[52] The four principles stipulated by Las Casas in this Latin work, like its speculative function in canon law, provided universal maxims for addressing the juridical independence of infidels in the New World from Spanish possession. By appealing to natural law and the law of nations, Las Casas could demonstrate that there was no legal distinction between believers and infidels in matters pertaining to property, political jurisdiction, and political liberty. The Dominican friar's brief yet systematic treatise represented a momentous synthesis of scholastic and juridical sources.

In the spirit of Vitoria's 1535 *Summa* commentary on restitution and Soto's *Relectio de dominio*, Las Casas began with the biblical doctrine of the image of God to explain the first legal principle concerning the division of things (*dominium rerum*), which referred to inhabiting a specific land and using its goods for sustenance. Certainly, every individual has a natural right to use things of creation by possessing what is necessary for the purpose of preservation. But a human being does not exist alone and isolated but always in community with others. The definitive historical moment in which the right of peoples came into effect was when human beings living together in society attained some kind of settlement. "Whence it follows," writes Las Casas, "that the common agreement or pact of the whole community or multitude, which is in accordance with the law of nations derived from natural reason, has introduced and approved that lands and material goods should be divided and apportioned."[53] Las Casas then asserted the standard scholastic rationale concerning the utility of the law of dividing goods for the sake of taking care of one's things, preserving social peace, and securing other common benefits.

Divided properties according to Las Casas and the Spanish theologians sharply contrasted with the idea of private property in Locke and other English

51 Hamilton, *Political Thought in Sixteenth-Century Spain*, p. 107.

52 José Cárdenas Bunsen, "Consent, Voluntary Jurisdiction and Native Political Agency" in Bartolomé de Las Casas' Final Writings, *Bulletin of Spanish Studies* 91, no. 6 (2014): 800. For more attention on the evolution of these Roman legal maxims in medieval Christian thought, see Harold Berman, *Law and Revolution: The Formation of the Western Legal Tradition* (Harvard University Press, 1983), pp. 132–143.

53 Las Casas, *Principia quaedam*, in *Tratados*, II, p. 1238.

colonial thinkers.[54] Division of things, although derived from natural reason, belonged properly under the universal domain of *ius gentium*, or positive human law, not a Eurocentric understanding of private property. Since humans live as social beings, individual appropriation was consequent of the common custom or political consent operative in the positive law of nations. Therefore, the idea of individual private property in a state of nature, especially over land, was mere legal and political fiction from a scholastic theological standpoint. Occupation of land for the Spanish theologians denoted political jurisdiction of some form according to the law of nations and not exclusive ownership according to natural law. No agricultural argument containing a European civilizational bias against other, especially collective, forms of property or forms of government could be asserted under the scholastic-juristic universal law of nations.

When Locke and other English colonists gazed at native inhabitants to determine if they had property in the earth itself and money, they concluded that its absence meant natives did not have organized political authority. In contrast, the Spanish Dominican theologians, using a variation of Aristotle's political taxonomy, observed the rational characteristics of Amerindian city life with rulers, marriages, laws, commerce, and religion. The division of goods and possessions entailed that some form of social and political organization was present according to the law of nations. The Spanish theologians were not after a superficial categorization of barbarians but instead a normative account of the juridical independence of native polities in the New World. Their scholastic-juristic notions of consent and the power of the people residing in the commonwealth would infuse their account of native life with robust political agency. Las Casas employed these ideas in a definitively humanist historical mode thus indicating a variant path of legal humanism for international thought informed especially by scholastic theology and canon law rather than Roman imperialism or Christian neo-Stoicism.

Like Soto, Las Casas also factored in divergent practices and customs for the law of nations. Yet the bishop put a civilian jurist gloss on this point by introducing the temporal distinction between a primordial law of nations and the secondary law of nations formulated by Bartolus of Sassoferrato.[55] The secondary law of nations could account for the existence of common customs that resulted directly from sin over time such as slavery, war, and other forms of bondage. The primordial law of nations, however, referred to things

[54] Mario Ruiz Sotelo, *Crítica de la razón imperial: la filosofía de Bartolomé de Las Casas* (Siglo XXI Editores, 2010), pp. 158–159.

[55] Las Casas, *Principia quaedam*, pp. 1252–1254.

that followed closely from the natural liberty endowed with humanity at creation yet still indicative of life after the Fall. Its original point of departure was "from the free consent of the people" (*ex consensu libero populi*) underlying separate political jurisdictions and the division of goods.[56] Even if the primordial law of nations was anterior temporally to the secondary of law nations, this did not imply for Las Casas that the former lost its normative weight. On the contrary, the legal recognition of Amerindian political independence and their original occupation of land and things in the New World rested on this fundamental *derecho* of native peoples, deriving its normative force from natural right.

Principia quaedam provided an incredibly concise theoretical formulation of natural law and the law of nations applicable to the Indies and international society more broadly. Consider Las Casas's summary of his third principle – a cornerstone for his thinking about world order: "All nations and peoples (*nationes et populi*), however much they be infidels, possess their separate lands and kingdoms, which they have inhabited originally. They are free peoples and do not recognize a political superior outside themselves, except their own."[57] The crucial role of the law of nations as a domain securing the independence of peoples, each with the requisite power of consent to form their own government, was a legacy of medieval jurist, Baldus of Ubaldis.[58]

Baldus was an authoritative legal commentator for Las Casas, yet one whose imperial tendencies, though not to the extent of his better-known teacher Bartolus, would need tempering in Las Casas by scholastic theological commitments. For example, Vitoria's repudiation of the medieval civilian doctrine of worldwide imperial sovereignty, the first unjust title of *De Indis*, directly targeted Bartolus's teaching that, "the emperor is *de jure* master of the whole world."[59] A key theological premise for Vitoria's counterargument was none other than the Thomistic axiom, which established that since political authority stems from human law, no valid enactment exists or has ever existed for a world government. Soto's *Relectio de dominio* also targeted Bartolus and his teaching on the emperor as lord of the world (*Imperatorem esse dominum totius*

56 Las Casas, *Principia quaedam*, p. 1252.

57 Las Casas, *Principia quaedam*, p. 1255.

58 On this important aspect of the people and *ius gentium* in Baldus's (and Bartolus's) international thought, see Canning, *The Political Thought of Baldus of Ubaldis*, pp. 104–106, and "The Medieval Roman and Canon Law Origins of International Law," in *Medieval Foundations of International Relations*, pp. 105–106; Monahan, *From Personal Duties towards Personal Rights*, pp. 21–32.

59 Vitoria, *On the American Indians*, q. 2, a. 1, p. 252.

orbis), among others, before he went on to cite the Thomistic political axiom to deny imperial jurisdiction over the lands of infidels.[60]

POLITICAL AGENCY AND CONSENT IN THE INDIES

The affair of the Indies brought out the deeper political implications of the scholastic-juristic view of the universal law of nations including Christians and infidels. Aquinas's axiom from 10.10 of the *Secunda Secundae* served as a normative theological claim about the lawfulness of native political sovereignty in the scholastic conception of world order. The human law that introduced political jurisdiction among infidel peoples, which derived from natural reason according to Aquinas, was none other than the law of nations for Dominican commentators addressing the New World. In the Valladolid *Apologia*, Las Casas read Aquinas's axiom under a jurist's gloss to mean all kingdoms (*regna*) are "under the law of nations, which is derived from natural law."[61] Dominican identification of the law of nations as a positive law deriving from natural reason and natural law, based in the theological doctrine of creation, provided support to what jurists had established according to the classical Roman law of first occupant or canonists had commonly identified as infidel rights. Without a normative theological basis, however, the deployment of Roman law and canon law in colonial contexts was notoriously prone to ambivalent interpretations about indigenous dominium, and argumentatively weak against a politics of dispossession.

Grounding political jurisdiction over land and propertied division of things in the universal law of nations instead of mere natural law illustrated how crucial both its positivity and rationality were for recognizing the rights of infidels in the New World. On the one hand, the universal law of nations stemming from natural reason could counter invasive European claims about the law of nations that excluded those deemed irrational or savage. The acknowledgment of a people's *ius* (or *derecho*), a power firmly established in natural reason and natural right, was a creative juridical resource for navigating and articulating native self-determination. On the other hand, placing the law of nations squarely in the domain of positive law, even while admitting a greater and lesser proximity to natural law, precluded civilizational arguments for dispossession reliant on claims that natives lacked civil codes and written laws. Usage, custom, and tradition were therefore instrumental in the Spanish Dominican recognition of genuine positive human law among

60 Soto, *De dominio*, nos. 27 and 32.

61 Las Casas, *In Defense of the Indians*, chap. 55, p. 334.

non-European peoples and the diverse expressions of specific practices in the law of nations.

At the normative core of the scholastic-juristic account of the law of nations was the idea of consent, deriving its force not just from universal natural reason, but also from natural *ius*. Which is to say, the natural liberty of all according to Isidore, Gratian, and the common opinion of the *ius commune*. Chapter 3 considered how Cajetan's political thinking shaped Spanish Dominican reflection on the people's natural right of consent – the efficient cause and power of political authority and sovereign rule. In addition to European expansion, the Spanish Dominicans were living during their own Castilian region's struggle of *comunidades* seeking greater independence from the Crown.[62] Originating from the Italian city-republics, the Roman legal glossators Bartolus and Baldus were another indispensable resource for Spanish ideas about popular consent, especially for Las Casas. The Dominicans would produce an account of the nature of political rule stemming from a distinct people recognized under the law of nations markedly different from the Westphalian imaginary of individuals in the state of nature. Their creative appropriation of the *ius commune* tradition, scholastic philosophy, and ecclesiology prompted a capacious view about the rational political agency of non-European native peoples as independent communities. To appreciate further their normative contribution to international thought through the law of nations, we must consider the constitutive basis for separate political jurisdictions and property in the consent of the people (*populi*).

The medieval jurists Bartolus and Baldus had granted the de facto political standing of independent commonwealths founded on popular consent yet still under the jurisdiction of a universal sovereign in principle.[63] Moving beyond this medieval jurist paradigm, the Spanish scholastic theologians promoted a universal law of nations free from imperial and papal jurisdiction to establish the de iure independence of all peoples in the world. Soto's 1535 *Relectio de dominio* was already attentive to the force of natural right (*ius naturale*) as the normative basis of every commonwealth's independent civil power.[64] Soto notably associated the notion of natural right with freedom and liberty. Therefore, dominium, whether taken in its natural expression of individual ownership of actions or in the conventional context of the law of nations as the division of property or political jurisdiction, was founded on liberty. Soto's clearest expressions concerning the constitutive power (*potestas*) of the people,

62 Monahan, *From Personal Duties towards Personal Rights*, p. 142.
63 Canning, "The Medieval Roman and Canon Law Origins of International Law," p. 104.
64 Soto, *De dominio*, no. 29.

or the commonwealth, often occurred in his rejection of arguments for worldwide imperial rule. Since the historical transference of political authority from the people to the ruler is consequent a people gathering and consenting to an election, at least in majority, the Roman imperial claim to universal rule implying the formal consent of the whole world was simply outrageous.[65] Neither Caesar's name nor fame had ever reached the peoples of the New World until European contact in 1492.

Consent at the level of the law of nations was especially relevant to the question of permissible seizure of metals in the New World. The abundant gold and precious stones taken from the sacred Peruvian shrines and holy sites, or *huacas*, the holy sepulchers and burial tombs, and the discovery of the silver mines of Potosí all in the Inca region during the 1530s and 1540s were well-known to the Dominicans. Vitoria's 1534 letter to Arcos, following the forced occupation and subjugation of the Inca, expressed loathing at the widespread robbery and plundering of the native peoples by *peruleros*. It was for him, to reiterate, a case of no uncertain restitution.

Soto expressed his normative position on native restitution in *De iustitia et iure*, where he followed his earlier position of *De dominio* locating the right of occupying or taking unclaimed things in the law of nations and not strictly natural law.[66] When he specifically treated *res nullius* with respect to Spaniards "who hasten to the Western continent in search of gold," he did so, tellingly, under the scholastic question of theft. It was not lawful for Spaniards to conduct these extractive mining expeditions, he claimed, "unless the (native) inhabitants were to consent or have left the treasures abandoned. That is because the regions have been divided by the right of peoples. And therefore although those things are in common for the peoples of those regions still foreigners may not seize those things against the will of the inhabitants."[67] Accordingly, back on the European continent, no country could venture into another's without proper consent.

Soto's deployment of *ius gentium* to establish the independence and autonomy of peoples rested on the right of consent over the distinct region's resources and riches. He made no appeal to providential commerce to justify

65 Soto, *De iustitia et iure*, lib. 4, q. 4, a. 2: "*[I]n quem transferat potestatem, requiritur publicus eius conventus ut faltem maior pars in talem consentiat electionem.*"

66 Soto, *De iustitia et iure*, lib. 4, q. 3, a. 1: "*Quod enim, inquit, ante nullius fuit, id naturali ratione occupanti conceditur. Et in hoc quid dicit, naturali ratione, intelligit ius gentium, id ex principiis naturalibus colligentium.*"

67 Soto, *De iustitia et iure*, lib. 5, q. 3, a. 3: "*[Q]ui ad Occidentalem continentem auri gratia advolant . . . nisi incolae ipsi consentirent: aut pro dereclictis eosdem thesauros haberent: nam regiones iure gentium divisae sunt: et ideo licet gentibus illius regiones sint res illae communis, tamen non possunt advenae incolis invitis easdem res usurpare.*"

the imposition of European interests against peoples ignorant of or sitting on their region's natural wealth. Annabel Brett has read this important example from Soto in discerning terms, noting that he viewed the world as comprised of "geographically separate political entities" with a stronger restriction on interpenetration than Vitoria.[68] As we will consider later in the chapter, Las Casas's *De thesauris* applied this teaching on the law of nations and world order to engage the Spanish occupation of Peru critically. Unlike the geopolitical hierarchy of the ancients or humanists based on climate or civilization, the Spanish scholastic theological account of the law of nations recognized the geopolitical significance of distinct regions (*regiones*) or lands (*terras*) inhabited and occupied by Noah's descendants after the biblical Flood.

In comparison to the English thinkers considered in the previous chapter, it is remarkable that Soto still made voluntary consent of the native inhabitants a requirement even if they held those material resources in common. In this instance, the first inhabitants would not only have the force of *ius gentium*, but also *ius naturale*. Even though the goods were not divided strictly among themselves, they were divided off from other peoples. Soto's normative argument outlined respect for native consent and self-determination without subjecting their common possession of the land to a European civilizational gaze from on high. His discussion of the law of nations allowed for the rectitude of *ius* to obtain independently of its proper exercise. Even if the form of property and the division of goods under the law of nations resulted in some evil like greed, or perhaps nonindustriousness among the people, the law of nations would not cease to lose its force or become defunct. As he clarified, "the equity of the law does not require that its end be achieved perfectly, because it is enough that the faculty (*facultate*) for it be established, which is suited to that end."[69] The conclusion followed that there could be no ideal or perfect form of property or government determining the presence or absence of the law of nations among diverse peoples. Remarkably, Christian Wolff's eighteenth-century Enlightenment view on the law of nations defended a similar position when he claimed that even several families inhabiting a territory do not lose common possession when there was no usage of the land.[70]

[68] Brett, *Changes of State*, p. 25. Similarly, see Cavallar, *Rights of Strangers*, p. 111.

[69] Soto, *De iustitia et iure*, lib. 4, q. 3, a. 1: "*Respondetur non esse necessarium ad aequitatem legis ut perfecte fine assequatur suum: satis quippe est illa pro sua facultate stabilire quae ad illum finem accommodantur.*"

[70] Wolff, *The Law of Nations*, chap. 3, §312. For more on Wolff's culturally sensitive account of moral cosmopolitanism, see Cavallar, *Imperfect Cosmopolis*, pp. 30–33.

The political importance of a people's right of consent in the Indies emerged at Valladolid specifically for Las Casas when he tackled the arguments of John Mair, who had justified taking political possession of indigenous peoples and their lands across the Atlantic because of barbarism. As noted in Chapter 3, Mair was the first to use Aristotle's natural slavery doctrine in asserting that brutish peoples without kingship, like the islanders of the Indies, could be fully subjugated in order to plant the faith there. Las Casas's rebuttal on this point brought into sharp relief a distinctive aspect of the Spanish scholastic theological view on politics informed by Aquinas and the jurists. Mair's argument forced Las Casas to consider the prepolitical foundations of civil authority in the people and to imagine its normative status apart from a distinct form of rule or government:

> For whatever right a king has, he has by the consent of his people (*populi habuit consensus*). If a king should die without heirs, the right of choosing (*ius eligendi*) a new king belongs to the people. Why, then, did John Mair want a commonwealth (*rempublicam*), and more than a king, to be deprived of choice when the jurisdiction and power of a commonwealth are more natural than the rule of a king, which derives its origin from the consent of the commonwealth? For it is obvious that a greater injustice is committed by depriving a community or people of its right of consent without any lawful cause than by depriving a ruler of his power, since the former is more opposed to justice ... [I]f the Pope deposes a king for some just cause, he cannot substitute another in his place, for the right of choosing a king, which belongs to the people by natural law, cannot be taken away from them.[71]

The establishment of governmental authority through the original voluntary consent of a people choosing a ruler was an expression of positive law par excellence. In his own way, Las Casas was getting at a crucial scholastic-juristic distinction between the authority of a chosen ruler and the natural power residing in the people similar to Vitoria's contrast between authority (*auctoritas*) and power (*potestas*). For Vitoria, the commonwealth as a multitude of people creates the king (*creat respublica regem*), and though it transmits authority to the ruler, it does not transfer the original elective power. However, the power remains defunct except under extreme situations.[72] Vitoria's initial explanation of public power's basis in natural right and God may have led to some confusion, making him appear as a divine right theorist. Yet by the time he presented his *Summa* lectures on law in the 1530s, it was clear that this scholastic political distinction was

71 Las Casas, *In Defense of the Indians*, chap. 56, p. 338.

72 Vitoria, *On Civil Power*, q. 1, a. 5, pp. 16–17.

required for justifying tyrannicide, a common opinion held among the theologians.

According to the distinction between the political authority of the ruler and the elective power of the people, Vitoria defended Aquinas's teaching on the lawful execution of a tyrant, or despot.[73] As Vitoria expressed in the *Summa* commentary, "if a king proves to be a tyrant in government the commonwealth can depose him, because even if the commonwealth has given away its authority it keeps its natural right to defend itself (*ius naturale defendendi se*); if there is no other way, it may reject its king." Vitoria, expanding upon Aquinas, referred to the subjective power of the commonwealth to exercise its natural right of self-defense prudentially in specific cases of tyranny. He followed this claim with a challenging proposition sure to dispel the view that he was a divine right theorist: the king does not possess all the powers inhering in the commonwealth. His specific example was that of *dominium rerum* or the commonwealth's possessions. A ruler "cannot make use of public things at his pleasure" but must always consider what is beneficial to the whole commonwealth. Vitoria then stressed the original elective power of the commonwealth further by considering a scenario in which a free (*libera*) commonwealth without a king or government can rightly give away a portion of its land if it so chooses. Contrastingly, an appointed king, who lacks the requisite power, could never give away what belonged to the commonwealth.[74] In other words, no political leader has the authority of transferring over land to foreigners that belonged to the people.

Vitoria acknowledged the freedom of a people or commonwealth as something categorically distinct from established political authority, which meant that a specific people could possess jurisdiction over land irrespective of whether or not a formal government was in place. Since this mode of power obtained as a right of peoples according to the law of nations, the Roman law of first occupant was suitable for designating such division over lands by its inhabitants. When Vitoria turned to the affair of the Indies, he relied on this scholastic categorical distinction for rejecting the sixth title for Spanish political possession in the New World purportedly based on the voluntary choice of the natives. This alleged though false title was contained in the so-called "choice" of the Requirement or assumed in Cortés's claim about Montezuma's willing transference of Aztec political rule to Spain. In actuality, Vitoria observed, both the Spanish threat of war against natives causing fear

73 Aquinas, *On Kingship*, in *On Law, Morality, and Politics*, Second Edition, eds. William Baumgarth and Richard Regan (Hackett Publishing, 2002), Book 1, chap. 6.

74 Vitoria, *On Law*, *ST*, I-II 105.2, pp. 200–202.

and the lack of a shared language eliminated any possibility of genuine freedom of consent present in the Indies. Vitoria further argued, using the scholastic-juristic distinction between rulers and peoples, that because the natives "already had their own true rulers and princes . . . a people (*populus*) cannot without reasonable cause seek new masters, which would be to the detriment of their previous lords. Nor, on the contrary, can the lords themselves create a new prince without the assent of the people (*sine assensu populi*)."[75] With respect to the Indies context, even if Montezuma had conceded his power to the Spanish Crown, the assent of the Aztec people was still required. Although Vitoria would never explicitly refer to Cortés or Pizarro as tyrants, the implications for doing so were immediately clear to Las Casas, as we will see momentarily.

A free people's right of consent was the defining issue for the Spanish Dominicans in their effort to recognize and promote native political independence. Scholastic juristic reflection emerging from the New World colonial context generated an innovative doctrine of popular consent distinct from modern contractarian thinkers. By acknowledging this normative claim bearing on matters of religion, government, and property, the theologians could deny, on moral and legal grounds, European assertions of colonial dispossession leveled by theocrats and imperial humanists alike. Vitoria, following Cajetan, provided the crucial philosophical distinctions for elaborating the original elective power of the people as belonging to the law of nations, which was derived from natural reason and natural law. However, as Las Casas consistently pointed out, ideas and principles alone were not enough. The fact (*el hecho*), or the realities of the case, were necessary to truly assess the cause of justice and right (*el derecho*). Moral theology and law required historical accounting and description of the actual situation. The Dominican bishop often invoked the expression of combining "*el hecho con el derecho*" to advance Amerindian freedom in the manner of the first Dominicans of Española.[76] According to Las Casas, Mair failed on both counts of assessing the facts and of right. And Vitoria, although quite perceptive about the affair as an erudite Dominican commentator on justice, had not fully reckoned with all the facts of the case.

With reports of Columbus and other Spanish travelers about the meekness and overwhelming kindness of native peoples in circulation around Europe, Mair still concluded that preachers there accompany armed soldiers. Denying the need for any consent from original inhabitants considered bestial, Mair

[75] Vitoria, *On the American Indians*, q. 2. a. 6, pp. 275–276.
[76] Las Casas, *Historia de las Indias*, III, cap. 3, p. 439.

assumed natives had to pay for the expenses incurred by Europeans sending preachers and soldiers or risk dispossession. He further claimed that Europeans could establish forts and residence in the foreign lands without the consent of a ruler or the people. All of this indicated for Las Casas that Mair, despite his nominalist and positivist predilection for history, disregarded "the real situation."[77] He knew neither law nor the facts (*ius et factum*). On this score, Las Casas even considered the limitations of his Dominican confrere from Salamanca, the "very learned" Vitoria, who entertained possible (or conditional) titles based on false premises and circumstances, some of which were a bit careless. Las Casas recognized at Valladolid that Sepúlveda and other imperial partisans later appropriated Vitoria's possible titles for their support of conquest.[78] Already in 1550, Las Casas offered a prescient warning about the easy appropriation of Vitoria's *De Indis*, if only in part, by aggressive colonial sympathizers.

Due to abiding concern with the reality (*el hecho*) of the Indies, Las Casas made an important humanist historical turn for Spanish international thought as a canonist and Dominican theologian. As early as the 1520s, after becoming a Dominican friar, Las Casas began his monumental three-volume *History of the Indies*. The singular purpose of this work was to assess the European historical record of injustices against native peoples in the Atlantic world, beginning with the Portuguese enslavement of Africans. The moral conviction running through the work was that the original inhabitants of these places had their own kingdoms and native rulers and lords, all of which demonstrated "the liberty of the peoples" (*libertad de los pueblos*).[79] With a lawyer's zeal and sensibility, Las Casas captured the crucial interplay between truth and justice for advocacy of free native peoples through the medium of historical narrative: "I have thought long and hard and often about the defects, the errors laid out above and the manifest, the harmful things that happened and still happen as a result. And (I have) thought how 'right is born and originates from the truthful accounting of reality' [*de la relación veridíca del hecho nace y tienen origen . . . el derecho*], as the jurists say. So I decided to write about the major events of the Indies, some of which I saw done, saw happen right before my eyes during my sixty and some years of life – for I was there present, in various areas, realms, provinces, lands."[80] Las Casas the Dominican missionary had

77 Las Casas, *In Defense of the Indians*, chap. 53, p. 327. Mair was "ignorant of the things themselves" (*ignorans res se*).

78 Las Casas, *In Defense of the Indians*, chap. 56, pp. 340–341.

79 Las Casas, *Historia de las Indias*, III, chap. 55, p. 19.

80 Las Casas, *Historia de las Indias*, Prologue, p. 19.

experienced the Indian world in a way the Salmantine theologians simply had not.

If the *History of the Indies* had been Las Casas's only account of the affair, then his advocacy would have remained a strictly negative task, a Black Legend, focused on narrating the extent of Spanish injuries toward the native inhabitants. However, Las Casas's *Apologética historia sumaria* (*Defensive History in Summary*), an ethnographic history of Amerindian customs and cultures considered already in Chapter 4, engaged in the positive task of defending the rational political agency of native peoples. Las Casas's *Apologética historia* was a work of utmost importance by using comparative ethnography to locate native customs and institutions within the law of nations and positive law.[81] Despite the work's inattention to legal sources explicitly, in contrast to his other works, it nevertheless must be considered within the broader corpus of Las Casas's juridical writings. By turning to ethnographic history, Las Casas could directly combat the popular descriptions of the natives as irrational creatures incapable of self-rule. These descriptions presented by Fernández de Oviedo and Fernández de Enciso made the arguments for war and coercion by Sepúlveda and Acosta more plausible. Las Casas argued to the contrary: natural reason and natural law, even outside of revelation, informed indigenous forms of labor, and their political forms and religious practices. The Dominican friar relied on personal experience and eyewitness reports, but also ancient historians and poets and theologians to demonstrate the economic and political prudence of native peoples in the history of civilizations. Comparative ethnography and empirical records from travelers and chroniclers, combined with theology and philosophy, were all crucial for this work's articulation of native political agency in normative and descriptive terms.

The Renaissance humanist dimensions of Las Casas's *Apologética historia* were apparent in his strategic use of Aristotle's political taxonomy filtered through a Ciceronian philosophical commitment to the unity of humankind. Book 7 of Aristotle's *Politics* provided six features of city life observable to a greater and lesser extent among the native inhabitants of the New World: laborers, artisans, warriors, aristocracy, priests, and judges or administrators of justice (see Figure 6.1).[82] According to the Aristotelian-Thomistic tradition, the existence of a city (*civitas*) or commonwealth (*respublica*) was necessary for the flourishing of rational social animals and for having definitive political

81 Cárdenas Bunsen, *Escritura y Derecho Canónico en la obra de fray Bartolomé de las Casas* (Iberoamericana, 2011), pp. 305–306.

82 Las Casas, *Apologética historia*, cap. 46, p. 523.

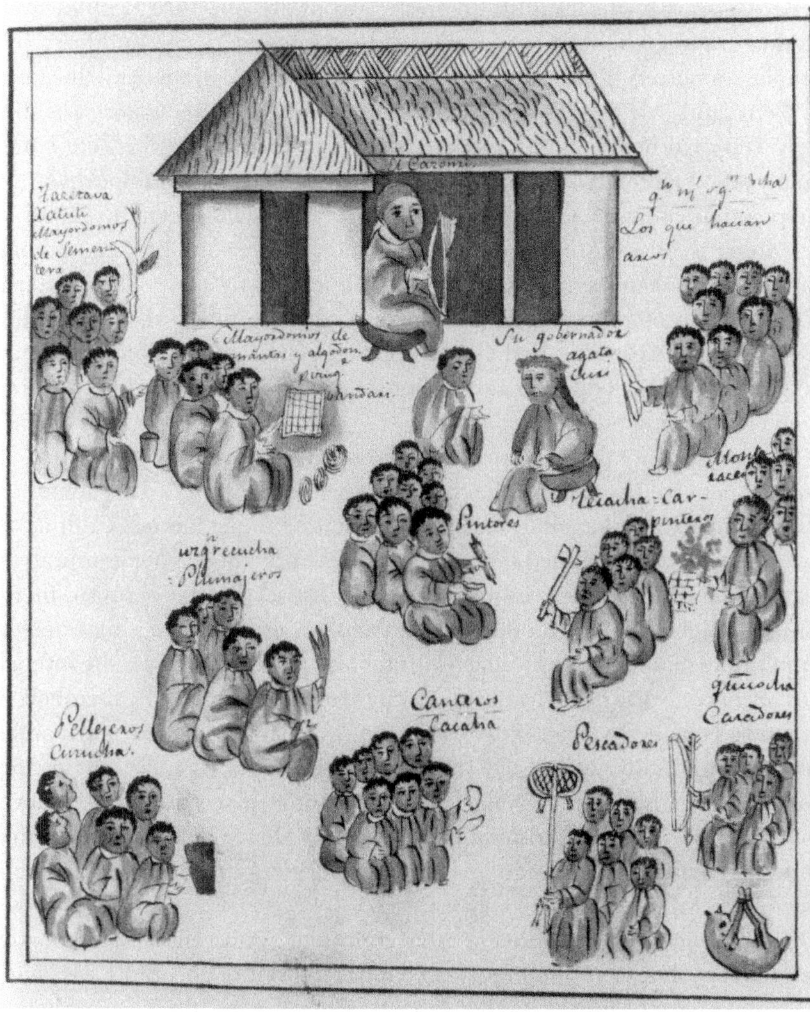

FIGURE 6.1 "Sixteenth-Century Spanish drawing of Michoacan natives broken up according to distinct social functions." (Source: Getty Images/Historical/ Contributor)

agency. To constitute an integral community or a people as self-sufficient (*per se sufficiens*) in a political and metaphysical sense, there had to be city life. It was precisely the claim about the absence of organized city life, and the characteristic marks of civilization, that both Spanish and English colonists used to designate numerous native communities as incompetent to rule themselves or as belonging to an anarchical state of nature.

Las Casas, like the English colonists, was aware of native peoples from Florida to the Caribbean islands who did not construct large buildings and temples, or possess highly stratified societies like the Amerindian civilizations of Peru and Mexico. Yet Aristotle's taxonomy to Las Casas was not a civilizational benchmark for assessing whether native peoples were either simply rational political animals or natural slaves, determined respectively by the presence or absence of city life. The taxonomic classification assisted in describing the various expressions of rationality and social life seen among native peoples who might possess all six qualities or only a few. The existence of a people or commonwealth did not depend on fulfilling all the qualities presented by Aristotle. Rather, Las Casas relied more heavily on an Augustinian and Ciceronian account of the city to include the innumerable peoples of the Indies.

Augustine's *City of God* provided the crucial definition of the city as "a number of people bound together by some tie of fellowship."[83] This definition of Augustine came largely from Cicero, who saw the commonwealth as an association of people united by a common sense of right and a community of shared interest.[84] On these terms, argued Las Casas, people organized themselves through social intercourse and peaceful accord to reside somewhere as a multitude of neighbors or citizens. In scholastic terms, this was the essence (*sustancia*) or being (*ser*) of a people or city (*pueblo o cuidad*), the members of whom had chosen to congregate in a city, town, or village. The true city, or the perfect community, was not defined by the existence of city walls or city buildings, but by people living together in some place allied "with love, concord, and peace."[85] Aristotelian political prudence rested on this more inclusive normative criterion of social association demonstrated through a common will.

Contrastingly, the so-called greater conveniences or enjoyments of life, described by Locke in the previous chapter, did not factor into Las Casas's expansive view of genuine political society. Consider the friar's description of city life among native inhabitants:

> In many parts of the Indies the peoples there do not have enclosed towns and municipalities nor very attractive buildings and elevated towers. Yet by living in peace, unity, and conformity, they do not cease being towns, villages, places, and cities. It is enough to live together with many or few neighbors in some good number so that there is a certain place, village, or city that can

83 Augustine, *City of God*, Book 15, chap. 8.
84 Augustine, *City of God*, Book 2, chap. 21.
85 Las Casas, *Apologética historia*, cap. 45, p. 491.

> suitably accommodate. Similarly, some gathering of homes among neighbors or extended family, composed of straw or some other kind of material, is enough. For they take from this earth only what is necessary, and they consider everything else, and it is, superfluous and excessive.[86]

From an Augustinian-Ciceronian standpoint, Aristotle's notion of the self-sufficient *polis* would acquire new valence through Las Casas's ethnographic history. The friar's appeal to the republican tradition of *civitas* enabled him to affirm peoplehood without the cultural elitism contained in imperial humanist readings. It was also significantly different from the Westphalian bifurcation of the Amerindian state of nature and civilized European society. An association of people bound together for the peaceful conservation of social life and its longevity was the interpretive frame for Aristotle's notion of the city as existing "for the sake of living well."[87] It was indicative for Las Casas that a city, community, or town had to be self-sustaining in the present and future for it to be considered a people. However, in no way did this require the exorbitant increase of wealth and the corresponding development of a slave labor society. Sustainable life together, rather than the accumulation of wealth or protection of private property among individual citizens, set the social aim of city life.

As Las Casas noted in his treatment of the Aristotelian notion of the city as self-sufficient (*por sí suficiente*), various peoples of the Indies lived in a simple manner, scattered among communities and settlements. He witnessed this first hand as bishop in the region of Guatemala, where the people there "do not want to have nor possess more than they have that is necessary to get through and sustain life." This "voluntary" poverty, as he called it, was not reprehensible, much less was it a defect of reason. On the contrary, it conformed to the teaching of Christ, who warned against storing up treasures on earth and caring too much for superfluous things. "Those who are truly Christian," wrote Las Casas, "have little concern to hold onto what is unnecessary and to accumulate more."[88] The mendicant spiritual dimensions of Las Casas's normative depiction here rang loud in a manner markedly different from the British colonial pursuit of life's greater conveniences through global commerce.

Oftentimes, scattered communities of those living by limited means were associated with a central governing agent by communication and trade. Yet

86 Las Casas, *Apologética historia*, cap. 45, pp. 491–492.

87 Aristotle, *The Politics*, Book 1, chap. 2, p. 37.

88 Las Casas, *Apologética historia*, cap. 46, pp. 525–526: "*[V]emos que los santo varones y los que verdaderamente son christianos curan poco de guardar lo superfluo y mucho athesorar.*"

Las Casas, in standard humanist fashion, also accounted for certain individuals and groups who do not congregate as a people but survive in isolation without social order.[89] Although rare instances of such groups hardly constituted a people in any meaningful sense for Las Casas, they still possessed reason and deserved treatment with the same respect and dignity that marked his ethic of evangelization.[90] Some natives of the wide region of Florida, whom for Acosta denoted the lowest barbarians on his civilizational scale, were for Las Casas examples of these herd-like groups inhabiting "the primitive state" (*el estado primero*) from which all humanity and peoples originally emerged.[91] Force of weapons and threats of violence, however, were not acceptable means of interacting with them in order to bring civility and the Gospel. Rather, Las Casas returned to Cicero's rhetorical account of the origin of civilization and the arrival of a wise teacher inducing the coarse (*silvestres*) with rational persuasion to live in a society with laws.

Unlike the state of nature marked by perpetual conflict among representative Westphalian thinkers, Las Casas claimed that a Christian encounter with those in the primitive state had to adhere to the peaceful order of divine providence, or "the universal way of mildness and love, natural and proper to human beings."[92] Gently attracting them into a shared society by respecting their free will as rational creatures made in the divine image was *the only way* to do so. Their consent, even on an individual or prepolitical level apart from organized social life, remained a prerequisite for incorporating them into a wider society or universal community of distinct peoples where living in concord with others, rather than in fear and seclusion, could bring greater human fulfillment.[93] In a similar vein, Wolff's Enlightenment international thought respected the freedom of either families or peoples, even the unrefined and barbaric, from ever being forced under the sovereignty of a more civilized foreign nation. Wolff specifically took aim at Grotius's contrary position, which permitted subjugation according to "the right to exact penalties from any who savagely violate the law of nature and of nations."[94]

Vitoria and Soto addressed the question of primitive-like or ungoverned persons under the scholastic treatment of Aristotle's natural slave, or those

89 Las Casas, *Apologética historia*, cap. 47.

90 Las Casas, *De unico vocationis modo*, cap. 5, §10, p. 100.

91 Las Casas, *Apologética historia*, caps. 47, 206, 207. Not all native Floridians belonged to this isolated state of life for Las Casas.

92 Las Casas, *Apologética historia*, cap. 209, p. 1339.

93 Jens Bartelson, *Visions of World Community* (Cambridge University Press, 2009), pp. 77–85.

94 Wolff, *The Law of Nations*, chap. 2, §§168–169.

groups inept at ruling over themselves as a commonwealth. In other words, those persons who do not live according to the Aristotelian political taxonomy in a discernible sense. Vitoria only entertained "merely for the sake of argument" this eighth possible title, which he did not call "just" or "lawful" the way he did in five preceding ones.[95] Even in this arguable instance, only if they were all considered inept (which they were not as he already indicated) could Spanish rulers govern them as children needing tutelage. Still, he argued in the first part of the *relectio* that children possess the image of God and have rights; therefore, they cannot be used for another's sake. Spain would be required to exercise benevolent charity toward them, loving them as neighbors and seeking their good and benefit by caring for their goods.

Soto acknowledged the possibility of natural slaves within single societies or outside society when encountering those who show no respect for pacts between peoples and attack travelers. Spaniards could respond to these aggressive and uncivilized persons by repelling or subjugating them, but only in defense. There is no strict right to rule over them politically because they are so-called natural slaves or to punish them for crimes against nature. If rulers or caretakers lawfully exert authority over natural slaves, these subjects cannot be regarded as property. Rather, they should be treated "just as free persons themselves."[96] What began for Vitoria and Soto under the heading of the natural slave became through their Christian hermeneutic a form of political dependency acknowledging dignity and rights of all subjects. Natural dependants were more like children in a legal sense and very different in theory and practice from Aristotle's wild beasts hunted down and brought under comprehensive subjugation by their masters as claimed by Gentili and Grotius.

In fact, the primitive natural state according to Las Casas's *Apologética historia* was an isolated phenomenon in the Indian world. Las Casas's general description of the native peoples of the Indies stood in stark contrast to the crude portrayal of irrational and savage natives by Sepúlveda, Acosta, Vázquez de Menchaca, and various English colonial thinkers. In addition to religion discussed in Chapter 4, two other prominent features of native communities across the Indies constituted their robust peoplehood – monarchy and agriculture – thus punctuating their respective political independence and division of goods. Religious customs, political governance, and the distinct usage

95 Vitoria, *On the American Indians*, q. 3, a. 8, pp. 290–291. Importantly, Vitoria also did not identify the possible titles of voluntary election (sixth) and alliances with natives (seventh) as lawful or legitimate when he concluded his discussion of them. It happened that these were the two titles claimed by Cortés in his taking possession of the Aztecs.

96 Soto, *De iustitia et iure*, lib. 4, q. 2, a. 2, p. 290: "*[S]ed tanquam liberis suique*." See also Soto, *In quartum Sententiarum*, p. 310, col. 2.

of land were all expressions of the universal law of nations, derived from natural reason and having the force of natural law.

Las Casas's ethnographic history of the law of nations had a radically different assessment of native political life than Acosta, Hobbes, and Locke, for whom nearly all, if not all, the Indians had no organized form of political governance. Beginning with the first encounter between Europeans and natives on Española, Las Casas followed the account of Fernández de Oviedo in identifying five different kings (*reyes*) who governed the entire island.[97] These rulers, or *caciques*, were comparable to the native sachems prominent among the Algonquian peoples, for example, of the Atlantic coast of North America. Whereas for Acosta and Locke, native chiefs were strictly warlords, Las Casas saw them as holding a customary status of governance in administering the people toward the common good by living peaceably together under a certain order of affairs. In contrast to the description of Acosta and later Locke, Las Casas saw in Española's example of kingship the norm across "these Indies universally."[98] The native monarchical arrangements, overall, were not tyrannies. Rather, they were just governments with political prudence oriented toward the specific community's welfare, however simple their organization.[99] Las Casas viewed these lords and rulers as natural political extensions of patriarchal relations between fathers and sons. Even so, native kingship did not belong to the strict necessity of the natural law, but instead the "more modern" (*más moderno*) law of nations freely established by the original consent of the people. Las Casas had to make this point to offset any Spanish colonial arguments favoring the *encomienda* as a hereditary natural right transferred from fathers to sons.[100]

The focus on native kingship in the Indies, from the caciques of the Caribbean islands to the Incas of Peru, challenged the political claims of Mair and Sepúlveda, each of whom denied native self-rule on the basis of ethnic subjugation. Another major obstacle in recognizing native political independence was the broad characterization of Indians as lazy and nonindustrious, a claim further justifying the forced labor system that demanded political submission. We observed in the previous chapter how English colonial thinkers relied on this description already present in Vázquez de Menchaca's legal humanism to advance an agriculturalist argument for improving underutilized land or wasted space and building cities. Since

97 Fernández de Oviedo, *Historia General y Natural*, primera parte, lib. 3, cap. 4, p. 66.

98 Las Casas, *Apologética historia*, cap. 197, pp. 1278–1279.

99 Las Casas, *Apologética historia*, cap. 197, pp. 1276–1277.

100 Las Casas, *Entre los remedios*, p. 747.

workers were the first social class of Aristotle's taxonomy, they were, according to Las Casas, the *sine qua non* for constituting a people. The "laborers and cultivators of the earth," observed Las Casas, produce the goods and fruit necessary "to sustain and maintain the city."[101]

Las Casas then indicated that the native peoples of the Indies exemplified this feature of city life more than anywhere in the world. They had all manner of farming and planting for the cultivation of crops and fruits, among them corn, avocados, and *sapotes*. The cassava root, for example, was especially important for making bread. Their utilization of the agave plant (*maguey*) was abundant for producing bread, wine, vinegar, syrup, and sugar. It also served medicinal purposes and provided linen for clothing. None of these examples of native cultivation of the earth required excessive labor from them, yet they were still able to meet the people's basic needs so that they never went hungry. Furthermore, Las Casas acknowledged like Hernán Cortés the indigenous use of cacao as money in the exchange of goods under King Montezuma.[102] Commerce and trade among merchants was common practice across the peoples of the Indies in search of necessary rather than superfluous goods.

Writing an ethnographic history of the positive law of nations in the Indies permitted Las Casas to defend native political independence and division of goods among cultivable lands using descriptive material from classical and early modern sources. The countless peoples of the Indies, in conclusion, were self-sufficient polities possessing legitimate rulers and ingenious laborers, with each aspect of city life contributing to the community's well-being. These basic features of city life embodied in laborers and kings, along with the manifold expressions of religiosity, were ubiquitous across the Indies. The combination of historical description and a normative commitment to the oneness of humanity made in the divine image provided an unprecedented argument for the economic, political, and religious agency of native peoples against European colonialism.

Soto, in his capacity as moderator of the Valladolid junta, had recognized the importance of Las Casas's descriptive task in refuting Sepúlveda's natural inferiority argument to support war and conquest. Against the Aristotelian claim of Sepúlveda that the natives were barbarians who could be hunted like "wild savage beasts" (*fieras silvestres*), Las Casas "told the history of the Indians at length, demonstrating that ... they are social and civil people who have large towns, houses, laws, arts, rulers, and government."[103] By demonstrating

101 Las Casas, *Apologética historia*, cap. 59, p. 578.

102 Cortés, *The Second Letter*, p. 94; Las Casas, *Apologética historia*, cap. 69.

103 Soto, *Sumario*, pp. 231–232.

the widespread political prudence of native peoples attentive to their diverse customs and practices, Las Casas thoroughly expounded the universal character of the law of nations in opposition to Sepúlveda's parochial humanist version designating the cultural vacuity of Amerindians.

Returning to the 1552 treatises published just after Valladolid, we see clearly what was at stake in Las Casas's articulation of a natural right of consent underlying rational political agency. The idea came out strongest in *Principia quaedam*, the most identifiably scholastic of Las Casas's juridical writings. Here Las Casas wrote that, "only in this manner, that is, by the election of the people, do any whatsoever have their just dominium and jurisdiction of kings over humans in all the world and in every nation. Any other manner (of dominium) would be unjust and tyrannical, except those constituted and introduced by divine mandate, as it occurred in the people of Israel (1 Kings 1, 8; Deuteronomy 17). Nevertheless, this divine mandate also concurred with the election, consent, and approval of the whole people (*totius populi*)."[104] Las Casas also considered the case of ancient Rome's transition from republic to empire, noting that the people "conceded all their power without losing their freedom to transfer their rule and jurisdiction." Whether in the case of a divine mandate or an imperial government, the elective power and liberty of the people of ancient Israel and Rome remained. These biblical and Roman historical examples were paradigms for recognizing the legitimacy of native kings, "*caciques* and *tatoanes*," or whatever name they call those who "receive from the whole society or multitude the supreme authority to rule in human affairs."[105] The respective rulers of native polities possessed the requisite *ius* or "power of judging" (*potestas iudicandi*) thereby setting the proper bounds of their jurisdiction over the people.

Although Las Casas was eminently concerned about preserving the liberty and right of native peoples to elect their rulers, his position on consent in the 1552 treatises did not represent the mature thought of his later writings, *De thesauris* (*On the Treasures of Peru*) and *Doce dudas* (*Twelve Doubts*). These final works, which he termed his "last will and codicil" dedicated to King Philip II, along with his posthumously published *De regia potestate* (*On Royal Power*), expressed the clearest juridical and theoretical account of the right of consent as a basis for political authority applicable to the Indies or anywhere else. These works illustrated not only a deeper engagement with Roman and canon legal sources, but also the crystallization of scholastic political thought for his legal reflection.

104 Las Casas, *Principia quaedam*, p. 1244.
105 Las Casas, *Principia quaedam*, p. 1246.

More than his Salmantine counterparts, the international thought of Las Casas expressed greater esteem for the public role of the papacy in the promotion of world order. This is hardly surprising since he was, after all, a canon lawyer formed in the *ius commune* tradition. His 1552 treatises still reflected a certain medieval *ius commune* bias toward the superior universal rule of the papacy and emperor that he later revised. The issue concerned the exact legal ramifications of the Alexandrine papal grant to the Spanish Crown now under a Holy Roman Emperor. Against theocratic papalists and royalists, Las Casas was clear that neither the faith nor Spanish political rule could be forced upon the natives against their will in the notorious manner of the Requirement. Religion and politics were inextricably wedded to the freedom of the will, as he demonstrated in his *Entre los remedios* (1552) before the Crown.[106] However, the question remained, what was the political status of those peoples who did freely embrace the faith without coercion and became baptized members of the Church?

The *Tratado Comprobatorio* plainly asserted that the "Supreme Pontiff is pastor and bishop of all infidels," a common canonistic opinion referring to Jesus's other sheep outside his fold.[107] Nevertheless, Las Casas was well-aware of the strong theocratic implications of this view advanced by medieval popes like Innocent IV. At this point in his career, Las Casas believed that the Alexandrine title had indeed granted to Spain political jurisdiction "*en hábito*," or potentially speaking, over infidels in the New World. Therefore, if the Amerindians freely embraced Christianity through baptism, they would automatically become subjects of the Spanish Crown, "*in actu*," according to the papal modal grant.[108] In another Sevillian treatise, *Treinta Proposiciones* (*Thirty Propositions*), Las Casas made a similar juridical claim about the modal grant in his nineteenth proposition. He proposed that all peoples of the Indies, following their voluntary acceptance of the faith and baptism, were obligated to recognize the universal rule of the Spanish Crown.[109]

Las Casas's native advocacy before the Crown during the 1540s and early 1550s affirmed the automatic incorporation of freely converted Amerindians into Spanish political jurisdiction, thereby exposing a limitation in his position reflective of his medieval legal sources Bartolus and Baldus. Both of these civil jurists, while formulating the de facto political independence of peoples, a most significant contribution, also adhered to the superior jurisdiction of the

106 Gutiérrez, *Las Casas*, p. 389.

107 Las Casas, *Tratado Comprobatorio*, pp. 938–939.

108 Las Casas, *Tratado Comprobatorio*, p. 1146.

109 Las Casas, *Treinta Proposiciones*, in *Tratados*, I, n. 19, p. 483.

Pope and emperor de iure. Although Las Casas did not support the "foolish assertion" of Roman imperial power as extensive over the whole world like Sepúlveda, he did follow Baldus's opinion at Valladolid that the Roman Emperor was the universal ruler of Christians.[110] However, Las Casas had to confront the abuse of this teaching by Sepúlveda, who saw it as justification for declaring war against native converts if they did not acquiesce to Spanish imperial rule. Las Casas immediately restated his position in yet another Sevillian treatise to avoid this seeming invitation to perpetual war with non-compliant natives. The natives were obligated to recognize Spanish rule after conversion. However, war was not acceptable even if they refused to submit since that would violate their welfare as a people.[111]

It would take the remaining juridical writings of Las Casas completed in the 1560s to work out the fuller creative implications of this shift in his political judgment that moved him in the more moderate direction of his Salmantine counterparts. The Dominican theologians at Salamanca, with their adamant denial of universal papal and imperial rule over infidels, evidently influenced his thinking. In the Sevillian treatises of 1552, Las Casas already acknowledged his indebtedness to Vitoria's *relectio* on ecclesiastical power and Soto's *De dominio* in developing a political view in between theocratic papalism and the secular governance of ecclesiastical affairs.[112] He sought to maintain the superiority of the Church's spiritual power without denying the integrity of temporal power among infidels. For this reason, he cited the Thomistic political axiom for working out this middle position.

Throughout an extraordinarily controversial career of legal advocacy on behalf of Amerindians, Las Casas maintained a twofold commitment to peaceful evangelization and the idea that there could be no sovereignty without a people's consent. Whereas he had formulated his commitment to the only way of peaceful evangelization clearly in his earliest writings, his view of popular consent evolved in innovative ways. What largely accounted for the development in his thought on consent was the unique symbiosis of scholastic theology and the tradition of *ius commune* on the subject of natural right and the right of peoples. The most salient expression of how his ideas matured through this creative correlation of scholastic and juristic thinking were evident in his final writings, which addressed Spanish restitution of native government and property in Peru, the native right of resistance, and the scope of possible European intervention. Attention to these aspects of his work,

110 Las Casas, *In Defense of the Indians*, chap. 21, p. 153.
111 Las Casas, *Aquí se contiene una disputa*, rep. 12, p. 433.
112 Las Casas, *Tratado Comprobatorio*, pp. 990–992.

alongside the Salmantine theologians, concludes our treatment of the distinct contours of this Spanish theological account of world order in the history of international thought.

THE NATIVE RIGHT OF RESISTANCE

Early modern ideas of resistance in Western political thought, among both Protestant and Catholic thinkers, has focused on the volatile European context of interconfessional strife and absolutist monarchs. From this standpoint, Calvinist and Jesuit theorists of resistance rightly attract the most attention from political theorists and intellectual historians.[113] However, as in the discussion of Cajetan's papalism considered in Chapter 3, we miss a sense of the wider international meaning of the right of resistance in early modern Christianity if our lens is restricted to the European continent of the seventeenth century. The sixteenth-century Spanish Dominicans, especially Las Casas, belong to this more radical political history in a transatlantic colonial context because of their deployment of infidel rights with emphasis on Amerindian consent to check and counter tyrannical European incursion.

Positive and negative expressions of freedom would take political form, respectively, through the Spanish theological treatment of the native people's right of consent and their right of resistance. Las Casas's final writings, the Latin *De thesauris* and *De regia potestate* and the Castilian *Doce dudas*, each relied on the Roman legal definition of liberty to contrast native political agency from imperial domination: "Liberty is the natural power to do whatever one pleases unless prohibited in some fashion by force or law."[114] And yet, this juridical definition of liberty, just like in his 1552 treatises, was read through Thomistic moral theological principles developed by his Dominican brothers at Salamanca. As Brian Tierney has penetratingly shown, this synthesis of juristic reasoning and Thomistic natural law contributed to Las Casas's most important theoretical achievement in the domain of natural rights.[115]

113 Skinner, *Foundations of Modern Political Thought*, vol. 2, part 3; John Witte, Jr., *The Reformation of Rights: Law, Religion, and Human Rights in Early Modern Calvinism* (Cambridge University Press, 2007); Harro Höpfl, *Jesuit Political Thought: The Society of Jesus and the State, c. 1540–1630* (Cambridge University Press, 2004).

114 *Digest*, 1.5.4; "*Libertas est naturalis facultas eius quod cuique facere libet, nisi si quid vi aut iure prohibetur.*" See the relevant references in Las Casas, *De thesauris*, cap. 16, p. 192; *Doce dudas*, cap. 11, p. 65; *De regia potestate*, in *OC*, 12, §1, nos. 4–5.

115 Tierney, *Idea of Natural Rights*, p. 276.

Importantly for Las Casas, the freedom to spread the faith must never detract from the fundamental liberty inscribed in all peoples according to natural law and the law of nations. These final writings continued to attest to the linkage between the peaceful ethic of evangelization and the promotion of spiritual and political freedom in the Indies. Reiterating the Dominican commitment to the only way of preaching, the octogenarian friar stipulated that "the only cause and end" of the papal concession of "the New World of the Indies" to the Spanish Crown was spiritual. The papal title entrusted to the kings was for the proclamation of the Gospel and conversion of the peoples there, certainly "not to make them greater rulers nor richer than they were already."[116] As he eloquently stated in *Doce dudas*, citing the Roman *Digest*, liberty was inestimable, and could "neither be measured nor sold for all the gold in the world."[117]

According to the apostolic method, the natives were free to embrace or refuse the Christian faith, just as they were free to listen or not listen to Spanish preachers.[118] Natives had the freedom to deny entry of preachers in their lands without threat of punishment. Las Casas resolutely maintained the shake the dust from your feet teaching from Matthew's and Mark's Gospel at the end of his career. With Pope Paul III's Dominican-inspired *Sublimis Deus* serving as the "new decretal" (*nuevo decreto*), Las Casas employed Church authority to strengthen Cajetan's "true and Catholic doctrine" of infidel dominium with a greater accent on freedom. With respect to the natives, "No King nor Emperor nor the Roman Church can wage war, nor disturb them in any manner so as to subjugate them against their voluntary freedom."[119]

The ecclesiological concept of the mystical Body of Christ present at Valladolid remained an important resource for defending native freedom in *De thesauris*. In this scholastic-inflected juridical work, Las Casas changed his position on the papal modal grant by abandoning his earlier idea about the automatic transference of Spanish rule over natives following their conversion. His revised interpretation of the papal concession depended on crucial theological and legal arguments. Against the forced incorporation of infidels into European jurisdiction, the mystical Body of Christ ensured a "voluntary incorporation" respecting freedom of the will among individuals and

116 Las Casas, *Doce dudas*, cap. 7, p. 51.

117 Citing *Digest*, 50.17.106. Las Casas, *Doce dudas*, cap. 11, p. 64.

118 Las Casas, *De thesauris*, cap. 42, p. 460; *Doce dudas*, cap. 10, p. 61.

119 Las Casas, *Doce dudas*, cap. 6, pp. 49–50: "*[N]ingún Rey ni Emperador ni la Iglesia romana las puede hacer guerra, ni por alguna manera molestarlas, para contra su voluntad sujetár selas.*"

peoples.[120] Las Casas once again applied Aquinas's teaching on Christ's mystical Body to elucidate the Church's voluntary jurisdiction over infidels according to the power of Christ and free will. Therefore, papacy and Crown could only attract nonbelievers to the faith through the way of peace, gentleness, charity, and example.[121] If natives did voluntarily embrace the Christian faith without coercion, then religious clergy could inform them about the papal title of Spain as their potential overseers. Nevertheless, native political consent was an absolute requirement. Papal concession granted Spain a possible "right to" (*ius ad rem*), or a title to rule, and not an actual "right in" ruling (*ius in re*) native converts over the demarcated geopolitical space of the New World.[122] Everything was now contingent upon voluntary consent of the natives.

The momentous shift away from automatic incorporation of natives into Spanish jurisdiction after conversion reflected the friar's evolving mindset steeped in the thought of Aquinas and the jurists. Aquinas's teaching on the mystical Body of Christ, along with the scholastic political axiom and Cajetan's appropriation of it, provided Las Casas with ample theological support for his mature legal interpretation of infidel dominium. Las Casas evidently revised his teaching from the 1552 treatises in light of Aquinas, Cajetan, and the Spanish Dominican theologians at Salamanca. After referring to their teaching, he corrected his view from the nineteenth proposition of *Treinta Proposiciones*:

> Just like before baptism, if after baptism they do not wish to admit our kings as their supreme rulers, there is no single judge in the whole world who has power to punish them by this cause .... Seeing that they have, according to their natural power, the right of consenting or dissenting from the oft-cited papal instruction, whatever their status. That is, whether *before or after* their conversion.[123]

Scripture generated additional legal support for mapping out a coordination of divine authority and royal power, as seen in the case of ancient Israel's kings Saul and David. Two juridical processes were operative here in the election of the Hebrew kings by both providence and the people of

[120] Las Casas, *De thesauris*, cap. 11, p. 140.

[121] Las Casas, *De thesauris*, cap. 40, pp. 442–444.

[122] Las Casas, *De thesauris*, cap. 29, p. 316; cap. 33, p. 356.

[123] Las Casas, *De thesauris*, cap. 27, p. 300. Emphasis mine: "*[T]am post baptismum quam ante, si nolunt Reges nostros recipere in principes supremos, nullus est iudex de mundo qui potestatem habeat illos, hac de causa, puniendi* .... *Quoniam in sua facultate naturali habent ius consentiendi vel dissentiendi sepe dicte institutioni papali, in utroque statu eorum, scilicet, vel ante vel post suam conversionem.*"

Israel.[124] Thus the Bible provided a theological basis for popular election. No universal judge could therefore deny a free people their right of electing (*ius eligendi*) a ruler over themselves. Not even God himself could violate the free consent of the people without causing them injury and harm. Due to the natural necessity of a people's voluntary consent in establishing the authority of a ruler to maintain justice, Las Casas elevated it to an irrevocable universal moral precept in the Thomistic sense.[125] Consequently, the Alexandrine title, a divine instruction of the Church, was ineffective apart from the authoritative intervention of native consent grounded in natural law and the law of nations.

The recognition of a subjective natural right to resist overreaching ecclesiastical and royal power in the New World illustrated the extent of Las Casas's radical politics against European forms of papal and imperial tyranny. Custom has established among all peoples the voluntary election of rulers from the beginning through "a treaty, pact, law, or convention" between the king and the people.[126] "The tyrant is one who," in the words of *Doce dudas*, "usurps by force, without just cause, the kingdoms and jurisdictions that pertain to true kings and rulers according to natural law and the law of nations."[127] Similar to Vitoria's letter to Arcos, when Las Casas confronted the case of Spanish seizure of the Inca Atahualpa and his dominion, the bishop friar forcefully asserted that the group of men (or *peruleros*) led by Francisco Pizarro were all tyrants and brigands. Beginning with the first entry (*primer ingresso*) to the New World, the Spaniards had been tyrannical aggressors, waging war and imposing forced labor to subjugate native inhabitants.[128] Spanish tyranny undermined the native people's custom of voluntarily electing their ruler. Its aftermath in the Indies demanded restitution of seized kingdoms and stolen property to promote justice for native victims and salvation for European oppressors.

Las Casas's indictment of Hernán Cortés was even more stinging because it had a personal dimension. While "tyrannizing New Spain," Cortés received unheeded instructions from the Spanish Crown in 1523 prohibiting him from

[124] Las Casas, *Doce dudas*, cap. 11, pp. 69–73.

[125] Las Casas, *De thesauris*, cap. 19, pp. 226–228. After referring to Aquinas, *ST*, I-II, q. 100, a. 8 on the immutability of the moral precepts, Las Casas wrote: "That precept, which ordains the establishment of a king through the consent and approval of the people, is moral and immutable."

[126] Las Casas, *De thesauris*, cap. 28, p. 307.

[127] Las Casas, *Doce dudas*, cap. 23, p. 112: "*Tirano es aquél que usurpa por fuerça, sin justa causa, los estados y principados que pertenecen a los verdaderos reyes y señores por derecho natural y de las gentes.*"

[128] Las Casas, *Doce dudas*, cap. 14, pp. 80–81.

establishing *encomiendas* and *repartimientos*, which were knowingly destructive to the natives on the Caribbean islands.[129] Moreover, from the moment Cortés encountered the peoples of Mexico, he had used coercion and trickery to overthrow them, most evident in the case of King Montezuma of the Aztecs. Las Casas knew the truth of the matter first hand from the mouth of Cortés, his onetime friend. As the friar recorded in *De thesauris*, when the two of them conversed in Mexico City years after the incident, Cortés claimed that Montezuma had voluntarily conceded his native throne to Spain. Las Casas contradicted Cortés by arguing that the conquistador had, in fact, employed the "fear and terror" of horses and weapons instead to force native compliance thereby undermining free consent.[130] Pressed further, Cortés laughingly admitted before others present that Montezuma had tried imploring them with gifts in order to leave more than thirty times. The conquistador had revealed his true ambition, and Las Casas did not hesitate to call the liar a tyrant.

Conquistadors were tyrants and looters precisely because they had denied native political consent by using the threat of war and punishment against innocent peoples to dispossess their kingdoms and property unlawfully. The prospects for any lawful transference of political authority presumed the scholastic-juristic distinction between the power of the people and the authority of the ruler. According to the Spanish Dominicans, lawful Spanish rule over native inhabitants of the Indies was possible if and only if the people offered consent, the necessary basis of establishing political authority. Vitoria, Soto, and Las Casas agreed on the point that the Crown could lawfully govern and administer justice in the Indies assuming the native peoples freely accepted Spanish sovereignty. Yet a nuanced difference between Las Casas and his Salmantine counterparts reveal the radical side of the canon lawyer's political thought.

According to the Salmantine theologians, the possibility of Spanish governance of the Indies following the lawful transference of political authority to another king rested on the power originating from the majority consent of a native people. Vitoria argued in his lecture on civil power, with Soto following, that since unanimous consent is impractical for achieving the interests of the commonwealth, "it is sufficient that the majority agree on one candidate for there to be a legal election."[131] In the case of the Indies, then, if a majority of native converts among a people decided to elect a Christian

[129] Las Casas, *Doce dudas*, cap. 31, p. 149.
[130] Las Casas, *De thesauris*, cap. 32, pp. 344–346.
[131] Vitoria, *On Civil Power*, q. 2, p. 30; Soto, *De iustitia et iure*, lib. 4, q. 4, a. 2.

ruler (domestic or foreign), thereby abandoning allegiance to an infidel ruler for the sake of promoting the common welfare, they could do so against the opinion of the minority.[132] The majority consent of the whole world to a single ruler may have demonstrated the implausibility of universal imperial sovereignty. But that did not preclude a situation whereby the majority among a single people could consent to foreign imperial rule such as the king of Spain overseas. On the rule of the majority as political principle, the Salmantine theologians were reliant on Roman legal precedent. Las Casas would appropriate theological and canon legal sources to articulate a more radical, indeed revolutionary, politics to account for the right of an Indian minority and even individual natives in matters of consent and resistance. As he saw it, majority consent was an insufficient legal principle in the case of transferring political rule.

Whether treating the specific affair of the Indies or offering a broader political theory, Las Casas's *De thesauris* and *De regia potestate* each identified the people's consent as the efficient cause of establishing political rule. Baldus's commentary on the *Digest* may have been the proximate source for Las Casas, yet we have seen how Cajetan's scholastic politics was in accord with the medieval Italian jurist on this point. The consenting people as the efficient cause of political authority was what enabled the *ius in re* to have effect beyond the mere title (*ius ad rem*) of Spanish rule in the Indies conceded by the papacy. Following Baldus, Las Casas distinguished the active principle of political agency in the electing people, and the passive principle residing in the elected ruler.[133] Where the active principle of the people was lacking, there could be no natural foundation for the efficient cause to attain realization. Despite transferring authority to the elected ruler, the people still retain their liberty and cannot have their rights violated by the king entrusted with their welfare. The people (*populus*), as O'Donovan outlined earlier in the chapter, were therefore a distinct reality anterior in principle and in time to government and kingship.[134]

A striking feature of Las Casas's treatment of the people's consent in the mature writings was his deployment of the mystical body (*corpus mysticum*) as a political concept for secular affairs. Indeed, the political and legal aspects of the mystical Body of Christ were understood for centuries in Spain since the Middle Ages.[135] Vitoria, for example, gestured at the secular political

132 Vitoria, *On the American Indians*, q. 3, a. 6, pp. 288–289.

133 Las Casas, *De thesauris*, cap. 29, p. 318.

134 Las Casas, *De regia potestate*, §4, no. 4.

135 José Maravall, "La idea del cuerpo místico en España antes de Erasmo," *Boletín informativo del Seminario del Derecho Político* (1956): 29–44.

implications of the mystical body when he emphasized the power of the commonwealth in matters of self-defense, which as "one body" can risk the lives of individual members for the sake of preserving common welfare and promising safety.[136] The conventional political application of the mystical body to secular affairs denoted Latin Christendom as "a single commonwealth and a single body."[137] Hence the majority of Christians in Europe could elect a single monarch to lead them against a tyrannical and aggressive infidel encroaching on their political borders, as the Ottoman Turks were often perceived.

Beyond Vitoria, Las Casas translated the mystical body into a philosophical political concept applicable to commonwealths as such and not strictly Christendom thereby anticipating the thought of Francisco Suárez. To account for the elective power of the people in a natural condition, the Spanish Jesuit scholastic Suárez did not appeal to an unorganized aggregate of individuals as social contract theorists of a Westphalian register were beginning to do in Europe.[138] Instead, a moral union was required in the act of forming distinct political communities with the power of electing a head to direct each people toward the common good. The community or perfect commonwealth is a moral bond of fellowship founded on consent, which possesses the requisite power of self-determination and self-governance.[139] That single unified body refers to the *corpus mysticum* residing in every commonwealth.

Las Casas also articulated a secular *corpus mysticum* but did so for a different political purpose than Suárez. *De regia potestate* identified the single bond of the mystical body as a "union of wills" in contrast to a composite union of organs in a physical body. Yet there was a sense in which Las Casas's political concept of the *corpus mysticum* reflected a richer ecclesiological indebtedness. Whereas Suárez invoked the mystical body to distinguish a unified political whole from disjointed individuals, Las Casas moved in the opposite direction. He sought to preserve the individual parts comprising the moral unity closer to Vitoria's discussion of the mystical Body of Christ in the *relectio* on ecclesiastical power. Unlike physical organs, which have no function apart from an organic whole, in a mystical body the union of wills presupposes individual persons (*suppositis*) as separate parts.[140] For this

136 Vitoria, *On Civil Power*, q. 1, a. 4, p. 11.

137 Vitoria, *On Civil Power*, q. 2, p. 31.

138 Skinner, *The Foundations of Modern Political Thought*, vol. 2, p. 165.

139 Suárez, *De legibus*, lib. 3, q. 3, no. 6.

140 Las Casas, *De regia potestate*, §22, no. 3, where he uses the scholastic philosophical term "*supposit*" to refer to a whole individual substance of a rational nature: "*Nam licet corpus physicum unitum sit ex partibus unione compaginis, corpus tamen mysticum unitum est solum*

reason, Las Casas was attentive to the consent required of every individual citizen even in an extended kingdom or empire. Although the king was the mystical head of the body of people, he could not transfer or alienate any part of his jurisdiction – a village, a city, a province – against the will of his respective citizens, no matter how small the region.[141] To do so would be like cutting off and injuring the body thus leaving it deformed. In particular, the Indies case established this universal juridical and political principle constraining alienation of rule without a people's consent.

The *corpus mysticum* as a political concept reinforced Las Casas's innovative ideas of consent and resistance for thinking about world order. These ideas received practical elucidation from the important Roman legal and canonistic maxim of *Quod omnes tangit debet ab omnibus approbari* ("What touches all must be approved by all"). In conjunction with the theological political concept of *corpus mysticum* and the canonistic *foris* principle, the *quod omnes tangit* maxim demonstrated Las Casas as belonging to a Christian legal tradition of "adapting ecclesiological and canon law concepts to political theory."[142] Though originally derived from Roman private law, the *quod omnes tangit* maxim became a principle of Church governance addressing issues of ecclesiastical appointments and taxation of clergy during the Middle Ages.[143] Its application in the New World safeguarded the legal immunity of the natives against Spanish theocratic claims based on the Alexandrine donation. Similar to his discussion of the *corpus mysticum* in the treatise on royal power, *De thesauris* and *Doce dudas* both utilized the Western legal maxim as a strategy for privileging the minority, or the individual, in the matter of lawful transference of political authority in the Indies.

The application of *quod omnes tangit* to the Amerindian case relied on a crucial canon legal distinction between a matter affecting a single body as a collective whole, and a matter touching upon every individual's right. Citing the legal commentaries of Pope Innocent III and Baldus, Las Casas noted the important distinction: "When something is common to the many, not as a collective or even a single body, but as individuals or concerning each one's right; then, truly, it is necessary for individuals to know and to consent. Subsequently, what is done by the many has no validity unless everyone agrees

unione voluntatis, non unione of compaginis, cum constet ex distantibus partibus sive suppositis."

141 Las Casas, *De regia potestate*, §22, nos. 1–2.

142 Pennington, "Bartolomé de las Casas and the Tradition of Medieval Law," *Church History* 39, no. 2 (1970): 151.

143 Monahan, *Consent, Coercion, and Limit: The Medieval Origins of Parliamentary Democracy* (McGill-Queen's University Press, 1987), pp. 97–111.

to it whether together or separately."[144] In a situation concerning the collective whole, the principle of the majority was sufficient; however, in matters affecting the rights of individuals, each person's consent was required.[145] With respect to the latter case, the Indies qualified because it involved a situation in which the decision for a foreign ruler went against what common agreement and custom had already established among the people. Even if the majority of the people freely accepted another political authority, they would still "act against liberty" (*contra libertatem*) in this instance, "which does not prejudice those who do not agree – that is, the remaining minority unwilling to consent."[146] Anyone affected by an action resulting in harm or loss of rights, regardless of social and political status, possessed the power to approve or disapprove it.

The concept of *corpus mysticum* recognized the constituent parts of the kingdom or commonwealth, from the greatest to the smallest town of people, as having juridical standing in matters affecting their political rule. Even more, the maxim of *quod omnes tangit* accounted for the juridical status of "every single individual person [*singulas personas uniuscuiusque*] of each province, city, town or place." The freedom of consent in deciding whether to accept the Spanish king as ruler pertained at the level of individuals as much as a city and a people. Since all the Indian peoples are free, they are endowed with a natural power and right of consenting to and resisting Spanish rule.[147] As Mario Ruiz Sotelo has observed, there is something truly astonishing in Las Casas's politics here: The revolutionary innovation of Las Casas was not his attention to the single individual as political subject as such, but rather, his recognition that the concrete political agent was "an Indian … dispossessed of goods, lands, family, of political power, of all rights."[148] The radical implications of Las Casas's politics emerge acutely in his historical treatment of the right of rebellion and resistance exercised, for example, by the Taíno *cacique*, Enriquillo.

Born Guarocuyá on Española and later baptized a Christian, Enriquillo was a relative of Caonabó, one of the original five rulers of the island before the arrival of Columbus and the Spaniards.[149] Enriquillo learned to read and write

144 Las Casas, *De thesauris*, cap. 17, p. 198.

145 Tierney, *Idea of Natural Rights*, p. 285; Cárdenas, "Consent, Voluntary Jurisdiction and Native Political Agency," p. 809.

146 Las Casas, *De thesauris*, cap. 17, p. 208.

147 Las Casas, *De thesauris*, cap. 17, p. 210. See also *Doce dudas*, cap. 11, p. 68.

148 Ruiz Sotelo, *Crítica de la razón imperial*, p. 205. See chap. 6 of this work for an illuminating account of Las Casas on consent and resistance.

149 Ida Altman, "The Revolt of Enriquillo and the Historiography of Early Spanish America," *The Americas* 63, no. 4 (2007): 587–614.

from Franciscan friars, and later married another native convert to the Church, Lucia. As a leader among the Taínos, Enriquillo and his people worked under a Spanish *encomendero* named Valenzuela who violently mistreated them. When it happened that Valenzuela raped Lucia and stole Enriquillo's mare, Enriquillo protested the abuses to Spanish authorities, only to be beaten and threatened. He finally made his way to Santo Domingo to raise his complaint before the *Audiencia* but to no avail. Civil authorities sent him back to Valenzuela. Enriquillo, along with other aggrieved Taínos, refused to return to the *encomienda*. When Valenzuela heard the news, he brought along a company of men to force the return of the natives. A skirmish broke out that left two Spaniards dead. Enriquillo and his men revolted and fled to the mountains in hiding. Over time, about 300 natives joined his resistance.[150] Enriquillo was marked a rebel yet proved quite formidable for his ability to sustain and protect his people apart from the rest of colonial society by cultivating crops and seizing Spanish weapons.

After a failed attempt by the Council of the Indies to grant Enriquillo liberty and pardon on peaceful terms due to mistrust, Las Casas intervened with another Dominican in 1533. They met and stayed with Enriquillo and his followers for about a month after which they helped secure a formal resolution with Spanish authorities: Enriquillo and resistance leaders would no longer work under Spanish *encomenderos* but would have their own land to settle.[151] Enriquillo was an important model for the peaceful relations between natives and Europeans, even the "recognition of at least limited rights of indigenous peoples" by royal officials during this initial phase of colonization.[152] Notably, this incident came just before Las Casas began drafting his treatise on peaceful evangelization, *De unico vocationis modo*, thereby demonstrating the practical experience and proven success informing the work later confirmed by the Verapaz example in northern Guatemala.

Enriquillo also provided Las Casas with a historical case for the native right of resistance. Las Casas was adamant that Enriquillo and his followers had always fought in self-defense. Their resistance on Española was an act of justice in the same manner as the Maccabean revolt from Jewish sacred history. Combining historical narration of the events (*el hecho*) with the language of right (*el derecho*), Las Casas made this extended declaration:

150 Las Casas, *Historia de las Indias*, III, cap. 125. See Francis Sullivan for an English translation of the episode, *Indian Freedom: The Cause of Bartolomé de las Casas* (Sheed & Ward, 1995), pp. 188–199.

151 Las Casas, *Historia de las Indias*, III, cap. 127.

152 Altman, "The Revolt of Enriquillo," p. 613.

> Enriquillo, and the small number of Indians on the island who remained following the cruel hands and horrible tyrannies of Spaniards, had a most just title to go after, destroy, punish, and eliminate the Spaniards as their supreme enemies – the destroyers of their once great commonwealths, as there had been on this island. All this the Indians were doing and permitted to do with the authority of natural law and the law of nations. It is more accurate to call it self-defense rather than war, strictly speaking. Moreover, Enriquillo had a fuller right as a prince because there was no other ruler left on the island. Therefore he could execute punishment and vengeance on every Spaniard found there. This cannot be denied as when those ignorant of *el hecho* and *el derecho* say that the ruler of the island was the King of Spain, and to him they should make their claim of justice. Such a false argument is mere flattery and nonsense. That is because the kings and native rulers of this island never recognized the Crown of Spain as their sovereign. From the moment of discovery until today, the Indians were tyrannized by actions lacking the cause of justice ... What is more, there was never any justice on this island, and nothing was ever done by Spaniards to make amends for their native neighbors, its inhabitants. And wherever justice is lacking, the one who is oppressed and injured can pursue it himself. That is the maxim of the jurists, a dictum and teaching of natural reason.[153]

The radical ramifications of Las Casas's teaching against Sepúlveda on the right to resist allegedly superior cultures at Valladolid had a real face in the person of Enriquillo, the legitimate native ruler on Española even after Spanish subjugation. In the case of the Inca descendants of Huayna Capac (or Guaynacapac), the immediate predecessor to Atahualpa, Las Casas would defend the full restoration of native sovereignty and possessions in Peru. The ruler Titu Cusi Yupanqui, residing in the Andes mountains, was the grandson of Huayna Capac and legitimate heir to the Inca throne (see Figure 6.2). As was his brother Tupac Amaru, who eventually led a rebellion against Spanish authorities that ended with his capture and cruel execution in 1572.

While these Inca successors were still alive, Las Casas directed his political proposal from *Doce dudas* to King Philip II. The Crown had the moral and legal obligation "under the penalty of eternal damnation, to restore those realms to King Titu Cusi, the successor or heir to Huayna Capac, and the other Inca lords, and to place in them all their authority and power."[154] The dispossession of native sovereignty and jurisdiction, like theft, was an obstacle to salvation for Europeans. Even if the native Peruvians consented to Spanish universal sovereignty following the exclusive peaceful urgings of the religious,

[153] Las Casas, *Historia de las Indias*, III, cap. 125.

[154] Las Casas, *Doce dudas*, cap. 40, pp. 196–197.

FIGURE 6.2 "Emperors of Peru." (Source: Getty Images/Hulton Archive/Stringer)

they would still maintain a degree of jurisdiction and power over their subjects. Las Casas continued to support the medieval juridical model of de iure universal sovereignty and the de facto independence of commonwealths though now with greater appreciation for consent after conversion according to the scholastic political doctrine. The power and freedom of a distinct people to live according to their laws, customs, and statutes, so long as it was not contrary to the faith, was compatible with superior Spanish rule.[155] Vitoria's reliance on the scholastic language of the commonwealth as whole and self-sufficient would similarly identify a people's political independence in terms of their own laws, assemblies, and magistrates. Such a commonwealth, complete in itself, possessed the requisite power from the law of nations to declare war in order to protect itself, even against members under the same single ruler irrespective of imperial approval. Reliance on custom as a force of law gave Vitoria's position even wider latitude to recognize that the right of waging (*ius gerendi*) war even belonged to a commonwealth that was not completely self-sufficient, a point relevant to both the *comuneros* revolt in Spain and native resistance in the Indies.[156]

Beyond the political power of the commonwealth, Las Casas made an additional claim about the individual right of self-defense among native populations. He favored an extreme scholastic view of tyrannicide in the Indies. Not only the Inca rulers and commonwealths can lawfully resist the oppressive Spaniards, but also "each individual person has the same right bestowed by natural law."[157] Put differently, each particular Indian has the individual right to wage war and eliminate a tyrannical enemy with similar authority as the deposed Inca ruler. This position contrasted with Suárez's scholastic view, which denied to a private individual the sole right of public authorities to wage war against enemies.[158] Vitoria also rejected the authority of the private person to kill another intentionally in accordance with the standard Thomistic teaching on self-defense.[159]

Although it might appear that Las Casas's humanism was closer to the Protestant natural lawyers Gentili and Grotius on this matter, the Dominican did maintain the scholastic jurisdictional view of punishment. Citing Cicero's distinction between two acts of vengeance, punishment and self-defense, Las Casas associated the former only with competent public

155 Las Casas, *Doce dudas*, cap. 41, pp. 200–201.

156 Vitoria, *On the Law of War*, q. 1, a. 2, pp. 301–302.

157 Las Casas, *Doce dudas*, cap. 27, p. 132.

158 Suárez, *On Charity*, in *Selections from Three Works*, ed. Thomas Pink (Liberty Fund, 2015), Disp. 13, pp. 933–934.

159 Vitoria, *On Homicide*, no. 20, pp. 84–85.

authorities and the latter with private individuals.[160] The ambiguity of Las Casas's position could explain why he preferred not to use the language of war in his discussion of violent native retaliation. Private individuals may be able to wage war in defense of their freedom and possessions, yet they cannot mete out punishment to their enemies. Only Enriquillo had that requisite power to exact punishment on the Spaniards as a legitimate ruler like the Inca descendants of Atahualpa. Despite his radical humanist juridical stance on resistance, Las Casas did not cease to inhabit the contours of scholastic political thought.

LAWFUL OCCUPATION AND THE CHRISTIAN ETHIC OF INTERVENTION

In addition to restoring native sovereignty, the matter of restitution also directly bore on the law of occupation concerning movable things or goods. Spanish occupation of material things in the Indies referred specifically to the extractive mining of gold and silver and the seizure of precious objects from shorelines, mountains, and sacred sites. Here too consent was an essential requirement for the Spanish Dominicans, as we saw in Soto's recognition that rational native peoples were the first inhabitants of the Indies.

Although Vitoria also emphasized the importance of consent in his limited treatment of lawfully occupying unclaimed things (*res nullius*), his position was prone to use for different political purposes by subsequent international thinkers. Attentive to this more complex background, Andrew Fitzmaurice has read Vitoria's historical reception with an eye to contrasting interpretations of his thought by strong partisans and critics of European colonialism alike.[161] Vitoria strictly rejected Columbus's alleged right of discovery in his third unjust title because it denied the fact, which Columbus himself observed, that the Indies were densely populated. Since native inhabitants occupied these lands and regions, it followed necessarily for Vitoria that consent was required for Spanish trade there and the occupation of things contained therein. This point becomes even clearer when turning to Vitoria's first possible just title for Spanish rule through war in situations involving travel and sharing resources with native peoples.

According to Vitoria, all trade and obtainment of goods by Spaniards in the Indies had to abide by two nonnegotiable norms for interacting with natives:

160 Las Casas, *Doce dudas*, cap. 28, p. 133.
161 Fitzmaurice, *Sovereignty, Property and Empire*, chaps. 2–3.

non-harmfulness and respect for native consent. Any harm or injury caused against the original inhabitants precluded the exercise of the right to travel and trade among them. If no harm was committed against natives and their homeland, then Spaniards were free to trade commodities like gold and silver with them individually, even against the wishes of respective rulers.[162] On this score, Vitoria consistently held that princes did not have absolute control over the property and goods of individual members of the commonwealth and could therefore not restrict trading when it was no threat to the well-being of the people. The most exploitative idea of Vitoria for subsequent colonialist sympathizers emerged when the theologian claimed that Spaniards could wage war to obtain their rights to travel and trade under the title of social intercourse and sharing goods (*naturalis societatis et communicationis*). Again, this probable argument assumed that Spaniards could prove they came in peace and had not deceived, tricked, or harmed the natives. Defensive war was permissible if violent native retaliation came after Spaniards sufficiently assured native inhabitants of their peaceful intentions. In this case, the natives could be considered innocent enemies fearful of Spanish aggression. Only treacherous enemies (*perfidis hostibus*) could be the proper subjects of political occupation and conquest.[163]

Despite a principled clarity, Vitoria's consideration of the right of traveling and trading had insufficiently accounted for facts about the Indies that his Dominican confreres at Salamanca immediately sought to clarify by the time of the theologian's death in 1546. Melchor Cano's *De dominio indorum* (1546) agreed with Vitoria that impeding travelers was injurious according to the law of nations. When applied to the Indies, however, Spaniards were evidently invaders (*invasores*) rather than passersby, lest one take Alexander the Great for a traveler.[164] If the Spaniards were genuine travelers seeking to trade peacefully, then native retaliation would violate the law of nations and present possible grounds for war. But the Spaniards overall were neither peaceful nor amicable in trade relations with Amerindians from the perspective of Cano. The seventeenth-century German critic of European conquest, Samuel Pufendorf, would also make a similar point about Vitoria's limits in his larger conflict with Grotius. In *De jure naturae et gentium* (1672), a moral science of the natural law, Pufendorf argued that such a "crude" right to travel

162 Vitoria, *On the American Indians*, q. 3, a. 1, p. 279.

163 Vitoria, *On the American Indians*, q. 3, a. 1, p. 282.

164 Cano considered the first six of Vitoria's possible just titles to claim rule in the Indies while excluding the title on making alliances with native friends and the title based on the mental ineptitude of the natives. In *De dominio indorum*, pp. 142–146.

and live among others was far too "indefinite" to avoid abuse by self-interested parties.[165]

Indirectly, Soto's treatise on the *Deliberation on the Cause of the Poor* (1545) also addressed the subject of genuine travelers, in this case the truly needy and indigent. Although this work focused specifically on aggressive Spanish laws restricting vagabondage and begging for alms, it had broader implications for international thought since it entailed the rights of citizens and foreigners throughout the kingdoms of Christendom.[166] Soto's defense of the poor's right of begging (*ius postulandi* or *ius mendicandi*) relied on his scholastic account of natural law and the law of nations in conjunction with the Christian duty of loving the poor neighbor. As he argued in the Spanish edition of the work, to refuse and expel strangers who are truly in need was a serious wrongdoing, "because according to natural law and the law of nations everyone has the freedom to go where they will so long as they are not inimical nor commit evil."[167] Remarkably, in the Latin edition of the work, Soto even acknowledged the right of infidels to beg and travel freely between European borders.[168] Cano and Soto, in distinct ways, qualified legitimate travelers by concretely addressing either the harmful motives of Spaniards in the Indies or the basic needs of the indigent.

Alongside the concern for legitimate or peaceful travelers, Vitoria also considered the prospect of occupation or co-possession of movable goods in the Indies as part of the law of nations. In principle, if Spaniards made it abundantly clear that their intentions were to visit the Indies and the native inhabitants still prohibited them from sharing in those things held and enjoyed in common by all other foreigners, then such unequal treatment was impermissible. Vitoria gave the prominent colonial example of digging for gold in common lands and rivers and fishing for pearls on coastal waters.[169] If this form of occupation extended to other travelers, Spaniards should likewise be able to partake of these goods yet do so without bringing harm to the native inhabitants.

To substantiate the legal argument for possession further, Vitoria cited the Roman law of occupation of unclaimed things (*res nullius*), thus likening the

[165] Samuel Pufendorf, *De jure naturae et gentium libri octo*, vol. 2 (Clarendon Press, 1934), Book 3, chap. 3, pp. 364–365.

[166] Brett, *Changes of State*, chap. 1.

[167] Soto, *Deliberación en la causa de los pobres*, in *Relecciones y opúsculos*, II-2, cap. 4, p. 237: "*Y la razón es, por que de derecho natural y de derecho de las gentes, cada uno tiene libertad de andar por donde quisiere, con tal que no sea enemigo, ni haga mal.*"

[168] Brett, *Changes of State*, pp. 29–30.

[169] Vitoria, *On the American Indians*, q. 3, a. 1, p. 280.

finding of gold deposits and pearls to taking fishes from the sea.[170] Nevertheless, as Vitoria had qualified already in the *Summa* question on restitution discussed in Chapter 3, foreign expropriation of things from an occupied land could only proceed if native inhabitants were willingly open to sharing. Relatedly, withdrawing mineral resources and soil deposits from inhabited lands under permission must never be inimical to the welfare of the local community. Were it the case that Spain held legitimate foreign rule in the Indies, for example, the Crown had no authority to export gold across the Atlantic against the consent and interests of infidel inhabitants.[171]

Soto, as noted, applied the Roman law of first occupant to the Indies case in his argument that Spaniards who zealously pursue gold must strictly adhere to the free consent of the native inhabitants to withdraw resources from the region. Even if the native inhabitants had not removed the mineral deposits from the earth themselves, they nevertheless had common possession of it as a collective juridical body because the goods resided within the boundaries of their occupied region. Exceeding Vitoria's limited reflections, the final legal writings of Las Casas had the benefit of this teaching from Soto's *De iustitia et iure*. Soto was a scholastic aid in elaborating the subject of lawful occupation, which outlined the material restitution required in the aftermath of the Spanish robbery of native treasures in either their sacred sites or mines in their lands, especially Peru. When Las Casas considered Spanish occupation of material goods in *Doce dudas*, he acknowledged that, "absent their permission we could not enter without causing them injury, and much less search (*escudriñar*) the land in order to see and know what it contained." After citing Soto's teaching on lawful occupation based on native consent in the West Indies, Las Casas applied it to show that both particular ownership and common ownership were present among native peoples possessing juridical independence:

> Those kingdoms and lands where the mines are have owners – whether they be kings or lords or particular persons or all of them – because all the land was shared ... and consequently everything contained therein is theirs and therefore someone else's. But we, having violently seized and usurped, like predators and tyrants, against their will ... We are thus obligated to restore all their gold and silver.[172]

[170] See Vitoria, *Comentarios*, 62.1, no. 26 and 66.1, no. 2.

[171] Vitoria, *On Self-Restraint*, q. 1, a. 5, p. 228.

[172] Las Casas, *Doce dudas*, cap. 36, pp. 178–179: "[A]*quellos reinos y las tierras donde las minas están tienen dueños, o los reyes y señores o personas particulares o todos ellos, porque toda la tierra estaba repartida ... y por consiguiente todo lo contenido en ellos y en ellas es de aquellos*

Similarly, Las Casas's work *On the Treasures of Peru* extrapolated the Roman law of first occupant from a scholastic theological perspective in extraordinary detail. He referred again to Soto's idea of geographically separated and therefore protected political entities under the law of nations, reinforced by both Scripture and the Roman jurists. In light of Soto's teaching, the friar raised a critical interrogative point for King Philip II of Spain suggesting the juridical egalitarianism of the scholastic law of nations: Would the King tolerate the French to enter Spanish provinces without royal consent to acquire precious metals?[173] Even the Book of Proverbs (22:28) attested to the law of first occupant for Las Casas in its prohibition of the removal of traditional boundaries established by ancestors. And, according to the *Digest*, consent factored in cases where the removal of trees or birds from another's land required the voluntary authorization of the owner.[174] Native customs concerning war on the Caribbean islands also signaled the importance of consent in tribal relations. Among the original Taíno *caciques* of Española, violating the consent constitutive of the law of nations and first occupancy had been a typical cause of war between the peoples as when they breached one another's territorial boundaries or infringed on fishing zones.[175]

By maintaining the scholastic political distinction between the authority of the king and the elective power of the people, Las Casas could avoid an autocratic conception of lawful occupation through his radical theory of consent. Like Vitoria, Las Casas believed the ruler was bound to the will of the people concerning the use and occupation of land. The Inca king did not have the authority to permit Spaniards to search out and mine precious metals in lands belonging to particular citizens such as estate holders.[176] Contrary to Sepúlveda and Acosta, Las Casas never accepted a providential justification for seizing and exporting gold in the Indies. Based on his personal failures, he knew better. After a botched attempt to settle a region of Venezuela with farmers and natives earlier in his career, Las Casas was well aware of the risk of buying Christ and the Gospel from European colonizers in a compromised attempt at securing peace through

y así es ajeno, pero nosotros havémosla tomado y usurpado violentamente como predones y tiranos contra su voluntad .... Que seamos obligados a restitución de todo el oro y plata."

173 Las Casas, *De thesauris*, cap. 38, p. 408.

174 *Digest*, 8.3.16; 33.2.12.

175 Fernández de Oviedo, *Historia General y Natural de las Indias*, primera parte, lib. 3, cap. 4, p. 66. The other cause of war typical among the Taínos was when they joined arms to defend themselves against Carib invaders.

176 Las Casas, *Doce dudas*, cap. 39, pp. 189–190.

economic means.[177] The indecent cause of Spanish presence in the Indies, evident to Las Casas by the utterly disastrous consequences of the entire affair, was to acquire gold and silver, not honor God and save souls. Christ had been defamed, the Holy Trinity offended, and the Christian name a cause for abomination. These activities at the hands of Spaniards were more tyrannical and cruel than any barbarous nation or cruel beasts.[178]

In addition to the mining of earth's rich deposits carried out by forced indigenous labor, there were also abundant precious objects subject to European seizure contained in Amerindian religious spaces like *huacas* and sepulchers. The charge of idolatry as a cause of war, as Sepúlveda decisively argued at Valladolid, made the sacred aspects of these shrines and burial sites lawful objects of dispossession. The Dominican theologians, as we have seen, had two interlocking legal arguments to prohibit further dispossession of native religious properties and to secure its restitution, both of which were reliant on the doctrine of subjective natural rights flowing from the divine image. First was their expansion of the Pauline *foris* principle into a political principle constraining Christian claims over non-European infidel sovereignties and properties. This powerful argument from canon legal tradition, as we have seen, undermined idolatry and other sins against natural law as a cause of punitive war waged Christian princes. The *foris* principle dismissed the grounds for lawfully dispossessing outside idolaters based on foreign judgement. But this argument in itself was not enough to posit the natives' lawful possession necessary for mounting claims of restitution.

The Roman law of occupation was a second resource to account for restoring the natives who were first possessors of the goods they used and owned. Use of these goods for idolatrous purposes did not delegitimize infidels of their possessions, especially their most sacred treasures. As Vitoria, Cano, and Soto consistently argued, the Indies were not unoccupied but inhabited by numerous infidel peoples whose goods belonged to the positive law of nations, which grace and divine law could not overturn. Going beyond the Salmantine theologians, Las Casas would expand upon the lawfulness of native possessions in religious matters. The royal platform at Valladolid had already allowed him to insist that infidel peoples could rightfully defend their religion from extermination according to natural law and the law of nations, even if

177 Las Casas, *Historia de las Indias*, III, cap. 138. For more on the failed Cumaná experiment in Venezuela, see Hanke, *Spanish Struggle for Justice*, chap. 5, and Gutiérrez, *Las Casas*, chap. 2.

178 Las Casas, *Doce dudas*, cap. 15, pp. 83–85.

their religious worship was erroneous and idolatrous. The ongoing Spanish injustice of dispossessing the Inca of their sacred treasures among *peruleros* only compelled Las Casas in his last will and codicil (*De thesauris* and *Doce dudas*) to elaborate the native right of holding religious possessions more forcefully.

Las Casas accounted for native restitution of Peruvian treasures by first addressing the extensive injury committed against persons of utmost honor and dignity – kings and lords. The dispossession of wealth and treasures entombed among the dead of high social standing was a supreme act of thievery acknowledged in the ancient wisdom of many cultures. Las Casas then argued that native non-Christians have "the same right" (*idem ius*) over their sacred treasures placed in their temples to idols as the precious things buried among the dead. The natives did not consider their temple treasures "abandoned objects neither did they renounce their ownership of them." Las Casas pressed further: "Not even now, after conversion, are their goods unoccupied [*vacantia*]. Rather the goods have owners, or those who personally offered the goods to idols. If they are still living, or are their heirs to those things, to them it pertains according to their laws and customs, by right of inheritance."[179] If the owners or their heirs were neither living nor traceable, then the wealth should go toward serving the oppressed and destitute in the Indies.

In the same manner that Las Casas finally did not accept the automatic transference of political authority to Spain following the conversion of native peoples in these later writings, neither did he support the automatic dispossession of sacred idols by the Church if natives became Christian. His argument rested on a moral and philosophical claim about the sincere intention of idolaters who, although objectively in error, believed that they had directed their idol offerings toward the true God for obtaining favor and benefits. The tacit or implicit proposal (*tacita vel implicita conditione*) here was that they would not have worshipped without belief in a god taken to be true and obliged accordingly by natural reason to make the offerings.[180] Honest or sincere error in religious matters may not deprive native inhabitants of their rightful sacred possessions, regardless of how idolatrous their worship. Under the Spanish occupation of Peru, inheritors had to be restored their sacred objects as a matter of justice and restitution. If they were now Christians, they

179 Las Casas, *De thesauris*, cap. 4, p. 60: "*Nec modo post conversionem suam sunt illa vacantia, sed dominos habent, scilicet, aut illi qui idolis obtulerunt in persona si extant, vel heredes eorum ad quos, secundum eorum iura vel consuetudines, pertinet succedere, hereditario iure.*"

180 Las Casas, *De thesauris*, cap. 4, pp. 62–66; *Doce dudas*, cap. 38, pp. 185–186.

could be encouraged to give their sacred treasures to benefit the Church and the poor, but this had to stem from their free consent just like the effective transference of political authority.[181]

In contrast to Vitoria, Las Casas never attempted to contrive probable arguments establishing the right of Spanish travelers and visitors to enter the Indies without hindrance. The facts on the ground (*el hecho*), of which the New World friar was intimately knowledgeable, precluded a probable case of reason whereby the natives might have come under the rule of Spaniards through a just war. From the beginning, the Amerindians were victims of conquest, theft, and oppression. If the Spaniards or their emissaries wished to enter, they needed express or tacit permission from the wronged native inhabitants. Otherwise, Spaniards will have committed an injury and therefore deserve violent resistance and forcible expulsion from native lands.[182] The right of sharing and acquiring goods (*ius communicandi et acquirendi*), like the right of war, was not an abstract claim of justice for Las Casas but always considered in view of the concrete circumstances.

Due to the existing damages and impunities, it was unlawful for Spaniards to partake of any goods with the native inhabitants or in searching after treasures and material resources residing in occupied land.[183] Native rulers, in particular, possessed the right to resist European incursion by refusing entry because of the subversive, long-term interests of Spanish adventurers. By way of political responsibility, native rulers had the freedom and authority from natural law and the law of nations to prohibit, as a matter of justice, any foreign nations who posed a threat to the common welfare of the people from conducting commerce with the people, or from surveying the land for digging.[184] The law of sharing goods through commerce and co-occupation had to be subordinate to the law of division distinguishing the freedom and independence of rulers and their peoples. Justice and solidarity stemmed from mutual recognition of independence first and could only then be followed by social interaction and, in extreme cases, intervention.

Since the wrongfulness of European expansion was so evident to Las Casas, and Spaniards had no just title to war in the Indies, it begged the question of whether the whole affair was ultimately a futile endeavor. Perhaps the most startling feature of the Spanish conscience in retrospect was not the imperial

181 Las Casas, *Doce dudas*, cap. 38, p. 187.

182 Las Casas, *De thesauris*, cap. 12, p. 146.

183 Las Casas, *De thesauris*, cap. 45, p. 506: "*Et ideo non immerito exclusi sunt hispani, naturali ratione ab omni bonorum temporalium communicatione cum indigenis querendi thesauros vel aliud temporale bonum illius orbis.*"

184 Las Casas, *De thesauris*, cap. 12, p. 150; *Doce dudas*, cap. 12, p. 75.

debate over the justice of conquest, but that the total abandonment of the Indies was a live question for some. The Spanish Dominicans had indeed pondered these matters in tandem. Las Casas, as previously noted, promoted the full restoration of Inca sovereignty and possessions. He claimed further, in his characteristic polemical style, that because the Spaniards were aggressive and invading tyrants, and the natives may wage just war against them in self-defense, it was not lawful for Spaniards to fight against natives to protect themselves. It was more fitting for a Spaniard "to flee or hide himself in order to save his own life. Indeed, there is recourse to withdraw completely from the lands of the Indians, unless something else be opposed."[185] Las Casas proposed, quite extraordinarily, an exit solution for Spain. The apostolic method of evangelization, which identified preachers as sheep among wolves who must leave from unwelcoming towns or risk martyrdom, only strengthened this idea as a viable ecclesial option among Dominicans.

Vitoria inhabited the Dominican spirit of evangelization and justice, but did not go quite as far as Las Casas, Soto, and Cano in his *relectio* on the Indies. Vitoria concluded his first lecture under the supposition that even if all the just titles to war against Amerindians were inapplicable, Spanish interaction with natives did not have to cease outright. In the absence of actual titles for Spanish rule over the native peoples, commerce and trade still allowed unharmful Spaniards to exchange things so they could receive from the natives possessed in abundance. Additionally, there were many goods that natives had left uninhabited or open for everyone to use.[186] Although Vitoria may have contributed to the emergent discourse of international commerce, it is important to note that he never articulated an economic doctrine of providence to the effect of Grotius and Gentili, or Acosta, Purchas, and Locke considered in the previous chapter.[187]

Trade and co-occupation gave license to Spanish presence in the Indies but the most important rationale to Vitoria for interaction remained the proclamation and preservation of the faith. If the number of native converts was widespread, then it would not make sense to abandon the Indies entirely at the expense of the new Christians there. Notably, Las Casas would take a similar view, qualifying his exit solution to the Indies, albeit not at the cost of letting the faith disappear. To abandon the New World completely would be

185 Las Casas, *De thesauris*, cap. 36, p. 388: "*[M]eliori modo quo possint, fugere aut se abscondere, ut salvent propriam vitam, immo, a terris indorum omnino recedere, nisi aliud obstaret.*"

186 Vitoria, *On the American Indians*, pp. 291–292.

187 Porras, "The Doctrine of the Providential Function of Commerce in International Law," in *International Law and Religion: Contemporary Perspectives*, eds. Martti Koskenniemi, Mónica García-Salmones, and Paolo Amorosa (Oxford University Press, 2017), p. 321.

immoral (or a mortal sin) for European Christians because of its detriment to converts and its dishonor to God. Nevertheless, were respectful and nonaggressive Spaniards to remain in the Indies for the benefit of the native peoples, it required two elements: a fundamental reconsideration of the spiritual purpose of their presence and restitution of native occupation. Only after Spaniards have gained sympathy from natives on behalf of good conduct, Christian example, and royal favors, could they even consider beginning to trade and share goods with the native inhabitants.[188]

Preaching the Gospel to all the nations facilitated, indeed sanctioned, ongoing interaction between European Christians and the non-European world across the Atlantic. The Dominican interpretation of the right of preaching conjoined to the apostolic ethic of evangelization and the Thomistic political axiom set clear parameters on Christian conduct during these interactions. Among the Spanish Dominicans, the right of teaching and the right of traveling were attempts to vindicate the Church's right of preaching on the authority of natural law and the law of nations. When Amerindians restricted preachers violently from exercising this right, Christians had a lawful claim of self-defense, perhaps even war, according to natural justice. Nevertheless, because the spiritual goal of converting natives was the overriding purpose of Spanish presence in the Indies, there were constraints based on both reason and faith to avoid using retaliatory force even if it was permissible. Inattention to these constraints, which the Spanish Dominicans including Vitoria knew all too well, would undoubtedly scandalize the purity of love taught by the Gospel and the forgiveness and salvation it promised to all.

Vitoria grounded his second possible just title of the freedom to preach in the right of traveling according to the law of nations and natural norm of hospitality. Yet he did not see the right of preaching (*ius praedicandi*) as a cover or failsafe measure for European expansion. On the contrary, if natives welcomed preachers in peace, there was absolutely no cause for war or conquest. A just cause for war in this scenario would exist if and only if natives placed violent obstructions in the way of preaching or conversion, thereby injuring innocent Spaniards or recent converts. When preachers were unjustly resisted, just like travelers, they could carry out this activity against the will of the inhabitants. Strictly speaking, this lawful cause of war still presumed that Spaniards had removed any justifiable reason for native retaliation by convincing the inhabitants that they were not there to the detriment of the native peoples. Assuming the highly specialized set of circumstances did indeed give

[188] Las Casas, *De thesauris*, cap. 36, pp. 390–396.

Spaniards a just cause of war, they must still "be prepared to forego some part of their rights rather than risk trespassing on some unlawful thing," always seeking to benefit natives and not profit themselves.[189]

The lawfulness of such a war did not necessarily require carrying it out since the brutal effects of war with its massacres and pillaging could entirely undermine justice and counteract the spiritual aim of native conversion. Vitoria reminded his listeners of an important point extrapolated from Aristotle's *Ethics* and the *Divine Names* of Pseudo-Dionysius: a good action can become evil in many ways by accident and circumstance.[190] The enforcement of this right to defend harmed innocent preachers (or converts) under the appropriate circumstances demanded absolute vigilance in order to prevent evangelization from becoming utterly scandalous. Whereas Vitoria considered this missionary strategy of pairing preachers and soldiers as lawful in principle yet dubious in concrete practice, Acosta transformed it into a new practical method of evangelization wholly applicable to the Indies.

The right of preaching as a possible title to war received more attention in Cano's treatise on Amerindian dominion, which had greater appreciation for native consent than Vitoria's account. Cano, similar to Las Casas and Soto, offered the scenario of an entire native community refusing the entry of preachers; in that instance, contrary to Vitoria, there can be no title to attack or defend.[191] Bartolomé de Carranza, a fellow Dominican theologian and attendee of the Valladolid junta, agreed with Cano that an infidel community had right of refusal to preachers. If an infidel community already possesses their own laws and customs according to *ius gentium*, they may see a foreign law and practice as threatening to their way of life.[192] Juan de la Peña, OP, a student of Vitoria who was Vespers (or evening) Chair of theology at Salamanca during the 1560s, would also take the position of Cano respecting a community's unanimous resistance to hear the Gospel preached against the view of Sepúlveda. One of the axioms of the freedom to preach required the freedom of people *not* to hear it. Jesus Christ confirmed this when he prepared his disciples to depart from unwelcoming towns by shaking the dust from their feet. Citing Soto's *Commentary on Book Four of the Sentences* discussed in Chapter 3, Peña concluded that if the faith cannot be forced through baptism,

189 Vitoria, *On American Indians*, q. 3, a. 2, p. 286.

190 See also Las Casas, *In Defense of the Indians*, chap. 28, p. 189.

191 Cano, *De dominio indorum*, 144. See Las Casas, *De thesauris*, cap. 40, p. 434.

192 Bartolomé de Carranza, *Ratione fidei potest Caesar debellare et tenere indos novi orbis?* In *Misión de España*, p. 42: "*[S]i tota respublica conveniret ut nollint audire aliam fidem, nec alias leges ab illis quas habent, isto non potest compelli, quia ipsi habent suas leges et nollunt alias.*"

then neither can it be forced upon someone who wishes to ignore it, since preaching is catechetical preparation for baptism. The Church does not possess a "greater right" (*maius ius*) to enforce baptism or preaching on the unwilling.[193]

Valladolid was the public imperial attempt to work out two divergent methods of evangelization and associated views of natural law and the law of nations. From the scholastic theological conception of world order framed by the mission to preach there also developed, alongside the political recognition of infidel polities, a Christian ethic of intervention. In extreme cases and under restrictive circumstances, Christians had a duty to protect the oppressed from tyranny. This duty and commitment to human solidarity conformed to a biblical ethic of loving one's neighbor rather than a neo-Stoic ethic of seeking friendship with others through providentially ordained world commerce. Among the Spanish theologians, the solidarity inscribed in neighbor love for international society was closely associated with both the natural right of defending the innocent from injury and the scholastic teaching on resisting tyrants, although both now expanded to address international society. Additionally for them, intervention had to abide by their Dominican ethic of evangelization rooted in the apostolic tradition.

The inclusion of non-Europeans in the New World as neighbors in the scholastic theological account of world order opened the prospect of intervening to protect the innocent in foreign infidel lands and to liberate them from oppression. At Valladolid, Las Casas understood this idea of intervention to belong to a "new case, not heard of until our times," involving those infidels who oppress and injure the innocent through human sacrifice and cannibalism, as reported by Spaniards among "some peoples of the Indian world" (*aliquas gentes indiani orbis*).[194] Scripture provided the all-important mandate, for example, from Proverbs 24:11: "Rescue those being dragged towards death."[195] Even Sepúlveda referenced this biblical passage along with the Samaritan example in his effort to sanitize a sacred humanitarian cause for

193 Juan de la Peña, *De libertate indorum contra Sepulvedam*, in *De bello contra insulanos: Intervención de España en América*, vol. 1, eds. L. Pereña et al. (CSIC, 1982), q. 3, no. 59: "*Hi infideles nullo modo possunt compelli ad baptismum. Ergo neque ad praedicationem Evangelii, quia praedicatio est catechismus baptismi suscipiendi. Probatur consequentia, quia Ecclesia non habet maius ius circa praedicationem Evangelii quam habeat ad conferendum baptismum. Non possunt compelli ad baptismum; ergo neque ut audiant ... De hoc videte Sotum* (In Quartum *dist. 5, quaest. Unica, art. 10*)."

194 Las Casas, *In Defense of the Indians*, chap. 28, pp. 185–186.

195 Daniel Schwartz, "The Principle of the Defense of the Innocent and the Conquest of America: 'Save Those Dragged Towards Death'," *Journal of the History of International Law* 9 (2007): 263–291.

war against uncivilized Amerindian peoples.[196] Spanish scholastic theologians introduced two important criteria so that intervention would not become a pretext for European imperial expansion.

According to one criterion, the Spanish Dominicans identified foreign intervention on behalf of innocent neighbors and allies as a defensive act rather than a punitive or vindictive one. They could do so invoking the canonistic *foris* principle, which received authoritative support from Session 14 at the Council of Trent, to restrict the punishment of anyone outside the political jurisdiction of the Church. Since the extension of ecclesiastical or Christian political power to punish infidels in foreign lands was impermissible, the use of force for defensive purposes abroad was a deviation from the scholastic-juristic norm of nonintervention applicable only in rare cases. When a case warranted the defense of foreign neighbors and no one else could, it had to abide by the strict conditions of minimal or proportionate use of force without bringing scandal to the Church's spiritual mission. Public authorities or princes, perhaps under papal request, were chiefly responsible for intervention.

Las Casas and Soto generated a second criterion at Valladolid directly in response to Sepúlveda's cause of saving the innocent from human sacrifice. The two Dominicans identified the precept to defend the innocent as a positive duty and secondary to the strict negative precept prohibiting the killing of innocent persons. As Soto tersely stated in his Valladolid summary, the negative precept "is narrower than the affirmative precept of defending the innocent."[197] Therefore, one cannot violate the negative precept against killing the innocent in order to fulfill the positive duty of protecting neighbor, which, according to Las Casas, was happening every time Spaniards attacked Amerindians and destroyed their communities for the sake of ending the practice of self-immolation and human sacrifice. Taken together, the Spanish Dominicans elaborated a normative framework for supranational society that could affirm the potential membership of everyone in the Body of Christ and the universal solidarity of individuals and peoples according to natural law and the law of nations.

To identify Vitoria as the chief originator of humanitarian intervention in the history of international legal thought is misleading.[198] Instead, he joined his Spanish Dominican confreres by inheriting a complex tradition of infidel rights with contradictory views on the politics of intervention. On the one

196 Sepúlveda, *Demócrates segundo*, pp. 61–63.
197 Soto, *Sumario*, 228. See also Las Casas, *In Defense of the Indians*, chap. 28-bis.
198 Neff, *Justice among Nations*, p. 124.

hand, Paulus Vladimiri justified intervention to protect infidels from unjustly invading Christians. Hernán Cortés, on the other, claimed he was rescuing infidel subjects from the state-sanctioned practice of Aztec human sacrifice. Coincidentally, Vitoria's fifth and seventh possible titles – defense of the innocent against tyranny and protection of allies and friends – were at least two arguments brought forward by Cortés in his self-promotional letters to Charles V. Other possible titles such as the protection of converts from tyrannical rulers forcing them to abandon the faith (third just title) or the papal protection of converts from infidel rulers (fourth just title) were additional redactions on the principle of protecting the innocent from injury.

Vitoria's *Summa* commentary already addressed lawful intervention in the New World when he referred to defending neighbors from practices of cannibalism and euthanasia on the mainland continent.[199] Although such practices violated the natural law, as did human sacrifices, these did not authorize war as a form of punishment. Vitoria insisted that war or lawful defense under these transatlantic circumstances must follow from an injury committed against one's neighbors irrespective of whether or not the native inhabitants bid the assistance of Spaniards.[200] The principal agents conducting defensive intervention were emperors and princes who, remarkably, did not require papal authorization on Vitoria's account.[201] Neither princes nor anyone else concerned for that matter had the power to punish mortal crimes, but only to defend their neighbors from oppressive tyrants, even to the point of shedding blood, across the Atlantic.

For Vitoria, the power of princes to defend infidels not under their jurisdiction from foreign tyrants stemmed from the natural law and the law of nations. His second Indies lecture concerning war established this right of princes on the authority of the whole world (*orbis totius auctoritate*).[202] In view of his earlier *relectiones*, Vitoria offered a case of the right of peoples having the sanction of the world. If princes carried out intervention on behalf of foreign infidels justly, it would be a public act of war according to the law of nations. Under private persons, intervention had to abide by the strict categorization of individual self-defense and conform to the scholastic model of jurisdictional punishment to exclude any private intention of killing or punishing oppressors.

199 Vitoria, "Lecture on the Evangelization of Unbelievers," p. 347.

200 Vitoria, *On Self-Restraint*, q. 1, a. 5, p. 225. He claimed it was even illicit for any regime (e.g., the Aztecs) to sacrifice its captives as an acceptable offering to God (q. 1, a.4, p. 214).

201 Vitoria, *On the American Indians*, q. 3, a. 5, p. 288; "Lecture on the Evangelization of Unbelievers," p. 347.

202 Vitoria, *On the Law of War*, q. 1, a. 4, pp. 305–306.

In contrast to later humanist jurists like Gentili and Grotius, Vitoria's aim of intervention was not to interrupt and punish the transgression of natural law but to protect the innocent from suffering concerted injurious action.[203] Such a distinction can clearly isolate the categorical difference between Vitoria's treatment of lawful intervention as a matter of defense and Sepúlveda's argument for a civilizing moral crusade in the New World. This distinction may have been difficult sometimes to discern in practice, as when Vitoria considered the possibility of forcing natives to abandon their violent religious practices altogether.[204] Still, the *foris* principle restricting Christian political judgment of non-Europeans was far less prone to abuse than the international right of punishment characteristic of imperial usages of legal humanism in colonial contexts. The scholastic natural law and the law of nations prevented defensive intervention from devolving into either private or public acts of punishment in an international state of nature accruing the rewards of slavery and the spoils of victory. Dominican rejection of a right to punish foreign violations of natural law, based on scholastic-juristic arguments, imparted a lasting, if largely unacknowledged, contribution to later international thinkers in the Westphalian ambit like Pufendorf and Wolff, both of whom were critical of Grotius's Innocentian doctrine of the right to punish and its abuse in colonial settings.[205] Even Vattel showed a sympathetic critical flair against Europeans, namely Spaniards, who subjugated Amerindians "to their greedy dominion" and unjustly "set themselves up as judges of the Inca Atahualpa."[206]

Lawful intervention to defend the innocent from tyranny and oppression was an innovative development from the Spanish theological conception of world order. The ethical doctrine could account for the juridical unity and solidarity of humankind without undermining the norm of nonintervention safeguarded by the right of independent peoples to consent or resist foreign rule and occupation. After Vitoria's passing, Las Casas and Cano uniquely approached the question of intervention in the New World not strictly from the standpoint of justice and the universal law of nations, but by appreciating the virtue of charity and the public role of the Pope as universal pastor. By locating intervention explicitly within the life of faith, they could place stronger restrictions on abuses of the doctrine and elevate the moral witness of the Church in the promotion of world order.

203 Schwartz, "The Principle of the Defense of the Innocent," p. 283.
204 Vitoria, *On the American Indians*, q. 3, a. 5, p. 288.
205 Tuck, *Rights of War and Peace*, pp. 159–161, 189.
206 Vattel, *The Law of Nations*, Book 2, chaps. 1, 4, pp. 265, 290.

When Cano turned to the subject of intervention in his *relectio* on the Indies affair, he regarded it as a lawful activity according to the title of charity rather than justice. He argued that intervention to protect the innocent from death, especially if it amounted to war, had to be a charitable act of defense strictly benefitting the oppressed, and not an invasion or conquest. It was certainly not an act of punishment, since Spaniards had no jurisdiction over foreign rulers or peoples. Cano employed two specific norms of *ius in bello* (right in war) to prevent intervention from becoming a humanitarian cloak for theft and avarice, which happened under many of the Spanish titles just like the ancient Romans.[207] First, proportionate and necessary force was the standard of intervention so that Spaniards did not cause more damage beyond the end of stopping the innocent people's destruction. Second, foreign occupation must conclude after achieving the objective of defense unless it was the will of the inhabitants to remain there. Taking consent seriously, Cano's view of lawful intervention presumed that the oppressed people called upon others for aid. If the oppressed chose to remain under tyranny, for example, to avoid a greater evil of widespread war and destruction, then authorization for intervention was lacking.[208] Although European Christians might have a just title to defend the innocent from the tyranny of state-sanctioned violence, it did not mean they should act accordingly if the results brought scandal to the faith or caused greater harm to innocent subjects.

What about the case of a tyrant preventing some of the people from hearing the preaching of the Gospel? A tyrant who prevented some of the people from listening to the Gospel preached could constitute lawful ground to intervene through war, a view shared by the Spanish Dominicans and the wider scholastic-juristic tradition. "Yet in no way," Cano added, "would it be expedient, considering those things that happen thereupon." Moreover, according to the Gospel mandate, Christians must be sheep among wolves rather than wolves armed with weapons.[209] This same principle of defending the innocent from tyrants also extended to Christian preachers according to Las Casas and Vitoria, as noted. In Chapter 4, we saw how Las Casas agreed with Vitoria that waging war against infidel rulers who maliciously attack and persecute preachers without valid reason was lawful. Yet in colonial context, neither the Spaniards nor the Portuguese had justifiable cause to go to war against Amerindians and Africans. Moreover, Innocent IV, like Sepúlveda, may have supported war to secure Christian preaching, but their arguments for

207 Cano, *De dominio indorum*, p. 108.
208 Cano, *De dominio indorum*, p. 106.
209 Cano, *De dominio indorum*, p. 144.

missionary war treated the hindrance of preachers as a punishable crime rather than lawful defense of the innocent.

The focus on infidel rights at Valladolid made the task of clarifying a Christian ethic of intervention more acute and necessary. Sepúlveda certainly couched his humanitarian cause in the biblical language of defending the innocent and rescuing the oppressed from human sacrifice and cannibalism. However, the underlying cause of punishing the publicly accepted crimes against natural law and not the lawful defense of the innocent from injury was what ideologically sustained his imperial-humanist brand of European colonial expansion.[210] Vitoria never lived to see the evolving debate on infidel rights in 1550 so we can only ruminate about his potential contribution to a Christian ethic of intervention had he been the moderator of the junta instead of Soto. Meanwhile, we cannot overlook the unique contribution of Las Casas at Valladolid on the issue of intervention when he delineated the public role of the papacy in promoting human solidarity for international society.

Rather than attenuating the role of the Church and papacy for intervention like Vitoria, Las Casas emphasized the Church's inherently political nature through the papal commitment to defend the innocent from oppression. His moderate position informed by the Salmantine theologians allowed him to qualify the temporal role of the international papacy in spiritual affairs. The *foris* principle's constraint on unlawful colonial expansion prohibited any ecclesiastical and Christian political claims to subjugate infidels. By appropriating this unimpeachable norm for a Christian view of international society, Las Casas deployed the medieval papal tradition of safeguarding world order without succumbing to the theocratic interventionism entailed in the power to punish sins against natural law among foreign peoples. However, it was not the universal law of nations that authorized Las Casas's interventionist rationale but, remarkably, the Church as mystical Body.

Bishop Las Casas put the matter concisely at Valladolid by giving political recognition to innocent infidels as members *in potentia* of the Body of Christ:

> [T]hose innocent persons belong to the Church potentially and therefore are under its protection. For this reason, it is the concern of the Church and the Pope, who is the head of the Church, to take care that they attain eternal salvation. But innocent persons would not attain this if they were killed. Therefore it is the concern of the Church and the Pope, to whom the pastoral

210 Sepúlveda, *Historia del Nuevo Mundo*, lib. 1, p. 60: "*Y tales indios violaban especialmente el derecho natural no solo porque rendían culto a los ídolos, sino también porque cometían numerosos homicidios, aprobados por todos, ya de inocentes, que eran sacrificados a los ídolos en altares impíos.*"

> care of the whole world has been entrusted by Christ, to prevent the slaughter of such innocent persons lest their souls, whose salvation should be of special concern, should perish forever. It is the business, then, of the Church and the Vicar of Christ, as the universal pastor and curate of the whole world, to exercise jurisdiction authoritatively in Christ's name in this case, not in order to punish or subjugate unbelievers by reason of their crime, since it is not the business of the Church "to pass judgment on those outside ... but of those who are outside, God is judge" (1 Cor 5:12–13), as has been proved at great length, but in order to take the steps necessary to prevent the slaughter of such innocent persons.[211]

In contrast to theocratic world order and the papal power to punish the sins of infidels, Las Casas presented another interpretation of papal power with a distinctive public responsibility: to care for the whole world by defending innocent nonbelievers from oppression so that they were not denied the possibility of receiving the gift of eternal life. As potential members of Christ's Body, every innocent person had protection not from the "lord of the whole world (*dominus mundi*) but the steward of the supreme Prince and universal Lord of the whole world."[212] The Pope was an apostolic herald of teaching truth and certainly not the judge of every nation.

Whereas early modern Westphalian political thinkers abandoned the traditional political role of the papacy for thinking about conflict in international society, Las Casas preserved it, yet shorn of its theocratic excesses to address the new case of the Indies. Vitoria also affirmed the international papacy but restricted its public role in the Indies to settling trade disputes among the rulers of Christendom or the removal of infidel authority over Christian converts.[213] In the case of possible intervention to protect innocent unbelievers, Vitoria turned exclusively to the law of nations and princes having the authority of the world, which kept the door open to justifying public acts of war for international society. Las Casas the canon lawyer took a different approach even though both he and Vitoria's views revolved around a scholastic conception of world order.

Anticipating later humanist natural lawyers of commercial empires, Las Casas viewed the rulers of the world as private persons in addressing sins like human sacrifice and cannibalism. Yet he did not conclude that individuals therefore inhabit an international state of nature with the executive right to punish these offenses in the absence of a higher authority. The Dominican

211 Las Casas, *In Defense of the Indians*, chap. 28, p. 186.
212 Las Casas, *In Defense of the Indians*, chap. 40, p. 260.
213 Vitoria, *On the American Indians*, q. 3, a. 2, pp. 284–285.

friar maintained the scholastic jurisdictional view of punishment, which denied private individuals any international right to punish violators. Consequently, as private persons the "rulers in the world … cannot pronounce judgment outside the boundaries of each individual kingdom." Private persons lack the authority to wage war yet they do remain obliged by natural law to set the innocent free when no one else can. The Pope as universal caretaker of the innocent could entrust the liberation of the oppressed to a Christian ruler or some other private person according to natural law and divine law. For Christians, then, intervening to rescue the oppressed constituted a merciful act, analogous to giving alms to the poor.[214]

As a matter of argument, Vitoria thought individual rulers did not require papal authority for defensive intervention. He also did not see the consequences of this argument at Valladolid under the rhetorical power Sepúlveda. To avoid the potential rivalry among European Christian rulers in a race "to free the oppressed" of the New World, Las Casas kept the papal office at the center. Ecclesiastical oversight of defensive intervention among non-European peoples had two additional purposes. First, it gave public authority to the act of intervention under the auspices of the Pope without empowering princes as private persons to wage a war. Second, with private persons formally carrying out only defensive intervention, an act terminating once the evil was thwarted, the Church must continue to "go further" and "care unceasingly for the salvation of souls, so that all peoples in the world may attain salvation."[215] The Church's particular solicitude can make sure that even defensive intervention does not cause scandal to the faith and that its long-term benefits for the innocent victims remain essential to the task.

At the twilight of a long and arduous career of native advocacy, Las Casas returned to the topic of intervention and world order in *De thesauris*. He reiterated the private, rather than public, legal status of rulers and officials outside their own territories where they cannot exercise jurisdiction and punishment.[216] In what would be his most experienced view on the question, he expanded the Christian political agency of the Spanish Crown, even though it had no effective power to judge the sins and crimes of native peoples, no matter how serious. Just as the role of the Pope was herald of truth, Spaniards could only teach non-European infidels by way of doctrine and especially good example, and assisted by divine grace, about a life in Christ that did not demand appeasing idolatrous gods through killing or consuming

[214] Las Casas, *In Defense of the Indians*, chap. 28, pp. 186–187.

[215] Las Casas, *In Defense of the Indians*, chap. 28, p. 187.

[216] Las Casas, *De thesauris*, cap. 39, p. 426.

innocent persons. The Crown had to persist in persuading them to end the violence against the innocent through every possible peaceful means and in a gradual way. He continued: "Now, if those unbelievers stubbornly refuse to abandon such practices, moderate force can be used to stop them. Yet it is not for the reason of punishing such crimes, nor to make them slaves, because this case cannot be treated appropriately by war. It is instead a kind of defense. In this way, our kings act like private persons who offer help to the oppressed against their oppressors."[217]

A lawful case of defensive intervention was one thing (*el derecho*). The reality (*el hecho*) in the New World was another. Las Casas immediately followed this point about intervention on behalf of the innocent by turning to "the doings of iniquitous men having incurable greed, who always look for occasions by pretending falsehoods about things which are not certain. They do this to the point of seeking the opportunity of plundering the goods of Indians and subjecting these persons under themselves, which they make every effort to do as tyrants and thieves up to this point in these lands of the West, quite frequently." Waging destructive wars to rescue natives from oppression was a greater evil than letting the innocent die under their religious laws and customs. The cruel wars in the Indies carried out by Spaniards were nothing short of "crimes against humanity" (*calamitas generis humani*) because of the incalculable slaughter of innocent human life.[218]

The very last written act of legal advocacy of the feeble yet resilient friar was a petition directed at Pope Pius V in 1566, the year of his death in Madrid.[219] It showed how much he believed in the public international role of the papacy as a leaven for hope rather than injustice in the New World. The petition was a brilliantly concise summary of his lifelong prophetic commitment to native freedom, native restitution, and the salvation of the whole world. In the letter, Las Casas requested that the Pope write a new decretal excommunicating any European who supported the following arguments of Sepúlveda at Valladolid: waging wars against infidels to remove idolatry or make conversion easier, or that infidels lacked true dominion or were incapable of receiving eternal life because of their alleged rudeness and savagery. The passionate friar exclaimed that such accusations did not apply to "those Indians whose rights I have defended till my death."[220]

[217] Las Casas, *De thesauris*, cap. 40, p. 434.

[218] Las Casas, *De thesauris*, cap. 40, pp. 434–436.

[219] See Document 26 in *Bartolomé de las Casas and the Defense of Amerindian Rights* for a complete translation of the petition to Pope Pius V.

[220] Las Casas, "Petición a su Santidad Pio V" (1566), in *OC*, 13, pp. 370–371.

In an utterly compromised context that did not admit the lawful intervention of the Crown on behalf of the innocent, the papacy and the bishops provided the final bulwark of defending the poor and oppressed from the death dealt by European colonial subjugation. Las Casas petitioned further: "[I]t is necessary that your Holiness order the bishops to defend this cause, becoming a wall of protection for them, even to the point of spilling their own blood, as they are obligated to do so according to divine law." The Church's role of witnessing to truth and justice for poor innocent persons was a powerful summons for a new kind of martyrdom across the Atlantic based in the apostolic ethic of evangelization. It was already happening in Las Casas's day, as the assassination of his Dominican friend Bishop Antonio Valdivieso at the hands of *encomenderos* in Venezuela painfully evoked. Crucially, Las Casas was calling attention to martyrs of the Church not killed by native nonbelievers, as had happened to his dear friend Luis Cáncer off the coast of Florida; but rather, martyrs murdered by those powerful Christians held captive to the idol of greed. In defiance, Las Casas shockingly stared at a "new situation" where even clerics were being swallowed up by their insatiable thirst for "getting rich and living large" while "converted subjects remain in such extreme poverty, and many of them die every day in utter misery because of the tyranny, hunger, and excessive labor."[221] The most dangerous form of idolatry, which Las Casas recalled numerous times because of his complicity in forced labor earlier in life, was to offer worship from the backs of the destitute in bondage. As the Book of Sirach 34 recorded, such blemished and unjust sacrifices that "take away a neighbor's living" and "deny a laborer wages" were tantamount to murder in the sight of God.

That the Spanish theologians saw the restoration of native occupation of sovereignty and possessions as a real possibility for a new world order is at once amazing and tragic in hindsight. When the British commercial empire arrived on the shores of North America the following century, it certainly distanced itself in appearance from the Spaniards. Yet the British too, like the Spaniards, took possession of their own idol, as Roger Williams perceptively admonished. The English god of land more than the Spanish god of gold would generate and justify a distinct mode of colonial possession and, concomitantly, a unique form of injury against innocent and displaced Native Americans and Black Africans forced to cultivate the land of slaveowners.

This latter idea and practice of possession through private property, which in many respects prevails in our world today, becomes more discernible by looking at its continuities and discontinuities with early modern Spanish

[221] Las Casas, "Petición a su Santidad Pio V," p. 371.

international thought. The Spanish Dominican contribution to world order, in which Las Casas emerged at its nexus point in Valladolid, is particularly important to this soulful introspection about the hemispheric colonial past in two ways. It can retain through the discourse of idolatry the acute capacity to criticize the ongoing land dispossession and the unprecedented wealth accumulation affecting, and injuring, the most vulnerable populations and their rights. It can also creatively foster a distinctly Christian hope in justice for, and solidarity with, the poor and dispossessed by means of a living faith tested through reliable theological convictions and radical examples. The Church universal and its papacy still offer an alternative way to practice world order by giving political recognition to the rights of neighbors, those innocent persons and peoples on the margins of neocolonial frontiers. Whether or not individual believers without staffs and purses choose to occupy this spiritual space, by sharing the saving love of the risen Christ with a broken world, shall remain a great dilemma prior to the judgment of the nations.

Conclusion

Much of the conceptual and historical repository for international legal thought emerging out of seventeenth-century humanist lawyers and natural philosophers was gleaned from early modern Spanish sources based on the encounter with the New World. That initial contact, incursion, and subjugation of native peoples through Christopher Columbus, Hernán Cortés, Francisco Pizarro, and many other so-called travelers, along with their indigenous allies, would culminate legally and politically for the imperial conscience at the Valladolid junta. If Westphalia, even in a demythologized sense, represents a crucial ideological turning point for the dominant story of modern international relations, it is a story that cannot ignore the historical significance of Valladolid in the development of the idea and practice of world order.

At the very least, Valladolid matters because the Protestant empires defined their distinctive colonial mission in contrast to Iberian Catholic models of evangelization in the New World that came to a head between Dominican Bartolomé de las Casas and royal chronicler Juan Ginés de Sepúlveda. Valladolid brought the non-European infidel on the periphery of a transatlantic empire to the center of legal and political controversy, which would inform modern political thought in remarkable ways. Religious wars outside Europe, it seems, were just as important as those inside Europe in the formation of modern political ideas. The concept of the state of nature, for example, a justificatory foundation for sovereignty among Westphalian thinkers, surfaced in an era gripped with fear of civil war in Europe. Yet the concept clearly had concrete political significance in the encounter and conflict between Europeans and natives of the Americas originally filtered through Spanish accounts. Early modern, largely Portuguese interactions with Africans merit similar treatment regarding the formation of Western European views on political sovereignty and dispossession.[1]

The ambivalence of modern international law comes into stark relief through Valladolid's attention to infidel rights. In seeking to overcome the evangelical impasse of Valladolid – the peaceful method of the apostles versus the coercive method of missionary war – seventeenth-century Protestant international thinkers discovered a more effective and salutary means of bringing Christianity to native savages through merchandizing and settlement, especially in the Americas. Francisco de Vitoria may have inferred this alternative approach of defending harmless travelers in his famous lecture on the Indies, but the Jesuit New World traveler José de Acosta would formulate it as a "new" method of evangelizing savage Americans. By redeploying this ideological third way within empires of commerce, seventeenth-century Protestant international thinkers no longer saw a conflict between spreading the faith and European expansion through the enforcement of rights to trade and to private property.

The political ramifications of this pacification with European expansion inaugurated by Acosta were indeed significant. In the apparent overcoming of the ideological conflict at Valladolid regarding Christian relations with infidels outside Europe, the doctrines of Spanish scholastic theology and Spanish imperial humanism were largely concealed from early modern and modern international legal thought. One the one side, Dominican repudiation of colonial violence and brutality mobilized European imperial competition against an Iberian Black Legend. However, the apostolic ethic of evangelization for thinking about relations with non-European infidels became an impractical method for commerce. On the other side, Sepúlveda's imperial humanism all but disappeared from international legal thought as part of an outmoded and crude argument for Romish conquest. But at least two features of his Spanish imperial humanism had a distinguished career in early modern and modern international relations: the Innocentian doctrine of an international right of punishment detached from papalist politics and the *res nullius* concept of Roman law applied to the imperial possession and improvement of uncivilized peoples.

By abandoning either approach of the apostles or the crusaders in favour of armed Christian commerce with non-Europeans, the emergent international thought under new Protestant empires obscured, rather than

[1] For a work that begins to chart this important path, see Herman L. Bennett, *African Kings and Black Slaves: Sovereignty and Dispossession in the Early Modern Atlantic* (University of Pennsylvania Press, 2019).

exposed, the ambivalent core of infidel rights, with its new discourse of universal natural rights addressing an international state of nature. Grotius, Purchas, and Locke each embraced key aspects of the Spanish theological interpretation of infidel rights to address the legal dominium of non-Europeans. Yet, in the American colonial context, universal natural rights were very often considered wholly compatible with a superior European right over land as private property based on the bifurcation of the state of nature with civilized society. If savages refused to comply, they were deemed enemies of the human race. The inimical side of Christian–infidel relations would persist under an influential civilizational and ethno-racial rubric of modern international relations supplied by Iberian sources: the civilized European versus the natural savage.

The ideological shift from Christian–infidel relations to international relations entailed the political recession of papal power in Western Europe and the demotion of scholastic theology amidst Protestant and humanist reforms. Nevertheless, this transformation did not signal the irrelevance or unimportance of religion for Protestant imperial powers. On the contrary, Christianity's message of salvation overlapped with the pursuit of profit and the generation of wealth through trade and land ownership. Plymouth governor Edward Winslow vividly expressed this point during the first half of the seventeenth century when he said America was the place where "religion and profit jump together."[2] With notable exceptions like Roger Williams, and others whose stories remain too dormant, the race for god land through cultivation of wasted space and the commodification of land under treaties met little legal resistance.

Above all, a neo-Stoic Christian humanist order developed during the seventeenth century that could link the world together through amity and solidarity aimed at mutually beneficial exchange. This providentialist doctrine of commerce sanctioned material and spiritual forms of exchange between civilized European Christians and the rest of the world. Anyone who refused to welcome the visitor or merchant was an affront to world order. Indeed, not a few Enlightenment thinkers of the next century from Adam Smith to Immanuel Kant were attentive to the injustices of global commerce at the hands of civilized European nations and stock company merchants.[3] For Smith, the only prospect of ever reforming such a patently troubled international society was to increase commerce,

[2] Pagden, *Burdens of Empire*, p. 126.

[3] Sankar Muthu, "Conquest, Commerce, and Cosmopolitanism in Enlightenment Political Thought," in *Empire and Modern Political Thought*, pp. 199–231.

especially among weaker states. Similarly, for Kant, the utopian hope of perpetual peace and the providential evolution of the human species all hung on commerce and the cosmopolitan right of visiting the regions of the earth. "The spirit of trade," Kant wrote near the end of the eighteenth century, "which cannot coexist with war ... will, sooner or later, take hold of every people."[4] Reforming unjust commerce through better and fairer forms of a providentially ordained commerce was not so much naïve as it was an indication of the truncated European imaginary of international society after Westphalia.

Our world today is not remotely different. There may no longer be a war against idolatry in the West but there is certainly a war against poverty. In an age of multinational corporations and international organizations where the sovereign state has lost its majesty, it is important to consider that this unquestioned noble cause in the age of global financial capital has its roots in the articulation and performance of providential commerce emerging from early modern European expansion. Growing food shortages, limited natural resources and minerals, and mass migration from the global South, compounded by increasing climatic shifts, indicate that poverty will continue to afflict the most vulnerable peoples, especially indigenous, in this twenty-first century and beyond. Rising economic inequality with the dawning plutocracy only heightens the imperative to see, judge, and act. How we think about poverty and how we respond to its multifaceted presence through practices of justice and solidarity matter immensely. The continued relevance of the Spanish theologians for international society becomes more detectable in the face of neocolonialism and neoliberalism in its various iterations aimed at land grabbing, deforestation, and foreign extractivism.

Without careful introspection into our hemispheric colonial past, we risk succumbing to new forms of dispossession and disempowerment under the guise of benefitting and alleviating the plight of the poor, of freeing them from oppressive systems and dictators. The absence of idolatry from the grammar of international thought may signal the welcome departure from an antiquated religious heritage in the West pitting true Christians versus infidels or heretics. Yet that dismissal has also, in turn, silenced a critical spiritual resource for seeing, naming, and rejecting those idols that destroy human relations and our planet. Las Casas poignantly called it the beloved and adored goddess of greed (*codicia*) at Valladolid.[5] Of course, moral critique and social resistance only go

4 Kant, *Perpetual Peace*, p. 92.

5 Las Casas, *Aquí se contiene una disputa*, rep. 11, p. 397.

so far without salt and flavor. We also need a complementary recognition and esteem for exemplars in our midst: those true believers who give of themselves to be in solidarity with the suffering poor and oppressed, just as the first Dominicans of the New World so powerfully demonstrated 500 years ago.

Bibliography

PRIMARY SOURCES

Acosta, José de. 1984. *De Procuranda Indorum Salute*. Edited by L. Pereña, V. Abril, C. Baciero et al. Madrid: Consejo Superior de Investigaciones Científicas.

2002. *Natural and Moral History of the Indies*. Translated by Frances M. López-Morillas. Edited by Jane E. Mangan. Durham, NC: Duke University Press.

Alexander VI. 1493. *Dudum Siquidem*. In Shiels, W. Eugene. 1961. *King and Church: The Rise and Fall of the Patronato Real*. Chicago: Loyola University Press, pp. 85–87.

1493. *Inter Caetera*. In Shiels, W. Eugene. 1961. *King and Church: The Rise and Fall of the Patronato Real*. Chicago: Loyola University Press, pp. 78–81.

Aquinas, Thomas. 1948. *Summa Theologica*. Translated by the Fathers of the English Dominican Province. New York: Benzinger Press.

On Kingship. 2002. In *On Law, Morality, and Politics*. Second Edition. Edited by William Baumgarth and Richard Regan. Indianapolis, IL: Hackett Publishing.

Aristotle. 1984. *The Politics*. Translated by Carnes Lord. Chicago: University of Chicago Press.

1998. *The Nicomachean Ethics*. Translated by David Ross. New York: Oxford University Press.

Augustine. 1953. *Saint Augustine Letters*. Volume 2. Translated by Sister Wilfrid Parsons. Washington, DC: The Catholic University of America Press.

2003. *City of God*. Translated by Harry Bettenson. London: Penguin Books.

2009. *The Works of Saint Augustine : I/12 Homilies on the Gospel of John 1–40*. Edited by Alan Fitzgerald, O.S.A. Hyde Park, NY: New City Press.

2014. *The Works of Saint Augustine : III/3 Sermons, (51–94) on the Old Testament*. Edited by John E. Rotelle. Hyde Park, NY: New City Press.

Bacon, Francis. 2000. *The New Organon*. New York: Cambridge University Press.

Bulkley, John. 1725. "Preface." In Roger Wolcott, *Poetical Meditations*, pp. 1–56. London.

Burns, S. J. and I. Robert, eds. 2001. *Las Siete Partidas*. Volume 2. Philadelphia: University of Pennsylvania Press.

Cajetan, Tommaso de Vío. 1882–1918. Commentary on Summa Theologiae, in *Sancti Thomae Aquinatis Opera Omnia*, Leonine edition. Romae: Ex Typographia Polyglotta.

1997. "Apology." In *Conciliarism and Papalism*. Edited by J. H. Burns and Thomas M. Izbicki, pp. 201–84. New York: Cambridge University Press.

Cano, Melchor. 1956. *De Dominio Indorum*. In Pereña, pp. 90–147.

2001. *De Locis Theologicis*. Edited by Juan Belda Plans. Madrid: Biblioteca de Autores Cristianos.

Carranza, Bartolomé de. 1956. *Ratione Fidei Potest Caesar Debellare et Tenere Indos Novi Orbis?* In Pereña, pp. 38–56.

Chazan, Robert, ed. 1980. *Church, State and Jew in the Middle Ages*. West Orange, NJ: Behrman House.

Cicero, Marcus Tullius. 1997. *The Republic and The Laws*. Translated by Niall Rudd. New York: Oxford University Press.

2005. *On Duties*. Translated by Walter Miller. Cambridge, MA: Harvard University Press.

Colección de Documentos Inéditos Relativos al Descubrimiento, Conquista y Organización de las Antiguas Posesiones Españolas de América y Oceanía. 1864–1884. Edited by Luis Torres de Mendoza, Francisco de Cárdenas, and Francisco Joaquín. Volume 1. Madrid.

Columbus, Christopher. 1960. *The Journal of Christopher Columbus*. Translated by Cecil Jane. New York: Clarkson N. Potter.

Cortés, Hernán. 1986. *Letters from Mexico*. Translated by Anthony Pagden. New Haven, CT: Yale University Press.

Cotton, John. 1634. *God's Promise to His Plantations*. London: Printed by William Jones for John Bellamy.

1643. *John Cotton's Answer to Roger Williams*. In *The Complete Writings of Roger Williams*. Volume 2. Edited by Lewis Diman, pp. 9–240. New York: Russell & Russell, 1963.

Covarrubias y Leyva, Diego de. 1957. "In Regulam Peccatum." In *Textos-Juridico-Politicos*. Spanish translation by Manuel Fraga Iribarne, pp. 81–103. Madrid: Instituto de Estudios Politicos.

Cushman, Robert. 1622. "Reasons and Considerations Touching on the Lawfulness of Removing out of England into the Parts of America." In *The Puritans in America: A Narrative Anthology*. Edited by Andrew Delbanco and Alan Heimert, pp. 42–44. Cambridge, MA: Harvard University Press, 2009.

Donne, John. 1622. "A Sermon Preached to the Honourable Company of the Virginian Plantation." In *The Sermons of John Donne*. Volume 4. Edited by Evelyn Simpson and George Potter, pp. 264–282. Berkeley: University of California Press, 1959.

Fernández de Oviedo, Gonzalo. 1851. *Historia General y Natural de las Indias*. Madrid: La Real Academia de la Historia.

Gentili, Alberico. 1612. *De Iure Belli Libri Tres*, Volumes 1 and 2. Translated by John C. Rolfe. Oxford: Clarendon Press, 1933.

Gratian. 1993. *The Treatise on Laws*. Translated by Augustine Thompson. Washington, DC: The Catholic University of America Press.

Grotius, Hugo. 2004. *The Free Sea (Mare Liberum)*. Edited by David Armitage. Indianapolis, IL: Liberty Fund.

2005. *The Rights of War and Peace (De Jure Belli ac Pacis)*. Volumes 1–3. Edited by Richard Tuck. Indianapolis, IL: Liberty Fund.

2006. *Commentary on the Law of Prize and Booty (De Jure Praedae)*. Edited by Martine Julia van Ittersum. Indianapolis, IL: Liberty Fund.

Hakluyt, Richard. 1584. "Discourse of Western Planting." In *New American World* 3, 70–123.

Hobbes, Thomas. 1996. *Leviathan*. Edited by J. C. A. Gaskin. Oxford: Oxford University Press.

1998. *On the Citizen*. Edited by Richard Tuck and Michael Silverthorne. Cambridge: Cambridge University Press.

2017. *Elements of Law*, in *Three-Text Edition of Thomas Hobbes's Political Theory: The Elements of Law, De Cive, and Leviathan*. Edited by Deborah Baumgold. Cambridge: Cambridge University Press.

Innocent IV. 1968. *Commentaria Innocentii Super Libros Quinque Decretalium*. Frankfurt: Minerva.

Innocent X. 1648. *Zelo domus Dei*. In Ehler and Morrall, pp. 194–198.

Kant, Immanuel. 2006. *Toward Perpetual Peace*. Edited by Pauline Kleingeld. New Haven, CT: Yale University Press.

Konetzke, Richard, ed. 1953. *Colección de Documentos para la Historia de la Formación Social de Hispanoamérica, 1493–1810*. Volume 1. Madrid: Consejo Superior de Investigaciones Científicas.

Las Casas, Bartolomé de. 1965. *Tratados de Fray Bartolomé de las Casas*, I and II. Mexico: Fondo de Cultura Económica.

1986. *Historia de las Indias*, I–III. Edited by Agustín Millares Carlo. México: Fondo de cultura economica.

1988–1990. *Obras Completas*. 14 Volumes. Edited by Paulino Castañeda Delgado. Madrid: Alianza Editorial.

1992. *In Defense of the Indians*. Translated by Stafford Poole. Dekalb: Northern Illinois University Press.

2000. *Apología, o, Declaración y defensa universal de los derechos del hombre y de los Pueblos*. Edited by Vidal Abril Castelló et al. Salamanca: Junta de Castilla y León.

Locke, John. 1991. "Some Considerations of the Consequences of Lowering the Interest, and Raising the Value of Money." In *Locke on Money*. Volume 1. Edited by Patrick Hyde Kelly, pp. 211–342. New York: Oxford University Press.

1996. *An Essay Concerning Human Understanding*. Edited by Kenneth Winkler. Indianapolis, IL: Hackett Publishing.

2003. *Two Treatises of Government and A Letter Concerning Toleration*. Edited by Ian Shapiro. New Haven, CT: Yale University Press.

López de Gómara, Francisco. 1979. *Historia General de las Indias y Vida de Hernán Cortés*. Caracas: Biblioteca Ayacucho.

López de Palacios Rubios, Juan. 2013. *Libellus de Insulis Oceanis (De las Islas del Mar Océano)*. Spanish translation by Paulino Castañeda Delgado, José Carlos Martín de la Hoz, and Eduardo Fernández. Navarra: EUNSA.

Machiavelli, Niccolò. 1996. *Discourses on Livy*. Translated by Harvey Mansfield and Nathan Tarcov. Chicago: University of Chicago Press.

2005. *The Prince*. Translated by Peter Bondanella. New York: Oxford University Press.

Mair, John. 1510. *In Secundum Sententiarum*. In Leturia, pp. 79–82.

1997. "A Disputation Concerning the Authority of the Council Over the Supreme Pontiff." In *Conciliarism and Papalism*, pp. 285–311.

Montesquieu, Charles de Secondat. 1900. *The Spirit of the Laws*. Volume 2. Translated by Thomas Nugent. New York: Colonial Press.

More, Thomas. 1989. *Utopia*. Edited by George Logan and Robert M. Adams. New York: Cambridge University Press.

Muldoon, James, ed. 1977. *The Expansion of Europe: The First Phase*. Philadelphia: University of Pennsylvania Press.

Quinn, David B, ed. 1979. *New American World: A Documentary History of North America to 1612*. Volumes 3 and 5. New York: Arno Press.

Nicholas V. 1455. *Romanus Pontifex*. In Ehler and Morrall, pp. 146–153.

Parry, John H. and Robert G. Keith, eds. 1984. *New Iberian World: A Documentary History of the Discovery and Settlement of Latin America to the Early 17th Century*. New York: Times Books.

Paul III. 1537a. *Sublimis Deus*. In Parish, pp. 310–311.

1537b. *Pastorale officium*. In Parish, pp. 304–305.

Peña, Juan de la. 1982. *De bello contra insulanos: Intervención de España en América*. 2 Volumes. Edited by L. Pereña, V. Abril, C. Baciero et al. Madrid: Consejo Superior de Investigaciones Científicas.

Pufendorf, Samuel. 1688. *De jure naturae et gentium libri octo*. Volume 2. Translation of the edition by C. H. Oldfather and W. A. Oldfather. Oxford: Clarendon Press, 1934.

Purchas, Samuel. 1625. *Hakluytus Posthumus or Purchas His Pilgrimes*. Volumes 1 and 19. New York: Macmillan Company, 1905–1906.

Recopilación de leyes de los reynos de las Indias. 1998. Madrid: Centro de Estudios Políticos y Constitutionales, 1998.

Schaff, Philip and Henry Wace, eds. 1895. *Nicene and Post-Nicene Fathers of the Christian Church, Second Series*. Volume 12. New York: Christian Literature.

Second Vatican Council. 1964. Dogmatic Constitution on the Church. *Lumen Gentium*.

1965. Pastoral Constitution on the Church in the Modern World. *Gaudium et Spes*.

Sepúlveda, Juan Ginés de. 1951. *Demócrates segundo, o de las justas causas de la guerra contra los Indios*. Edited by Angel Losada. Madrid: Consejo Superior de Investigaciones Científicas.

1963. *Tratados políticos de Juan Ginés de Sepúlveda*. Spanish translation by Angel Losada. Madrid. Instituto de Estudios Politicos.

1966. *Epistolario de Juan Ginés de Sepúlveda*. Edited by Angel Losada. Madrid: Ediciones Cultura Hispanica.

1987. *Historia del Nuevo Mundo*. Spanish translation by Antonio Ramírez de Verger. Madrid: Allianza Editorial.

1997. *Apologia*. In *Obras completas*, III. Edited by Angel Losada, revised by A. Moreno. Salamanca: Ayuntamiento de Pozoblanco.

Smith, Adam. 2000. *The Wealth of Nations*. New York: Modern Library.

Soto, Domingo de. 1561–2. *Commentariorum fratris Dominici Soto … in quartum Sententiarum*. Salamanticae: Terranova.

1967. *De iustitia et iure libri decem*. Madrid: Instituto de Estudios Politicos. Facsimile of Salamanca 1556.

1995. *Relecciones y opúsculos*, I. Edited by Jaime Brufau Prats. Salamanca: Editorial San Esteban.

2011. *Relecciones y opúsculos*, II-2. Edited by Jaime Brufau Prats. Salamanca: Editorial San Esteban.

Suárez, Francisco. 1973. *De Legibus*. Edited by L. Pereña, V. Abril, P. Suñer. Madrid: Consejo Superior de Investigaciones Científicas

2015. *Selections from Three Works*. Edited by Thomas Pink. Indianapolis, IL: Liberty Fund.

Teoría y leyes de la conquista. 2008. Second Edition. Edited by Francisco Morales Padrón, Universidad de Sevilla.

A true declaration of the state of Virginia. 1610. In *New American World*. Volume 5. pp. 248–262.

Torquemada, Juan de. 2000. "In Honor of the Roman Empire." In *Three Tracts on Empire*. Edited by Thomas Izbicki and Cary Nederman, pp. 113–125. Sterling, VA: Thoemmes Press.

Vattel, Emer de. 2008. *The Law of Nations*. Edited by Béla Kapossy and Richard Whatmore. Indianapolis, IL: Liberty Fund.

Vázquez de Menchaca, Fernando. 1564. *Controversiarum illustrium aliarumque usu frequentium libri tres*. Edited by Fidel Rodríguez Alcalde and Calixto Valverde y Valverde. Valladolid: Talleres Tipográficas Cuesta, pp. 1931–1934.

Vitoria, Francisco de. 1932–1952. *Comentarios a la Secunda secundae de Santo Tomás*. 6 Volumes. Edited by Vicente Beltrán de Heredia. Salamanca: Biblioteca de teológos españoles.

1960. *Obras de Francisco de Vitoria*. Edited by Teofilo Urdanoz, OP. Madrid: Biblioteca de Autores Cristianos.

1991. *Political Writings*. Edited by Anthony Pagden and Jeremy Lawrance. Cambridge: Cambridge University Press.

2008. *On Homicide and Commentary on* Summa Theologiae II-II Q. 64. Translated by John P. Doyle. Milwaukee, WI: Marquette University Press.

2017. *Relecciones jurídicas y teológicas*, Tomos I-II. Salamanca: Editorial San Esteban.

Vladimiri, Paulus. 1965. *Opinio Hostiensis*. In *Paulus Vladimiri and His Doctrine Concerning International Law and Politics*, Volume 2, edited by Stanislaus F. Belch. pp. 864–884.The Hague: Mouton & Co.

Williams, Roger. 1643. *A Key into the Language of America*. In *The Complete Writings of Roger Williams*. Volume 1. Edited by James Hammond Trumbull. New York: Russell & Russell, 1963, pp. 77–279.

1644. *The Bloody Tenent of Persecution*. In *The Complete Writings of Roger Williams*. Volume 3. Edited by Samuel L. Caldwell. New York: Russell & Russell, 1963.

1963. *The Letters of Roger Williams*. In *The Complete Writings of Roger Williams*. Volume 6. Edited by John Russell Bartlett. New York: Russell & Russell.

Winthrop, John. 1629. *Reasons to Be Considered for . . . the Intended Planation of New England*. In *The Puritans in America*, pp. 71–74.

Wolff, Christian. 2017. *The Law of Nations Treated According to Scientific Method*. Translated by Joseph Drake. Indianapolis, IL: Liberty Fund.

SECONDARY SOURCES

Adorno, Rolena. 2007. *The Polemics of Possession in Spanish American Narrative*. New Haven, CT: Yale University Press.

Åhrén, Mattias. 2018. *Indigenous Peoples' Status in the International Legal System*. New York: Oxford University Press.

Alexandrowicz, C. H. 2017. "Paulus Vladimiri and the Development of the Doctrine of Coexistence of Christian and Non-Christian Countries." In *The Law of Nations in Global History*, edited by David Armitage and Jennifer Pitts. Oxford: Oxford University Press, pp. 53–61.

Altman, Ida. 2007. "The Revolt of Enriquillo and the Historiography of Early Spanish America." *The Americas* 63(4): 587–614.

Anaya, James. 1996. *Indigenous Peoples in International Law*. New York: Oxford University Press.

Anghie, Antony. 2007. *Imperialism, Sovereignty, and the Making of International Law*. Cambridge: Cambridge University Press.

Armitage, David. 2000. *The Ideological Origins of the British Empire*. Cambridge: Cambridge University Press.

2013. *Foundations of Modern International Thought*. Cambridge: Cambridge University Press.

Arniel, Barbara. 1996. *John Locke and America: The Defense of English Colonialism*. Oxford: Clarendon Press.

Baber, R. Jovita. 2009. "Categories, Self-Representation, and the Construction of the Indios." *Journal of Spanish Cultural Studies* 10(1): 27–41.

Bain, William. 2013. "Saving the Innocent, Then and Now: Vitoria, Dominion and World Order." *History of Political Thought* 34(4): 588–613.

2014. "Rival Traditions of Natural Law: Martin Wight and the Theory of International Society." *International History Review* 36(5): 1–18.

2015. "Thomas Hobbes as a Theorist of Anarchy: A Theological Interpretation." *History of European Ideas* 41(1): 13–28.

ed. 2017. *Medieval Foundations of International Relations*. New York: Routledge.

Bartelson, Jens. 2009. *Visions of World Community*. New York: Cambridge University Press.

Bartlett, Robert and Angus MacKay, eds. 1989. *Medieval Frontier Societies*. Oxford: Clarendon Press.

Bejczy, István. 1997. "*Tolerantia*: A Medieval Concept." *Journal of the History of Ideas* 58(3): 365–384.

Belda Plans, Juan. 2000. *La Escuela de Salamanca y la renovación de la teología en el siglo xvi*. Madrid: Biblioteca de Autores Cristianos.

Bennett, Herman L. 2019. *African Kings and Black Slaves: Sovereignty and Dispossession in the Early Modern Atlantic*. Philadelphia: University of Pennsylvania Press.

Benton, Lauren and Benjamin Straumann. 2010. "Acquiring Empire by Law: From Roman Doctrine to Early Modern Practice." *Law and History Review* 28(1): 1–38.

Berman, Harold. 1983. *Law and Revolution: The Formation of the Western Legal Tradition*. Cambridge, MA: Harvard University Press.

Beuchot, Mauricio. 1994. *Los fundamentos de los derechos humanos en Bartolomé de las Casas*. Barcelona: Editorial Anthropos.

2013. *Filosofía y política en Bartolomé de las Casas*. Salamanca: San Esteban Editorial.

Biermann, Benno. 1971. "Bartolomé de Las Casas and Verapaz." In Juan Friede and Benjamin Keen, eds. 1971. *Bartolomé de las Casas in History: Toward an Understanding of the Man and His Work*. Dekalb: Northern Illinois University Press, pp. 443–484.

Borschberg, Peter. 1999. "Hugo Grotius, East India Trade and the King of Johor." *Journal of Southeast Asian Studies* 30(2): 225–248.

Boucher, David. 1998. *Political Theories of International Relations: From Thucydides to the Present*. Oxford: Oxford University Press.

Boucher, David and Camilla Boisen. 2017. "The Medieval and Early Modern Legacy of Rights: The Rights to Punish and to Property." In William Bain, ed. 2017. *Medieval Foundations of International Relations*. New York: Routledge, pp. 149–165.

Bowden, Brett. 2005. "The Colonial Origins of International Law: European Expansion and the Classical Standard of Civilization." *Journal of the History of International Law* 7: 1–23.

2009. *The Empire of Civilization: The Evolution of an Imperialist Idea*. Chicago: University of Chicago Press.

Bowe, Gabriel. 1955. *The Origin of Political Authority: An Essay in Catholic Political Philosophy*. Dublin: Clonmore & Reynolds.

Boyarin, Jonathan. 2009. *The Unconverted Self: Jews, Indians, and the Identity of Christian Europe*. Chicago: University of Chicago Press.

Brading, David. 1993. *The First America: The Spanish Monarchy, Creole Patriots and the Liberal State, 1492–1867*. New York: Cambridge University Press.

Brault, Gerard J. 1978. *Song of Roland: An Analytical Edition*. University Park, PA: Pennsylvania State University Press.

Brett, Annabel S. 1997. *Liberty, Right and Nature: Individual Rights in Later Scholastic Thought*. Cambridge: Cambridge University Press.

2006. "Scholastic Political Thought and the Modern Concept of the State." In Annabel Brett and James Tully, eds. 2006. *Rethinking the Foundations of Modern Political Thought*. Cambridge: Cambridge University Press, pp. 130–148.

2011. *Changes of State: Nature and the Limits of the City in Early Modern Natural Law*. Princeton, NJ: Princeton University Press.

Brett, Annabel and James Tully, eds. 2006. *Rethinking the Foundations of Modern Political Thought*. Cambridge: Cambridge University Press.

Brierly, James L. 1958. *The Basis of Obligation in International Law and Other Papers*. Oxford: Clarendon Press.

Brown Scott, James. 1934. *The Spanish Origin of International Law: Francisco de Vitoria and His Law of Nations*. Oxford: Clarendon Press.

Brufau Prats, Jaime. 1989. *La escuela de Salamanca ante el descubrimiento del Nuevo Mundo*. Salamanca: Editorial San Esteban.

Brundage, James. 1976. "Holy War and Medieval Lawyers." In Thomas Patrick Murphy, ed. *The Holy War*. Columbus, OH: Ohio State University Press, pp. 99–140.

Brunstetter, Daniel R. 2017. "Bartolomé de las Casas (1484-1566)." In Daniel Brunstetter and Cian O'Driscoll, eds. *Just War Thinkers: From Cicero to the 21st Century*. New York: Routledge, pp. 92–104.

Bull, Hedley. 1981. "Hobbes and the International Anarchy." *Social Research* 48(4): 717–738.

1984. "The Emergence of a Universal International Society." In Hedley Bull and Adam Watson, eds. *The Expansion of International Society*. Oxford: Clarendon Press, 117–26.

2000. *Hedley Bull on International Society*. Edited by Kai Alderson and Andrew Hurrell. Basingstoke: Palgrave Macmillan.

2002. *The Anarchical Society: A Study of Order in World Politics*, 4th edn. New York: Columbia University Press.

2002. "The Importance of Grotius in the Study of International Relations." In Hedley Bull, Benedict Kingsbury, and Adam Roberts, eds. *Hugo Grotius and International Relations*. New York: Oxford University Press, pp. 65–94.

Buzan, Barry. 2004. *An Introduction to the English School of International Relations*. Malden, MA: Polity.

Carlyle, Robert Warrand and Alexander James Carlyle. 1928. *A History of Medieval Political Theory in the West*. Volume 5. Edinburgh and London: William Blackwood & Sons.

Canning, Joseph. 1987. *The Political Thought of Baldus de Ubaldis*. Cambridge: Cambridge University Press.

2017. "The Medieval Roman and Canon Law Origins of International Law." In *Medieval Foundations of International Relations*, pp. 102–116.

Castañeda Delgado, Paulino. 1970. "La politíca española con los caribes durante el siglo XVI." *Revista de Indias* 30: 73–130.

1971. "La condición miserable del indio y sus privilegios." *Anuario de estudios Americanos* 28: 245–335.

1990. "Las doctrinas sobre la coacción y el 'Idearium' de las Casas." In *Obras completas*, Volume 2, xvii–xlii.

1996. *La teocracía pontifical en las controversias sobre el Nuevo Mundo*. México: Universidad Nacional Autónoma de Mexico.

Castilla Urbano, Francisco. 2012. "La consideración del indio en los escritos sepulvedianos posteriores a la Junta de Valladolid." *Cuadernos americanos*, 26 (4): 55–81.

Cárdenas Bunsen, José. 2011. *Escritura y Derecho Canónico en la obra de fray Bartolomé de las Casas*. Madrid: Iberoamericana.

2014. "Consent, Voluntary Jurisdiction and Native Political Agency in Bartolomé de Las Casas' Final Writings." *Bulletin of Spanish Studies* 91(6): 793–817.

Carro, Venancio D. 1951. *La teología y los teólogos-juristas españoles ante la conquista de América, Segunda Edición*. Madrid: Biblioteca de Autores Españoles.

1971. "The Spanish Theological-Juridical Renaissance and the Ideology of Bartolomé de Las Casas." In Juan Friede and Benjamin Keen, eds. *Bartolomé de las Casas in History: Toward an Understanding of the Man and His Work*. Dekalb: Northern Illinois University Press, pp. 237–277.

Cavallar, Georg. 2002. *The Rights of Strangers: Theories of International Hospitality, the Global Community, and Political Justice since Vitoria*. Aldershot: Ashgate Publishing.

2011. *Imperfect Cosmopolis: Studies in the History of International Legal Theory and Cosmopolitan Ideas*. Cardiff: University of Wales Press.

Cavanaugh, William T. 2002. *Theopolitical Imagination*. New York: T&T Clark.
Chafuen, Alejandro A. 2003. *Faith and Liberty: The Economic Thought of the Late Scholastics*. Lanham, MD: Lexington Books.
Chazan, Robert. 1980. *Church, State and Jew in the Middle Ages*. West Orange, NJ: Behrman House.
Christov, Theodor. 2016. *Before Anarchy: Hobbes and his Critics in Modern International Thought*. New York: Cambridge University Press.
Clark, Ian. 2005. *Legitimacy in International Society*. Oxford: Oxford University Press.
Clayton, Lawrence A. 2012. *Bartolomé de las Casas: A Biography*. New York: Cambridge University Press.
Clayton, Lawrence A. and David M. Lantigua, eds. 2020. *Bartolomé de las Casas and the Defense of Amerindian Rights: A Brief History with Documents*. Tuscaloosa: University of Alabama Press.
Cohen, Jeremy. 1999. *Living Letters of the Law*. Berkeley: University of California Press.
Coleman, Janet. 2000. *A History of Political Thought: From the Middle Ages to the Renaissance*. Malden, MA: Blackwell.
Condorelli, Mario. 1960. *I fondamenti giuridici della tolleranza religiosa nell'elaborazione canonistica dei secoli XII-XIV*. Milan: Giuffre.
Crawford, Neta. 2002. *Argument and Change in World Politics: Ethics, Decolonization, and Humanitarian Intervention*. Cambridge: Cambridge University Press.
Cronon, William. 2003. *Changes in the Land: Indians, Colonists, and the Ecology of New England*. New York: Hill & Wang.
Cunill, Caroline. 2011. "El indio miserable: nacimiento de la teoría legal en la América colonial del siglo XVI." *Cuadernos intercambio* 8(9): 229–248.
Davis, G. Scott. 1997. "Conquest and Conscience: Francisco de Vitoria on Justice in the New World." *Modern Theology* 13(4): 475–500.
Deagan, Kathleen and José María Cruxent. 2002. *Columbus's Outpost among the Taínos*. New Haven, NJ: Yale University Press.
Deckers, Daniel. 1991. *Gerechtigkeit und Recht: Eine historisch-kritische Untersuchung der Gerechtigkeitslehre des Francisco de Vitoria, 1483–1546*. Freiburg: Verlag Herder.
Deusen, Nancy van. E. 2015. *Global Indios: The Indigenous Struggle for Justice in Sixteenth-Century Spain*. Durham, NC: Duke University Press.
Dunne, Timothy. 1997. "Colonial Encounters in International Relations: Reading Wight, Writing Australia." *Australian Journal of International Affairs* 51(3): 309–323.
Dumont, Jean. 1995. *La Vraie controverse de Valladolid: premier débat des droits de l'homme*. Paris: Criterion.
Duve, Thomas. 2008. *Sonderrecht in der Frühen Neuzeit: Studien zum ius singulare und den privilegia miserabilium personarum, senum, und indorum in Alter und Neuer Welt*. Vittorio Klostermann.
Ehler, Sidney Z. and John B. Morrall, eds. 1954. *Church and State Through the Centuries: A Collection of Historic Documents with Commentaries*. Westminster, MD: Newman Press.
Elliott, J. H. 1963. *Imperial Spain, 1469–1716*. New York: Penguin Books.
2006. *Empires of the Atlantic World*. New Haven, NJ: Yale University Press.

Erdmann, Carl. 1977. *The Origin of the Idea of Crusade*. Translated by Marshall Baldwin and Walter Goffart. Princeton, NJ: Princeton University Press.

Espinel, José Luis. 1995. *San Esteban de Salamanca: Historia y Guía*. Salamanca: Editorial San Esteban.

Fernández-Armesto, Felipe. 2009. *1492: The Year the World Began*. New York: HarperCollins.

Fernández-Santamaria, José. 1977. *The State, War and Peace: Spanish Political Thought in the Renaissance, 1516–1559*. Cambridge: Cambridge University Press.

Fitzmaurice, Andrew. 2007. *Humanism and America: An Intellectual History of English Colonization, 1500–1625*. New York: Cambridge University Press.

2014. *Sovereignty, Property and Empire, 1500–2000*. Cambridge: Cambridge University Press.

2017. "The Problem of Eurocentrism in the Thought of Francisco de Vitoria." In José María Beneyto and Justo Cordi Varela, eds. *At the Origins of Modernity: Francisco de Vitoria and the Discovery of International Law*. Switzerland: Springer, pp. 77–93.

Folgado, Avelino. 1960. *Evolución historica del concepto del derecho subjetivo*. Madrid: San Lorenzo de El Escorial.

Friede, Juan and Benjamin Keen, eds. 1971. *Bartolomé de las Casas in History: Toward an Understanding of the Man and His Work*. Dekalb: Northern Illinois University Press.

Getino, Luis G. Alonso. 1930. *El maestro fr. Francisco de Vitoria*. Madrid: Imprenta católica.

Gómara, Francisco López de. 1993. *Historia General de las Indias*. Lima: Comisión Nacional del V Centenario del Descubrimiento de América Encuentro de Dos Mundos.

Góngora, Mario. 1975. *Studies in the Colonial History of Spanish America*. Translated by Richard Southern. Cambridge: Cambridge University Press.

Grayzel, Solomon. 1989. *The Church and the Jews in the XIIIth Century*. Detroit, MI: Wayne State University Press.

Gross, Leo. 1948. "The Peace of Westphalia: 1648–1948." *American Journal of International Law* 42(1): 20–41.

Gutiérrez, Gustavo. 1993. *Las Casas: In Search of the Poor of Jesus Christ*. Translated by Robert R. Barr. Maryknoll, NY: Orbis Books.

Guzmán Brito, Alejandro. 2009. *El derecho como facultad en la neoescolástica Española del siglo XVI*. Madrid: Iustel.

Hamilton, Bernice. 1963. *Political Thought in Sixteenth-Century Spain: A Study of the Political Ideas of Vitoria, Soto, Suárez, and Molina*. Oxford: Oxford University Press.

Hanke, Lewis. 1937. "Pope Paul III and the American Indians." *Harvard Theological Review* 30(2): 65–102.

1995. *All Mankind is One*. Dekalb: Northern Illinois University Press.

2002. *The Spanish Struggle for Justice in the Conquest of America*. Dallas, TX: Southern Methodist University Press.

Harrison, John and Peter Laslett. 1965. *The Library of John Locke*. Oxford: Oxford Bibliographical Society.

Harrison, Peter. 2005. "'Fill the Earth and Subdue It': Biblical Warrants for Colonization in Seventeenth Century England." *Journal of Religious History* 29 (1): 3–24.

Hernández Martín, Ramón. 1986. "Primeros Dominicos del convento de San Esteban en América." *Ciencia Tomista* 113: 317–342.

1992. "Interrelaciones de misioneros y teólogos ante las problemas de América." In *La Iglesia en América: siglos XVI–XX*. Madrid: Editorial Deimos, pp. 103–125.

1995. *Francisco de Vitoria: Vida y pensamiento internacionalista*. Madrid: Biblioteca de Autores Cristianos.

Herzog, Tamar. 2018. *A Short History of European Law: The Last Two and a Half Millennia*. Cambridge, MA: Harvard University Press.

Höffner, Joseph. 1957. *La Ética Colonial Española del Siglo de Oro*. Madrid: Ediciones Cultura Hispanica.

Höpfl, Harro. 2004. *Jesuit Political Thought: The Society of Jesus and the State, c. 1540–1630*. New York: Cambridge University Press.

Housley, Norman. 2002. *Religious Warfare in Europe, 1400–1536*. Oxford University Press.

Ince, Onur Ulas. 2018. *Colonial Capitalism and the Dilemmas of Liberalism*. New York: Oxford University Press.

Irving, Sarah. 2016. *Natural Science and the Origins of the British Empire*. New York: Routledge Press.

Isaac, Benjamin. 2004. *The Invention of Racism in Classical Antiquity*. Princeton, NJ: Princeton University Press.

Izbicki, Thomas. 1978. "An Argument from Authority in the Indies Debate." *The Americas* 34(3): 400–406.

Jennings, Francis. 1975. *The Invasion of America: Indians, Colonialism, and the Cant of Conquest*. Chapel Hill: University of North Carolina Press.

Jennings, Willie James. 2010. *The Christian Imagination: Theology and the Origins of Race*. New Haven, CT: Yale University Press.

Keal, Paul. 2003. *European Conquest and the Rights of Indigenous Peoples*. Cambridge: Cambridge University Press.

Kedar, Benjamin Z. 1979. "Canon Law and the Burning of the Talmud." *Bulletin of Medieval Canon Law* 9: 78–82.

1988. *Crusade and Mission: European Approaches toward the Muslims*. Princeton, NJ: Princeton University Press.

1992. "*De Iudeis et Sarracenis*: On the Categorization of Muslims in Medieval Canon Law." In José Rosalio and Castillo Lara, eds. 1992. *Studia in Honorem Eminentissimi Cardinalis Alphonsi M. Stickler*. Rome: LAS, pp. 207–213.

Keen, Benjamin. 1990. *The Aztec Image in Western Thought*. New Brunswick, NJ: Rutgers University Press.

1998. *Essays in the Intellectual History of Latin America*. Boulder, CO: Westview Press.

Keene, Edward. 2002. *Beyond the Anarchical Society: Grotius, Colonialism, and Order in World Politics*. Cambridge: Cambridge University Press.

2005. *International Political Thought: A Historical Introduction*. Malden, MA: Polity.

Kingsbury, Benedict and Adam Roberts. 2002. "Introduction: Grotian Thought in International Relations." In *Hugo Grotius and International Relations*, pp. 1–64.

Kingsbury, Benedict and Benjamin Straumann. 2010. "Introduction: The Roman Foundations of the Law of Nations." In Benedict Kingsbury and Benjamin Straumann, eds. *The Roman Foundations of the Law of Nations: Alberico Gentili and the Justice of Empire*. New York: Oxford University Press.

Koskenniemi, Martti. 2011. "Empire and International Law: The Real Spanish Contribution." *University of Toronto Law Journal* 61(1): 1–36.

Kraynak, Robert. 1983. "Hobbes on Barbarism and Civilization." *Journal of Politics* 45 (1): 86–109.

Langella, Simona. 2011. *Teología y ley natural: estudios sobre las lecciones de Francisco de Vitoria*. Translated into Spanish by Juan Montero Aparicio. Madrid: Biblioteca de Autores Cristianos.

Lantigua, David M. 2016a. "Faith, Liberty, and the Defense of the Poor: Bishop Las Casas in the History of Human Rights." In Timothy Shah and Allen Hertzke, eds. *Christianity and Freedom*, Volume 1: *Historical Perspectives*. New York: Cambridge University Press, pp. 176–209.

2016b. "The Image of God, Christian Rights Talk, and the School of Salamanca." *Journal of Law and Religion* 31(1): 19–41.

2019. "Religion within the Limits of Natural Reason: the Case of Human Sacrifice." In David Orique, OP, and Rady Roldán-Figueroa, eds. *Bartolomé de las Casas, OP: History, Philosophy, and Theology in the Age of European Expansion*. Leiden: Brill, pp. 280–309.

Lauterpacht, Hersch. 1946. "The Grotian Tradition of International Law." *British Yearbook of International Law*.

Lecler, Joseph. 1960. *Toleration and the Reformation*. Volume 1. Translated by T. L. Westow. New York: Association Press.

Leturia, Pedro. 1930–1. "Maior y Vitoria ante la conquista de América." *Anuario de la Asociación Francisco de Vitoria* 3: 44–78.

Linder, Amnon. 1997. *The Jews in the Legal Sources of the Early Middle Ages*. Detroit, MI: Wayne State University Press.

Lobato Casado, A. 1988. "El obispo Garcés O.P. y la bula Sublimis Deus." In *Actas del primer congreso internacional sobre los dominicos y el nuevo mundo*. Madrid: Editorial Demos, pp. 739–796.

Losada, Angel. 1973. *Juan Ginés de Sepúlveda: a traves de su "Epistolario" y nuevos documentos*. Madrid: Consejo Superior de Investigaciones Científicas.

Lotter, Friedrich. 1989. "The Crusading Idea and the Conquest of the Region East of the Elbe." In Robert Bartlett and Angus MacKay, eds. *Medieval Frontier Societies*. Oxford: Clarendon Press, pp. 267–306.

Lupher, David. 2006. *Romans in a New World: Classical Models in Sixteenth-Century Spanish America*. Ann Arbor: University of Michigan Press.

MacCormack, Sabine. 1991. *Religion in the Andes: Vision and Imagination in Early Colonial Peru*. Princeton, NJ: Princeton University Press.

MacMillan, Ken. 2006. *Sovereignty and Possession in the English New World: The Legal Foundations of Empire, 1576–1640*. New York: Cambridge University Press.

Malcolm, Noel. 2002. *Aspects of Hobbes*. Oxford: Oxford University Press.

Maravall, José. 1956. "La idea del cuerpo místico en España antes de Erasmo." *Boletín informativo del Seminario del Derecho Político*: 29–44.

Mayer, Alicia. 2019. "Controversial Cases on Humanitarian Doctrines: Bartolomé de las Casas's Intellectual Legacy among New England Puritans." In *Bartolomé de las Casas, O.P.*, pp. 167–193.

Medina, Miguel Angel, OP. 1983. *Una comunidad al servicio del indio: la obra de Fr. Pedro de Córdoba, 1482–1521*. Madrid: Instituto Pontificio de Teología.

Mignolo, Walter D. 2011. *The Darker Side of Western Modernity: Global Futures, Decolonial Options*. Durham, NC: Duke University Press.

Miura, Nagamitsu. 2013. *John Locke and the Native Americans: Early English Liberalism and Its Colonial Reality*. Cambridge: Cambridge Scholars Publishing.

Moloney, Pat. 2011. "Hobbes, Savagery, and International Anarchy." *American Political Science Review* 105(1): 189–204.

Monahan, Arthur P. 1987. *Consent, Coercion, and Limit: The Medieval Origins of Parliamentary Democracy*. Montreal: McGill-Queen's University Press.

1994. *From Personal Duties towards Personal Rights: Late Medieval and Early Modern Political Thought, 1300–1600*. Montreal: McGill-Queen's University Press.

Muldoon, James, ed. 1977. *The Expansion of Europe: The First Phase*. Philadelphia: University of Pennsylvania Press.

1979. *Popes, Lawyers, and Infidels: The Church and the Non-Christian World, 1250–1550*. Philadelphia: University of Pennsylvania Press.

1994. *The Americas in the Spanish World Order*. Philadelphia: University of Pennsylvania Press.

1999. *Empire and Order: The Concept of Empire, 800–1800*. New York: St. Martin's Press.

Muthu, Sankar. 2012. "Conquest, Commerce, and Cosmopolitanism in Enlightenment Political Thought." In *Empire and Modern Political Thought*, edited by Sankar Muthu. New York: Cambridge University Press, pp. 199–231.

Nederman, Cary J. 2000. *Worlds of Difference: European Discourses of Toleration, c. 1100–1550*. University Park: Pennsylvania State University Press.

2013. "Civil Religion—Metaphysical, Not Political: Nature, Faith, and Communal Order in European Thought, c.1150–c.1550." *Journal of the History of Ideas* 74 (1): 1–22.

Neff, Stephen C. 2014. *Justice among Nations: A History of International Law*. Cambridge, MA: Harvard University Press.

Niebuhr, Reinhold. 1959. *The Structure of Nations and Empires: A Study of the Recurring Patterns and Problems of the Political Order in Relation to the Unique Problems of the Nuclear Age*. New York: Scribner.

Noreña, Carlos G. 1975. *Studies in Spanish Renaissance Thought*. The Hague: Martinus Nijhoff.

O'Donovan, Oliver. 1996. *The Desire of the Nations: Rediscovering the Roots of Political Theology*. Cambridge: Cambridge University Press.

2005. *The Ways of Judgment: The Bampton Lectures, 2003*. Grand Rapids, MI: Eerdmans.

Oakley, Francis. 2015. *The Watershed of Modern Politics: Law, Virtue, Kingship, and Consent (1300–1650)*. New Haven, NJ: Yale University Press.

Orique, OP, David. 2018. *To Heaven or to Hell: Bartolomé de Las Casas's* Confesionario. University Park, PA: University of Pennsylvania Press.

Pagán, Luis Rivera. 1992. *A Violent Evangelism: The Political and Religious Conquest of the Americas*. Louisville, KY: Westminster/John Knox Press.

Pagden, Anthony. 1982. *The Fall of Natural Man: The American Indian and the Origins of Comparative Ethnology*. Cambridge: Cambridge University Press.

1990. *Spanish Imperialism and the Political Imagination: Studies in European and Spanish-American Social and Political Theory, 1513–1830*. New Haven, NJ: Yale University Press.

1995. *Lords of all the World: Ideologies of Empire in Spain, Britain, and France, c.1500–1800*. New Haven, NJ: Yale University Press.

2012. "Conquest and the Just War." In *Empire and Modern Political Thought*, pp. 30–60.

2015. *The Burdens of Empire: 1539 to the Present*. Cambridge: Cambridge University Press.

Parish, Helen Rand and Harold E. Weidman. 1992. *Las Casas en México: Historia y obra desconocidas*. México: Fondo de Cultura Económica.

Parry, John H. and Robert G. Keith, eds. 1984. *New Iberian World: A Documentary History of the Discovery and Settlement of Latin America to the Early 17th Century*. Volume 2. New York: Times Books.

Pennington, Kenneth. 1970. "Bartolomé de las Casas and the Tradition of Medieval Law." *Church History* 39(2): 140–61.

Pereña Vicente, Luciano. 1956. *Misión de España en América, 1540–1560*. Madrid: Consejo Superior de Investigaciones Científicas.

1982. "La intervención de España en América." In Juan de la Peña, *De bello contra insulanos*. Madrid: Consejo Superior de Investigaciones Científicas, pp. 21–134.

Pérez Fernández, Isacio. 2001. *El Derecho Hispano-Indiano*. Salamanca: Editorial San Esteban.

Peterson, Mark. 2019. *The City-State of Boston: The Rise and Fall of an Atlantic Power, 1630–1865*. Princeton, NJ: Princeton University Press.

Phillips, Jonathan. 2007. *The Second Crusade: Extending the Frontiers of Christendom*. New Haven, NJ: Yale University Press.

Philpott, Daniel. 2001. *Revolutions in Sovereignty: How Ideas Shaped Modern International Relations*. Princeton, NJ: Princeton University Press.

Piñón, Jr., Santiago. 2016. *The Ivory Tower and the Sword: Francisco Vitoria Confronts the Emperor*. Eugene, OR: Pickwick Publications.

Pitts, Jennifer. 2013. "Intervention and Sovereign Equality: Legacies of Vattel." In Stefano Recchia and Jennifer M. Welsh, eds. 2013. *Just and Unjust Military Intervention: European Thinkers from Vitoria to Mill*. New York: Cambridge University Press, pp. 132–153.

2018. *Boundaries of the International: Law and Empire*. Cambridge, MA: Harvard University Press.

Porras, Ileana. 2014. "Appropriating Nature: Commerce, Property, and the Commodification of Nature in the Law of Nations." *Leiden Journal of International Law* 27: 641–660.

2017. "The Doctrine of the Providential Function of Commerce in International Law." In Martti Koskenniemi, Mónica García-Salmones, and Paolo Amorosa eds. *International Law and Religion: Contemporary Perspectives*. Oxford: Oxford University Press, pp. 313–333.

Porter, Jean. 2005. *Nature as Reason: A Thomistic Theory of the Natural Law*. Grand Rapids, MI: Eerdmans.

Recchia, Stefano and Jennifer M. Welsh, eds. 2013. *Just and Unjust Military Intervention: European Thinkers from Vitoria to Mill*. New York: Cambridge University Press.

Reichberg, Gregory, Henrik Syse, and Endre Begby, eds. 2006. *The Ethics of War: Classic and Contemporary Readings*. Malden, MA: Blackwell.

Reid, Jr., Charles. 2011 "The Rights of Self-Defence and Justified Warfare in the Writings of the Twelfth- and Thirteenth-Century Canonists." In *Law as Profession and Practice in Medieval Europe: Essays in Honor of James Brundage*, edited by Melanie Eichbauer and Kenneth Pennington. Aldershot: Ashgate Publishing, pp. 73–92.

Reséndez, Andrés. 2016. *The Other Slavery: The Uncovered Story of Indian Enslavement in America*. Boston, MA: Houghton Mifflin Harcourt.

Restall, Matthew. 2018. *When Montezuma Met Cortés*. New York: HarperCollins.

Riley-Smith, Jonathan. 1986. *The First Crusade and the Idea of Crusading*. Philadelphia: University of Pennsylvania Press.

Robledo, Antonio Gómez. 1989. *Fundadores del Derecho Internacional: Vitoria, Gentili, Suárez, Grocio*. México: Universidad Nacional Autónoma de México.

Rommen, Heinrich A. 2006. *The State in Catholic Thought: A Treatise in Political Philosophy*. Lexington, KY: Cluny Media.

Rosalio, José and Castillo Lara, eds. 1992. *Studia in Honorem Eminentissimi Cardinalis Alphonsi M. Stickler*. Rome: LAS.

Ruiz Sotelo, Mario. 2010. *Crítica de la razón imperial: la filosofía de Bartolomé de Las Casas*. Mexico: Siglo XXI Editores.

Rus Rufino, Salvador. 2018. "Fernando Vázquez de Menchaca." In *Great Christian Jurists in Spanish History*, edited by Rafael Domingo and Javier Martínez Torrón. Cambridge: Cambridge University Press, pp. 157–172.

Russell, Frederick H. 1975. *The Just War in the Middle Ages*. Cambridge: Cambridge University Press.

Ruston, Roger. 2004. *Human Rights and the Image of God*. London: SCM Press.

Schmidt, Sebastian. 2011. "To Order the Minds of Scholars: The Discourse of the Peace of Westphalia in International Relations Literature." *International Studies Quarterly* 55(3): 601–623.

Schmitt, Carl. 2006. *The Nomos of the Earth*. Translated by G. L. Ulmen. Candor, NY: Telos Publishing.

Schwartz, Daniel. 2007. "The Principle of the Defense of the Innocent and the Conquest of America: 'Save Those Dragged Towards Death'," *Journal of the History of International Law* 9: 263–291.

Scott, James Brown. 1934. *The Spanish Origin of International Law: Francisco de Vitoria and His Law of Nations*. Oxford: Clarendon Press.

Seed, Patricia. 2001. *American Pentimento: The Invention of Indians and the Pursuit of Riches*. Minneapolis, MN: University of Minnesota Press.

Sharman, J. C. 2019. *Empires of the Weak: The Real Story of European Expansion and the Creation of the New World Order*. Princeton, NJ: Princeton University Press.

Shiels, W. Eugene. 1961. *King and Church: The Rise and Fall of the Patronato Real*. Chicago, IL: Loyola University Press.

Sierra, Vicente D. 1953. "En torno a las Bulas Alejandrinas de 1493." *Missionalia Hispanica* 10: 73–122.

Simpson, Lesley Bird. 1966. *The Encomienda in New Spain*. Berkeley and Los Angeles: University of California Press.

Skinner, Quentin. 1978. *The Foundations of Modern Political Thought*, Volume 2, *The Age of Reformation*. New York: Cambridge University Press.

2008. *Hobbes and Republican Liberty*. New York: Cambridge University Press.

Stern, Philip J. 2011. *The Company-State: Corporate Sovereignty and the Early Modern Foundations of the British Empire in India*. New York: Oxford University Press.

Straumann, Benjamin. 2015. *Roman Law in the State of Nature: The Classical Foundations of Hugo Grotius' Natural Law*. Translated by Belinda Cooper. Cambridge: Cambridge University Press.

Strauss, Leo. 1953. *Natural Right and History*. Chicago: University of Chicago Press.

Sullivan, Francis. 1995. *Indian Freedom: The Cause of Bartolomé de las Casas*. Kansas City, MI: Sheed & Ward.

Taylor, Charles. 1989. *Sources of the Self: The Making of Modernity Identity*. Cambridge, MA: Harvard University Press.

Tierney, Brian. 1988. *The Crisis of Church and State 1050–1300*. Toronto: University of Toronto Press.

1997. *The Idea of Natural Rights: Studies on Natural Rights, Natural Law, and Church Law, 1150–1625*. Grand Rapids, MI: Eerdmans.

2007. "Vitoria and Suárez on Ius Gentium, Natural Law, and Custom." In *The Nature of Customary Law*, edited by Amanda Perreau-Saussine and James B. Murphy. Cambridge: Cambridge University Press, pp. 101–124.

Todorov, Tzvetan. 1999. *The Conquest of America: The Question of the Other*. Translated by Richard Howard. Norman, OK: University of Oklahoma Press.

Tolan, John. 2002. *Saracens: Islam in the Medieval European Imagination*. New York: Columbia University Press.

Trelles, Camilo Barcia. 1949. *Interpretación del Hecho Americano por la España Universitaria del Siglo XVI*. Montevideo: Institución cultural Española de Uruguay.

Tuck, Richard. 1999. *The Rights of War and Peace: Political Thought and the International Order from Grotius to Kant*. Oxford: Oxford University Press.

2012. "Alliances with Infidels in the European Imperial Expansion." In *Empire and Modern Political Thought*, pp. 61–83.

2013. "Grotius, Hobbes, and Pufendorf on Humanitarian Intervention." In Stefano Recchia and Jennifer M. Welsh, eds. 2013. *Just and Unjust Military Intervention: European Thinkers from Vitoria to Mill*. New York: Cambridge University Press, pp. 96–112.

Tully, James. 1993. *An Approach to Political Philosophy: Locke in Contexts*. Cambridge: Cambridge University Press.

Ullmann, Walter. 1949. *Medieval Papalism: The Political Theories of the Medieval Canonists*. London: Methuen.

Ulloa, Daniel. 1977. *Los predicadores dividos: Los Dominicos en Nueva España, siglo XVI*. México: El Colegio México.

Valenzuela-Vermehren, Luis. 2012. "The Politics of Legitimacy and Force in International Relations: Vitoria and Rawls on the 'Law of Peoples' and Recourse to War." *Revista de ciencia política*, 32(2): 449–478.

Washburn, Wilcomb. 1959. "The Moral and Legal Justifications for Dispossessing the Indians." In *Seventeenth-Century America: Essays in Colonial History*, edited James Morton Smith. Chapel Hill: University of North Carolina Press, pp. 15–32.

Wey Gómez, Nicolás. 2008. *The Tropics of Empire: Why Columbus Sailed South to the Indies*. Cambridge, MA: MIT Press.

Wheeler, Nicholas. 2000. *Saving Strangers: Humanitarian Intervention in International Society*. Oxford: Oxford University Press.

Wight, Martin. 1987. "An Anatomy of International Thought." *Review of International Studies* 13: 221–227.

2002. *International Theory: The Three Traditions*. New York: Continuum.

Williams, Jr., Robert A. 1990. *The American Indian in Western Legal Thought: The Discourses of Conquest*. New York: Oxford University Press.

Witte, Jr., John. 2007. *The Reformation of Rights: Law, Religion, and Human Rights in Early Modern Calvinism*. New York: Cambridge University Press.

Wolfson, Adam. 2010. *Persecution or Toleration: an Explication of the Locke-Proast Quarrel, 1689–1704*. Lanham, MD: Lexington Books.

Zavala, Silvio. 1953. *The Political Philosophy of the Conquest of America*. Translated by Teener Hall. Mexico: Editorial Cultura.

1981. "Hernán Cortés ante la justificación de su conquista." *Revista de Historia de América* 92: 49–69.

1991. *Las conquistas de Canarias y América*. Las Palmas: Cabildo Insular de Gran Canaria.

Index